War, Peace, Survival

War, Peace, Survival

Global Politics and Conceptual Synthesis

Robert C. North
STANFORD UNIVERSITY

E 7.0

Westview Press
BOULDER, SAN FRANCISCO, AND OXFORD

For Elizabeth Katrynka

Copyright © 1990 by Westview Press, Inc.

Published in 1990 in the United States of America by Westview Press, Inc., 5500 Central Avenue, Boulder, Colorado 80301, and in the United Kingdom by Westview Press, Inc., 36 Lonsdale Road, Summertown, Oxford OX2 7EW

Library of Congress Cataloging-in-Publication Data
North, Robert Carver.
    War, peace, survival : global politics and conceptual synthesis /
Robert C. North.
        p.   cm.
    Includes bibliographical references.
    ISBN 0-8133-0682-5 — ISBN 0-8133-0683-3 (pbk.)
    1. International relations.   2. International organization.
I. Title.
JX1391.N56   1990
327—dc20   89-48927
                                                                    CIP

Printed and bound in the United States of America

   The paper used in this publication meets the requirements
         of the American National Standard for Permanence of Paper
         for Printed Library Materials Z39.48-1984.

10   9   8   7   6   5   4   3   2   1

Contents

Preface

This book was begun many years ago, long before I was adequately prepared to write it. Preliminary chapters on international conflict, arms races, and crises were drafted in the early 1960s, but except for several journal articles—most of them co-authored with colleagues—few of these materials were published. I thought that Ole Holsti's book *Crisis, Escalation, War*—along with articles published by him, by Richard Brody, and by others—presented most of the significant work that had been done. In any case, I was looking for a conceptual framework within which any number of partial theories could be compared and, in the long run, tested. The framework I was groping for was more a set of generic, even universal, *processes* that would be found to function across societies and through time and to encompass social, psychological, technological, economic, political, military, and other phenomena and somehow capture their interplay. I soon learned by hard experience that this framework was easier to propose than to recognize or construct.

In 1968, I began working with Nazli Choucri on a study of national growth and international violence leading up to World War I, which we reported on in *Nations in Conflict*. As I saw it, this (and subsequent analyses) helped to explain the growth, development, relative capabilities, and constraints of national and international structures within which the "black box" functions of our earlier studies—the cognitions, affects, decisions, and associated phenomena—could be located.

So far, so good, but the disturbing problem was that I could not see then, or for several years thereafter, how the different sets of functions could be linked. The answer did not come to me until the late 1970s when suddenly, while I was caught in a gridlock within sight of the campus, it occurred to me that bargaining, as theoretically developed by William Riker, Glenn Snyder, Paul Diesing, Thomas Schelling, William Zartman, and others, combined with leverage was ready-made for linking the relevant processes together.

This insight, which had eluded me for so long, is only one example of my intellectual indebtedness to colleagues in a number of disciplines— through their writings, in face-to-face discussions, or from their marginal comments. In the course of these exchanges, I was increasingly struck by the extent to which these valuable concepts, insights, and partial theories on war, peace, and human adaptability have been parceled out—and then fenced in, discipline by discipline, without readily available opportunities for comparison or interchange. I hope colleagues in these disciplines will forgive me for whatever false steps I have taken as a stranger in their territories.

In recent years, I have been strongly influenced by Karl Popper's *Objective Knowledge: An Evolutionary Approach* and its rationale for indeterminacy in our relations with the universe and especially with each other, and also by Werner Heisenberg's *Physics and Philosophy: The Revolution in Modern Science.* Many realists and other theorists in the fields of international and global politics have appeared to look for analogies between principles of mechanistic, nineteenth-century physics and the dynamics of political power. In the meantime, dating from the Copenhagen "revolution" of the 1930s, physicists, distinguishing between "fact" and our knowledge of it, have moved away from mechanism and determinism toward "uncertainty," probability, and even a certain amount of randomness. If such a "revolution" is considered appropriate for physics, it may be overdue for the "uncertainties" on all levels of human activities and relationships. I do not mean that numbers and observed regularities are unimportant—only that I wish to cast them in probabilistic modes.

Within this context, the chapters that follow proceed from assumptions of *equifinality* (different causes may lead to the same or similar outcomes) and *multifinality* (the same causes may lead to different outcomes). In addition, causality tends to be *multidirectional* ("up," "down," "sidewise," and recursive). As a result, individuals and states shape and are shaped by each other as well as by the international and global systems. Such complexities strain conventional assumptions of rationality and help explain, retrospectively, sudden shifts in human affairs such as those that occurred in the USSR and elsewhere in the Eastern bloc during the late 1980s.

Inescapably, in a task pursued for the better part of three decades, I owe much to many more students, colleagues, and others than I can thank here. Significantly, after all of these years, I am still indebted to the late Harold Fisher and Easton Rothwell, who helped me start the research, and to Heinz Eulau for his caustic comments and realistic encouragement. In the early 1960s, I had the further good fortune of working briefly with social psychologist Charles Osgood, and I have been strongly influenced by his Graduated Reciprocation in Tension Reduction (GRIT) approach, which I take to be one of the more promising approaches to the development of a global diplomacy for peace. For well over two decades Hayward Alker has served as a generous adviser and stimulating critic. Tom Milburn has never popped into my office on his way somewhere without dropping off a valuable new insight tempered by his training as a social psychologist and his years of experience in government research. Richard Largerstrom was of great help in developing the lateral pressure concept. And the whole world, in my view, should listen carefully to John Platt, who has thought more about how to deal with its (our) problems than anyone else I know.

Many students working on various phases of the investigation made valuable contributions, and in pursuing research of their own, many—including Dina Zinnes, Ole Holsti, Edward Azar, Michael Haas, Randolph Siverson, and Joshua Goldstein, to mention only a few—have become prominent in the field. To this group should be added Richard Ashley, whose book *The Political Economy of War and Peace* had its genesis in his MIT dissertation. Finally, in my files I keep a folder of valuable critiques of the unfolding conceptual framework written by Brian Sayre, an innocent victim of a highway accident that terminated all too soon an extremely promising career in the social sciences.

Deriving from interactions among three "master" variables (population, technology, and resources), such processes as uneven growth and expansion (lateral pressures), decisionmaking, and international violence have been linked within a unified framework during more than two decades of collaboration, still ongoing, with my colleague (and onetime graduate student) Nazli Choucri. Critiques of the lateral pressure concept by Bruce Russett and Harvey Starr have provided valuable insights and correctives.

In writing this book, I have been indebted to Kenneth Waltz, Robert Gilpin, Robert Keohane, John Ruggie, Stephen Krasner, George Modelski, A.F.K. Organski, Jacek Kugler, Bruce Bueno de Mesquita, and others whose provocative ideas have shaped recent progress in the field. I can only hope that others can gain as much from my writing as I have gained from theorists of neorealism, structural realism, hegemonic stability, and power transition. More recently, among colleagues who read earlier versions of the manuscript, Gabriel Almond, Alexander George, and Robert Keohane were especially helpful, as was Emanuel Adler, a younger scholar with combined Latin American and Middle Eastern experience and a capacity for incisive thinking.

Once the manuscript had been submitted for publication, Helen Milner (as referee) made painstaking and specific comments, criticisms, and suggestions that led to successive revisions and an organizational transformation of the book for which I am deeply grateful. Behind it all were the patience, guiding insights, and incisive editorial recommendations of Spencer Carr.

Early phases of the research leading to this book were supported by the Ford Foundation (with the good offices of Carl Spaeth, Clarence Thurber, and the late David Munford), the Office of Naval Research, the Advanced Research Projects, and the Stern Family Fund. Later aspects were undertaken with grants from the National Science Foundation. Soon after my retirement, I received two year-long grants, as professor emeritus, from the Provost's Office of Stanford University (funded by the Ford Foundation) to help in manuscript preparation. Then three colleagues—Alexander George, Ole Holsti, and Randolph Siverson—generously dedicated the royalties of their book *Change in the International System* to a special research fund that greatly helped in the final preparations of this book.

The earliest drafts of some of the chapters were typed by Helen Grace, who, until her retirement, kept my files in order (they have been threatened by forces of disequilibrium ever since). More recently, Gaye Passell typed subsequent chapter drafts, and Helen Morales transferred them to disks. As the manuscript has been readied for press, I have benefited from the research assistance of Luchao Xu for data updating and Catherine Shapiro and Ian Bremmer for checking sources.

In presenting these acknowledgments, however, I am profoundly aware that the ultimate responsibility for the book and its unconventional perspectives is solely mine.

Robert C. North

1

The Contemporary World and Its Problems

In 1968, we saw for the first time ever, through Apollo lenses, the earth suspended in space, a sphere that seemed the size of a volleyball, alone, isolated, but encompassing the whole of humanity. We imagined we could see ourselves moving on the surface of the globe, and a few years later, peering into the night sky, we could almost discern our fellows walking on the moon. "Viewed from space," astronomer Carl Sagan (1982:3) wrote, "the Earth seems exquisite and serene."

Paradoxically, however, with this spectacular human intervention among natural forces, we could at the same time comprehend how dependent we were upon the earth, its resources, the sun, and each other. Standing with our own feet planted firmly upon the earth, moreover, if we looked about us, we could find "the majority of humanity leading lives of misery and despair." Concurrently, the United States and the Soviet Union were investing vast resources in weaponry capable of destroying the nations they were intended to protect.

Sagan reminded us that the world's total arsenal of targeted nuclear weapons could destroy human technology and possibly the whole species. But the only concrete solution to the danger of nuclear war that anyone had put forward was mutual deterrence by threat of reciprocal destruction.

According to estimates published by International Physicians for Prevention of Nuclear War, an all-out nuclear engagement between the USSR and the United States in the mid-1980s would have killed more than 200 million men, women, and children immediately and would probably have injured another 60 million. In addition, communication and transportation facilities would have been demolished; food and water would have been extensively contaminated; stores of antibiotics, blood plasma, and drugs would have been destroyed; 80 percent of hospital beds would have been demolished; and 80 percent of physicians would have been killed by blast and fallout (Adams and Cullen, 1981:170–177, 242). In effect, every human being had a nuclear missile nudging his or her back. At the moment when schisms among nations had never been deeper, Henry Kissinger (1957:3) observed, humanity had found at its disposal "the means to destroy itself." No one was more than thirty minutes from destruction.

Nuclear war was condemned as the central terror of an era. Jonathan Schell (1982:226) called for a new beginning, a reinvention of politics and of the world. "We must lay down our arms," he wrote, "relinquish our sovereignty, and found a political system for the peaceful solution of international disputes." Others took what they thought to be a more pragmatic view. While many people suggested a rule of law to prevent "minor clashes from becoming major ones," Herman Kahn (1960:229) conceded that he was "not very hopeful" of success. Kahn (1960:569) thought peacekeeping required "a balance of terror," and physicist Edward Teller (1962:229) called for the "courage" to use nuclear weapons.

How could Schell's "optimism" and the "pragmatism" of Kahn, Kissinger, and Teller be reconciled? Surely there were scholars or diplomats able to solve these problems and comprehensively address issues of war and peace. But the field of international politics was in disarray. The problem was not lack of ideas but an overload of partial theories so unconnected that it was difficult to relate, compare, and choose among them.

Since then, the years have slipped away, and the world has changed. The United States and the Soviet Union are speaking civilly with each other, but both sides continue to build weapons, many critical issues remain unsettled, and new problems are arising. The world seems to be at a junction point, and although the cold war world as we have known it is not likely to reappear, the television evening news still shows battles raging, terrorism seems to be endemic, millions of people starve, both developing and industrialized nations are deeply in debt, and scientists warn us of unprecedented environmental threats. The rhetoric of recent decades no longer seems appropriate, but time has been too short for a new idiom to develop.

During the autumn of 1989 millions of unarmed citizens in Eastern European countries, demonstrating in the streets, dismantled their totalitarian regimes in a matter of weeks. These events have been hailed as putting an end to the cold war and opening a new historical era. But can these societies transform themselves economically, or achieve the democratic freedoms they seek? There are no ready answers.

Challenge to Theory and Practice

In the early years after World War II, the explosion of nuclear bombs over Hiroshima and Nagasaki, and the establishment of the United Nations, many people—including scholars and policymakers—were confident that ways could be found to counter the potentially catastrophic implications of the new weaponry. But events during the cold war years seriously eroded such optimism as debates in the field of international relations and global politics drove otherwise sober scholars and practitioners to vivid metaphor. International political theory was dismissed as less a "seamless garment" than "a thing of shreds and patches"; and teachers and research scholars were called "travellers in a houseboat," shuttling back and forth between "islands of theory."

Critics took writers of all persuasions to task for not coming to grips with what seemed like near chaos in the field. The same errors were made again and again and the same criticisms leveled. Critics likened scholars to the fabled blind men investigating an elephant, one seizing the trunk, a second hugging a leg, a third tugging at the tail. Findings seldom accumulated. No one knew what the whole animal looked like or how the parts fitted together. Efforts by luminaries in the field to clarify issues only fueled more controversy. Hedley Bull (1966:361) contrasted "classical" approaches (which were derived from philosophy or from law by scholars often dismissed as bookworms) and "scientific" approaches (which sought empirical procedures for verification and were practiced by scholars often referred to as number-crunchers). Classicists criticized scientists for treating political phenomena as "natural events," searching for "a critical experiment" or "powerful equation," and trying to emulate nineteenth-century physicists. Scientists, for their part, took classicists to task for endlessly rewriting Thucydides. A third group thought that both approaches had important contributions to make and that the challenge was to reach agreement on some basic assumptions and central axioms.

Much excellent research and writing have been done since these charges were leveled, but war and peace issues continued to be discussed in terms of cold war "deterrence" strategies and narrowly conceived "security" studies, even as new isues—worldwide debt, environmental and other problems—began impinging upon these discussions. Such "islands of theory" remained largely unconnected. Why have better linkages not been achieved? Why does the field remain so splintered? We have no reason to expect an entirely satisfactory answer or a perfect solution, but we might gain ground if competing (and partial) theories could be located and compared within a more unified context than is currently available. What we hope to do in this book is to derive and link together three critical *processes—war, peace,* and *survival*—from a common set of interconnected variables interacting within a unified conceptual framework.

The Need for a Conceptual Framework

An adequate framework should be capable of encompassing a range of differing theories that scholars and policymakers find useful. By reviewing and comparing assumptions and axioms within such a context, we might be able to formulate, test, and retest theories more effectively and facilitate the accumulation of findings.

In the field of international relations and global politics, the development and testing of current theories and their application to practical policymaking leave a number of fundamental questions unanswered. In addressing the question of where we should look for the major causes of war, Kenneth Waltz (1959:236–238) sought to make manageable the "bewildering" variety of possible answers by locating them under three headings: within the individual human (first image); within individual states (second image); and within the international system (third image). Others have proposed a fourth image, an emerging global system of which the other three images are component parts.

In *Man, the State and War*, Waltz concluded that the deterrence strategies of the late twentieth century—the fear of modern weapons and of the destruction of the world's civilizations—would not be sufficient to establish effective conditions for peace and that world government remained unattainable. On the contrary, short of "tremendous" changes in "man" and "state" (the forces in world politics), war would be "perpetually associated with the existence of separate sovereign states." At the same time, however, without the third image—the framework of international politics—neither the importance nor outcomes of first and second image forces would be subject to assessment or prediction.

Subsequently, in *Theory of International Politics*, Waltz (1979:6, 61) pursued the issue. Prediction was not enough, he asserted. We would like to "exert some control"; to do that, we need a theory to "explain laws" and tell us "whether we can exercise control and how we might go about doing so." Waltz then presented a theory that won widespread attention for its parsimony and elegance. The problem he set out to explicate was "how to conceive of order without an orderer." To do so, Waltz (1979:6, 89) drew on microtheory (theory of markets) for an analogy to the market with states operating as units of the system.

On the basis of an analogy he drew between money as a market medium and power in competition among nations, Waltz (1979:90–99) saw states, in pursuit of their individual interests, creating an international system that imposes itself between each state and the outcomes of its actions—a force that the individual state cannot control. Consequently, international structures vary only through changes in the international system's organizing principle, which is essentially anarchic or, "failing that, through variations in the capabilities" of states. Particular international structures—notably the balance of power, he thought—are predisposed toward war (Waltz, 1979:90–99). Issues of war and peace were thus reduced to functions of power redistributions—an old idea elegantly remodeled that does not tell us much about the source(s) of power *nor about the responsibility (if any) of human beings in deciding how it is to be used or misused.*

Our intention is to address these questions—starting with the individual human being as the only sentient (and hence identifiably responsible) unit in the three (or four) image structure. Who, if not individual humans, singly or in concert, developed the idea and reality of the state? How successfully can we infer why and how they did it and what bearing, if any, these questions have on issues of war, peace, and survival? Where do we look for the "causes" of war and the potentials for peace? In "human nature"? In "evil" kings and dictators? In the structure and other characteristics of the state? In the international system? Is war "inevitable," or are there ways of avoiding it? Can we find answers to these questions in the three (or four) images?

Other questions come to mind. Are there verifiable connections between events on any two or more of these organizational levels? Do decisions and actions on one level, for example, affect events upon one or more of the other two (or three)? If so, in what ways? To date, not much progress has been made toward linking these levels. To what extent could a more unified, if tentative, conceptual framework encompassing all three (or four) levels help us deal with competing (often contradictory) theories and partial theories in the field of international relations and global politics? What are the possibilities for developing a generic context in which competing hypotheses and partial theories can be compared and contradictions and seeming irrationalities examined?[1]

This book makes no claim for the early emergence of a new general paradigm but does propose that prevailing paradigms (in the sense of more or less coherent sets of assumptions and/or beliefs) are inadequate for today's realities. According to Thomas Kuhn (1970:77), the emergence and acceptance of a new paradigm require reconstruction of the field using new fundamentals and changes in its elementary generalizations, methods, and applications. We think it is none too soon to launch this endeavor, but we recognize that in the "plastic" social sciences particular theories may not be wholly "falsified" in the course of what Imre Lakatos (Lakatos and Musgrave, eds., 1970:118–124) called "progressive problem shifts." We assume that the emergence of a new paradigm will require years of theoretical formulation, testing, reformulation, and retesting along several conceptual, theoretical, and methodological paths. Meanwhile, in practical pursuit of peace and survival, this book builds up to a pair of critical questions: How can national leaders deal with an adversary's hostile move, and how can they respond responsibly to an "untrustworthy" adversary's offer of conciliation? Is there a viable alternative somewhere between appeasement and attack?

The Influence of Existing Paradigms

None of us can escape the influences of our respective cultures, the history of our nations, or the conventional paradigms to which we have been exposed directly or indirectly. To one degree or another, the concepts and theories touched upon in this book have affected the thinking that underlies it. In this regard, five paradigms deserve acknowledgment for the reason that most political thinking in modern times—including the proposed framework—derives from one (or more) of them: mercantilism, liberalism, Marxism-Leninism, realism, and idealism. Mercantilism, liberalism, and Marxism-Leninism are essentially perspectives on political economy. Mercantilism and liberalism have been shaping influences in Western thought and to a large extent in the general theory and practice of foreign policy and diplomacy worldwide, whereas Marxism-Leninism has played a challenger role for the better part of a century.

Realism (and neorealism, its contemporary variant) is widely recognized as the prevailing paradigm today. Idealism, favored by many during the early days of the League of Nations and again with the establishment of the United Nations, fell casualty to cold war exigencies. (Space allows for only brief consideration of the five paradigms here, but in subsequent chapters they will be discussed where particularly relevant.)

The aim of a mercantilist regime was to enable the populace to obtain sufficient income to support itself as well as supply the state with revenue for regulating the economy, maintaining public services, and guaranteeing national security. This regime emphasized the maintenance of a trade surplus and the acquisition of "treasure"—silver, gold, jewels, and other less "mutable" and less "perishable" commodities thought to represent "wealth at all times and all places." The connection between money and goods was represented in balance-of-trade theory—a perspective often identified today as characteristically mercantilist. Believing that a gain in wealth, power, or other advantage by one state necessarily exacted a comparable loss on the part of other state(s) in the system, mercantilists expected intense competition for raw materials to give rise to international conflict. This meant that a country's economic activity, especially its trade, should be subservient to national interests and security requirements and that military and naval forces should be kept up to optimal strength (Heckscher, 1935:II, 17; Petty, 1899:259; Viner, 1958:286).

In contrast to mercantilist ideas, classical liberal theory defended freedom of the individual from economic and political restraints, economic competition, and self-regulating markets. Classical liberalism, which derived mainly from the theories of Adam Smith but was traceable to the writings of Socrates and the Stoics, saw a harmony within natural economies and between trading nations. While recognizing economic growth as a primary function of divisions of labor, Smith (1937:397, 625) saw possibilities for comparative advantage/positive sum outcomes from thriving markets. But the optimal functioning of domestic markets depended upon foreign markets.

Free trade, a balanced budget, and the gold standard were hallmarks of classical liberal theory. Smith believed that a gain in wealth, power, or other advantage by one state need not inflict a comparable loss or disadvantage upon others. As for colonies, he thought that the costs of empire outweighed the benefits. In a free-trade environment, the costs of using force in pursuit of economic interests outweighed gains. Immanuel Kant (1939) concluded that commerce and war were essentially incompatible—a view elaborated upon in recent times.

Such assumptions about the benign implications of the trading state stood in sharp contrast to Marxist-Leninist doctrines, according to which divisions of labor arose from the development of productive forces and contributed to contradictions between individual interests and the interests of the community. This basic conflict gave rise to uneven distributions of wealth and status, the development of classes (and conflicts between them), and the establishment of the state, which emerged, according to V. I. Lenin (1932:20) "where, when, and to the extent that such contradictions could not be reconciled." Each state was shaped by the mode of production prevailing at the time. Technological, economic, and other underlying elements of production and class struggle also created a "superstructure" of social, economic, and political relationships, including cultural values, laws, and institutions (Marx and Engels, 1947:16–23; cf. Engels, 1962:306). As changes in productive forces occurred, every class that struggled for mastery had to wrest political power for itself and abolish the old form of society in order to represent its own interest as the general interest. Force served to "deliver an old society pregnant with a new one" (Marx, 1967, 1:386).

Karl Marx expected early fulfillment of his prognostication that the proletarian revolution and the collapse of the capitalist order were close at hand, but fifty years later, as Lenin was rising to prominence in Russia, capitalism was still thriving and conditions for the proletariat were steadily improving. Lenin (1939:13) concluded that the bourgeoisie, with superprofits obtained by investment in the colonies (and semicolonies such as China) had been able to "bribe" the labor "aristocracy" with high wages and thus stave off the revolution. Meanwhile, the bourgeoisies, with the help of armies of colonial recruits, were fighting an "imperialist war" among themselves (World War I) over a redistribution of the colonies. Lenin (1939:12) predicted that world revolution would break out not in the industrialized countries as Marx had expected but in colonial regions where the "capitalist chain" was weakest. Future wars—fought among major capitalist powers competing for colonial markets, raw materials, and cheap labor—would put an end to capitalism. Having achieved power in the Soviet Union during World War I, the Marxist-Leninist regime—challenging the Western democracies—had the effect of strengthening and stimulating further developments in realist thinking (cf. Communist International, 1920:12, 19–20, 32–33; Lenin, 1932:33, 84).

Derived in large part from a combination of mercantilism and liberalism, modern realism proved readily adaptable for cold war strategies. In describing the realist (or "power") approach, Hans Morgenthau (1968:2–3, 161–168) presented society and its politics as governed by objective laws with roots in human nature. Central to realist thought was the possibility of developing a rational theory capable of reflecting these objective laws, however imperfectly, and the possibility of distinguishing between truth and opinion in international politics. As a signpost, Morgenthau used *interest defined in terms of power* to connect reason as a theoretical tool with the realities to be understood. Politics as an autonomous sphere of action and understanding was thus set apart from other spheres "such as economics (understood in terms of interest defined as wealth), ethics, aesthetics, or religion."

Power turned out to be an elusive concept, however. Of numerous definitions (several to be discussed in Chapter 5), one defined power as the ability of one person (or organization) to get others to do—at a cost acceptable to themselves—what they otherwise would not do. Another definition used power as a synonym for capability. The aspiration for power by various nations, each trying to maintain or to overthrow the status quo, produced a *balance of power* (an ancient concept) and policies for preserving it. But scholars disagreed as to whether a balance of power, or any particular power configuration, was war prone or peace prone. In recent years, political economy has made important contributions to realist theory, but the logic of economics and the logic of power are rarely linked persuasively.

Deriving their perspectives from the same philosophical and political heritage, idealists normally shared with realists many of the same assumptions, values, and predispositions. Both drew heavily upon classical mercantilist and liberal traditions, and in domestic politics, both inclined toward pluralism, respect for the rule of law, and related concepts. The formulation and implementation of much foreign policy—even in non-Western and nondemocratic states—was frequently characterized by combinations of realist and idealist elements. Yet the two approaches were often treated separately in theory and practice (even juxtaposed), and partisans of the two "schools" were commonly at odds.

The nature of humankind, individually and collectively, was a major topic of idealist-realist debates. Even more than conventional liberals, idealists tended to emphasize the essential goodness of humankind and to trust the human potential for reason, perfectability, and, possibly, transcendence. They often envisaged an order deriving from principles universally recognized as valid, moral, and attainable "here and now." Assuming the adaptability of human nature, they were inclined to explain failures of the social order on faulty knowledge, and for remedies idealists tended to rely on education, reform, and, at the extreme, cautious and judicious use of force (Buzan 1983:248–249). In stark contrast, realists assumed the world, with all its imperfections, to be a rational result of forces inherent in human nature. To improve the world, one had to cooperate with these forces, not oppose them.

Each of these paradigms has strengths and weaknesses; much can be gained by comparing some of their fundamental assumptions and concepts. Mercantilists and classical liberals both assumed a linkage between economic and political elements in international politics, but they disagreed about the implications and consequences, and neither stated clearly what connections they saw between the two sets of phenomena. Whereas mercantilists emphasized economics at the expense of politics, classical liberal theorists tended to treat economics and politics as largely separable and semiautonomous spheres of activity. Both identified power as a central variable, but their definitions lacked precision. Neither developed a systematic theory of change.

Marxist-Leninists allowed for change through the dialectic, a concept that drew on Marx's view of mid-nineteenth-century physics and tended to be mechanistic, virtually impossible to test, and often confusing. Class struggle was located at the core of the process, but when two worker factions were in conflict (Stalinists vs. Trotskyites, for example), it was often difficult to ascertain "objectively" which group was "reactionary" (thesis) and which was truly "progressive" (antithesis). Fundamentally materialistic, Marxist-Leninist theory also contained strong idealist elements (such as the hypothesis about the "withering away of the state"). Despite its ambiguities, the overall theory was presented as "scientific."

If realists, emphasizing "power," and idealists, emphasizing preferred outcomes, had merged their ideas, some important advances toward conceptual synthesis might have been achieved, but they too often allowed their differences to blind them to such possibilities. In effect, realists tended to emphasize "what is" (the realities of the here and now), whereas idealists pursued "what ought to be" (possibilities and preferences for the future).

None of the paradigms defines power adequately or goes far enough in identifying its sources, how it is distributed, under what conditions distributions occur, or under what circumstances a balance of power (or other power configuration) is war prone or peace prone. All tend to treat state and international systems as *states of being* rather than as *processes of becoming*—except Marxism-Leninism, which presents us with an improbable theory of development, "progress," and "peace" resulting from bitter conflict. Despite the contributions of anthropology, sociology, and psychology to the field of international relations (especially the relevant psychological aspects of deterrence, crises, war, de-escalation, and peace), none of the paradigms systematically or persuasively relates human cognitions, affects, needs, wants, desires, and demands with the sources of "power" as influence (persuasion) or with the mechanisms by which power is distributed.

Perspective for a Conceptual Framework

The discussion in this section may seem remote to the reader who is accustomed to conventional balance-of-power approaches and who might justifiably ask, "What has *this* to do with international relations and global politics?" The answer is simple and utilitarian. In the nuclear era we need new conceptual tools to help us make sense of the rapidly changing conditions in the world as well as the plethora of partial theories current in the field. Conventional theories of international politics, including some recent "refinements," have tended to postulate the state and international systems as a set of assumptions rather than an interplay of elements and variables. Here, by contrast, we place human beings in a natural environment and use several intensively interactive processes to help explain state origins, historical adaptations, and transformations from the distant past to the immediate present. Our goal is to link the elements and processes most relevant to war, peace, and survival within a single conceptual package. Such a linkage occurs when an action on one side of an organizational or systemic boundary affects conditions in another system, subsystem, or environment (Rosenau, 1969b:61).

Some of the language and concepts in our "assembly manual" may seem unorthodox and remote from concerns of modern politics, but we have found them useful for opening up and analyzing problems that (1) cut across image levels, (2) are dynamic (with processes functioning from the past through the present and into the future), and (3) are intensely interdependent (involving actors who initiate and respond to activities that combine demographic, technological, economic, political, and environmental undertakings in complex ways). In this context, individuals, states, the international system, and phenomena on the global level are processes of becoming.

Most readers will gain by pursuing the reasoning of this chapter step by step and by resisting the natural disposition to fit the framework into a conventional approach to the field. Some of the concepts may seem elusive, but if considered carefully, they may become "commonsensical."

Let us start with the concept of *nesting*. Within an overall system, the four images (or system levels) nest roughly like Chinese boxes—the individual human being into the national system, the national system into the international system, and the international system into the global system. This arrangement reminds us that *individual human beings are the prime actors on all four image levels* as well as in systems on intermediate levels, such as the family and the corporation.

In such a nested arrangement, a system is molecular (a component) relative to the system(s) that encompasses it but is molar (a whole) with respect to the systems it encompasses. A central puzzle we want to solve is how to connect the four images. They are not inert building blocks or Chinese boxes; rather, they vibrate, oscillate, fluctuate, and sometimes are transformed in the course of continuous human activity, but except for the individual person (a biopsychological system), they are not organic. Obviously, neither members of a family "system" nor the institutions of a state are joined by tissues or ligaments; they are joined by kinship and/or interpersonal and national "ties," common or overlapping interests, strong expectations and habits, feelings of loyalty, and interdependencies. The next question is, What holds the national, international, and global systems together?

In this regard, we must draw a distinction between actor systems, such as the individual and the state, and the international and global systems, which seldom, if ever, "decide" or act as units. The United Nations, for example, is not a full-blown international "government"; it is a partial or limited actor lacking the overriding power and legal sanctions required to enforce its decisions, especially those seriously opposed by the more powerful of its member states. As will be discussed in subsequent chapters, the third and fourth images are essentially interactive ecological systems in which human beings are relatively dominant.

An interactive, or "dynamic," approach tends to emphasize functions or processes rather than conditions, which are like high-speed snapshots of critical dimensions or variables in more or less continuous change. Within such a dynamic framework, a process approach is useful because of its capacity to accommodate and help to explain change in different, usually interactive variables (population, available resources, knowledge and skills, capabilities, power, and the like) through time and within, between, and among states and image levels. Within this four-image framework we can distinguish the nature, source(s), direction(s), rate(s), and outcome(s) of change—from peace to war to peace, from prosperity to depression to prosperity, and so forth. Cooperation, competition, conflict, and configurations of power, war, peace, and associated phenomena can be explained better as interactive processes than as neatly labeled conditions or states of being.

First Image: The Individual

Strictly construed, the individual (the first image) is the sole thinking, feeling, acting system in politics, as contrasted with the state (the second image), which is only analogous (or isomorphic, perhaps) to a human actor. The two systems share similar functions (decisions and actions result from each), but the structures responsible for these functions are different.

Presented from the perspective of an individual human being as an actor system, the following seven processes link him or her to other actors (individuals, groups, or organizations, including the second image, or state) in revealing ways:

1. *Information and resource processing:* how the central nervous system of the human being transforms needs, wants, and desires into demands; food and other raw materials into psychic and muscular energy; and resources from nature into tools, mechanical power, machines, weapons, goods, and services

2. *Demands, capabilities, actions, and linkages:* how demands combine with capabilities to produce actions

3. *Feedback, "learning," adaptation, and "social evolution":* how individuals learn and adapt to changing circumstances and how collectivities, including families, organizations, institutions, states, and whole societies, can be said to adapt, "learn," and evolve through the experiences of their human components.

4. *Bargaining, leverage, and coalition formation:* how individuals, singly and collectively, try to persuade others to act or not to act in certain ways; how bargaining and leverage activities contribute to group decisions, establish linkages, and promote cooperation, conflict, coalitions, and countercoalitions within and among units on the same or different image levels

5. *Uneven growth and development:* how individuals and social systems grow (decline, perish), enhance their capabilities, and expand their activities and interests

6. *Cooperation, coalition formation, and unification:* how cooperation comes about, facilitates organization, and often maintains "peace" but also contributes to hostile conflict, violence, and war

7. *Conflict escalations:* how human needs, demands, values, beliefs, interests, expectations, and actions often collide, how one actor's search for well-being may appear to threaten the well-being of another actor, and how negative leverages escalate

From this perspective, individuals interacting in groups, coalitions, and coalitions of coalitions (including the state as second image) speak and act for the encompassing collective in many different ways. Thus, in humans, cognitive, affective (emotional), and muscular subsystems undergird and empower the functions; in the state, institutionalized decision and action subsystems of individuals are the structural components. To assert that Great Britain "decides," Iran "threatens," the United States "insists," or the USSR "protests" is a mode of verbal shorthand, a reification of the state. Human beings, singly or in groups, make all decisions and perform all actions that occur within and between states.

For purposes of analysis, we can view the individual human being as an information and resource processing organism. Through our central nervous systems we receive "messages" involving cognitions, sensations, and affects (emotions) that report on our internal and external environments and generate basic needs for food, water, air, living space, and other necessities. Such reports provide evidence of our lifelong dependence upon resources from "outside," which we require in pursuit of dynamic equilibria between our internal and external environments. Through metabolic and associated processes we then transform these resources into energy for living and performing "work."

We also develop psychological wants or desires for outcomes and objects that we *think* we need above and beyond basic necessities of life. Often the boundary between basic needs and psychological wants and desires is difficult to ascertain. A person may survive a long time without medical care, for example, but in modern times more and more people are beginning to view preventive health care as a "necessity."

A *demand* is a determination deriving from a need, want, or desire to narrow or close a gap between a perception of fact (what is) and a preference or value (what ought to be). This definition emphasizes not only the actor's purpose, goal, or objective but also the location, condition, or state of being that she or he wants to change. In order to close is/ought-to-be gaps, we begin at birth to make demands upon ourselves, upon other people, and upon institutions. The strength or magnitude of a demand can be measured in terms of the effort, time, money, deprivation, or other costs associated with closing the gap. A student thinking about a medical career has many such costs to assess.

In making a *decision*, we determine first (consciously or unconsciously) whether to continue our ongoing activity (or state of being)—our perception of what is—or to make a change toward our perception of what ought to be. If we chose the latter, we then select a means, mode, or course of action. In order to narrow or close such an is/ought-to-be gap—and possibly approach or establish a dynamic equilibrium—an individual person requires some amount of energy (physical and psychological) and *capability* if the task is to be accomplished.

Capability derives from combinations of physical energy (strength); appropriate knowledge, skills, and adeptness (technology); and resources. Overall, we tend to succeed insofar as we are able to approximate a satisfactorily dynamic (moving, adaptive, changing) but stable equilibrium (stable because it maintains integrity and adaptibility through stages of growth and development). The maintenance of such an equilibrium may be frustrated, however, by inadequate or faulty information and by the tendency for events in our internal and external environments to change (often at different rates). The internal environment changes because of each person's growth, maturation, and altered needs, wants, and desires (from infancy through old age); the external environment undergoes alteration because of demographic, technological, economic, and political changes and the effects of these changes on the natural and social environments.

Balancing Internal and External Environments

Whenever we act to close one discrepancy, another gap—a problem, constraint, or cost of some kind—tends to open or widen. In addition, each of us lives on a "frontier," or threshold, between past and future. This means that we are continually drawing on a recollected past as we plan for a necessarily uncertain future. Thus, insofar as many of our needs, wants, desires, and demands are unsatisfied, we find ourselves in a partial disequilibrium, which, if not unduly disturbing, leads us on and induces us to continue "working," learning, adapting (but "normally" a trifle "off balance"), and moving toward, rather than maintaining, a true equilibrium.

Demands combine with capabilities to produce *actions*, but depending upon his or her physical capacities, knowledge, skills, and access to resources, each person is constrained by realities of the natural and social environments. Strong demands (high motivation) may compensate for low capability, just as high capability can compensate for low demand (motivation). In general, however, if a task or long-term purpose is too difficult, a person must obtain more resources, seek further information, increase his or her knowledge and skills, elicit help (cooperation), or pursue an alternative.

Individuals (and social actor systems) act across the boundaries between their internal and external environments. For example, reaching into the external environment, we obtain food to satisfy our internal hunger or information, knowledge, and skills to inform and guide our actions; concomitantly, we marshall our internal capacities to accomplish external tasks. Consciously or unconsciously, we all tend—somewhat like bicycle riders or tightrope walkers—to monitor and adjust our behavior to the consequences of our actions. Thus, in trying to achieve and if possible maintain a dynamic equilibrium between our (continually changing) internal requirements and (frequently changing) external environments, our central nervous systems—through senses, cognitions, and affects (emotions)—report "back" and evaluate outcomes of our ongoing behavior (the extent to which it is on or off course in our effort to narrow or close is/ought-to-be gaps). Such *feedbacks* can be positive (when the outcome induces us to continue what we are doing (whether or not it is enjoyable or "good" for us) or negative (when the outcome discourages us from continuing what we are doing, even though it may be pleasurable or "good"). Beginning at birth (if not before), and insofar as they are accurate, feedbacks help us assess the successes and failures of our actions.

There are two major types of feedback—learning, as when by trial and error we learn to walk, and goal-seeking, as when we "steer" our bicycles to class. We all relied upon trial-and-error testing and feedback processes when we learned to talk, read, write, do algebra, drive a car, make love, fly a bomber, or earn a living.

We can distinguish between feedback and feed*forward*, which refers to our psychological processing of and responses to phenomena projected into the future. For example, in high school we imagined being an attorney, we established that as a goal, and then we went after it. Once we passed the bar examination, we stopped that activity and pursued something else— joining the family partnership, working for a firm, or setting up a practice of our own.

As individuals, in the course of a lifetime, we go through many physical, intellectual, emotional, attitudinal, and behavioral changes that result partly from maturation and partly from experience, adaptation to changing circumstances, and learning. Generally, such growth and development tend to be uneven. Physical growth may outpace intellectual growth for a while, and then the reverse may occur. Socially, our parents or friends may see us maturing faster during some stages of our lives than at others. We may also notice differences between ourselves and friends. Some are early bloomers, and others blossom late. Such tendencies are likely to proceed unevenly within and between individuals. Making demands upon and adjusting to changes in our internal and external environments during our lifetimes, we normally grow and develop rapidly in our early years, then "settle down" or taper off somewhat later on, and eventually begin to decline physically and intellectually. What we accomplish varies with our innate capabilities, dispositions, and knowledge and skills, which tend to increase during much of a lifetime as we learn and mature. Allowing for more or less random factors, the more advanced our knowledge and skills, the more widely our activities and interests are likely to expand during our more active years.

Individuals Dealing with Each Other

The course of our lives is shaped not only by physical and intellectual knowledge and skills but also by our dealings with other people. Central among our interactions with family, friends, co-workers, supervisors, and others are the means of persuasion we use to influence them (and they use to inspire, guide, or persuade us). These activities include various strategies and tactics of *bargaining, leverage,* and *coalition* (alliance) *formation,* which most of us begin learning almost from birth (Riker, 1962; Snyder and Diesing, 1977). Even small babies bargain and leverage by smiling, gurgling, dimpling, whimpering, and screaming—often with remarkable success. Lessons we have all learned from bargaining and leveraging with parents and siblings have affected us in powerful ways. The means of persuasion (the positive and negative *incentives* we use—promising, encouraging, rewarding, threatening, coercing, punishing) have left their lifetime marks on us.

Bargaining and leveraging are not the only ways in which people deal with each other, but negotiations, including various means of persuasion, account for a large part of our daily interactions (Iklé, 1964). If we stop to think about it, most of us can remember bargaining and leveraging to get what we wanted from parents, siblings, playmates, even teachers and enhancing our influence by gaining allies in a competition or conflict. We may recall also how we made group decisions by mobilizing a coalition in support of a favored option (Cyert and March, 1963:29–34).

Bargaining and leverage refer to verbal and/or nonverbal interchanges that occur when one person perceives his or her ability to gain a desired outcome as depending on the attitude or action of another person. Efforts by one bargainer to influence the attitudes or actions of another are called incentives, inducements, leverages, or side payments. Such efforts at influencing or persuading can be positive or negative and can involve rewards, pressures, threats, coercion, "carrots," "sticks," punishment, violence, and so forth. Leverage can be explicit or implicit (by innuendo or gesture). We bargain and try to persuade whenever we want some other person to help us reduce our sense of disequilibrium (or approximate a moving equilibrium).

A bargaining move contains three critical elements: a *contingency* (If . . . , unless . . .); a *demand* (an indication of the response that is expected); and a *leverage element* (explicit or implied). As used in these pages, a bargain is concluded whenever (and for whatever reasons) two or more "bargainers" decide explicitly or tacitly to accept as the status quo (for a time, at least) a particular relationship resulting from an exchange of leverages.

The strength of a leverage move can be assessed objectively in terms of the costs (in time, money, health, forsaken alternatives, or other "losses") the initiator has been willing to incur; or the leverage's strength can be assessed subjectively in terms of the way the leverage move is perceived and evaluated by the target party or by others, including the initiator (whose perceptions of costs and benefits may differ from those of a detached observer). Whatever the feelings that people harbor toward each other, the quality of their relationships (cooperative, competitive, conflictual, violent) and the outcome depend in considerable part upon the quality of leverages used (Schelling, 1960; cf. Zartman, 1976:28, 33).

Bargaining and leverage can lead to cooperation or to competition and/ or conflict. When two (or more) individuals leverage each other, each seeking an advantage involving loss to the other—but within some framework of rules and "fair play"—we say that a competition is taking place. An example is provided by two merchants, each trying to outsell the other. Some negative leveraging may occur, but neither tries to put the other out of business.

Conflict usually implies a contradiction of some kind, a situation in which two mutually exclusive values or outcomes are being pursued. When an individual feels compelled to choose between two contradictory courses of action, he or she is said to confront an internal conflict. By contrast, a social conflict occurs when two (or more) individuals (groups, nations) pursue mutually exclusive objectives (he wants the heat turned up, she wants it down, he wants to drive faster, she wants him to slow down, he wants a trip to Las Vegas, she insists on going to the beach). Conflicts are endemic to human relations; the critical issue is whether the *means of resolution* are perceived as fair or unfair, coercive or accommodative, nonviolent or violent.

Bargaining and leverage can also lead to cooperation and the formation of a *coalition* (alliance) and/or a *coalition of coalitions* (a large firm, political organization, state, or other extensive organization or institution). As a component of one or more of these collectivities, each person plays a role and deals in various ways with other members and with people outside the coalition. In whatever coalition(s) and/or coalition(s) of coalitions she or he participates, including the state, the individual brings to it (them) a complex of personal beliefs, capabilities, habits, dispositions, and idiosyncracies. Influence within a coalition can be relatively equally distributed, "democratic," and egalitarian, or influence can be grossly unequal, "authoritarian," or "totalitarian."

Second Image: The State

Historically (and prehistorically), people have formed coalitions in order to do what no individual could accomplish alone. Complex organizations, including states, are coalitions of coalitions. By definition, a state (the second image), however primitive, cannot exist without a population of some size and a *regime* or government of one sort or another. For practical reasons, a state also requires a society with some minimal level of technology (it is difficult to imagine a state-level society in a Stone Age world) and access to resources including some territory. All the activities occurring within a state are accounted for by individuals (singly or in concert)—a simpleminded observation often overlooked in studies of state institutions.

The Emergence, Growth, and Development of States

The emergence of the first states in prehistoric times has been explained variously, but there are good reasons for believing that population increases, technological advances, and uneven resource distributions were contributing factors. The need for basic resources—food, water, fibers, metals, minerals, living space, energy, and so forth—rises with population increases. The more people there are, the greater is the demand for the materials required for subsistence (a simpleminded consideration often overlooked until more and more people move into an area where water is scarce, for example). Whatever the minimal amount of resources needed by an individual for survival in a particular environment, a thousand people will require a thousand times as much, a million people a million times as much. In order to obtain more resources, people develop technology (intellectual, physical, mechanical, and organizational knowledge and skills), which enables them to acquire new resources and use old resources for new purposes.

Development often alleviates and sometimes exacerbates a society's disequilibrium. Technologies help us find new resources, but they also create needs for new resources. In general, the more advanced the technology, the greater is the amount and range of resources required to support it (how many resources from how many places are needed to build a jet aircraft?). In addition, the more advanced the technology, the greater are likely to be the amount and range of resources above subsistence requirements people perceive as necessary. We need consider only the new "necessities" created by developments in medical technology in recent decades. Finally, although energy is never destroyed, each application (or consumption) of resources reduces energy to a less usable form and generates waste (often including toxics).

In state-level societies—city-states and empires of the past as well as nation-states and multinational states of today—differential levels and rates of population growth, access to knowledge and skills, and resource availabilities in various sectors of the populace have contributed to institutionalized asymmetries (potential disequilibria) in the distribution of capabilities and leverage potentials and in the formation of classes, interest groups, elites, and regimes. This perspective distinguishes us from Marx, who saw contradictions between individual and community giving rise to other inequalities. In short, we identify population/technology/resource ratios rather than (admittedly real) individual/community contradictions as the more useful analytical base point.

Occupying a threshold position between a state's internal and external environments, the chief executive and his or her regime must monitor and try to coordinate continuous "flows" of domestic and foreign events that occur "inside" and "outside." As a result, the demands of society are only partially met (as soon as inflation is reversed, people worry about recession, and vice versa, and yesterday's ally may become tomorrow's adversary). At the same time, a leadership must draw on the past while developing policies for an uncertain future and balance demands of tomorrow against others later on. Yet leaders must decide. If too many crucial demands are unmet, the society may decline and even disintegrate.

In subsequent chapters, we show how disequilibria in prestate societies contributed to the development through adaptation and sociocultural evolution of states with overarching *regimes*, or governments, with a capacity for domestic regulation, a degree of domestic stabilization, and defense against attack from the outside. Consisting of interconnected and relatively stable leadership and bureaucratic roles, regimes commonly invoke values, customs, traditions, and laws while "disciplining" a society according to some inherent "constitution," social "contract/bargain," or "social habit structure" that serves to constrain tendencies toward disequilibrium to one degree or another. Eastern European events of the last weeks of 1989 demonstrated how quickly a regime can collapse if established habit structures fail to adapt to critical changes in a society's domestic or external environments.

By whatever means they achieve office, individual leaders and bureaucrats constituting a regime bring with them some prerequisites or qualifications (whether constitutionally stipulated or established ad hoc by superior bargaining and positive and/or negative leverage potentials—brute force, at the extreme). These leaders also bring a full array of personal attributes, dispositions, and idiosyncracies, including, perhaps, a compelling drive to capture an elusive personal (and/or state) equilibrium. In ancient states and empires, powerful families often monopolized high-level, interlocking leadership and bureaucratic offices.

In the course of ruling and administering, governmental leaders and bureaucrats in effect draw upon the resources available to them in order to bargain with and apply leverages to their subordinates and the public at large in order to ensure compliance and active support to the extent possible. Similarly, they draw upon state and their own capabilities in order to expand their influence externally and maintain security from outside attack—all in the proclaimed interests of economic, political, and strategic security (generally interdependent) and achievement of a stronger, better regulated, more rapidly growing social order. In so doing, rulers and bureaucrats respond to feedbacks (subjectively interpreted) from their previous policies and activities.

This does not mean that the rank and file of a society is without capability and bargaining and leverage potentials. In principle, a people can bring down a regime merely by refusing to comply, although this tends to be easier said than done. But even in a powerful dictatorship or tyranny, people can combine their efforts in various ways to limit what a regime can do, and in modern democratic states, citizens rely on the ballot box, letters to the editor, lobbies and other interest groups, demonstrations, and other leverages to influence local and national leaders and bureaucrats.

Among states so conceived, tyrannies, dictatorships, modern totalitarian regimes, and democracies can be distinguished by comparing distributions of knowledge, skills, capabilities, access to decisionmaking and combinations of positive and negative leverages employed, together with safeguards against misuse, if any. Depending on the structural arrangement of elites, or "estates," some regimes develop and maintain public and private sectors with varying degrees of economic and/or political responsibility and authority, free economic enterprise, secret balloting, free speech, and so forth. Others concentrate economic as well as political authority, regulation, and control in a single, highly centralized, "total" regime of leaders and bureaucrats who think, plan, and act in the name of the society. Both types can be identified as self-organizing, however, because the populace, through its attitudes and activities (including indifference, fear, greed, ambition, compliance, appeasement, and collaboration) contribute to and preserve the warp and woof of interactivity holding state and society together. Conversely, people can self-disorganize the state when enough of them turn against it.

State-Level Decisions and Actions

State decisions, policymaking, and actions are commonly written about and discussed in three major ways: The state is reified (we say that Russia mobilized in 1914); a "strong leader" is said to decide and act for the state (Kaiser Wilhelm invaded Belgium); or the decisionmakers (the chief executive and members of the cabinet or board, advisers, or staff) present various options and then bargain and leverage among themselves until a coalition forms in support of a particular course of action. Later, top bureaucrats or officers in the field and their staffs, charged with implementing the decisions, select specific activation strategies and procedures in similar ways (Cyert and March, 1963:28, 36; Riker, 1962:107). Even in the second case, the presence of a "strong leader" does not preclude bargaining and leverage processes. On the contrary, even a tyrant or dictator who may appear to be all-powerful and not dependent upon support from his generals or advisers is likely to consult, and even negotiate, with his advisers and generals. A Caligula or a Hitler must continually bargain with, apply positive and/or negative leverages to, and mediate between his ambitious aides and henchmen (who may be expected to compete for his time and favor) in line with his own judgments, preferences, goals, and idiosyncratic fantasies. If he fails too often, his dominance may be undermined. In short, all leaders, whatever their capabilities, must bargain, "twist arms," and perhaps instill fear to obtain support for their policies and thus transform individual "preferences" into a collective will.

We can conceptualize state leaders and bureaucrats as planning, developing policies, making decisions and conducting domestic affairs, all within the second image system. In fact, however, they occupy an authoritative position at the boundary between their own state and the international system. When they turn their attention externally, they must first debate, plan, decide, and begin organizing internally in order to implement policy and action externally in the third image environment. In these terms a truly "sovereign" chief of state (prime minister, president, or dictator, for example) is a legitimate actor in both systems and can thus be viewed as the ultimate spokesperson for the state on both second and third image levels.

Third and Fourth Images:
The International System and the Global System

Strictly construed, an international system (the third image) may include any two or more states that regularly interact with each other positively and/or negatively. Conventionally, however, the concept of the international system dates from the mid-seventeenth century, when it referred to the major powers of Europe. Since then, the meaning of the term has been expanded to include all the states of the world, although major powers tend to be emphasized. Only rarely have all the countries of the globe been studied as components of the third image as a whole.

Consisting of states that proclaim their own independence and "sovereignty," the international system has no overarching authority, or regime, and therefore cannot be treated as an actor system. It is true that the United Nations and its agencies have limited powers of regulation, but its sanctions are severely constrained by veto in the Security Council, and lesser states are often protected to the extent that they are clients of one or another major power or superpower. Essentially, the constraints of the international system are the outcome of all the nations, but especially the stronger ones, interacting with each other. In terms of its components, their functioning, and their relations with each other and with the physical environment, the international system approximates an ecological system in which the human elements are dominant. To conceptualize the international system as a unified actor system is to reify it. In principle, the state could exist without an international system (as many states did in earlier periods of history), but the modern international system could not exist without states.

Demands, Capabilities, and National Expansion

Population growth and technological advancement generate demands and affect national capabilities and influence in various ways. As we have indicated, demands increase as population increases. Knowledge and skills make new resources available and find new applications for old resources that were previously considered of little or no use. But technology also requires new resources, and as new expectations are generated, wider ranges and larger amounts of raw materials and other resources are likely to be in demand. In addition, a society's access to resources depends in considerable part upon its power—its capabilities and influence.

Realists, whose theories and perspective prevail in the field of international relations and among foreign policy makers in general, usually view state-level regimes as acting to maximize or optimize power much as economists assume that a hypothetical "economic man," commercial and industrial organizations, and whole economies pursue maximization or optimization of wealth. Power is more difficult to define (or measure) than wealth is, however, and theoreticians, writers, foreign policy makers, and the public at large often slide from one meaning to another unaware of what they have done. Rooted in the three master variables (population, technology, and resources) and resulting demands (especially those that are unmet), the power perspective of this book is more dynamic, more interactive, more complexly interdependent than that of most realists.

In general, we would expect the people in a society and their regime to use domestic resources first if only for reasons of availability. Insofar as arable land, foodstuffs, building materials, energy in various forms, and other resources (including labor and manufactured goods) are in short supply and/or can be obtained more cheaply elsewhere, people reach out beyond national borders to obtain them by trade or other means. Such tendencies on the part of a number of nations often lead to competition and to a disposition on the part of traders, investors, national leaders, bureaucrats, and even the public at large to establish foreign interests and concepts of economic, political, and strategic security, including an expectation that their respective governments will use their power (involving, on occasion, armed force) to protect resource access and other aspects of security as variously defined.

However, the expansion of national interests is not always the outcome of a search for resources narrowly conceived. John Maynard Keynes (1936:38) saw "population pressures" and competition for markets as common "causes of war," and Harold Lasswell (1935:121) asserted that "prosperity expands markets, intensifies contact, sharpens conflict and war." Historically, nations have expanded and defended such activities and interests as the conversion of "heathens" and the enhancement of national prestige and influence. In many instances, however, national interests have been mixed—for example, the search for spices as well as "souls," free land along with religious freedom, or the desire for prestige. But national prestige is often so intertwined with the pursuit of economic, political, and strategic capabilities and influence that it is difficult to ascertain where one ends and another begins.

In these pages, a tendency for a people to expand their activities and interests for any purpose whatsoever is identifiable as a manifestation of *lateral pressure*—a relatively neutral concept similar to what Pitirim Sorokin (1857:565) called economic expansion and economist Simon Kuznets (1966:334–348) referred to more generally as *outward* expansion. Generally, the strength of a country's lateral pressure correlates with its *power*, a concept that is widely, almost universally, used but that is rarely well defined.

As we see it, the lateral pressure phenomenon—the *uneven* expansion of national activities and interests (both governmental and private)—is an outcome of power as *capability* (power$_1$) and is a manifestation of power as *influence* (power$_2$). In combination, these two types of power commonly contribute to issues of war, peace, and survival. Both types of power have "subjective" as well as "objective" components; that is, in any particular situation they tend to be dependent on how they are perceived and assessed (often differentially) by the people involved.

Measurable in terms of gross national product (GNP), GNP per capita, import and export strength, military expenditures, troop levels, armaments, or other indicators, power$_1$ is synonymous with economic, political, military, and overall generalized capability. In the abstract, the assessments of a nation's capability are often assessed one way by its leaders and bureaucrats, another way by its allies, and a third way by its adversaries. The same nation's "real" power$_1$, remains objectively uncertain, relative to the capability of other states, until it has been demonstrated by success or failure.

Power$_2$, which includes many social and psychological components (cohesion, integrity, "will," "vision," determination, and the like) refers, in contrast, to one actor's influence over another. Influence is often defined as "the power to produce an effect without apparent exertion of force" or "the capacity of causing an effect in indirect or intangible ways." How much influence country A possesses in any particular situation depends also in considerable part on B's readiness to be influenced—in leverage terms, "persuaded." A country that is capable of transforming its inherent capabilities into widely extended and effective influence can be said to possess *power outreach*.

The Outcomes of Lateral Pressure

The outcomes of lateral pressure are not predetermined. On the contrary, they depend on the interactions, competitions, interdependencies, and conflicts of the countries of the world and the ways in which such phenomena are perceived, evaluated, and acted on. Overall, the consequent activities and relationships define the international system at any particular time. The various combinations of these subjective and objective power considerations contribute to an uncertainty and a paradox.

The Power-Uncertainty Problem. One way of clarifying power$_1$, power$_2$, and the uncertainty phenomenon on a national level is to begin with their sources—individual human beings developing and applying capabilities and influence in order to improve the probability that their personal demands will be met. If we imagine a state-level society as a pyramid of human interactivity, then millions of rank-and-file individuals at the base are developing their capabilities and influence in various ways, bargaining and leveraging among themselves and forming coalitions and coalitions of coalitions (social, economic, political, and so forth)—horizontal and vertical networks of interactivity. We can envisage these interactivities as linking people with each other, however remotely, and with national leaders, bureaucrats, and the regime.

Because of the relative and interdependent aspects of capability (power$_1$) and influence$_2$—in combination and as applied to another nation—the outcome tends to be uncertain, a phenomenon that can be referred to as *power uncertainty.* Powerful "conquerors" like Napoleon and Hitler have commonly run afoul of the power/uncertainty phenomenon—partly because they overassessed their own nation's power and influence relative to the potentials of their adversaries and partly because they failed to foresee how other nations would combine against them. In terms of power/uncertainty the critical issue pertains to the extent to which all of these interactivities combine to constrain tendencies toward disequilibrium and contribute to the state's coordinated power and influence relative to the power and influence of other states in the international system.

The recent Vietnam and Afghanistan wars illustrate the uncertainty problem. By most rule-of-thumb criteria the United States had more power$_1$ in economic, political, and military areas than did North Vietnam or the Vietcong, and both the Washington regime and large sectors of the public—including many who opposed the war—took for granted that the combined power and influence of the United States was more than adequate. There was loose talk about "paving Vietnam over with high-yield bombs, if necessary to 'win.'" In the end, however, the United States had an insufficiency of the potent capability/influence combination—just as the USSR suffered an insufficiency and consequent defeat in Afghanistan. So much for the power-uncertainty problem.

The Security Paradox. The paradox of security is even more unnerving in some respects. By security we mean a sense of feeling well defended, protected, and safe. Like power$_1$, security implies an intense interdependence among economic, political, and strategic components. And like power$_2$, security includes more or less intangible social and psychological variables— a sense of well-being or confidence, for example, in dealing with the present and planning for the future. But there are realities in economic, political, and strategic relationships that render security to some degree elusive and paradoxical.

In general, the higher the level of a country's aggregated and unsatisfied demands and the higher its economic, political, and military capabilities (power$_1$), the greater is the probability that the country's external activities and interests will intersect with the activities and interests of other countries in negative ways, and the greater is the likelihood that conflicts (and possibly war) may eventuate—especially to the extent that unfolding events leave the nation's leaders and populace feeling blocked and frustrated.

When there is an intersection or collusion of the activities and interests of two countries with grossly unequal capabilities, the weaker is likely to be penetrated and possibly dominated, exploited (intentionally or unintentionally), and even absorbed by the stronger. On the other hand, when the expanding activities and interests of two (or more) high-capability countries intersect or collide, the leaderships involved (in principle) have two choices. If interactions between the two countries are confined to positive or relatively low-level negative leverages, serious conflict may be avoided, friendly competition fostered, or cooperation achieved.

Whenever accelerating negative leverages are exchanged, however, there is a risk that conflict and a crisis may be generated, escalations empowered, and violence triggered. In Chapters 7 and 10 we consider circumstances under which a crisis may de-escalate, but here we are concerned with trends toward crises and wars by two or more adversaries in pursuit of their own security. *Insofar as each side seeks to enhance (and defend) the security of its expanding economic, political, and/or military activities and interests, its rival or potential enemy may be predisposed to interpret such defensive moves as a threat to its own activities and interests.* Common to such sequences is a positive feedback phenomenon referred to as the *conflict spiral*, in which a move by one actor so widens the cybernetic (is/ought-to-be) gap of the adversary that the latter responds with a tit-for-tat increase in its own leverage and thereby incites additional retaliation by the first actor. *Once caught in such an escalation, it often follows that if either party makes a conciliatory move, the adversary is likely to dismiss it as a deception or accept it as an opportunity to be exploited.*

Caught in situations of paradox, decisionmakers commonly experience the inherent contradictions as *dilemmas*. At this point we need to reemphasize that neither the uncertainty of power nor the security paradox is "inevitable" or deterministic in the sense that any particular outcomes are utterly beyond human control. In principle (and usually in fact), being the outcome of human decisions and actions, both the power-uncertainty problem and the security paradox can be avoided or resolved in a number of ways—by a willingness by both sides, for example, to negotiate peacefully and patiently, to submit to mediation or adjudication, and so forth. The "determinism," in short, is social rather than material or physical (like the law of gravity) or mechanical: Through their perceptions, beliefs, fears, habit structures, and other human attributes, people shape their own unintended consequences and many of their disasters.

Against this background, our line of investigation into problems of war, peace, and survival is to examine as carefully and thoughtfully as we can the human activity variables that contribute to power uncertainty, to the security paradox, and also to alternate options and possibly more favorable outcomes for the future.

Here let us remind ourselves that in a framework of nested systems, each actor system acts upon—and in a sense mediates between and tries to "balance"—its internal (molecular) and external (molar, encompassing) environments. Although not an actor system, strictly speaking, the international system is defined and kept in motion by the power distributions and interactivities of states that affect conditions and events not only within internal environments of the third image (individual states and their internal environments) but also within the encompassing fourth image, or global environment.

The Need for a Global System Concept

Originally, the international system referred only to a cluster of newly emerged nation-states in Europe. During three or four centuries, the concept was expanded as original member states acquired overseas empires. More recently, with the dissolution of these empires, former colonies have joined as component states, thus expanding the system. Even now, however, there are extensive parts of the planet—the oceans, their respective "floors," and space, for example—that are not organized as states and are not subject to the direct or formal jurisdiction of any government. Various international conventions regulate certain human activities in these regions, but their status remains ambiguous. We locate them within the fourth image.

The fourth image concept is invoked with increasing frequency these days. We refer to *world* population, *world* development, *world* trade, *world* finance, the *World* Bank, *global* pollution, *global* ecology, *world* war, *global* catastrophe, and, when we speculate about the future, a possible *world* government. The concepts of *world economy* and *world market* are widely used. Yet the fourth image, or global system, has not been extensively developed or widely accepted as an analytical concept, even though there seems to be an increasing need for it. Often it is used as a synonym for the international system, which, as conventionally defined, is a relatively narrow concept that is not easily expanded to accommodate the challenges to humankind as they unfold today.

Embodying the dynamic interactivities of individuals within and between coalitions on a rich but increasingly crowded planet, the complicated issues of war, peace, and survival require a broader, more encompassing view that includes twenty-first-century expansion of human activities, interests, competitions, and potentials for cooperation well beyond international borders. Thus, the fourth, or global, image, as we define it, distinguishes between natural and social environments and allows for the systematic investigation of the ways in which they interact on land, in the sea, in the air, and in space and for the outcomes.

As we see it, the earth, its geological and geographical features, its flora and fauna, and its surroundings (including the sun) provide a unique and indispensable environment for life as we experience it. For the time being, at least, this is the ultimate molar image, the source of our energies, and the field in which our aspirations are conceived and our lifetime activities carried out—like the first, an image we could not do without. We could not exist without the planet and the delicate balances of its natural features. Even relatively minor alterations in natural environment—climate, weather, and atmospheric conditions included—could make our survival difficult, if not impossible. Meanwhile, our expanding activities and interests exert increasingly threatening pressures on both social and natural environments.

In a sense, the natural environment holds us all hostage, but the implications have become increasingly more complicated as exponential population growth and advances in technology have enabled human beings to expand their activities and interests into remote enclaves of the planet (and into space) and increasingly to intervene in natural processes, often blindly and without foreknowledge of consequences. Meanwhile, fundamental powers and processes of the fourth image remain dominant over—and disrespectful of, even oblivious to—our regimes and boundaries. Once we have released our toxins into the soil, water, and air, for example, nature's processes take control. Whatever we do that drastically interferes with the natural system can have global repercussions. Only a four-image framework can demonstrate the extent to which war, peace, environmental, and other current problems impinge on each other. Against this four-image background, then, we are ready to see how individual humans (the first image) and their needs, wants, desires, demands, capabilities, and actions create, constitute, constrain, shape—and are constrained and shaped by—the other three.

Notes

1. The conceptual framework developed in this book draws from the writing of Ludwig von Bertalanffy and other general systems theorists. Recognizing analogs (or isomorphisms) in the structures and attributes of organismic, social, and ecological systems, general systems theory facilitates identification of linkages and cause-effect relationships within and between them. Aspects of this approach can be useful for studying how first (individual), second (state), third (international), and possibly fourth (global) images relate to each other. Although general systems is a generic paradigm of structure, attributes, and change, not a theory of politics, a number of political scientists have adapted it for the study of international politics. But with a few major exceptions, the attempts have been partial, even piecemeal.

PART 1

First Image: The Individual

2

The Individual in Primal Environments

Having identified two central problems (the power-uncertainty phenomenon and the security paradox as sources of war and obstacles to peace) and our line of investigation, we are now ready to consider the first image—the individual in primal environments—as the generator of a sociocultural evolutionary thrust resulting, through millennia of adaptation, in the historical development of the second, third, and fourth images as we know them today. But first we need to explain why, in a study of states and the international and global systems, we dwell on the individual at all. In this regard, our focus arises from a widespread tendency to treat the state as if it possessed a reality and integrity apart from the individuals who constitute it, shape it, and commonly invoke its "authority." In fact, because individuals are the only thinking, feeling, and acting units in any social system, we have to take into serious account how they "work," or more specifically, what they bring with them when they fill leadership, bureaucratic, or even rank-and-file roles within any organization.

Individual Cognitions, Affects, and Motivations

But can we understand the individual apart from his or her social contexts? Is it not risky to discuss the individual, qua individual, apart from family, neighborhood, community, and nation? Is this not like studying Robinson Crusoe upon his remote island before Friday's arrival (but worse because Crusoe had a physical environment at least, however limited)? Most of us, by contrast, are lifelong social dependents.

Although we take these objections seriously, spotlighting the individual imposes upon us a certain discipline, provided we do not lose sight of the individual's social (as well as physical) environments. For example, with family and other institutional contexts firmly in mind, we can gain from a brief consideration of the individual's central nervous system and its interactions with physical and social environments—reminders of how dependent we all are upon our surroundings and upon each other. In addition, we can recognize how individuals bring neurobehavioral processes as well as personal values, predispositions, idiosyncracies, beliefs, motivations, and limitations to the roles they play.

In this chapter, we view the individual from three perspectives: (1) as a being sensitive and responsive to internal and external experience who continually generates personal needs, wants, desires, and demands; transforms raw materials into physical and psychological energy; and at the same time learns lessons from deciding and acting in both environments; (2) in dyadic relationships as cooperator, competitor, or adversary; and (3) as a bargaining and leveraging member or participant in coalitions, specifically family and other prestate societies.

Why a prestate society? What does it have to do with war, peace, and survival at the beginning of the twenty-first century? The answer is simple. Modern states are so complex that it is difficult to understand what they are and how they got started. Most of us just take them for granted; fear them as adversaries or merely as unpleasant realities like bad weather, taxes, and death; or glorify them on independence day and give our lives in their defense. An investigation into prestate society may illuminate modern states—particularly in regard to how human beings organize and govern themselves—in ways impossible to discern from a more contemporary analysis.

Of course, prestate societies were different from our own. But a large part of these differences can be accounted for by two levels of technology (knowledge and skills)—theirs and ours—and the uncounted millennia of experience between them. Succeeding pages will suggest that the psychological and affective processes of our ancestors' central nervous systems—their thinking, perceiving, feeling, believing, expecting, deciding, and acting functions—were much like ours, although the *content* was different. As with us, what they thought about depended upon what they perceived, experienced, believed, expected, and hoped for. There were fewer of them, their knowledge and skills were more limited (as we measure these things now), but they knew a great deal about their relatively undisturbed natural environments, and they were remarkably adept in their adaptations. Their beliefs derived directly from their perceptions of and experience with these relatively "untouched" surroundings and from traditions passed along from their forebears.

In this chapter, we are concerned less with our ancestors' physical and mechanical technologies (crucial though they were for human survival) than with their organizational knowledge and skills, which centered in the family. We shall start with the needs, wants, desires, and demands of the individual and then move along to motivations, intentions, decisions, and actions. All of these phenomena, we shall discover, are conditioned and sometimes sharply altered by such factors as cognitions, memory, habits, and beliefs as well as by continually changing events and conditions of physical and social environments. The second part of the chapter will direct our attention to how individuals—members of families, extended families, and other prestate collectives—dealt with each other. Relevant, too, are some of the ways in which interactions among members contributed to the maintenance of the collective, to how group decisions were made, and to how perseverant behaviors and responses to nature and to each other led to changes in social structures and institutions. Also fundamental to the discussion is how population growth and advances in technology (knowledge and skills) affected the family and contributed to adaptation and institutional change.

The Interdependence of Body and Mind

In Chapter 1, we considered how inescapably dependent our bodies, minds, cognitions, affects, beliefs, and actions are upon sustained access to food, water, air, and other resources from the natural environment. By transforming these materials through the body's metabolic processes we "stay alive" and advance our ability to cope with natural and social environments. In so doing, however, we transform our physical surroundings and also generate other, less tangible "needs," wants, and desires such as physical safety, economic security, affiliation (a sense of belonging), a measure of order and predictability in our lives. In addition, we want affection from loved ones; a sense of self-esteem; fellowship with friends, neighbors, and fellow workers; and opportunities for self-realization or self-actualization (Maslow, 1978). Anthropologists and others who have lived intimately with Stone Age survivors in remote enclaves of the earth affirm that our remote ancestors had feelings and aspirations similar to our own, although differing in specific content.

Today, however, the possibilities are vastly greater for those of us who also want "success," riches, and/or power or control over others—aspirations that for our remote ancestors were so severely limited as to be scarcely imaginable in terms we take for granted today. Who among them, for example, could aspire to a multimillion dollar fortune, the power of a modern dictator, the composition of a symphony, or discoveries about the shaping powers of DNA? (Subsequent chapters will suggest ways in which development of the second image—the state—made such aspirations conceivable and, for at least a few, attainable.)

Many if not all of these (and other) needs, wants, and desires appear to be intensely interdependent. Some amount of sustenance is necessary if a person is to pursue security, just as some measure of security is essential if sustenance is to be maintained. So, too, the maintenance of affiliation depends upon sustenance and some degree of security. Such interconnectedness implies networks of needs, wants, desires, and demands (all translatable into is/ought-to-be terms). Commonly, when one need or want is satisfied, another takes its place, with the result that few of us are ever fully satisfied.

Capabilities and Demands

Individuals differ with respect to the nature and levels of their *capability*—the ability to perform "work" (physical, social, intellectual, artistic) and accomplish specific tasks. There are numerous kinds of capability, including muscular strength, general and/or specific knowledge, skills and talents, bargaining and leverage potential, experience, "wisdom," charisma, and so forth. Some of these capabilities tend to be genetically endowed, whereas others are acquired through training or practice. Specialized capabilities pertain to particular trades, professions, arts, or services. In prestate societies, divisions of labor and specializations were limited by prevailing technologies, but arrowmakers, bone- and woodcarvers, shamans, and other specialists were commonplace. In all societies, *demands* (determination deriving from a need, want, or desire to narrow or close an is/ought-to-be gap) tend to combine with particular capabilities in order to yield particular "work" outcomes. In some endeavors, strong inner demand (motivation) can often compensate for inadequate capability, and up to a point superior knowledge, skills, and capability can compensate for low demand (a kind of "steamroller" effect). We will return to this consideration when we discuss incentives further along.

Cognitions, Feelings, and Affects

Cognitions are whatever knowledge, opinion, or beliefs we have about ourselves and the physical or social environments as well as about whatever information we have at hand (Zajonc, 1968:321). Without cognition, we could not remember the past, comprehend the present, or envisage the future. Cognitions and *feelings* (sensations, sensitivities) have much in common and tend to be interdependent; some psychologists see them as "almost inseparable" (Allport, 1958:223). Much the same can be said about *affects* (emotions)—the positive or negative feelings associated with (or responsive to) cognitions of what is (has been, will be) and of what ought to be. (Strongly negative feelings about what is (a push) or strongly positive feelings about what ought to be (a pull) can intensify motivation to close a *gap* between perceived fact and felt preferences.) What we identify as needs, wants, and desires, and what we do about them, will depend upon our cognitions tempered by our feelings and affects.

Despite these similarities and close interdependencies of process, people commonly perceive and feel differently about the same situations, events, and other people. In effect, none of us understands "reality" except through deeply personalized cognitions, feelings, and affects. This means that much of what each of us takes to be "real" is deeply personal and subjective and is influenced by our individual temperaments, family backgrounds, and training and experience. Even Stone Age hunters could disagree about how many buffalo were represented by a cloud of dust on the horizon, and today's economic, financial, and political "experts" are often at odds about theories and predictions.

Values, Beliefs, and Attitudes

In order to survive and function, every person during the course of development acquires *values, beliefs,* and *attitudes,* which are closely interconnected. Values refer to assignments of worth (relative or absolute) that make it possible for an actor to select from among—or set limits upon—behavioral actions that are considered desirable. A belief is a habit or state of mind that identifies what the believer accepts as true or false, right or wrong, good or bad, acceptable or unacceptable. And an attitude is a cognitive and/or affective disposition toward a person, action or activity, condition, option, event, or likelihood. Values, beliefs, and attitudes shape each other: We value our beliefs; believe in our values; changes in either beliefs or values may alter our attitudes; and if for one reason or another our attitudes begin to change (through experience, therapy, or a religious event) our values and beliefs may also change. In this chapter we are concerned primarily with beliefs, but values and attitudes are nearly always implicit.

As we become cognizant of objects, situations, events, or other people, we tend to evaluate them. From a wholly detached perspective, none of them is inherently "good" or "bad"; we make those judgments ourselves. As Shakespeare observed in *Hamlet* (II, 2259), "There is nothing good or bad, but thinking makes it so." Or, as Saint Paul told the Romans, "There is nothing unclean of itself, but to him that esteemeth any thing to be unclean, for him it is unclean" (Romans 14:14). Obviously, it is not always easy for us to deal with real-world people that way. We commonly attribute values to them and their idiosyncracies (and they to us and ours). In fact, we often polarize them according to aspects we identify as good or bad, white or black (the grays tend to be overlooked). You and I may not trust those strangers out there, and they probably do not trust us (and sometimes you may not be sure about me).

In practice, then, our beliefs tend to be whatever we perceive to be true or real (personal constructs) about our physical and social environments and the whole universe (the earth is flat for those who believe it to be flat). The beliefs of most of us tend to be strongly influenced, positively or negatively, by the beliefs and attitudes of our family members, teachers, religious counselors, and other authority figures.

Among prehistoric hunters and gatherers, people lived and interacted so closely with the natural environment that they often tended to anthropomorphize not only animals but even inanimate objects; these ancestors were sensitive to their respective "spirits" and "intents." "Truth" often differed from one kinship group to another, but much of what appeared obvious and "rational" to them would seem irrational to many of us. At the same time, those of us living in highly industrial societies today often remain remote from the natural world and ill at ease, even threatened, when forced to become more intimate with it.

However strange the beliefs of an African Bushman or Australian aborigine even today may seem to us, we may assume that his or her beliefs provide a more or less coherent way of organizing and making sense of what would otherwise seem chaotic, senseless, perhaps terrifying. Beliefs, in short, enable people to construct more or less manageable "models" of their external and internal environments, of past and future events, of how other people relate to each other, and of intricate abstractions such as war, peace, and survival. Beliefs are thus indispensable, but from time to time we must remind ourselves that they may simplify and structure the real world in ways that can be misleading. Could a "flatworlder" navigate a spaceship to the moon? Can a person who believes that the world was created a few thousand years ago study fossils or australopithecine remains to the satisfaction of a modern anthropologist? The round world is still populated by some holdout flatworlders; they *know* it is flat because they can *see* that it is flat. In effect, we choose, maintain, defend, but seldom fully adjust to or totally reject our images of reality. Yet now and then, a new insight may compel us to abandon a cherished belief. If this were never to occur, we could not adapt to changing realities.

Motivations and Values

As opposed to being acted upon, as beliefs are, motivations generate dispositions to act and values help to shape our motivations (if I favor the underdog, I may be motivated to support him). The concept of *motivation* includes the phenomena of needing, wanting, and desiring, but it generally refers more to the feelings or emotions involved than to the more cognitive concept of intent. Motive thus encompasses specific needs, wants, and desires (as well as more enduring tendencies and dispositions such as greed or lust) and is translatable into the broader notion of gap. The stronger my positive feelings about what ought to be, the greater will be my motivation to narrow or close the gap between that outcome (goal) and what is, with the following proviso: Depending upon my capabilities, the wider the gap (beyond some threshold point), the lower my motivation is likely to be. (If I am a D student in high school, I may not be sufficiently motivated to prepare myself for medical school—unless, for example, I am a highly intelligent foreigner not yet in sufficient command of English.) People are motivated by desires to avoid pain, punishment, or disadvantage; to be well regarded; or to gain advantage. (Anger, fear, hope, and other negative and positive affects also contribute to and often intensify motivation.)

Motives are commonly mixed and difficult to distinguish analytically. A shaman among hunters and gatherers might perceive him- or herself as a mediator between the vicissitudes of nature and the interests of members of the band but find advantage also in opportunities for influencing their behaviors. Similarly, a student today may favor teaching college English but decide on medicine in order to help sick people (and "incidentally" to make more money). A U.S. president, extending economic aid to other countries, may foresee an advantage down the road in terms of markets for U.S. goods. Self-assessments of motive are likely to be suspect, especially when high stakes are involved.

All motivations, as well as attitudes, decisions, and actions, involve *values*—the relative worth, utility, or importance that a person attributes to an object, person, type of behavior, course of action, experience, and so forth. Values also affect our goals and our selection of behavioral options; we are taught that the means we choose may nullify the ends we pursue. A clear distinction must be drawn, however, between values that are *professed* (but not necessarily observed) and those that are *validated* by suitable behavior (our true values help shape and are revealed by our actions).

We have no way of knowing other people's true motives (or intents); we can only infer what those appear to be. The motives (and intents) we attribute to another person—particularly if he or she is a competitor or adversary—may be quite different from what that person intends or a third observer perceives. Often, we do not fully understand or even recognize our own motives, let alone those of anyone else. The human tendency is to perceive the best in one's own motivations and to impugn the motives of competitors, rivals, superiors, inferiors, and adversaries (you and I do not trust their motives, and sometimes you may wonder about mine).

Memory and Habit. Associated with motivation are memory and habit. Memory can be defined as the store and capacity for recalling or reproducing what has been experienced and/or learned in the past. Habit refers to a tendency or pattern of behavior acquired by frequent repetition manifested in the regularity or frequent repetition of performance. Without memory and habit the basis for our motivations would be extremely narrow, and we would have difficulty in relating to our physical and social environments. A distinction needs to be drawn between motives relating to memory of past observations or experiences (he decided to attack because he wanted to preempt the enemy) and motives oriented toward the future (later he withdrew in order to repel a threat to his flank).

Memory defines what responses have been associated in past experience and contributes to *habit*—the behavior patterns acquired through frequent repetition (and increased facility of performance) in response to similar stimuli in the past. Memory of responses and their association can be flawed, however, and habitual responses that have developed strength in the past may not be appropriate when applied to a new circumstance (generals are often charged with fighting the previous war all over again in a new situation).

Inducements, Incentives, and Expectations. The concept of motivation also encompasses inducements and incentives, which are specific events, expectations, or outcomes that are evaluated or interpreted in ways that bias an actor toward some particular behavior. Broadly construed, inducements and incentives refer to a sense of being drawn, pulled, or attracted toward some perceived quality or value on the ought-to-be side of a gap. More specifically, an *inducement* is a consideration (positive leverage) offered by one party in an exchange or bargaining situation in order to encourage a particular response from the other party (the headman offered food to the strangers in order to induce friendly behavior; the president offered asylum in order to induce the dictator to abdicate).

Incentive, on the other hand, refers to the magnitude of a particular satisfaction that an actor in an exchange situation expects to accrue if a certain act is performed (for the strangers from afar, the hope of obtaining food and rest was a strong incentive for friendly behavior; the possibility of winning the nomination was sufficient incentive to keep the candidate hard at work on the campaign trail). At the third image level, we may infer that Neville Chamberlain's expectations at Munich ("peace in our time") provided him with a strong incentive for what has been interpreted ever since as his "appeasement" of Adolf Hitler. Another incentive—Harry Truman's anxiety about Soviet expansion into Western Europe—yielded for the West a seemingly more favorable outcome through the Marshall Plan and the North Atlantic Treaty Organization (NATO).

The concept of *expectation* is closely associated with incentive and can be construed in two ways. A person's motivation is likely to be strengthened by positive expectations of outcome and weakened by negative expectations of circumstance (if a major war appears imminent and I am registered in the draft, my motivation for entering a Ph.D. program in the classics is likely to be dampened). But expectation may also refer to a person's subjective assessment of probable outcome in terms of his or her self-concept (a student may have high scores in the Graduate Record Examinations but be aware of a strong tendency to procrastinate).

The Making of Decisions

In Chapter 1, we differentiated power (a capability) from decisionmaking, policy formation, and the selection of courses of action, which can be conceptualized as *steering*. We must immediately qualify this distinction, however, because in terms of decision and action, power and steering are often so interactive and interdependent that boundaries are difficult to draw. (For a crude example, recall that some boats can be steered by varying the flow of power applied to the right and left propellers; analogously, more money to the military may "steer" a society toward lower standards of health.) But there is a different point to make, and again a maritime metaphor may help. Power *differential* distinguishes a kayak or dugout canoe from a capital ship, but each must have a power *source*, and both must be susceptible to steering. The point of this is that a boat cannot be steered without a source of power, and a boat with power but no steering is not manageable. Analogously, whereas a state cannot make effective decisions beyond the limits of its power, a powerful state can become unmanageable through inept decisionmaking.

Decision—a determination to act in order to narrow or close a gap between a perception of fact (what is) and a perception of value (what ought to be)—is a highly generic concept. It can apply to any decision, at any time, and in any situation, whether made by a nation, firm, individual, or my programmable thermostat, which can "decide" what the temperature of my house should be, "act" accordingly, or "change its mind" several times in twenty-four hours if so directed. The gap view of decisionmaking is especially useful in the study of international politics because the boundaries for decision are explicit: The perceived actual state of affairs and the preferred condition and the difference between them—the "cost" of reducing or closing the gap—can often be identified and measured in one currency or another (time, effort, money, forfeiture of a valued alternative).

Situations triggering decisionmaking may originate within the individual (hunger, toothache), in the outside environment (change of temperature, charging buffalo), or both interactively (dismissed after twenty years with his firm, an accountant—feeling desperately inadequate in the contemporary business environment—signs up for an extension course in computing). As commonly conceived, the making of a decision involves at least three segments: a determination to act (to narrow or close a perceived gap) or not to act; the selection, in the first instance, of a mode of action (or action sequence), a plan; and the implementation of the action. Whether or not the action occurs will depend upon the strength of the demand (motivation, will) and the level of capability. Generally, our decisions and actions are shaped by the way we (individually) perceive and interpret objective realities, whereas outcomes tend to be constrained by objective realities as they *really* are—available tools and resources, for example, or miscalculations of cost (U.S. forces in Vietnam, Soviet troops in Afghanistan).

People often have difficulty choosing between alternative courses of action, especially when both alternatives are unsatisfactory. For example, should a hunter in pursuit of a polar bear proceed across thin ice or take a long leap to the nearest floe? Should I testify against the Mafia boss or go to jail for contempt of court? Should the United States, or the USSR, proceed against an adversary (and accept more casualties) or withdraw with consequent losses of prestige and face? Then there are quandaries (choosing between mutually exclusive but equally desirable options). Should a hunter go after the elk or the moose? Should I vacation in Hawaii or the Caribbean? Should a national administration invest a one-time tax windfall in Acquired Immune Deficiency Syndrome (AIDS) research or in an upgrading of education?

Inherent in the making and implementing of decisions are many if not most of the cognitive, sensory, and affective phenomena touched upon in previous sections of this chapter. Many of these can be integrated into the elusive processes of scanning, comparing, assessing, selecting, planning, and trial-and-error adjusting functions. A tracker takes into account the terrain, wind, and habits of his prey; a surgeon reviews the patient's symptoms, medical history, results of specific tests, diagnoses, risks of operating or not operating, and so forth. Involved in the assessing function are the identification of constraints and obstacles and the comparing of probable gains and costs. Because of the multiplicative relationship between motivation and capability, a high level of one may substitute for a deficiency of the other (Vietcong against the United States, the U.S. "steamroller" effect in Grenada).

Planning and Feedforward

In reaching a decision, a person's brain makes psychic preparations for each act in the form of molar-molecular hierarchies of instructions or processes that control the order in which intricate sequences of action are to be performed. As a plan is implemented, consequent activities may be manifested as comparable, but more substantial, hierarchies of means and ends. (Check any cookbook.) In each hierarchy, the "higher," or "controlling," component is molar (adjust the dial), the controlled elements molecular (oven temperature is changed) (Miller, Galanter, and Pribram, 1960:1, 32).

Inherent in the making of any plan is feed*forward*, a "looking ahead" to the decisionmaker's definition of purpose and goal and selection (and readjustment in response to anticipated obstacles) during the planning stage. Is the deerhunter proposing to act alone, or is he thinking of organizing a drive? Is the surgeon ready to operate, or does she consider consulting a senior colleague? Is the head of state ready to declare war, or does she seek advice from the cabinet one more time?

Feed*back*, by contrast, refers to the success-and-error messages resulting from measures undertaken and corrections made in response. Feedback will continue as long as the decision is being implemented. As a navigator steers for an intermediate reference point (a headland, perhaps), any deviation from that vector is *positive* feedback that must be corrected by a negative adjustment. As the vessel nears the reference point, however, a new heading is required. Thereafter, any positive deviation from course must be checked by a negative adjustment, until a new reference point is selected. In principle, any course of action (and alterations therein, including policy changes) will be subject to analogous feedbacks. As the hunter moves forward, he changes course as the lead buck stamps a foot in alarm. The surgeon responds to a drop in the patient's blood pressure. A diplomat breaks off negotiations when the adversary regime mobilizes its troops.

Two modes of feedback can be distinguished. The first is *reflex behavior,* which is inborn, genetically determined in detail, and not appreciably modified by individual experience. Such simple feedbacks amount to the reinsertion of information for the relatively unsophisticated, short-term regulation and control of a person's activities. The second feedback mode is *learned behavior,* which is not inborn or genetically determined in detail but is markedly modified by personal experience. From walking a tightrope to performing a surgical operation or executing a troop withdrawal, action sequences involve parallel and sequential feedforward and feedback loops that must be coordinated if we are to undertake and complete the activity.

Even a simple act can be the outcome of complex cognitive, affective, and muscular activities (Granit, 1977:160). In order to perform so simple an act as picking up a pen to sign his declaration of war, Woodrow Wilson had first (as an aspect of his plan) to mobilize an array of brain cells, nerve fibers, muscles, ligaments, bone assemblies, and other bodily components and processes—the "simple" sequences of his overall task (Chein, 1962:11). A juggler's activities may appear to be more complex, but during the previous night the president suffered the psychic and affective agonies of formulating a plan that contradicted some of his most deeply held convictions.

Acts—the Implementation of Decisions

Human acts (actions, activities, behavior) may be verbal or nonverbal. In either case, each act requires some release or application of energy by the central nervous system, the glandular-affective system, the muscular system, and so forth. In the implementing of many acts, tools (or weapons) are required to augment the human activity involved. Even a relatively "simple" molar activity such as fashioning a flint arrowhead can involve many complex patterns of molecular activity. To fly a jet fighter or a spaceship is obviously more complicated. In general, the more advanced the technology, the greater the number and the more complex are likely to be the hierarchies of functions and possibilities for error.

In decision and action situations, the closing of a gap almost always exacts a cost of some kind—energy expended, time that might have been used for another purpose, and so forth. This means that a decisionmaker consciously or unconsciously balances expected costs against expected benefits. The bear is cantankerous, but the hunter's family is short of food. If I go to the mountains fishing, I'll miss a beach party, but I prefer fishing to beach partying. The president is told to expect a thousand casualties if the island is invaded.

As a general rule, we act when we assess benefits as outweighing costs, and we defect when we expect the costs to outweigh the benefits. If we are risk averse, however, we may tend to be unduly cautious; whereas if we like to take chances, we may discount risks somewhat (Before it gets darker, I think I'll take the ski jump one more time). Assessing costs, risks, and outcomes requires the calculation of probabilities, which we often do without awareness that we are making such calculations.

Dyadic Interactions

Most of us spend a large part of our lives interacting with other persons. This means that when two people cooperate, compete, fight, or make up, each is exercising similar sets of processes or functions—even though the personal motivations, values, habits, dispositions, expectations, and idiosyncracies of one may be different from those of the other. I may be ambitious, aggressive, dogmatic, and ruthless, whereas you are outgoing, generous, reasonable, and gentle, but our cognitive and affective processes are essentially true copies. At the same time, however,—and here is the rub—we filter our perceptions of people, events, and other "realities" through personal lenses, beliefs, and preferences.

Insofar as two people interact, they can do big things in one direction or another. This is to say that dyadic interaction (positive and/or negative) is not additive, not merely A + B, but multiplicative, something like A × B but potentially much more than 2 × 1. Whether for cooperation, competition, or conflict, two people interacting can multiply an array of capabilities, potentials, and fears by an array of capabilities, potentials, and fears—an often explosive combination for "good" or "evil." The crux of human relations—the positive/negative switch—operates as soon as two people begin to interact. Here we are close to the security paradox, as subsequent pages will reveal (Chein, 1962:11, 15).

As soon as two (or more) individuals begin to interact, the probability is high that conflicts will occur. This observation is complicated by the fact that insofar as the central nervous system of the individual functions autonomously and is also sensitive to and often constrained by events in the external environment, the individual must often deal with inner and outer conflicts that may be closely linked. A gatherer or hunter who had a falling-out with the headman might contemplate leaving the band. In many prestate societies, however, such a defection could jeopardize the defector's existence, and subsequently the individual might stay on indefinitely, buffeted from within and without. Today, after a bitter argument with an overbearing boss, a worker with a large family might find himself in a similar predicament, or husband and wife may cling to a marriage neither can abide. Similarly, a head of state may hesitate to withdraw from a troublesome alliance.

Still another kind of inner conflict involves choosing between a course of action likely to serve more immediate interests at the cost of longer term advantage. Should the successful hunter give a feast for the band or smoke the buffalo meat to see them all through the winter? Should country A raise taxes now or let the next administration, or generation, fix the deficit? Should developing country B clear-cut a forest now to pay off its debt or save extensive woodlands for the future?

External conflicts are inescapable within dyads; they emerge soon after the honeymoon, if not on the way to the altar. Such conflicts can occur because two (or more) actors cannot occupy precisely the same space or possess (exclusively) the same object at the same time. Often the successful completion of a task at hand requires assistance that is being withheld, or the decisionmaker undertakes a project blocked by someone else. Or personal values differ. The young hunter wants to go faster, whereas the older slows down. *She* wants the electric blanket warmer; I prefer it cooler. Israelis and Palestinians both lay claim to the West Bank and the Gaza strip.

In many conflicts, the central issue is not the critical one. Sometimes the means take over and determine the outcome. The young hunter slows down a bit, and the older moves a bit faster. She gives me a blanket of my own for Christmas. The Israelis and Palestinians agree to sit down and talk.

The hierarchical (although continually fluctuating) characteristics of plan and action can add to the complexities of conflict (as well as efficiency). When two (or more) parties interact, the hierarchical character of plans and actions greatly complicates and often obscures the relationship. We are now dealing with processes organized on several molar/molecular levels on both sides of the relationship. In order to do something to (or for) B, A may have to do something else, not subsequently but first (or simultaneously) in order to complete the action (Chein, 1962:11). A molar behavior on either side of the dyad is thus a motive for the molecular behavior(s) it includes.

If I want to borrow your power mower, I cross your yard, knock on your door, and make my case. If a disagreement or conflict ensues, you may not be responding negatively to my request to use your machine, but to the fact that I trampled your zinnias on the way over. Between us we have demonstrated that means can condition ends. In order to strengthen its bargaining position, country A explodes a powerful new weapon immediately before a summit meeting on arms control with country B; the negotiations collapse.

These homely parables have at least two major implications for human relations. B may approve of A's molar purpose. You applaud my readiness to cut my grass but reject my preparatory means (cutting across your flower bed). Or during the Vietnam War, you may have supported my son's right to protest but condemned his trashing of the university's administration building. Nation B welcomes A's decision to negotiate but distrusts the motive behind its weapons testing.

Beyond this, from a broader, more inclusive perspective, the hierarchical organization of the plans and actions of two (or more) interacting parties have implications for the assessment of motivations and responsibilities of both. Thus, an act that A performs (as the outcome of a motivation generated by interaction with B) may be viewed not only as an A-act but also to some degree as a B-act. Because both have contributed, although perhaps disproportionately, they may be said to have produced an A/B outcome. Your refusal to lend me your mower and my locking the gate between our yards are both I/you acts. The outcome, moreover, can seldom be attributed solely to either participant. In these terms the U.S. airlift to Berlin and the shooting down by the Soviets of a U.S. U2 spy plane can both be viewed as A/B acts, as can the U.S. downing of an Iranian passenger aircraft, for that matter.

Dissonances of Inner and Outer Conflicts

A special kind of disequilibrium resulting from interplays between internal and external environments can lead to *cognitive dissonance*, which refers to a psychologically disturbing discrepancy between a state of affairs that a person has chosen or accepted and information that calls the utility or desirability of that condition into serious doubt (right after I buy the $25,000 sports car I've scrimped for, a consumer protection agency reports that its fuel tank is lethally exposed in case of a rear-end collision). Somewhat comparably, those of us who are, or have been, inveterate smokers know the feeling when we have been warned about the danger of lung cancer. The possibility of contracting the disease is anxiety producing, as is our physicians' disapproval or the complaints of our nonsmoking spouses, but we are already addicted to cigarettes. What can we do?

In his theory of cognitive dissonance, psychologist Leon Festinger (1957) dealt with the psychic discomfort that often results from such incongruities and helped to clarify options. A person experiencing cognitive dissonance will not only try to reduce it but may also avoid information and situations perceived as likely to increase it. In principle, such a person has three options for dissonance reduction or elimination: (1) change relevant beliefs, attitudes, and behavior (quit smoking); (2) reinterpret or alter information about the situation that contributes to the contradiction, by denial perhaps (no link between smoking and cancer has ever been proved); or (3) act on the environment in ways calculated to change it (support research for a harmless cigarette).

Similarly, in a famine winter a headman proposes a deer hunt in the Ghost Hills, but the shaman of the band warns of dire misfortunes that have occurred there in the past. What can the headman do? He can overcome his fear of spirits and kill a deer on his own; persuade himself and the band that the shaman is pursuing her own interests and that past misadventures in the hills were accidents that had nothing to do with malicious spirits; or propose to drive or induce the deer out of the hills into safe territory. (By analogy, nation B may decide to disregard A's weapons test and proceed with the negotiations, test a weapon of its own, or refuse to negotiate.)

Reducing dissonance at one source does not guarantee, of course, that it may not emerge elsewhere. Although external factors help trigger and shape feelings of dissonance, the conflict itself is internal. Relations with other people are a common source of the sense of disequilibrium that is often associated with such uncertainties and inner conflicts. Whenever inner and outer phenomena are linked in such situations, the individual has no choice other than to meet the problem with whatever adjustments he or she can make in the interplay between the two environments.

Another kind of dyadic conflict involves the dissident and the collective—the frustrated young hunter and the band, the skeptic among true believers, the whistleblower in a defense plant, or the revolutionary in a society of reactionaries. Marx used this fundamental contradiction between individual and collective as a departure point for his theory of class conflict, establishment of the dictatorship of the proletariat, and the eventual withering away of the state. While recognizing the same basic contradiction (including potentials for class conflict), we follow a different line of reasoning in our approach to war, peace, and survival by focusing upon uneven population growth, technological advancement, access to resources, and bargaining and leverage potentials.

Bargaining, Leverage, and Coalition Formation

In attempts to satisfy our inner needs, wants, and desires (for sustenance, companionship, and help in meeting the exigencies of life), we have two main choices—to increase our individual coping capabilities or to seek assistance on a more or less sustained basis (to form a coalition). Probably the oldest institutionalized coalition is the family (or some variant of the family as we define it), and whatever we know or can learn about this institution may help us find out important things about ourselves, humanity at large, and more extensive organizations such as the state.

In considering coalitions, we refer to virtually all groups, communities, and organizations in which individuals to one degree or another share and pursue some common interest and joint actions, however indirectly. Coalitions are characterized by the bargaining and leverage activities that participants undertake in dealing with each other and in influencing or altering the external environment. People voluntarily join some coalitions, but they may be coopted into others, and we are born into still others such as our families, communities, and nations.

The motivations of our forebears in developing communities of different sizes and characteristics have often been explained by a desire for social affinity, a cooperative "instinct," or other elusive concepts. Probing as far back as feasible into the prehistory of human organization and cooperation, some investigators have postulated that "reciprocal altruism" is a key to the transformation of a "social apelike creature" into human beings (cultural animals living in highly structured societies) (cf. Leakey and Lewin, 1978:153–155; Sahlins, 1965:144). There are grounds for this perspective. Altruism and the desire for affinity have been strong elements in the establishment of many groups and organizations. Generally, however, altruism does not seem to rank high among motivations driving most current and past organizations. Self-interest (individual, group, corporate, and national) appears to possess more explanatory strength in most coalition behavior than altruism does. Among manifested self-interests, moreover, economic and political security and security from attack seem to be almost universally pursued.

Near the core of the coalition idea (whether on a prestate, state, or other level) are human concerns about cooperation and conflict. We usually cooperate in order to further self-interest(s), and conflict commonly emerges from efforts to defend (or extend) what we perceive as self-interest. Whenever two people seek cooperation, there is at least a tacit (although often unrecognized) assumption that both have, or can find, some common interest(s) or goal(s). This is true even though a search for an agreement or bargain may evoke vague statements of objective and give rise to so much disagreement and uncertainty about subgoals that participants may appear to be pursuing different objectives. Even after the bargain is sealed and the coalition is operating, the contention can, and often does, continue with almost neverending internal bargaining, leveraging, and reformulating of ends and means (Zartman, 1976:8; Cyert and March, 1963:28).

The strength of a coalition depends upon the diversified and often uneven but combined capabilities of its members. Each member has a weight, which is the amount of strength she or he adds to, withholds from, or conceivably turns against the whole. This weight can be assessed in terms of productivity and accommodative and/or coercive leverage potential (Snyder and Diesing, 1977:65). The maintenance and effectiveness of a coalition in turn depend to a large extent upon the distribution or redistribution of gains and costs or losses incurred in the course of the coalition's functioning. Each member, in short, may be expected to participate more or less voluntarily as long as the gains of participation tend to outweigh the costs (or the costs of defection outweigh the costs of participating) (Schelling, 1963:31). Generally, a member with greater weight can contemplate defection with more equanimity than can a member with lesser weight.

A successful coalition has weight or capability apart from that of any single member. Thus, a coalition can increase its capabilities in two major ways: by enhancing the capabilities of its members and/or by increasing their numbers. The larger the membership of a coalition, however, the greater is the volume of demands for food and other resources. This means that coalition capabilities will decline unless resource availabilities increase. The implications are clear: A coalition that cannot help its members to satisfy their demands or in so doing exacts too high a price is not likely to survive in the long run.

Bands and Chiefdoms

Notable among the undertakings not readily accomplished by an unassisted human individual are procreation and rearing of infants. It seems reasonable to speculate, therefore, that the husband/wife, Adam/Eve, nuclear family combination (or its equivalent) is one of the earliest evidences of coalition formation. But some anthropologists believe that the hunting and gathering band came first. However that may be, throughout the greater part of their existence as a species, human beings appear to have lived in band-sized communities of one description or another. Until twelve thousand or thirteen thousand years ago, such communities were probably the only organized human societies.

Family groupings—whether nuclear, extended, or bandlike—are not commonly thought of as coalitions, especially because most of us are introduced to our families by being born into them. From primeval times, however, procreation and the raising of offspring have provided core organizing principles and a prime example of interdependence and the need for some type of bargaining. Thus, the establishment and maintenance of a family are the outcomes of bargaining and leveraging between bride and groom (or their respective families) and culminate in a coalitional bargain manifested (if not by formal marriage vows) by procreation, joint parental responsibility for offspring, and neverending efforts to ward off disequilibrating tendencies.

Possibly the most primal of human collectives, the hunting and gathering band (essentially an extended family), constituted a social, economic, and political nexus from which all other human organizations evolved. As such, this prestate collective provides a useful model for other collectives that are *self-organizing* and *self-regulating*, that *lack overarching regimes* (centralized governmental sanctions), and that are thus almost purely *democratic*. In addition, the long trend of sociocultural evolution throughout the world from band to more complex organizational forms can help us understand how the earliest states may have come about and why. Beyond all this, moreover, an examination of hunting and gathering bands may provide clues about how states "behave," and why, and suggest how a comparison of prestate level institutions may be useful in helping us to solve some of the difficult problems we face in an increasingly globalized world. As will be touched upon in Chapter 10, moreover, there may be modern analogs to prestate institutions that could be used in the long-term pursuit of human survival.

Band Organization as Leverage for the Individual

Hunting and gathering bands of the distant past can be envisaged as "coalitions" of relatives. Almost nothing is known about the size of human populations during the hunting and gathering stage, but scholars generally assume that much of the earth was still uninhabited and that existing populations were sparsely distributed—at least 2 square miles per person being required for an economy at that technological level.

The band amounted to an organization facilitating the acquisition, transformation, and distribution of energy (food, fuels) and other natural resources. The social configuration was relatively symmetrical in that, with allowances for age and sex, distribution of resources, capabilities, benefits, and influence over others was roughly equal. Leadership tended to emerge on an ad hoc basis, the leader owing his or her position to age, experience, wisdom, skill as a hunter or gatherer, oratorical powers, or other personal characteristics. The leader's incumbency in that role was contingent upon the acquiescence of the group. The leader had no way of enforcing his or her will upon others; any attempt to do so would probably result in the formation of a coalition against the leader. He or she might exchange gifts (or barter) but could not accumulate sufficient wealth or power to institutionalize any coercive potential. Individual possessions tended to be limited to whatever a person could carry on his or her back. Anything more would be an impediment.

The shaman, often a distinctive figure in prestate societies, derived influence from an understanding of wild herbs and their properties and from specialized knowledge about the world of spirits and related mysteries—often including the sun, moon, and stars. Nature was so vast and awe-inspiring that the individual used all available assistance in working toward a flexible equilibrium between external and internal environments. The shaman foreshadowed clerics, including those with political aspirations and power.

Hunters and gatherers had cognitive and affective systems similar to our own. Given the similarities, we can ponder how without governments, legal statutes, courts, attorneys, police, or prisons, hunters and gatherers dealt with each other as well as they seemingly did. We may assume, however, that their perceptions of and feelings about themselves and their environments were deeply influenced by their small numbers and by where and how they lived. Their understandings of nature—the immediate loci of all the resources required for their survival—were intimate, as were their relations with each other.

Most band decisions were the outcome of discussions, bargaining, non-violent leveraging (persuasion), and the reaching of a consensus, or near-consensus in support of an option—more or less on a "Quaker meeting" basis. With the possible exception of small children, a band functioned as its own regime, which was open in the sense that everyone usually knew what everyone else was doing and where each stood on critical issues. Feedbacks tended to be immediate or nearly so. People could not afford to make many serious mistakes in relations with the natural environment or with each other. Immersed as they were in the natural environment and its vicissitudes, members of a band tended to share—more directly and equally than we—both the costs and benefits of everyday living.

The beliefs and customs of hunters and gatherers, however fanciful they may seem to us, were probably adaptive under the circumstances. People commonly respected and felt reverence for rocks, springs of water, and other inanimate objects, as well as herbs, trees, and animals of the forests or deserts. Groups in many parts of the world expressed formal regrets to the game animals they were about to kill. Within and between bands, ritualized exchanges of gifts often substituted for concepts of barter and commerce of a later era, and in more complex chiefdoms, gift-giving had leveling effects.

Hunting and gathering bands increased the capabilities and security of their individual members by providing a milieu that was socially, economically, and politically supportive. By living in such a coalition, each individual gained emotional support and fellowship from other members, assistance in child-rearing (built-in child care) and in obtaining food and other resources, and an enhanced measure of protection against attack from the outside. Combining oral history (including a certain amount of cultural myth) with custom and ritual, bands also developed *ideologies*, or systems of shared beliefs, that enabled individuals with discrete personal cognitions and affects to identify communalities and thus coordinate their activities with those of other members and contribute to the integrity of the group.

This does not mean that there was no conflict. Living out their lives face to face with the same relatives would have been enough to ensure endemic conflict, frequent dissent, and occasional violence. With allowance for differences in technology and its conditioning effects, we can probably assume that many of the intrafamily abuses we are familiar with today occurred also in hunting and gathering bands. The main, and extraordinary, constraint was the intimate and lifelong dependence of band members upon each other. Ultimately, for most participants, the gains in lifetime security and affinity were worth the contributions expected of them by the coalition as a whole. For a lone individual, moreover, or a solitary couple with offspring, potential separation from the community (ostracism, exile) could be a fearsome prospect. In short, the probabilities are that for most community members the advantages far outweighed the social costs.

Among some hunting and gathering bands, violence, both domestic and external, was rare. In others, murders and feuds occurred, but in the absence of complex military organization and authority as we know it today, warfare was undisciplined in the sense that a leader could not prevent defection. Some studies, however, have reported war parties with "high degrees" of centralization and obedience to command, presumably because of the "need for unison" if the warriors were to succeed in battle (Otterbein, 1970:26–27). Hunting parties sometimes clashed in pursuit of game, and the people of one band defending their hunting grounds might collide with people of another band defending theirs or in search of elusive game. Pillage as a quick source of wealth was limited in prestate societies as long as possessions were perceived as burdensome (MacDonald, 1973).

Some anthropologists conclude that the hunting and gathering band may have been one of the more efficient organizations throughout the millennia of sociocultural evolution. Population growth was relatively self-regulating; a woman carrying and feeding more than one small child was at a disadvantage (as were the children). This constraint, combined with the accumulation of appropriate knowledge and skills throughout uncounted generations (and allowing for natural catastrophes), was a major factor in allowing a band in a reasonably favorable resource environment to approach a steady state (input equaling output).

Individual Learning and Social Adaptation

What counts in organismic evolution is not mere survival but the contribution of the individual or group to the gene pool of the next and subsequent generations (Mayr, 1976:183). A "successful" individual or group has a greater probability of producing effective offspring than an inferior one does. Those who adapt best to the environment and its potentially destabilizing changes tend to be favored (Simpson, 1949:221). A particular individual varying, however slightly, in ways that favor itself within the complex and varying conditions of living may be expected to have a better chance of contributing to the "naturally selected" gene pool.

Contemporary perspectives on biological evolution also stress behavior as an important element in the process of adapting, although there is uncertainty about the nature of the relationship. Swiss psychologist Jean Piaget (1978:147) saw organisms, their behavior, and their environments coordinated from the moment of inception of life. According to Piaget, behavior provides indispensable linkages between organism and natural and social phenomena and governs advances in the "supersession of adaptation." With resource acquisition, social organization, and other behavioral phenomena playing such a major role in the ability of individuals to survive and reproduce, the relevance of behavior in the initiation of new evolutionary events becomes self-evident. Such considerations involve special human applications of what Piaget meant when he called behavior "the motor of evolution"—with the tendency of high-capability individuals and groups to expand their activities and interests "outward," thus widening the (resource) environment and increasing individual capabilities and those of the group.

Social psychologist Donald Campbell (1969:69–85) interpreted sociocultural evolution in terms of trial-and-error human variability (including feedforward and feedback) in response to variabilities in physical and social environments. Associated with these activities, as he conceived of them, was a human capability for eliminating or avoiding many dysfunctional behaviors and—through individual memories, myths, legends, rituals, and other customs—for retaining, propagating, and reinforcing those that seemed to "work." In this way, knowledge, skills, and some wisdom were transmitted from generation to generation and were gradually, often painfully, revised and refined; people transmitted at least a part of what they learned from generation to generation (Mayr, 1978:55). The catch was that environments were also changing as a result of "natural" reasons and the expanding capacity of human beings to intervene in physical as well as social processes, often with unintended consequences. Such changes contributed to the disequilibria that kept individuals and communities busy trying to set things straight.

We may infer that variations in human activities and relative capabilities within and between organizations on all levels (commonly at different rates) constitute a primary requirement for social as well as individual adaptation and development. Variations are manifested through such mechanisms as population growth and decline and technological change, variable accesses to basic resources, and fluctuations in the ways people deal with the physical environment and with the outcomes of their interactions with others. In this regard, bargaining and leverage activities not only account for a large proportion of human interactions within, across, and between organizations; they function also as trial-and-error probing and learning mechanisms for change in individuals, institutions, and social and natural environments (Stebbins, 1971:178; Aldrich and Pfeffer, 1976:4).

In their interactions with natural and social environments, people tend to select those behaviors that appear generally to yield advantages that outweigh costs. The extent to which such behaviors are adaptive in the long run can be determined only in retrospect, however, and even then a seemingly favorable course of action may prove to be maladaptive as circumstances change.

Innovating individuals can introduce variation into a society by purposely departing from established behavior patterns. Innovation need not be consciously planned; indeed, it often results from unplanned, clumsy attempts to emulate others who are thought to have been successful. The randomness inherent in many natural processes (as well as in human behavior) can also be a significant contributory factor (Aldrich, 1979:39). In general, those social-environmental settings that provide the greatest possibility and range of variation are likely to produce the most advances (Campbell, 1969:73).

Although individual organizations "rise" and "decline" with time, overall, their complexity and form tend to increase and vary with the level of technology and the amount of energy converted in the system (Adams, 1975:304). In view of the technological level that prevailed in prehistoric times, the limited population size of the hunting and gathering band was a distinct advantage. Band membership may have averaged about twenty-five members, although some may have been twice or three times as large. But if the numbers increased much more, heavy strains were likely to be imposed upon game and other resources. The band might then split up, allowing newly independent groups to move farther afield, or new technologies might be developed to improve access to new resources or find new uses for old resources. Anthropologists commonly characterize hunters and gatherers as conservative, however, meaning that sociocultural evolution, although exponential even then, was at the "slow" end of the growth and development curve. Evolution proceeded from limited population and technological bases at low rates of growth and development. Because overall population sizes were small relative to the expanse of territory and resources, environmental "pollution" (toxics included), depletions, and scarcities tended to be localized. Nevertheless, during the course of millennia, numbers of hunting and gathering communities in various parts of the world did respond to population growth, new technologies, and the management of resources in ways that eroded the hunting and gathering band and gave rise to the chiefdom.

Tribes and Chiefdoms

With population increases, accelerating advances in knowledge and skills, and rising needs and demands for food and other resources, humans developed new organizational units—tribes and chiefdoms. The concept of tribe is controversial among anthropologists. Many identify the tribe as an adaptive response (resulting from uneven development during millennia) to more "advanced" organizations, primarily chiefdoms and eventually states (Service, 1962:126; Fried, 1967:124–125).

Chiefdoms emerged as societies with growing populations and advancing knowledge and skills expanded across two or more ecological zones in which quite different technologies were appropriate (hunting, herb gathering, and ocean fishing, for example, and possibly early forms of horticulture). This expansion encouraged population growth and technological advances and generated further resource demands. Under such circumstances, population/technology/resource ratios allowed the accumulation and aggregation of product surpluses and the centralization of materials in the hands of the more efficient members.

When and where the first chiefdoms appeared is a matter of speculation; surely they emerged at different times in widely separated parts of the world beginning about the twelfth millennium B.C. Divisions of labor increased. Barter within and between communities became institutionalized in more advanced chiefdoms.

With population growth and technological development, these new societies required more systematic regulation of the exchange and distribution of raw materials and goods from various ecological zones. By accepting responsibility for such supervision, headmen and -women increased their average potentials to a point where they became chiefs with authority to plan and organize exchanges of goods and deploy public labor. Nevertheless, chiefs lacked the institutionalized political power that kings and queens of even the most archaic states were able to exercise. The chief's dominant influence derived not only from custom, prestige of the position, and force of personality but also from new opportunities for accumulating wealth. These opportunities were constrained, however, by potlatch and other "giveaways" (Lenski, 1970:138; Service, 1962:150).

The advantageous position of the chief was further enhanced with advances of knowledge and skills but was constrained by his or her (matriarchies were not uncommon) lack of a legalized monopoly of violence (of reliable sources for effective coercion) to enforce his or her will. Even such limited centralization of power and influence enabled chiefdoms in some parts of the world to achieve remarkable levels of production.

Chiefdoms (and tribes) developed clan structures (*sodalities*) based originally upon kinship ties and extending across organizational frontiers as band populations became too large for self-regulation. Relatives belonging to a particular clan (eagle, raven, deer, bear, wolf, or other) in one community maintained close filial relationships with members of the same clan in another community (cf. Service, 1962:126; and Fried, 1967:124–125). Such arrangements linked groups that would otherwise have tended to drift apart. These arrangements were forerunners of the ways in which present-day religions, political parties, commercial organizations, labor unions, and professional societies often cut across national boundaries.

In modern terms, chiefdoms were less "egalitarian" than hunting and gathering bands and less "democratic." Scalp-taking, headhunting, human sacrifice, cannibalism, and slavery, which were rare or situational among hunters and gatherers, became commonplace and more or less institutionalized among technologically more advanced chiefdoms of the world. This may be evidence that what we refer to as human values do not necessarily advance with levels of technology. On the contrary, as knowledge and skills advance and as new instruments and institutions become available, we may use them for new "evil" as well as new "good."

Chiefdoms were characterized by ranking but not by stratification (the emergence of social and economic classes). Rank societies possessed mechanisms for limiting member access to status positions founded on the basis of sex, age, or personal attributes (Fried, 1967:53–109). In view of the component hierarchies of wealth, rank, and status, the structure of a chiefdom was highly asymmetrical as compared with a band but less so than the structure of even the earliest states. There was no concept of "sovereign regime" as yet, but chiefs of tribes and chiefdoms were commonly advised by more or less institutionalized councils of elders or subchiefs. In a rank society, leaders could lead, but they might not be obeyed (Farb, 1968:133).

Growth, Development, and Transformation
at the Chiefdom Level

Among prestate societies in general, warfare as it developed in historical times was probably out of the question. Populations were small compared with subsequent standards, were widely dispersed, and were thus buffered from each other by space and travel time. Until the domestication of draft animals and the invention of the wheel, travel was on foot (raft or canoe), and a war party had no way of transporting supplies beyond what each warrior could carry on his or her person. Weapons (sticks and stones at first, later spears, axes, bows and arrows) had limited range and effectiveness. Large campaigns, protracted attacks, and sieges did not—indeed, could not—occur.

Despite these limitations, as the populations of prestate societies grew and as their knowledge and skills advanced, many of them produced formidable warriors—as the armies of states and empires of a later age (through the nineteenth century, in fact) often discovered when they invaded the territories of tribes and chiefdoms. Some appeared to be much more warlike than others, however.

Comparative studies of large numbers (some thousands) of prestate societies in terms of "peacefulness" and "war-proneness" suggest that those communities less likely to become involved in relatively large-scale violence were characterized by (1) common recognition that the activities of individual members contributed to general survival and well-being; (2) customs and activities that allowed optimal opportunities for the individual to achieve self-fulfillment; and (3) transactions among individual community members and between communities that were reciprocally reinforcing rather than destructively competitive or conflictual (Gorney, 1971). Retrospectively, however, the peace-prone societies appear to have been at a disadvantage. As the millennia advanced, the more peaceful societies were pushed aside, if not overrun, by more powerful and warlike societies or were destroyed by societies with superior technologies.

The threshold for the more successful chiefdoms in several parts of the world was provided by agriculture, especially in river valleys. In such locations, some of the more advanced of these societies built elaborate irrigation systems that paved the way for large-scale "hydraulic" production in arid or semiarid regions. More production fed more people, supported more enterprises, and created unprecedented surpluses for the chief to aggregate, "invest," bargain with, and distribute. These new capabilities in turn initiated a transformation of both chiefdom and chief, who could now reward subchiefs and warriors on a more sustained basis.

Such developments set the stage for a major "evolution" in the human condition—the apparently independent emergence in several parts of the world of the first pristine states. From this point forward, an intricate interweaving of economic, political, and strategic (military) knowledge and skills progressively dominated, shaped, and transformed humanity.

PART 2

Second Image: The State

3

The Growth and Development of States

So far we have been concerned primarily with the individual in social contexts, specifically in the family and prestate societies. This chapter examines the growth and developmental processes of states—the emergence of the first, or pristine, states and the development of the state from its ancient (or archaic) to its agrocommercial (and industrial) forms. We expect this procedure to help us understand the behavior of modern states as well as the intensely dynamic structures of present-day international and global systems.

The Emergence of Pristine States

The word *pristine* refers to the first states, which evolved from chiefdoms or other prestate societies several thousand years ago. As phenomena of the uncertain past, these first states appear to have emerged independently in widely separated parts of the world (in the Nile, Tigris-Euphrates, and Indus valleys and in China, Peru, and Mexico). Once a pristine state had been established, all subsequent states in that region—including offshoot or successor regimes—were secondary, derivative, or emulative institutions. (Modern states, together with those of recorded history, qualify as secondary states.) Speculation about the emergence of the first states is thus hampered by the necessity of working backward from what we know about current and historical state-level institutions.

Fortunately, the secondary states that followed—the ancient or archaic states of Egypt, Sumer, Assyria, Persia, Greece, Rome, Peru, Mexico, and so forth—left archaeological and/or written records of their activities. The structures of these states differed in various ways. Many were patriarchal; administrative officers were private officers of the monarch and/or vassals with sworn obligations to a feudal lord. Others (often evolving from one or possibly both of the other two) were bureaucratic; administrative subsystems were more centralized, possessed limited autonomy, and pursued goals that might be relatively independent from those of the monarch. Such differences, however, were essentially variations on the fundamental elements, processes, and relationships that distinguished the state from prestate institutional forms.

Although state institutions have undergone many changes since ancient times, and new institutions have developed, the earliest known, most archaic states probably bore a closer resemblance to modern states than they did to bands, chiefdoms, or other prestate forms. By definition, in fact, the same constituent elements and necessary processes are inherent in states today. This suggests that we may gain in our understanding of state behavior in modern times if we piece together the processes that created the first states several thousand years ago.

Explanations for the emergence of state forms of organization fall into two main categories—*voluntaristic* and *coercive*. According to voluntaristic theory, certain peoples renounced their individual sovereignties spontaneously and united with other communities to form a larger unit—the first state. For example, Jean-Jacques Rousseau (1916:VI, I, 109) thought that when individual humans could no longer maintain themselves in a state of nature, they formulated among themselves an association—a social contract—in which the community as a whole committed itself to defense of the property of each "associate."

Coercive theories assume that disciplined organization and a threat or application of violence—coercive leverage—were necessary for the genesis and maintenance of state forms and that human beings initially subjected themselves to emerging state authority against their will and in response to superior force. David Hume (1889:I, xxi) thought that most governments had resulted initially from usurpation, conquest, or both without regard for the will of their people, who might subsequently acquiesce, however, through a habit of obedience. Similarly, in the nineteenth century, Herbert Spencer (1891:64–72, 80–81) presented a revolutionary theory of the state in which warfare was a leading factor. According to Spencer, wars between societies— the causes of "all such improvements"—led to the building of governmental structures. These coercive theories draw upon three distinct but interrelated applications of organized violence: (1) armed force associated with defense against threat or attack from outside; (2) defense of the society's external activities and interests (including the penetration and/or conquest and exploitation of weaker populations); and (3) reliance on armed force as an ultimate sanction for the maintenance of domestic "law and order" and security against crime, dissidence, revolution, civil war, or external threat or invasion.

Thomas Hobbes (1950:144) postulated the emergence of states by voluntary institution as well as by coercive acquisition. The people of a community might band together in a commonwealth to "live peacefully among themselves" and protect themselves against coercive annexation. Other scholars who have put forward a combination of voluntaristic and coercive hypotheses have specified that state forms have emerged in situations in which a powerful tribe or chiefdom began conquering, absorbing, and controlling weaker communities around its periphery. The chief and the tribe's warriors could then present themselves as "protectors" of the people they had conquered and thus be justified in demanding subservience.

This supposition leaves a critical issue unsettled, however. Did such an outcome result from simple aggressiveness, or were there underlying considerations? We have several clues that help to explain the emergence of state forms and their evolution in recent millennia. At the time of the first pristine state (perhaps 5000–4000 B.C.), global populations may have numbered about 50 million (up from a possible 5 million around 8000 B.C.), with a doubling time of a bit more than fifteen hundred years. In considerable part these increases could be attributed to advances in knowledge and skills—primarily agriculture and the development of metal tools and weapons. Combination of larger populations and more advanced technologies led to exponential increases in demands for resources together with pressures on land and water for irrigation. A core problem within many societies at the time was how to provide a reasonably secure environment for the mobilization and deployment of labor and management for higher levels of food production.

These conditions suggest the relevance of the master variables and their interrelated growth and development processes put forward in Chapter 1. Conceivably, in widely separated regions of the world where states emerged independently, population growth, technological development, and access to basic resources proceeded unevenly within and among prestate societies. As a consequence, at least one chiefdom achieved a larger population and more advanced knowledge and skills than did neighboring chiefdoms (and/ or bands). In time, this chiefdom, having depleted local resources in satisfying its rapidly increasing demands, extended its activities and interests outward (lateral pressure) by "penetrating" and conquering its less advanced neighbors and annexing their territories and (presumably) more abundant resources. Anthropologist Robert Carneiro (1970:133) added to this scenario the notion of containment, or superscription—a blockage of possible escape for the victims by mountains, rivers, or even surrounding population densities. Whether this was a necessary condition remains moot (Service, 1978:39–46).

Conquests under such circumstances provided a bonus that the invading chief may have intended from the first or that may have been an adaptive afterthought. Several, if not most, regions of the world where states developed indigenously had one factor in common. All were areas of land suitable for large-scale, labor-intensive agriculture (provided water was available or could be made so through large-scale irrigation), and conquered communities provided a bonanza in slave, corvée, or other modes of more or less forced labor (early manifestations of "institutional" or "structural" violence). Some scholars conclude that early states could not have been established or long maintained without slavery or some comparable institution to provide the necessary pools of cheap labor.

As a result of such conquests, the victorious war chief now possessed the makings of a state—a territory under the chief's control, armed forces for imposing law and order within and maintaining security against attack from without, a productive population with differential bargaining and leverage potentials, and subchiefs to whom authority could be delegated. Presenting himself as the "protector" of his domain and its people, the chief need only to "bargain" with and apply leverages to the populace in order to obtain a sufficient share of their agricultural surplus for maintaining and rewarding his warriors and subchiefs and meeting other costs of "administration." Such were the sources of production, established obligations, and customary reciprocations for holding the new arrangements together. The test for "statehood" was whether the "bargains" held firm and processes of "governing" functioned effectively.

Once such bargaining, leveraging, coalition-maintaining arrangements had been stabilized, people in nearby villages—pursuing economic, political, or strategic security—might negotiate their own bargains with the war chief, who (in modern Mafia style) would guarantee protection in return for a share of the crops. With these further surpluses, he could expand his domain peacefully or by mounting expeditions against communities (and their croplands and water resources) farther afield. Concurrently, he could impound larger gangs of forced labor (prisoners captured in raids) for the construction of larger, more sophisticated, and productive hydraulic systems. In addition, he could build pyramids, temples, and fortifications to defend the populace and their (his?) territory against rival warlords.

These potentials available to early kings opened the way, in principle at least, for three possible relationships deriving from state uses of violence that can be recognized in nations today: "legalized" (institutional, structural) violence as a sanction for the maintenance of domestic order; violence used to conquer and subject other societies and territories; and violent leverages applied in order to influence weaker states in substantial ways without conquering or annexing them.

The Establishment of Regimes

With the maintenance of stable authority over an ascertainable and defensible domain, the chief became king, his sons princes, and the warriors a ruling elite. The council of subchiefs or elders was now a royal court. With the proliferation and institutionalization of domestic and external transactions, the king and his lieutenants began developing a bureaucracy to keep accounts, manage the labor force, raise taxes, and allocate crops and other resources among the society's classes and sectors (Almond and Powell, 1966:190–212). Archaeological evidence suggests that "counters" for keeping track of goods (and possibly corvée or slave labor) may have led to the gradual development of alphabets and numerical systems.

We need not assume that all early states were formed the same way, however. Hobbes (1950:xxiv, 144) thought that some "city"-states might have emerged as federations formed by communities trying to protect themselves against marauders. The feature distinguishing such a federation would have been the voluntary aspect, the consideration that all partners to the federal bargain presumably subscribed to it of their own free will, although under coercion from outside forces. Historians and archaeologists have noted that such "republican" federations often emerged from trade centers situated within clusters of small islands, such as the Greek archipelago; on chains of lakes, as in ancient Switzerland; near river crossings; or where caravan routes converged. Within such "trading states," a citizenry of independent merchants often constituted a governing elite that chose leaders from within itself through debate, votes, lots, or other noncoercive, relatively egalitarian, "coordinated" means. Rights of citizenship were not universal, however. Slaves, foreigners, workers, and women were usually excluded.

From the start, both agrarian kingdoms and republican trading states developed rules and institutionalized codes of behavior—*regimes*—to provide ways of defining relationships and responsibilities, making state decisions, resolving disputes, keeping the economy working, and maintaining military and/or naval forces. Ruling elites in both kingdoms and city-states, like national leaders today, had three prime objectives: to protect and if possible enhance their authority and that of their regime; to mobilize sufficient social, economic, and political resources for implementing major policies; and to minimize discrepancies between a preferred state of affairs and the ever-changing realities of the domestic and external environments. Thus, as states proliferated in various parts of the world, their security interests tended to emerge along three dimensions: (1) *structural* (economic) *security* (a viable balance or ratio between the size of a state's population and demands) relative to the level (and characteristics) of its technology (ability to produce) and resource availabilities; (2) *regime security* (the capacity of the government to protect itself from domestic disorder or revolt); and (3) *strategic security* (the ability of the state to defend itself from external coercion, attack, or invasion and guarantee itself access to resources beyond its borders).

In domestic terms, every state had to possess the capacity for defining, specifying, and enforcing property rights—the means for ordering social, economic, and political affairs within a society. Property rights described the individual and group incentives within the system—the institutionalized carrots and sticks—and sustained the authority to tax and "exclude"—that is, to allocate rights, privileges, statuses, and resources. These powers were not absolute, however—even in a dictatorship or tyranny. Rulers possessed a comparative advantage in violence, and in varying degrees this included the pursuit of both personal and national objectives. Such advantage was limited, however, in that some proportion of the demands (individual and aggregated) of influential citizens, special interest groups, powerful coalitions, and the populace at large had to be met.

In addition, the leadership had to regularize and institutionalize acquisition of resources from internal and/or external environments, oversee the trans-formation of these resources into goods and services, and distribute them. As growing populations and advancing knowledge and skills stimulated demands, the tendency to expand activities and interests (lateral pressure) often became irresistible. In pursuit of resources (and markets), trading states were likely to build more merchant (and naval) vessels, whereas agrarian kingdoms might conquer more territory (with populations included). Neither was very good at doing both, but Athens, Rome, and numerous other commercial city-states transformed themselves into empires by territorial conquest. Characteristically, the expanding activities and interests of a powerful state were likely to penetrate weaker states and thus to one degree or another influence and possibly dominate and exploit them. Whenever the expanding activities and interest of two or more states collided, moreover, there was risk of conflict, crisis, and, possibly, war.

In language of a later era, regimes of both types implied state "legitimacy," "sovereignty," and the right—the obligation—to use legalized coercion (negative leverage) as well as positive incentives for the maintenance of internal and external security, stability, and the authority of the state itself. All such powers and obligations were limited, however, even in despotisms and dictatorships, by a readiness of the populace to comply. How much compliance and support a regime could expect from the populace depended upon prevailing capabilities and bargaining potentials. Outcomes would also depend upon the capabilities of the populace, its possibilities for coalition formation, and its assessments of the benefits and costs of compliance relative to the costs and benefits of defection.

As suggested by historian Otto Hintze, the integration and evolution of domestic institutions were powerfully influenced by the interplay of internal and external activities and events, including diplomatic interchanges, alliances, trade, international conflicts, crises, wars, victories, and defeats (Hintze, cited in Gilbert, 1975:160–163). Over time, and partly as an outcome of internal/external interplays, the fundamental bargain or social contract—the "charter" for a functioning regime—might be taken for granted. In return for some minimal combination of economic, political, and bodily security (safety, well-being), many people offered support for the emergent king and other members of the ruling elite. They in turn used this support to achieve and implement binding decisions—an exchange of specific support and compliance in return for favorable responses to fundamental demands.

From this perspective, the state was a behavioral structure of thousands or millions of individuals all making decisions that in the aggregate affect the lives of all. At the frontier between the state and the rest of the world stood the queen, king, prime minister, president, or dictator acting through the regime—bargaining and exerting leverages on his or her aides, advisers, generals, and local chiefs—in efforts to minimize the disequilibrium created by ever-changing events in domestic and external environments. Once a state was established, various sectors and interest groups competed for resources to the extent that their capabilities allowed.

Perseverant bargaining and leverage exchanges in ancient states, especially to the extent that at least minimal demands were met, thus served as linkages in emergent social structures and often became institutionalized through custom and legal arrangements. But any major alteration in the incentive structure (denying resource access considered just or customary, for example) could alter perceptions about the fairness of the system and (depending again upon the distribution of power$_1$ and power$_2$) could affect the stability of the system.

Although kingdoms and republican city-states differed substantially in structure and the means employed in governing, their regimes served many of the same purposes—to keep society and government in working order, protect the state from external attack, and maintain a "secure enclave" within which the society as a whole could function effectively. From this perspective we may conclude that organized violence was a major factor in providing the protected environments within which the great civilizations of the past could take root, constrain disequilibrating tendencies, and even flourish for a time.

Internalization of State Security Values

Criteria for social, economic, political, and military security, insofar as they have been formulated, have tended to be established by state regimes. Not uncommonly, such arrangements have been incorporated through generations of practice into the value and belief systems of the rank and file as well as the ruling elites—to the point where a subject was willing to give his or her life for the exploiting tyrant. We may assume that the ruler and dominant elites did what they could to shape a belief system, an ideology, in support of the regime and favorable to themselves (rulers often presented themselves as gods or at least as divinely appointed). Although the extent to which such belief systems were initially accepted by lower classes may not have been substantial, the long-term trend was in that direction. Seeking to explain the internal cohesion of state-level societies, sociologist Émile Durkheim (1960) put forward the idea of *conscience collective*—a sense of shared values, beliefs, reciprocal expectations, and common community so all-encompassing that the individual does not question this collective but may even defend it against personal interests.

As such arrangements became institutionalized, a ruler gained the wherewithal to make and enforce binding decisions of the kind desired by his or her more reliable supporters and "clients" in a political analog to economic exchange. With this capability came possibilities for a wide range of positive and negative leverages to collect more "taxes," recruit more warriors and bureaucrats, impound more corvée (or slave) labor, and enforce top-level decisions.

In their pursuit of domestic economic and political security, states through their leaders relied upon and invoked the ideology that prevailed in the society. Characteristically, ruling elites discouraged or suppressed economic and political ideas and undertakings perceived as threatening to their programs, the regime, and their interpretations of the society as a whole. In order to retain power$_1$ and power$_2$, however, even a tyranny had to ensure that some proportion of rank-and-file, retainer, and bureaucrat demands were reasonably well met. A ruling elite was thus challenged by necessity to grant some groups a measure of initiative, independence, or autonomy while still denying them latitude sufficient to threaten sovereignty.

The ideology of agrarian kingdoms and empires usually centered on the monarch and higher nobility. In some, the social, economic, and political belief systems were closely integrated with a dominant religion (the king or queen might also serve as high priest). Many archaic states in Mesopotamia and elsewhere were theocracies. In Egypt, the pharaoh was a god, and hence the regime was divine. City-state ideologies, however, often involved concepts of individual rights and collective responsibilities (at least among the citizenry) deriving in part from the values and requirements of commerce. (In subsequent chapters, we shall see how state ideologies, like state structures, have tended to "evolve" with population growth and technological advancement.)

Agrarian kingdoms (and empires) tended to be strong in a military sense, but their structures were such that it was not possible to secure the active support and loyalty of more than a small part of the populace (Gilpin, 1981:120–121). City-states, while attracting the active support and loyalty of the citizenry, were severely constrained in their ability to generate $power_1$ and, beyond narrow borders, $power_2$. City-states also were often riven by competing domestic factions. Despite the differences between agrarian kingdoms and city-states, they shared a tendency to pass through "life cycles" of change to which present-day states are not immune.

State Life Cycles:
Growth, Development, and Decline

States do not stand still; they are subject to continuous change. Uneven growth and development among domestic variables (population, technology, territory, resource access, allocations to production, defense, and so forth) will tend to increase or decrease a state's *absolute* capabilities ($power_1$). Its bargaining and leverage potentials ($power_2$), however, and its rank among states with which it interacts will be constrained by its levels and rates of growth relative to levels and rates of growth of other nations. Thus, over time, states tend to "leapfrog" each other.

Although the emergence, growth, development, and decline of states cannot be separated from the sociocultural evolutionary trends resulting from such changes (and from responses to them), history suggests that during its existence each state proceeds through an identifiable life cycle from emergence through a phase of rapid growth to an apogee of growth and development. This high point in the cycle is likely to be followed by a leveling off—a mature phase—after which come decline and eventual extinction. At some point (after generations, centuries, or, conceivably, a millennium) the constraints upon disequilibrium are weakened (or disrupted from the outside) and the state collapses or is transformed by a thoroughgoing revolution.

Pertaining to the life "history" of an individual state, such cycles should not be confused with the long-term sociocultural evolution of overall state forms (from agrarian kingdoms and city-states to agrocommercial nation-states and thence to modern nation-states, for example). But the life cycle of a "fallen" state (ancient Athens, for example, or Rome) may well have contributed to such an overall institutional transformation in ways that are not realized until many centuries after its collapse.

Growth refers to an increase in quantity, "size," volume, or level, whereas development implies a qualitative change, generally positive, from less adaptive to more adaptive to changing circumstances, but not without costs. If a country's population grows (increases) faster than its technological advances, development—adaptive change for that country—will be constrained or blocked. And to the extent that many states suffer similar constraints, pressures will build for some subsequent state(s) to provide evidence sooner or later of a sociocultural adaptation—from an agrarian economy to a mixed agrarian/commercial economy, for example—"resolving" that particular constraint.

In the life cycles of states, periods of decline are not deterministic in any absolute sense, but they are highly probable—not because of iron laws but because of the potentially destructive interlinkages of social, economic, political, and military phenomena with which societies, their regimes, and their leaders must continually deal. The source of many of these dysfunctional possibilities can be located in the contradictions, paradoxes, and dilemmas that arise when large numbers of people deal with each other.

The roots of a country's power$_1$ (capability) and power$_2$ (influence, leverage) extend down to the knowledge, skills, and capabilities of individual members of the populace interacting within second image environments and to the opportunities available for these individuals to bring their energy to bear on local and national enterprises. To a large extent, societal outcomes are the result of producers' and consumers' small decisions and actions as they are aggregated, transformed, and applied on various means/end levels within the society. Many, if not most, of these decisions and actions pertain to questions about who gets what, when, and how. Presiding over these complex interactions are economic, political, and military elites that sometimes generate, sometimes block, often help coordinate, and to varying degrees regulate production processes, taxation, and the allocation and distribution of the goods and services within the regime and society at large (Almond and Powell, 1966:195–199).

Within a state, bargaining and leverage potentials can be envisaged as differentially "pumping" and distributing resources, services, statuses, and influence through the society according to how capabilities are distributed. Consequently, we can learn much about a society and its regime by identifying the major sources of its materials, goods, and services and by charting their "flows" and destinations.

Uneven Growth and Takeoff

Kuznets (1966:6–11) identified state-level technologies as resulting from growing populations, widely dispersed, generating more and more demands for basic resources. In adapting to such ramifying pressures, certain societies created mechanical and organizational knowledge and skills "early in the histories of emergent states." Such innovations, Nicolas Rashevsky (1959:287–300) thought, were most likely to occur when a concentration of population took place in an environment favorable for transportation and communication—in an archipelago (as in ancient Greece), at a river crossing, near a river's mouth, or at a juncture of major trade routes. Such a concentration of people had to be large enough to produce a critical mass of innovators, whom Rashevsky took to be limited to a small proportion of any society's population, whatever the level of knowledge and skills. Similarly, Karl Deutsch (1957:28, 137) saw state-level societies emerging first in relatively advanced core areas, which as knowledge, skills, and production capabilities developed became centers of expanding systems.

Clearly, in the course of such a society's early growth, a large part of the demands made—and to an even greater extent the demands met—pertained to essential resources, goods, and services. During these early stages, competitions probably occurred among people of unequal capabilities and interests and thereby contributed to the development of new divisions of labor (*differentiation*), the strengthening and *centralization* of the regime, the establishing of local enterprises and local governmental institutions (*individualization*), the organizing of small bureaucracies where none existed (*mechanization*), and the development of minimal but expanding functions of communication, transportation, commerce, finance, and education (Bertalanffy, 1968:54–75). Because the centrifugal (dispersing, disintegrating) tendencies were probably still strong, every step toward survival, growth, and expansion could be traced to efforts by many people and the centralized leadership to aggregate, transform, organize, bureaucratize, regulate, and coordinate the expanding activities (and interests) of the society at large.

At some point, if the economy and production capacity continued to expand, a state-level society would attain a point of *takeoff* (the exponential growth represented by the forward slope of a sigmoid or logistic curve). An excess of energy and other resource and "work" inputs (productive "investments") over outputs (not to be confused with commercial imports and exports) characterized the forward slope of an expanding society's growth curve.

Where appropriate resources were available, a country's takeoff phase was manifested by an exponential increase in rate of productive investment relative to national income or net national product. (Takeoff also included the rapidly increasing capability of a society to produce more at relatively lower unit costs in labor and resources.) Meanwhile, rising demands and expectations contributed to further organizational complexity. Ensuing dynamics constituted both cumulative outcomes of knowledge from major innovation and effects of the new institutions to which it contributed.

From Takeoff to Apogee

The period from takeoff to apogee (the high point or apex of growth and development) tends to be extremely variable and may differ substantially from country to country. Eventually, however, the growth rate may be expected to taper off.

From the start, in growth processes, numbers generate numbers multiplicatively (by the square, the cube) across dimensions (population, mechanical and organizational technologies, resource demands and so forth) unevenly. More people generate more demands; more technology generates more goods and services and more demands; more demands generate more pressures on basic resources; more demands for resources, goods, and services create more incentives for regulative institutions, more pressures on institutions, more pressures of institutions on people, and more pressures of people on resources.

As a society and its economy grow and develop demographically, technologically, economically, and politically, and as larger volumes of energy and other resources move through the system, major changes take place in both the domestic and external environments. Among these changes are those that rank and file and more influential elites have, through their individual and collective activities, instituted, expanded, and rendered increasingly complex. Insofar as domestic and state capabilities and bargaining and leverage potentials increase absolutely and relative to those of other states, private and public activities and interests and the national power outcome (the search for resources, markets, investments, cheap labor, and measures for their defense) can expand beyond national frontiers. In the past, such lateral pressures into the external environment often included territorial conquest as well as trade, exploration, and investment.

With takeoff, the rate of growth and development may be expected to increase insofar as (1) technology outpaces population growth and access to resources continues to increase (through trade or territorial access compensating for domestic shortages); (2) investment in basic scientific research and development and investment in capital enterprises exceed investments in consumer goods and military allocations; and (3) public and private economic and political institutions develop with and are generally adaptive to technological change. In modern times, growth and development are facilitated by basic scientific research and development. Also critical are investments for capital-producing enterprises immune to erosions by consumerism or military expansion. Economic and political institutions that enhance communications, the diffusion of knowledge and skills, productive employment, and adequate incentives are similarly relevant. If such conditions are encouraged and as the society's level of technology continues to advance and its productivity to expand, any apparent decline is likely to be temporary.

Such trends in a country may persist for decades, generations, or even centuries and be furthered *and* constrained by comparable growth and development on the part of countries with which it closely interacts. Eventually, however, a peaking, or apogee, will occur, followed by a leveling off of growth and development rates—a near steady state in which inputs approximate outputs. Unfortunately for analytic and policy purposes, a country's true apogee can be identified only after the decline has become irreversible. Until that point is reached, an input/output balance may be a temporary phenomenon in that the possibility remains (in principle at least) that the country can reorganize, reinvigorate, and possibly reconstitute itself for a new cycle of growth and development.

Characteristically, as a country climbs a logistic curve toward its unidentifiable apogee, a cornucopia may appear to have been established, whereas in fact a life-cycle clock is already ticking—not deterministically but because dysfunctional trends are allowed to persist. Exponential but uneven changes in some of the society's growth and development variables begin to operate as constraints on the system. We might imagine that a social, economic, political, and (possibly) military trap has been set to spring decades, generations, or possibly centuries later (depending upon how decisions affect the country's life cycle). With growth, development, and expansion proceeding unevenly, demands for goods, services, security, and wealth increase exponentially, as do the bureaucratic, military, and overall costs of governing. At the point at which output begins to exceed inputs, disequilibria between domestic and external events (and overall perceptions of is and ought to be) cease to be manageable.

Because many societies of the past—China and Persia, for example—are still identifiable after many political transformations, the true life span of many states is difficult to ascertain. We can safely observe, however, that historical states did suffer eventual decline followed either by disintegration or by radical transformation. Somewhat paradoxically, one of the most powerful elements in the emergence and evolutionary development of states— warfare—is often a critical factor in their demise. In this regard, the history of Rome provides a classical example of growth, development, expansion, decline, and disintegration—from early amalgamation of tribes along the Tiber River through the republican period to an apogee of early imperial grandeur, postapogee leveling off, decline, and destruction by wave upon wave of "barbarian" invaders (Huns, Vandals, Visigoths).

The Roman Collapse and
a New European Environment

Many factors contributed to the Roman Empire's decline and fall (debased currency, overextended frontiers, exorbitant taxes, domestic discontent, rising labor costs, and so forth). In terms put forward in Chapter 1, however, the collapse occurred in large part because overall the population of the Italian peninsula and of the empire as a whole had outpaced the advancement of knowledge and skills. Then, as production costs overtook productivity, the cost of administering and policing the colonies began exceeding the benefits (especially under barbarian pressures from north, east, and west). Meanwhile, the imperial bureaucracy was becoming increasingly ineffective (as well as overgrown and expensive).

With continentwide dismemberment of the Roman Empire, populations in western Europe declined; communications, trade, and market capabilities shrank; and the circulation of money virtually ceased as concentrated political power and influence were dispersed among local kings, princes, and warlords and people hoarded coins and precious metals. Having contributed to the empire's disintegration, intruding barbarians continued to sweep across much of Europe, spreading havoc and preparing the way for new ideas and ways of doing things.

As the Roman Empire disintegrated, the imperial structure burst apart with the result that bits and pieces of it took shape as independent principalities, warlord regimes, and other feudal holdings. The imperial collapse put an end to established property rights and cleared the way for new relationships characterized by fragmented political structures, warrior elites, and personal ties of fealty between lord and tenant. Supporting this superstructure economically were peasant serfs tied to the soil of the great manorial estates who owed a substantial part of their labor and crops to the lord and possessed a minimum of bargaining and leverage potentials. At the same time, with the shrinkage of trade and the shortage of money, merchants were hard put to survive.

The Roman Catholic church was powerful in civil as well as ecclesiastical politics, and the monastic movement was strong. Meanwhile, power on much of the Mediterranean rim devolved upon the Arab empire that was emerging from Arabia and expanding its activities, interests, and dominion from the Middle East across North Africa into Spain and eastward into the Pacific. In our history books, these are often presented as grim times, but the Roman Empire's collapse and the fracturing of European institutions that resulted appear to have provided an environment that made development of new economic and political institutions more feasible. Metaphorically, the young "nation"-states that emerged in Europe were a clutch of young phoenixes rising from the ashes of the Roman Empire.

Although nations (communities of people sharing common antecedents, culture, and language) are often presumed to have created the new state structures, we shall see that the process may have been more interactive, with changes in state structure (feedbacks) providing incentives for new loyalties and hence new "nations." Or we may find population increases combining with the new knowledge, skills, and resource availabilities to yield interplays between the two tendencies—new structures resulting in shared community values "at the top" combined with population pressures and new knowledge and skills emerging "from below." These processes were not simple. Rapid population growth was almost always accompanied by intense pressures on arable land, competition for inadequate resources, and unemployment. But new technologies (knowledge and skills plus tools), while making new resources (and more efficient uses for old resources) available, also required higher levels of collective effort and created more stimulus to nationalistic sentiments and collective security.

Technological Diffusion

Although commonly referred to as dark, the Middle Ages in Europe benefited from the introduction of critically useful knowledge, skills, and tools that ultimately helped transform much of Europe from near stasis into an international society of economic, political, and technological leadership. Borrowed in part from elsewhere (China, India, and the Middle East in particular) and refined or put to new uses by Europeans, the new technologies were developed in a number of different spheres—notably agriculture, commerce, finance, navigation, manufacturing, and warfare. In this new Western environment, each of these technologies played a critical role in the integration of elements from agrarian-based empires and commercially based city-states of the past into the agrocommercial nation-states of the future.

Among influential agricultural developments were the curved plowshare, iron horseshoes, and the horse collar. The greatest single advance in agricultural technology, however, may have been the replacement of the two-field system of crop rotation with the three-field system. Based on calculations made by historian Lynn White (1962:71–72), productive acreage, and presumably crop output, may have risen by at least 50 percent as a result of this change. Combined with the new availability of lands to the east, this gain in productivity substantially increased European food supplies, which then contributed to population increases, sustained by and contributing to further advances in agricultural production and the enhancement of other knowledge and skills. Overall, however, for the better part of a millennium, growing populations in western Europe were outpaced by exponential advances in knowledge and skills. These exponential advances led to even further advances in technology (organizational as well as mechanical) and eventual world leadership in commerce, manufacturing, exploration, science, and politics. As early as the tenth century, the new "spirit of enterprise" was preparing the way for the beginnings of capitalism and an aggressive mode of statecraft, which in combination contributed to the development of nation-states and the structure of an international system.

Many technological advances of the time were not so much inventions as regenerations of knowledge, skills, and specialized activities retained, however inertly, from the past or borrowed from elsewhere. Merchants were adapting the commercial and financial skills that Arabs had been employing throughout the Mediterranean basin since the late seventh century and that had roots in India and China. The concept of zero, which was fundamental for the development of capitalism as well as modern science, reached Europe from India by way of the Middle East. By A.D. 1000, China—populous, skilled, and rich for its time—possessed technologies (including textile manufacture) and a rudimentary market-regulated economy that began impinging on Europe, where new possibilities were seized upon and developed. These influences shifted the course of world history into "a thousand-year exploration of what could be accomplished by relying on prices" and "private advantage as a way of orchestrating behavior on a mass scale" (McNeill, 1982:22).

Gradually market economies reemerged, and increasing numbers of serfs left the manors to which they were bound and went in search of wage labor in expanding towns. Many of their children, grandchildren, and descendants pursued "security" in personal terms and became the artisans, clergy, lawyers, physicians, financiers, merchant princes, bourgeois aristocrats, and statesmen of the future. Of those peasants who remained on the manors, more and more were freed from a bondage whose structural violence was only a few steps removed from slavery.

With a renewal of population growth, which boosted demand, and technological advances, which provided resources, goods, and services (but also raised demands), market economies reemerged, and monarchs of the time, perceiving a need for larger tax revenues as an instrument of power (capabilities and influence) were persuaded to encourage and extend trade. Such extensions required the enforcement of property rights over larger areas and thus contributed to the extension of activities (and often power outreach) beyond established borders. Over time, the costs—as well as the benefits—of foreign trade were increasingly internalized. Thus major developments within the state affected its external activities and vice versa.

In pursuit of commerce, European merchants (especially in the city-states of Amalfi, Genoa, Florence) developed or adapted from Muslim usage new economic and contractual techniques—deposit banking, bills of exchange, loan mechanisms, insurance protection, and other commercial technologies—to facilitate long-distance transactions. Such innovations also facilitated the growth of large-scale market economies and outward expansion of trade, territorial holdings, and national interests (D. North and Thomas, 1973:95; Miskimin, 1969:19).

New military technologies (longbow, pike, gunpowder, new organizational techniques, and discipline, plus the availability of funds to hire mercenaries) provided ambitious rulers with coercive leverages for collecting taxes and harassing lesser warlords. In addition, a number of talented kings induced litigants to appeal decisions of local judges to the royal court, successfully monopolized coinage, levied troops from ducal territories, and expanded their authority over ever-larger territories (Guizot, 1869:75).

Increasingly, people from all walks of life responded to pressures of everyday life in new ways. Depending upon circumstance, locality, time, and the strength, ambition, or other disposition of the king, any two or more of such special interests might align themselves in a coalition to enhance their respective positions and thereby invite formation of an adversary coalition. The relative impact of such participation in the affairs of a society helped shape its structure and form of government (Huntington, 1968:76, 90).

As these developments occurred, the consequences became manifold: new demands, new knowledge and skills, new specialized capabilities, new individual roles, new classes and elites, new coalitions, new adversaries, new nation-states, new expansionist tendencies (lateral pressures), and the beginnings of an international system. Associated with these phenomena was a developing body of new ideas, beliefs, and worldviews. As an outcome of such changes, the demands, expectations, capabilities, and bargaining and leverage capabilities of diverse classes, estates, and elites in western Europe—notably the Crown, medieval church, greater nobility, gentry, merchants, and peasants—underwent significant changes.

Many reasons have been advanced to explain why these trends and changes originated in Europe rather than elsewhere. According to Rashevsky, western European geography was especially favorable for communication, transportation, and commerce—a long shoreline (relative to land area) combined with navigable lakes and rivers, a natural environment favorable for interactivity and innovation. In addition, the collapse of the Roman Empire had "freed up" a continent receptive to new knowledge, skills, and demands and new economic and political developments. Money was becoming available in greater amounts, there was growth in market forces, "free" labor was available, and opportunities for trade were expanding. Now required for orderly management of the new technological, economic, and social forces were larger political units capable of defining relationships, protecting commerce, and enforcing property rights over greater areas and larger populations.

Emergence of the Nation-State

If agrarian empires and commercial city-states had been deficient in terms of loyalty and organizational scale, respectively, feudal institutions were deficient in both. The agrocommercial nation-state turned out to provide a context for inducing mass loyalty within a large and often expanding state structure, but it is doubtful that anyone foresaw or "invented" it. Like so many other adaptations in human history, the nation-state emerged as (in part because) individuals (notably feudal warlords turned king, jealous nobles, determined navigators, and restive peasants) pursued their varied, sometimes disparate interests.

Uneven growth and development within and between small kingdoms, principalities, city-states, and other political entities contributed to expansions of the activities and interests of some at the expense of others, which were often conquered and annexed by the stronger rival. Additionally, some states gained power, influence, and territory from marriage bonds, which preserved kinship ties as an important economic and political variable. As with the emergence of agrarian-based pristine states, warfare seemed to rank with technological advancement in the development of nation-states founded on a combination of agriculture and commerce. In order to wage foreign wars, kings and their generally expansionist regimes had to raise troops (increasingly mercenaries), which tended to place a burden on the peasantry. In order to supply and pay these mercenaries, money had to be raised by whatever means were available—through sale of offices and privileges, fines and confiscations, forced loans, or extraction (taxes) (Tilly, 1981:119).

Extraction took many forms, but European monarchs tended to favor taxable commerce, which often led to the strengthening of navies. The administering of such proliferating activities generated larger bureaucracies, as did the putting down of peasants resisting military conscription. The waging of war thus exerted powerful pressures in both internal and external environments. Domestically, necessities of war required bureaucracies for conscripting, commandeering, "disarming, and taxing subjects." These bureaucracies enhanced the state's coercive power. Externally, regimes used capabilities and leverages so generated to extend their activities, interests, and power outreach; penetrate weaker states; or collide with the activities, interests, and policies of other strong states (Tilly, 1981:47–48).

The conquest of England in 1066 by William, Duke of Normandy, was one of the earlier and more influential of the many wars contributing to the emergence of the nation-state. In effect, William, through his army, established a foreign dynasty in England while maintaining his dukedom in France. This situation contributed to a series of Anglo-French wars during the next four centuries, all of them influential in shaping what became a powerful French nation-state matched by an equally powerful English nation-state.

In the ensuing centuries, William's successors conquered, absorbed, and partially integrated Wales, Scotland, and Ireland. Meanwhile, during the late twelfth and early thirteenth centuries, Philip Augustus of France (r. 1179–1223) and his son Louis VIII (r. 1223–1236) took control of neighboring principalities and brought about fundamental changes in the political configuration of Europe by administering these principalities directly. Using an array of political, economic, administrative, legal, and military leverages, Philip Augustus and his successors established a new order of jurisdiction in France, appointed magistrates and councils in every town, organized a national militia, strengthened the royal court (which invited appeals from ducal courts), promoted their own currencies to the detriment of ducal coinage, and conquered one French principality after another (Guizot, 1869:75).

A common royal strategy was to offer inducements to middle and lower level estates (bankers, traders, clergy, lesser landlords, and petty nobility) at the expense of autonomous dukes and other powerful nobles or warlords. As a result, relatively homogeneous and comparatively powerful national kingdoms were established in both France and England at a time when the collapse of imperial power in Italy and Germany was reducing those countries to "a scattering of small territorial and city-states" (McNeill, 1963:541–542). Wars between France and England were assured, however, as a succession of French kings turned their attention to a succession of English monarchs, who largely through nuptual alliances dating from the days of William of Normandy obtained title to about half of all the French fiefdoms.

Using an array of political, economic, administrative, legal, and military leverages, ambitious monarchs in France (Louis IX, Philip the Fair), England (Edward I, Edward II, the Tudor monarchs), Spain (Ferdinand and Isabella,

Charles V, Philip II), and elsewhere extended their activities and interests and unified their domestic domains. French monarchs gained sovereignty over Burgundy, Normandy, Maine, Anjou, Touraine, Gascony, and so forth. Spanish monarchs drove out the Moors and unified Castile, Aragon, Catalonia, and other parts of the Iberian Peninsula. Under these circumstances, the conquest of "foreign" lands and the putting down of domestic resistance were not easily distinguished.

Manufacturing, Commerce, and the Rise of Capitalism

To underscore warfare at the expense of other, even more fundamental factors contributing to development of nation-states would be a serious error. The period under scrutiny provides a sharp reminder that multicausality and social complexity prevail in human outcomes. What we find is a convergence of interest between unlikely partners—monarchs and an emerging capitalist class. The basis of this convergence is not difficult to identify. For warfare and "statemaking," monarchs required access to resources that were "embedded in local communities," whereas merchants, being specialized in the pricing and exchanging of goods in "larger and larger markets," were in a position to facilitate the seizure of whatever was needed, provided the incentive was right (Tilly, 1981:49).

In previous pages, we have emphasized the strong influence of population growth upon the emergence and growth of states, but beginning in the early 1300s, Europeans suffered a devastating famine that contributed to decades of pestilence (notably the Black Plague of 1348–1351), a severe decline in population, and outbreaks of rebellion and war lasting into the fifteenth century. The consequences of these developments were complicated to say the least. Even as the value of land increased, the precipitate flight (and death) of large numbers of peasants led to greater competition among landlords in attracting tenants. Thereafter, each new disaster suffered by the landlords strengthened the bargaining position of the peasants, who, raising their own new demands, had the effect of increasing those of the society as a whole (D. North and Thomas, 1973:72–73; Miskimin, 1969:45). With the general decline in population, meanwhile, and a depressed volume of trade, people tended to rely more heavily on the coercive forces of centralized states for regulation of economic activities. As in Mafia-dominated societies of a later era, people were ready to pay high prices for domestic protection against peasant rebellions, marauding pillagers, and foreign invasions. Such tendencies, along with continuing technological change, the persistence of a money economy, and increases in scales of warfare, steadily enhanced state power and influence (D. North and Thomas, 1973:72–88).

Domestic cooperation between rulers and capitalists was linked with overseas collaboration between the two. The outward expansion of a state's activities, interests, and influence was often facilitated by financiers and merchants who relied upon the armed forces of the regime for protection in hostile environments (McNeill, 1982:121). Through the end of the thirteenth century, England figured in the commercial life of Europe as an exporter of raw materials such as wool, hides, coal, lead, tin, and grain. As exporters of wool, London merchants developed a direct interest in the diplomatic practices of Edward II (r. 1307–1327), and because the Crown was heavily dependent upon merchants for loans, they exerted influence upon foreign affairs (Keen, 1973:163–179). The expanding trade of France under Philip VI (r. 1328–1350) and of England under Edward III (r. 1327–1377) contributed to the Hundred Years' War, although dynastic and other interests were also at issue. Meanwhile, as English sovereigns expanded their activities and interests northward, French kings allied themselves with Scottish leaders and supported the resistance of Robert Bruce and others.

Once commercially dependent upon the Hanseatic trading system, English merchants struggled for three centuries to strengthen their grip on foreign trade. Under Richard II (r. 1377–1399), Parliament passed a navigation act in 1382 that restricted imports and exports to English ships, and as English commerce came to subserve English power, the Crown became dependent on the merchants and the House of Commons, where, along with landed gentry, this class was strongly represented. A struggle over the wool tax developed among Crown, exporters, and Parliament, where the wool growers had strong leverage. The outcome was a compromise through which the Crown received the tax revenues, Parliament set levels, and merchants achieved a monopoly of trade (cf. Williamson, 1922:19; D. North, 1981:155).

As trade expanded from the Mediterranean during the late Middle Ages, merchants and bankers of Amalfi, Genoa, Florence, Amsterdam, the Hanseatic towns, London, Paris, and elsewhere relied upon economic and contractual instruments to facilitate long-distance transactions. Through new applications of capitalist theory and method, commercial elites—the bourgeoisie—enhanced the power of regimes, even as emergent nation-states provided bureaucratic and executive guarantees and legal protections far beyond what simpler and more localized feudal institutions had achieved.

Centuries later, Marx (1965:25), an implacable foe of capitalism, charged the emerging bourgeoisie with substituting "naked, shameless, direct, brutal exploitation" for the lord, vassal, and serf relationships of the Middle Ages, yet credited the capitalist class with playing a "most revolutionary part" in putting an end to "all the feudal, patriarchal bonds" of the Middle Ages and tearing apart "motley feudal ties that bound man to his 'natural superiors.'" Emerging nation-states required capitalism, and capitalists needed nation-states.

Meanwhile, invention of the rudder and of more effective methods of navigation were liberating seafarers from the necessity of following coasts, and by the close of the fourteenth century the seven seas were accessible to Europeans. As the mariner's compass (developed in China) became available, the seamen of Portugal, Spain, France, Holland, and England opened a more adventurous and enlightened era of navigation and expansion. A French vessel sighted the Canary Islands in 1330; in 1418 the Portuguese began colonization there; and in 1431 a shipmaster from Bruges discovered the Azores. The activities and interests of European nations-states began expanding to the far reaches of the world.

Behind the western dynasties that presided over the early commercial and industrial economies were phalanxes of opulent merchant and banking families who provided bourgeois resources crucial to the state-building and centralizing policies of kings and their advisers. Crucial also to the differentiation of cabinet, legislative, and judicial offices was direct access to agricultural resources, which could be mobilized only with rising productivity and the development of the princely leverages needed for enforcement of government claims.

In a later era, Marx (1848) explained the emergence and development of domestic institutions primarily as the outcome of class struggles, and undoubtedly unending competition and conflict among classes, estates, and elites played an important role. As emphasized by Hintze (cited in Gilbert, 1975), however, constituent institutions—the constitutions—of states were also shaped by their external environments (relations with other states) and by interactions between the two. As Hintze saw it, the councils, cabinet ministries, and parliaments of later times could be traced back as modifications and adaptations of germinal offices and institutions developed in feudal environments and identified as outcomes of domestic external interactions.

The bargaining, leveraging, and coalition-forming activities of commercial and financial elites, the dependence of agriculturally based elite on loans to finance their military activities, and conflicts between the ruler and ambitious or alienated nobles contributed to an enhancement of state capabilities and the emergence of new and ever more complex institutions. At the same time, successful state-building and the tendency toward concentrations of urban populations and increased government expenditures provided entrepreneurs with unique and invaluable opportunities for capturing economies of scale and contributed to the development of capitalism.

Did the impetus for capitalism come from domestic sources or from international trade? The answer is probably both. It is difficult to envisage the growth and expansion of capitalist enterprise aside from the availability of domestic knowledge, skills, labor, at least minimal resources, and consumer demand in combination with raw materials, markets, and some measure of foreign labor. In the long run, surely the interplay between domestic and foreign phenomena provided capitalism with its explosive economic power. Along with these economic considerations, however, historian Paul Kennedy (1987:76–86) saw warfare—and the demand for "money, money, and yet more money" to pay for it—as providing the "most sustained boost" to Europe's "financial revolution" between the early sixteenth century and the defeat of Napoleon.

Between the end of the fifteenth century and the end of the eighteenth, several European countries entered an epoch of merchant capitalism (mercantilism) that was characterized by spectacular increases in knowledge and skills pertaining to science, navigation, weaponry, and domestic production (notably mining, textile manufacturing, and shipbuilding) and step-by-step innovations in organization. Increases in the bargaining power of merchants and the lesser gentry contributed to the emergence of legislative bodies and constrained the centrist and absolutist tendencies that had been building up among European monarchs.

Unlike modern economic theory, which emphasizes the values of want-satisfying commodities, seventeenth- and eighteenth-century mercantilist thought was concerned with acquiring and storing precious metals. A major aim was to maintain a trade balance that enabled an influx of gold and silver, which contributed to the country's wealth and power. Only bullion imported made amends for bullion exported. Increasingly, colonies were relied upon to supply commodities that were unavailable at home "and which otherwise would have to be imported from a foreign country, and might require payment in bullion" (Williams, 1966:9, 30). The encouragement of exports and the discouragement of imports were the two great engines by which the mercantilist system sought to enrich the home country through an advantageous "balance" of trade.

Statesmen of the era saw mercantilist practice as a means of transforming economic capability into power as an end in itself. It was the state, not the nation at large, that absorbed mercantilist attention in order to make economic activity subservient to the state. The state's first interest was power, which it could not resign "without resigning its own paramount interest" (Heckscher, 1935:II, 15–17, 31). The expectation was that one nation could get rich by drawing capital out of the other nations (Viner, 1958:6–7). What Charles Tilly (1981:137) attributed to France during much of the sixteenth and seventeenth centuries was characteristic of other nation-states of the time. Statemaking and continual warmaking combined to put recurring demands on capital, labor, and commodities, and concurrently, "each new surge of warfare" generated popular resistance and a need for more taxes to invest in more power for enforcement of domestic law and order.

Westphalia and the New Nation-States

We cannot assert with confidence when and where the first nation-state was established. The Spanish state appeared as the Moors were expelled and as power was centralized under Ferdinand and Isabella at the nobility's expense. Nation-state structures, moreover, differed from country to country. In Spain and France, these structures were absolutist, whereas in England and the Netherlands, such tendencies diminished as monarchs bartered away property rights in exchange for revenue and as representative assemblies succeeded in exerting further constraints upon the Crown (D. North and Thomas, 1973:86–87).

What is relatively clear is that the 1648 Treaty of Westphalia, which terminated the Thirty Years' War, formally recognized nation-states. In addition to the thirteen international hostilities constituting the Thirty Years' War, Quincy Wright (1965:642–643) listed seventeen more in which western European nations were engaged between 1600 and 1650. The Congress of Westphalia brought together for the first time all the major European powers, which achieved through negotiation two multilateral treaties (Osnabrück and Münster) legalizing a new order in Europe and opening a new era in international relations but not in peace (Mangone, 1951:47).

Ancient agrarian kingdoms and empires of later eras owed their genesis and survival to the concentration of power in the hands of a monarch, a bureaucracy, and a noble ruling class. Republican city-states also relied upon a concentration of power, but in principle at least, the citizenry and/or its representatives were active shareholders in the civic enterprise and a source of constraint on the exercise of power. During the course of centuries, the emerging agrocommercial states, through the creation of sufficient economic surpluses, induced a succession of estates to challenge royal power and thus to gain larger shares of influence over extraction, allocation, nationalism, exercise of power, and claims of sovereignty, however limited in terms of effective control. Like its predecessors, the new nations-states, however powerful, operated to maintain a moving equilibrium (if not a constrained disequilibrium).

The Westphalian treaties served as a relatively early milestone in the displacement of the agrarian empire and the city-state by the agrocommercial nation-state, which increasingly merged nationalist loyalties and passions with state requirements for compliance, active support, ardent patriotism, and the internalization of state ideologies. These sociocultural adaptations greatly strengthened the nation-state as the organizing principle of a new international order (Gilpin, 1987:4–7). In the succeeding centuries, nation-state societies—notably Great Britain, Holland, the Scandinavian countries, and postrevolutionary France—unified processes of centralization and coordination within their respective regimes (monarch → cabinet → prime minister → parliament → voting citizenry). This was achieved through adaptive, largely trial-and-error initiation, practice, and gradual institutionalization of "horizontal" and "vertical" bargaining and leverage modes.

In actuality, because of the way they have evolved, most large countries today (the USSR, for example) and many smaller ones (notably Lebanon) are more multinational (or at least multiethnic) than national. The level of cultural and political integration often depends upon the extent to which component national (and/or ethnic) populations have retained their respective territorial bases, languages, and coherent cultures. (Even Great Britain encompasses identifiably Scottish, Welsh, and Irish components.)

As it turned out, the peace negotiated at Westphalia was short-lived. During the late seventeenth and early eighteenth centuries, the five littoral states of the new international system—Spain, Portugal, Great Britain, the Netherlands, and France—fought a series of bitter wars on the high seas and in Europe, Asia, and the Americas. Wright listed eighty-seven wars fought by countries in western Europe between 1650 and 1825. Along with uneven growth and development, the expansion of national activities and interests, and the establishment of far-flung colonial empires, this incessant warfare contributed to the domestic development and structuring of individual states, the establishment of commercial (and later industrial) empires, and the establishment of the third image (the international system).

So far we have been concerned primarily with some of the institutional consequences of uneven growth and development among populations, technologies, and resource accesses during several millennia of institutional adaptation on the second image level. Before proceeding to the third image, however, let us consider the more or less generic decision- and policymaking processes of the state and some of the ways in which they contribute to the encompassing international system.

4

State Decisionmaking

Chapter 3 considered how the uneven growth, development, and expansion of prestate societies may have contributed to the independent emergence of the first states in several parts of the world. The chapter also discussed how second image institutions appear to have evolved during some thousands of years from archaic, agrarian-based kingdoms and empires and commercial city-states to the agrocommercial and industrial nation-states of the modern era. The central purpose of this chapter is to present and defend a pluralist explanation of state decisionmaking and to move from the second image toward the third by showing how processes of information distribution and interpretation, bargaining, leveraging, coalition formation, decisionmaking, and associated activities impinge on, help to shape, and are shaped by the third image.

Unitary Rational Actor Versus
Pluralistic Assumptions

The nature of the two images and interplays between them indicate that the state—which is characterized by an overarching regime with a monopoly of legal power within its "sovereign" borders—is a true social actor system with the capacity to maintain a "security zone" within and protection against attack from without. By contrast, as we shall discuss in Chapter 5, the international system is no more than the complex and vibrant structure or pattern of interplays and shifting relationships among its member states. This perspective underscores unique properties of the state and the role of the regime and its prime minister, president, dictator, or other chief executive as an authoritative decisionmaker in domestic and external environments.

As pointed out in earlier chapters, an underlying problem confronting the chief executive and his or her regime is that both the internal and external environments of the state are subject to continual change as well as interplay. In addition, the chief executive, located between past and future, must draw upon the past and act in the present in order to deal effectively with environments that do not yet exist. Because of these inherent instabilities and uncertainties, the best that can be said of even the shrewdest chief executive is that he or she is working to achieve an equilibrium that is forever in the making.

Given such uncertainties, the concern of this chapter is to discover (1) what the nature of the state as decisionmaking actor is; (2) how states "perceive," "compare," "weigh," and "evaluate" events in the two environments; (3) how the state, through its regime and executive, "decides" and "acts" in neverending efforts to meet demands and exploit often contradictory potentials originating in the two environments; and (4) what initiatives, if any, a state may be expected to take.

The possibility of addressing these issues satisfactorily is limited by the fact that states, being part social habit pattern and part conceptual abstraction, cannot think, feel, evaluate, or act in the way that a human does. Yet much of the conventional wisdom and theoretical literature of international politics relies upon a vocabulary that appears to attribute personality, cognitions, affects, and actions to the state. In part, this has been a linguistic convenience because it is difficult to discuss the abstract concept of the state except by reification of its structure and activities. The danger in this convenience is that we may slip into analyzing the state *as if* it were a living, thinking, deciding, and acting organism.

Unitary Rational Actor Assumptions

Conventional approaches to international politics (notably realist and neorealist theories) have tended to treat the state as a unitary rational actor. If this tendency is pursued too rigidly, however, the theorist, analyst, or decisionmaker risks exclusion of information that can be vital to an understanding of how states "really" work. In Chapter 3, we postulated the origin of early states as resulting from a coalition imposed on weaker coalitions by a powerful invader (or from voluntary coalitions formed in opposition to such states). Insofar as this proposal is a reasonable approximation of prehistorical reality, the concept of the generic state as a unitary rational actor is subject to critical scrutiny from the start.

The concept and reality of second image institutions have become more complicated since the first state emerged, but many of the potential conflicts and internal fracture lines remain. When a state has internal trouble—as the United States did during its Civil War and China, the USSR, and Lebanon do today—the persisting lines of potential cleavage erupt and the overarching regime suffers agonizing strains and may split apart or collapse. Such outcomes are the extreme, but the neverending challenge of an effective state is how to constrain disequilibrium, correcting for the ubiquitous contradictions, arationalities, and disunities inherent in the pursuit of dynamic (moving) equilibria.

An underlying difficulty with the unitary actor concept is that it serves as an assumption and a definition; it places the United States and all the other countries of the world in the same basket. In fact, if we were to use degrees of cohesion, consensus, or dissent as indicators, great differences would be evident between Japan, for example, as a relatively unitary nation and numbers of Third World countries. By the same token, however, if we were to measure our own country (whichever it is) year by year, we might find significant variability in these indicators throughout its history (the United States, for example, before and after Franklin Roosevelt and during administrations from Harry Truman to George Bush). This does not mean that "working" assumptions of unity and rationality cannot be theoretically and analytically useful, but care must be taken under such conditions if critically relevant information is not to be disregarded, overlooked, or underevaluated.

The risks of relying exclusively on rational actor assumptions are somewhat comparable. These assumptions have been so fundamental to the "classical" model of foreign policy decisionmaking, however, that the question of whether or not leaders under scrutiny could have rationally undertaken a given action has often been obscured or overlooked (Allison, 1971:13).

According to the (minimal) assumptions of utility theory (the criterion of right conduct is the usefulness of its outcomes), state actors have perfect information about the consequences of their actions (given another state's choice) and clearly identified, defined, and limited options. They can attach precise payoff values to each set of outcomes and calculate "the payoffs of their rational opponent over all possible outcomes" (Jervis, 1971:125). Although assumptions of maximization may be replaced by the concept of *satisficing*—the idea that the actor is pursuing some less than maximal level of aspiration—a number of important questions may remain unanswered. Whose aspirations are pursued? How are aspiration levels determined? (Axelrod, 1972:43–44).

From an analysis of social choice mechanisms in economics and politics, Nobel Prize–winner Kenneth Arrow (1963:1–6, 18, 28, 30, 56) concluded that only *actual behavior* can indicate the meaning of utility as a concept, and insofar as any behavior can be explained by a given utility function, "such a course of behavior can be equally well explained by any other utility function which is a strictly increasing function of the first." (Roughly, any given behavior that can be explained by variable x can also be explained by some variable y that increasingly varies with x.) Without measurable utility, moreover, "we cannot have interpersonal comparability of utilities a fortiori."

In their development of the mathematical theory of games, John von Neumann and Oskar Morgenstern (1944:8–9) defined rationality in terms of a basic assumption that the aim of all participants is money, or some equivalent, which is taken to be divisible, substitutable, freely transferable, and identical with whatever utility or satisfaction each participant desires. A game in this context refers to a situation in which the outcomes for two or more interacting participants are conjoined and neither is certain which outcome will occur (Tedeschi, Schlenker, and Bonoma, 1973:3). Game theory, which is inherently interactive, has clear advantages over decision theory in the study of social functions in which behaviors are exchanged or traded off in pursuit of some goal or outcome. As compared with money, however, exchanges of behavior lack a clear order of fungibility, and rationality in many intensely subjective real-world games is often difficult to sustain.[1]

A country's foreign policy or specific action may emerge, in fact, as an inconsistent or shifting compromise resulting from the "pushing and hauling" of powerful domestic interest groups, rival bureaucratic interests, or military services and advisers competing for favor and influence. Decisions reached under such conditions may differ substantially from what was originally intended (Snyder and Diesing, 1977:75) and may include unexpected side effects.

In discussing the limitations of the utility approach as manifested in game theory, Richard Cyert and James March (1963:29–30) addressed two major considerations and a consequence. The first of the considerations is that game theory assumes a "fixed booty" available as side payments (positive leverages) for distribution among members of a coalition. This assumption is nullified, however, by the consideration that a "winning coalition" in politics does not have a fixed booty or conservation of utility. Consequently, in politics the side payments available for distribution among coalition members must necessarily depend on the composition and structure of the coalition, and the overall utility of side payments must differ according to the distribution of capabilities and bargaining and leverage potentials within the coalition.

Similar stipulations have been advanced in game theory, which requires that once side payments have been made, a joint preference ordering is defined, and then side-payment bargaining (leveraging) settles the conflict. To a large extent, however, leverages of reward in political coalitions take the form of policy commitments—the trading off of certain goals or subgoals in order to win support for a main or central goal (Riker, 1962:19–20). A recalcitrant member of a coalition adopts the organizational goal for a price. For political bargaining, terms must be flexible enough to accommodate side payments that are distributable according to variations in the complementarity of policy demands—a phenomenon that represents a special case of preference ordering (Luce and Raiffa, 1957:50) combined with a special process in the specification of goals (Cyert and March, 1963:50).

Any search for an alternative or optimal strategy has costs. A choice or trade-off must therefore be made between potentially favorable solutions that are more costly to pursue and less likely to be found and more obvious strategies and outcomes that are less acceptable but quicker and less costly to obtain. In many situations, however, the combinations of possible moves and outcomes for all participants are too large to allow calculation in whatever time is available. Under such circumstances, to speak of an optimal solution can be misleading.

In seeking to reconcile such differences, Herbert Simon (1955:76–77) suggested that "rationality" be used only in conjunction with appropriate limiting adverbs. A decision is "objectively" rational if it maximizes preferred given values; "subjectively" rational if it maximizes an outcome *perceived* as desirable; "consciously" rational if means are consciously adjusted to ends; "personally" rational if it is oriented to the objective of the individual; and "organizationally" rational if it is oriented toward goals of the organization. But what if (as suggested by Cyert and March) there is no such thing as an organizational goal? What if the organization's goal is, in fact, a compromise—essentially an outcome of a bargaining process (as many collective outcomes are)?

One common solution has been to designate the prime minister, president, dictator, or other executive leader as state spokesperson. Within a war decision model, Bruce Bueno de Mesquita (1981b:15) identified "the strong leader" as speaking and acting for the state, which can thus be accepted as a "rational actor." This convention provides a convenient way of circumventing a complex problem, but it does not help us to understand the complicated ways in which internal and external processes and events interact and how the chief executive and his or her regime can most effectively *work toward* an equilibrium.

In national decisionmaking, there are two main sources of irrationality, policy, and action—one personal, the other structural. Woodrow Wilson's post–World War I effort to "save" the League of Nations—to guarantee U.S. support for it—provides an example of personal irrationality affecting national policy. In trying to gain U.S. support for the league, Wilson felt compelled to spurn the "mild reservationists" in the Senate, whose support was indispensable for his purposes, and appeal to the people—a course "which he must have known held little hope of success." Reason would have required him to stay in Washington and compromise, but an emotional sense of necessity "forbade him doing so." Feelings "which he could neither understand nor bear to examine nor resist" impelled him toward actions that jeopardized the league he was struggling to save (George and George, 1964:291–292).

Structural sources of irrationality include subjective (and often conflicting) perceptions, expectations, goals, and interests from one organizational level to another. What is rational for the individual may not be—indeed is unlikely to be—wholly rational for any group or organization of which he or she is a member. Conversely, what is rational for a group or an organization, including the state, will not be wholly rational for any component part. "Two soldiers sit in a trench opposite a machine-gun nest," wrote Simon (1955:76). "One of them stays under cover. The other, at the cost of his life, destroys the machine-gun nest with a grenade. Which is rational?" Today, terrorists are skillful at creating situations that defy solutions that all or most victims can accept as rational.

The limitations of rationality as an assumption are well known, but most analysts recognize that the analysis of decision and action—of planning and prediction of any sort—becomes exceedingly difficult without such an assumption. Failure by many theorists to take these various considerations into account can be seriously misleading. An important factor that is neglected by utility and game theory models is the interplay between adversary and alliance (coalition) bargaining. Adversaries commonly have allies, and alliance considerations often play a role in moves against adversaries, but much of the information the utility model accepts as given may not be available in such a bargaining sequence.

Simon (1985:295) thought that in situations in which the decisionmaker had no advance knowledge of either alternatives or consequences and could not be certain even of his or her own goals except during the "problem-solving process," the assumption of rationality by itself could not provide an adequate basis for predicting outcomes unless conditional relationships had been made explicit and relevant empirical details about the decisionmaker were available. But within the international system, rational calculation of risks and probable outcomes by any one state can be obfuscated by the behavior of other states over which the calculating state has no reliable control. This uncertainty often expands as a conflict escalates.

Rational, unitary actor assumptions may provide an indispensable baseline or standard against which second image realities can be measured for deviance, but care should be taken that the standard is not confused with the reality. Reliance upon rationality as an assumption places a heavy burden upon the way it is defined, and the unitary actor concept can obscure many of the inconsistencies and contradictions that are virtually endemic to organizational decisions. By contrast, a dynamic, generic approach includes no prior assumptions about the degree of unity in a state or the rationality of its decisions and actions. A dynamic approach leaves these considerations to be found empirically through analysis.

Some Pluralistic Counterassumptions

In the real world, neither a regime nor a whole state is a unitary (or even a conglomerate) actor unit. Both are fluctuating, only partially stabilized patterns of individual human beings performing interacting, often interdependent, and partially conflicting roles. Each individual is pursuing a personal equilibrium, just as each responsible leader is trying to harmonize domestic with external changes, argue issues as she or he sees them, apply whatever leverages can be brought into play, and look for help (allies) from whatever corner.

Inescapably, each participant brings to the bargaining and leverage interchange the beliefs, perceptions, values, memories, innate capabilities, experience, unconscious bias, habits, predispositions, expectations, idiosyncracies, and character flaws that are likely to influence his or her decisions and actions. In a sense, these are commonplace realities, but they open the way for the confusions and irrationalities that may surface when personal attributes combine or collide in a bargaining and leverage milieu. Such possibilities indicate that a pluralistic approach should allow for both rational and nonrational components in any sequence of intense or high-stake interchange (Snyder and Diesing, 1977:332).

When applied to decisionmaking, the "bounded rationality" model proposed by Simon (1985:293–294) drops assumptions of homogeneous good and perfect ability to calculate and replaces them with assumptions of the "heterogeneity of goods." This latter concept includes reliance on media that are not easily compared; alternatives the whole of which is not ascertainable at the start of the decisionmaking; and, even for the alternatives that are known, an assumption that the probability of achieving specific "goods" cannot be calculated with any precision.

From a pluralistic viewpoint, second image decisionmaking may approximate what Cyert and March (1963:32, 99, 266, 269) had in mind when opposing "adaptively rational" systems to the customary idea of "omnisciently rational" systems. An adaptive system is characterized by the existence of a number of conditions (states of being) of the system (actor, participant, bargainer). At any given time, the system "prefers" some of these conditions to others. There are also external sources of disturbance or shocks to the system that cannot be controlled and a number of internal decision variables that are manipulable according to some decision rules. Each combination of external shocks and decision variables changes the condition of the system. Thus, given an existing condition, an external shock, and a decision, the next condition is fashioned (Cyert and March, 1963:99–100).

In ways that are crudely analogous to individual decisionmaking, individuals engaged in reaching for a group decision are constrained by activities and interests in both internal and external environments. External constraints on the second image level comprise phenomena outside national jurisdictions—primarily the activities of other states. Internal constraints may be found within the group itself, within the bureaucratic environment, and/ or within the country at large.

Contributing to the decisions and activities of societies and their governments are tens of millions of constituents making billions of decisions weekly and bargaining and leveraging as best they can in order to get and keep jobs, acquire the "necessities" for survival, educate their children, improve their own lot if possible, and snatch a few pleasures along the way. If too much goes wrong, these constituents may be in serious trouble (Schelling, 1978:21). When aggregated, such demands, decisions, responses, and outcomes (purchases made, items sold, workers hired and fired, loans granted, money saved, taxes paid or withheld, ballots cast, and so forth) affect both economic and political decisionmaking on the second image level. The impact of such activities and their aggregations on national decision- and policymaking varies according to how and to what extent information about them is transmitted to and interpreted and acted upon by the regime.

Although communications—compared with other activities—often require few resources, information transactions by themselves may not always accomplish much. If information is to be translated into useful outcome, resources and further knowledge and skills are almost always required. Useful information implies a need for resources and knowledge and skills, and to the extent that access to either of these is blocked or otherwise unavailable, effective decisionmaking will be constrained or brought to a standstill (Cyert and March, 1963:32). (Other constraints are ideological, psychological, bureaucratic, or structural.)

Information Loss and Distortion

Underlying the transfers and interpretations of information (and disinformation) among leaders, bureaucrats, and the citizenry that impinge upon decisionmaking on the second image level are individual beliefs, including ideological elements that are more or less widely shared. Since World War I, there has been a growing tendency to explain the policies and behaviors of countries, especially adversaries, in ideological terms. Narrowly defined, *ideology* refers to the integrated assertions, theories, and aims of a particular socioeconomic or sociopolitical program or regime. The concept of ideology carries a connotation of a belief system that is widely shared (or imposed).

Beliefs, Belief Systems, and Ideologies on the National Level

Martin Seliger (1976:13–27, 143–147) distinguished between two categories of ideology: restrictive and inclusive. *Restrictive ideology* refers to specific political belief systems. Marx and Engels, who developed the first elaborate ideological theory, used the term "ideology" restrictively and pejoratively, particularly in their focus on "bourgeois ideology." *Inclusive ideology*, according to Seliger, refers to all political belief systems. In either case, ideology and politics are inextricably interlinked.

Broadly construed, an ideology might include views of the universe, human roles within it, and people's relations with each other—the what has been, is, ought-to-be, and will-be terms that prevail within a community or society at any given time. Defined in this way, an ideology on the second image level might be expected to include core assumptions and values along with inconsistencies and outright contradictions. Within such a framework, there presumably is space for overlaps in beliefs and also for more restrictive, less widely shared belief systems and subsystems.

As restrictively defined, ideology provides powerful cognitive and affective tools for bargaining and leverages applied by leaders to influence constituents, by the rank and file to influence regimes and other large institutions, and by special interest groups and revolutionary movements to influence the populace and/or government or to incite rebellion. On the second image level, a central function of a successful ideology is to energize the populace— by appeals to nationalistic values and patriotic sentiments—to support the regime and comply with its imperatives (often at the expense of the rational calculus of individual benefits, costs, and other individual interests). Of major concern to regimes in this regard is the "free rider" who "consumes the good at no personal expense or little expense" (D. North, 1981:52; Gilpin, 1981:16, 104, 169). As employed by a skillful head of state, adviser, or bureaucrat, ideology provides a powerful instrument for persuading, and even coercing, free riders (and freethinkers) into compliance, if not active support, and isolating the true recalcitrants.

As analytic concepts, ideological phenomena are often difficult to define or analyze rigorously. Thus, it may be useful to rely on functions (and indicators thereof) common to all societies, such as bargaining, leveraging, and coalition formation, in order to find out how various states employ these generic processes in determining and rhetorically defining who gets what, when, how, why, and with what outcomes. Then, insofar as such functions are performed in particular modes, according to identifiable strategies, and with characteristically patterned outcomes, we may be able to characterize these functions as more or less "nationalistic," "totalitarian," "democratic," "socialist," "communist," or whatever.

Psychological Constraints on Communications

Information available to higher officials for making individual (or group) decisions can be constrained in two seemingly contradictory ways. Officials may be exposed to more information than they can effectively sort out and evaluate, or information may be lost in the course of information transfers or bureaucratic management. Even seemingly overwhelming flows of information may have been subjected to selective processing, if only because information cannot be gathered or transmitted except selectively. Information for the chief executive and bureaucratic offices responsible for making a policy decision tends to be passed along from bottom to top or from periphery to center in a manner something like this:

$$\text{molecular} \longrightarrow \text{molar} \longrightarrow \text{molecular} \longrightarrow \text{molar}.$$

Typically, a part of such information may be lost, enlarged upon, or reinterpreted at any molecular/molar nodal point.

Some essentially psychological constraints are also organizational (information-gathering agencies and personnel have limited time, budgets, and energy), some are more mechanical (transmission mechanisms have limited capacities), and some are partly sociological (what a speaker, writer, or other information sender means can be interpreted differently by a receiver in a different milieu or subculture). Communication from foreign environments can be even more severely constrained. Already shaped (perhaps unintentionally) by biases of culture and personal dispositions, a written report submitted by a U.S. vice-consul about a political uprising in central Africa may cross many desks before it reaches a high-level decisionmaker. Or it may be filed somewhere along the line or condensed to a paragraph or perhaps a sentence in a more comprehensive document. In fact, the original meaning of a message may be altered intentionally or unintentionally in the course of any transmission, condensation, interpretation, evaluation, or change of context.

Additionally, differences in the way sender and receiver or two or more recipients perceive, recall, feel about, or interpret events can impede information exchanges, as can individual differences in belief or expectation. These considerations pertain to participants in group decisionmaking and to the ways in which they, as individuals, perceive and respond to each other and to friends, allies, competitors, rivals, and adversaries as well as to events, issues, and various possible policies and courses of action.

Professional gatherers and transmitters of information—intelligence agents included—maintain what is essentially a bargaining and leverage relationship with their bureaucratic superiors. They agree to produce some amount or continuing flow of information in return for rewards of one kind or another—fee, salary, recognition, possibility of promotion, and the like. Under such circumstances, such purveyors may tend to emphasize the types of information they think their principals desire or expect—the kinds of news that a newspaper or television editor considers of interest to his or her public, for example, or alternatively, the kinds of intelligence that an official of the Central Intelligence Agency (CIA), KGB, or other agency views as vital. In the former case, the reporter's bias is likely to be in the direction of scandals, accidents, disasters, crimes, riots, crises, and violence, whereas the bias of an intelligence agent may tend to reflect the ideology and policies of the regime and the assumptions and expectations of superiors. Secrecy, moreover, can exact heavy costs in administrative efficiency. There is always a possibility that one's own spy may be a double agent working for the adversary or for both countries at once or that one's covert agents are pursuing agendas of their own. Whatever its advantages, secrecy can obscure accountability for state activities—in police states and in democracies.

Professionals gathering information for different purposes may invoke quite different values. A news reporter may consider it desirable to be accurate but even more desirable to be read. The intelligence agent, by contrast, cannot afford to be wrong too often (therefore, his or her reporting may be conservative), but the agent may prefer not to be too consistently right (especially in predicting the improbable) lest he or she be suspected of collusion with the enemy (providing information that the latter wants transmitted). In either case, transmitted information can be, and all too frequently is, distorted (often without the awareness of either the purveyor or the recipient) by aspects of the bargaining process. Thus, Roberta Wohlstetter (1962:72–74) reported how agencies of the U.S. government drew differing conclusions about Japan's intentions and messages before Pearl Harbor because they interpreted incoming information in very different contexts; officers in the field discounted Washington's caveats.

Bureaucratic Constraints on Communication

Glenn Snyder and Paul Diesing (1977:349) compared treatment of information by decisionmakers according to their respective levels in the bureaucratic hierarchy. On a lower, molecular level is a bureaucrat who has internalized the values and beliefs of his own department and thus identifies its welfare with that of the nation as a whole. In the process of coalition-building, of which decisionmaking in large part consists, his activities may become increasingly partisan. "He supports the strategy favored by his department." Operating on a higher, molar level, on the other hand, is the president, prime minister, dictator, foreign secretary, or other decisionmaker, together with aides and assistants who have responsibility for the country as a whole. Their inclination may be to identify the interests of the constituencies that put them into office with the interest of the nation as a whole.

The participation of each ministry, bureau, or other organizational unit in the identification and evaluation of policy options tends to be shaped by its own parochial views and interests. During the bargaining, coalition-forming process, each component of a government develops its own preference ordering by rationalizing an interpretation of its responsibilities and how they contribute to the national interest. Whatever bargaining advantages they possess are then used to influence the executive's choice of policy.

Because bargaining and leverage advantages are unevenly distributed among leaders, advisers, and bureaucrats, there is no assurance that those with superior competence in a matter up for decision can compete successfully with those having superior power and influence. Therefore, whether through cynicism or inadvertence, each actor unit is likely to produce its own partisan evaluation of options under scrutiny and to discredit the analyses of adversaries. This tendency may persist until a group with sufficient status forms a coalition in support of an option and thus validates a decision that is binding on all participants who recognize its authority.

In view of the proportions of organizational "rationality" and "reflective" subjectivity in thinking and acting that tend to vary from person to person and with changing circumstance, we would expect to find collective decision- and policymaking characterized by comparable variability. Insofar as disparate perceptions, affects, and individual interests contribute to the bargaining, leveraging, and interplays, however, we might find additional inconsistencies and rationalities (or irrationalities) characterizing many coalitional consensuses.

Although the prime minister, president, or dictator appears to possess overriding power and influence in a government, bureaucrats and other advisers often find ways of manipulating information flows. A certain amount of secrecy may be unavoidable in carrying out a delicate task, but reliance on it blocks information exchanges and contributes to policy contradictions and associated arationalities. During the autumn of 1941, Japanese decisionmakers were hampered by limitations on the information made available to them by the armed forces. "I was astonished at our lack of the statistical data," Foreign Minister Shigenori Togo complained, ". . . but even more, I felt the absurdity of our having to base our deliberations on assumptions, since the high command refused to divulge figures on the number of our armed forces, or any facts relating to operations" (Ike, 1967:188). (Classification of documents and other forms of secrecy are often used to protect incompetence, bad judgment, or peculation—thus endangering a society's security and overall well-being.)

Decisionmaking at the "Top"

Writers in the field commonly distinguish "rational," "utilitarian," "organizational" (individuals from rank and file contributing in varying degrees to governmental decisions and actions), "bureaucratic" (decisions shaped or made by governmental bureaucrats), "cybernetic" (the "system" acting to close a gap between the real situation and a preferred outcome), and other decisionmaking and action models as if they were separable and somehow optional. In the real world, however, each of these represents no more than one of innumerable manifestations of generic decision and action. Any decision process leading to an activity is likely to manifest elusive shadings of rationality, utility, organizational, and bureaucratic perspective. If any one of these perspectives is more generic and inclusive than the others, it is probably the cybernetic in that virtually any other decisionmaking model can be subsumed within or translated into it.

Conditioned by incoming information, personal beliefs, and ideological considerations, national leaders are under pressure to make decisions. Some of these can be deferred indefinitely, but others cannot be delayed. In circumstances of the latter sort, a responsible decisionmaker cannot escape an ultimate decision, but he or she seldom reaches it in isolation. Faced with the prospect of declaring war, Woodrow Wilson secluded himself in his study late into the night, but the bargaining and leveraging (with advisers as well as critics) had already occurred.

As in the bureaucratic model (Allison and Halperin, 1972:27), participants act less through "consistent sets of strategic objectives" than in line with national security as they construe it and with their interpretations of domestic, regime (organizational), and personal interests. Harold Lasswell (1958:38) characterized the motives of political leaders as private motives/displaced upon public objects/rationalized in terms of public interest.

In the course of decisionmaking, however, all participants tend to find themselves under bargaining and leveraging pressures that run counter to their personal values, objectives, outcomes, and incentives. In such circumstances, each participant must decide how far to bend in modifying his or her attitudes, position, and behavior. Each person's position will depend upon personal interests, conception of role, and responses to pressure.

Whatever his or her personal interests and perspectives, a responsible head of state (in principle, if not in practice) confronts the challenge of pursuing national growth and development—economic, political, and strategic security—and maximizing efforts to constrain tendencies toward disequilibrium. Within this context, the essence of the leader's task is the persuasion of other players "that his version of what needs to be done is what their own appraisal of their own responsibilities requires them to do in their own interests" (Allison, 1971:176–177). Responses of other players to the leverages of a superior are likely to depend in part upon the amount of disagreement or consensus in the decisionmaking group and the distribution of authority and other sources of leverage potential within the system. Variable distributions of capabilities and bargaining and leverage potentials contribute to different structural patterns among the decisionmakers. Often, but especially in times of crisis, leaders, seeking to stir patriotic or nationalist feelings in support of what might appear to be draconian policies, invoke national myths—widely shared stories derived from the oral or written history of a nation and extolling its traditions, rectitude, and past glories.

Unless a regime is in the throes of an extreme internal crisis, the prime minister, president, dictator, or other chief executive normally has the greatest leverage potential and the ultimate decision capacity. In return for his or her confidence, however, the chief executive expects judgments and recommendations from ministers, aides, and advisers (who are likely to have specialized diplomatic, economic and financial, military, or other knowledge and skills that the executive needs before a decision is made), and the chief executive also wants assurance of their loyalty, vigorous support, and discretion after a determination has been made. Even a dictator is likely to sense—as Hitler discovered in the final days of World War II (if he did not fully appreciate it before)—that effective power depends upon such support from leading civilian and military officers (or gauleiters who represent major interests or are guarantors of public compliance). The president, prime minister, or dictator who lacks the ability to generate and motivate coalitions is in deep trouble.

By relying on the power of their regimes, as well as on whatever charisma and other sources of influence they may possess, national leaders are often able to influence public beliefs, attitudes, and behavior in remarkable ways. In pursuing support for themselves and their policies, they can identify friends and enemies and interpret events in self-serving ways. This is possible even in pluralistic countries where the press is relatively free—as Lyndon Johnson demonstrated in 1964 with respect to the Gulf of Tonkin affair and as Ronald Reagan attempted in his antiterrorist policies in the mid-1980s. As in both of these efforts, however, such definitions and interpretations may be called into question by the course of subsequent events (as Johnson and Reagan discovered, each in his own way). In totalitarian states, dictators can grossly manipulate public images of foreign (and domestic) events for many years.

Options for Social Choice

We have identified generic decisionmaking as occurring whenever an individual, group, or coalition contemplates (consciously or unconsciously) acting to narrow or close a gap or discrepancy between a perception of fact and a perception of value. Each of us is likely to encounter hundreds or thousands of situations in the course of any given day, and within a whole society the aggregation of such situations can be astronomical—some are entirely personal, whereas others reverberate (in aggregate, if not singly) on the second image level.

In dealing with the more disturbing of their gaps, members of the rank and file bargain with and apply what leverages they can to influence their peers, local authorities, and representatives of the regime. Similarly, in pursuit of their own interests and perspectives, private and governmental elites probe, test, evaluate, and act upon whatever opportunities they pursue "below" them and "above" them in social, economic, political, and associated hierarchies. Over time, the conscious and unconscious self-monitoring of activities—the accumulation and collectivization of personal observation and experiences—contributes to changes in the physical and social environments of the community (or state), to adaptation, and to a kind of social learning, often without serious disruptions of relatively stable local and national structures.

The behavior of governments can in turn be identified less as deliberate choices than as interactivities within a large organization encompassing many bureaucratic components, each with its own interests, biases, and idiosyncratic purposes. In such an organizational context, individuals—from rank and file to head of state—contribute in varying degrees to particular governmental decisions and actions. From this perspective, national leaders rise or fall, and organizations prosper or decline, depending on domestic support and the extent to which domestic demands are satisfactorily met (Allison and Halperin, 1972:58).

Insofar as it serves conveniently as an all-purpose generic decisionmaking concept, the gap, or discrepancy, approach encompasses a considerable array of particular, more specialized processes and patterns for reaching decisions. In general, regimes through their leaderships try to enhance their own power and influence and that of the state, but they must also make tributary decisions pertaining to the sources of power, to the extraction and transformation of its elements, and to strategies and actions pertaining to its uses.

Arrow (1963:1–2, 5–6, 18, 23, 27–30, 56, 80–86, 90–95, 110–113, 120) identified several ways in which social choices are made—Quaker meeting (search for consensus), voting, market mechanism, dictation, oligarchy, and convention or code. Despite their differences, these decision procedures can be viewed as efforts to close gaps between real (or anticipated) conditions and preferred outcomes as follows:

- *Quaker meeting consensus*—reasoned consideration and evaluation of the pros and cons, advantages and disadvantages, and costs and benefits leading to a consensus. Leverage is inherent in the compelling logic of the presentations, comparative evaluations, and, possibly, the charisma of the discussants.
- *Voting*—an aggregation of individually registered preferences leading to a plurality, majority, or other decisive threshold of acceptance. Bargaining and leverage typically occur prior to the balloting, the outcome being measured according to the rules and patterns of aggregation.
- *Market mechanism*—an exchange of offers (or bids) in a proposed exchange of goods and/or services. The leverage may be applied beforehand (advertising) or in a bidding process of one kind or another. When prices are fixed, the buyer in effect rejects or accommodates to the seller's leverage (price, display, advertising).[2]
- *Dictation*—decisionmaking by a dictator, whose power derives from an aggregation of political, organizational, military, and other capabilities and from control over communications combined with

rewards for compliance and punishment for noncompliance (extreme threat, torture, and execution). The effectiveness of the dictatorship depends upon an elite (and ultimately upon a rank-and-file) willingness to comply and upon the immediate support of critically placed subordinates whose loyalty must be "bargained for" with carrots (special privilege and/or tightly controlled delegations of power) and sticks (possibilities of purging, imprisonment, torture, or death).

- *Oligarchy*—organizational decisionmaking by a small group of leaders of roughly equal capabilities who use bargaining, leveraging, and coalition forming around specific alternatives.
- *Convention or code*—decisionmaking "by a widely encompassing set of traditional rules" or codified values and operating procedures; a constitution by consensus that constrains conflict and "illegal" leverages within tolerable limits.

In an *ideal* dictatorship, Arrow conceded, only one will is involved in choice, and in an *ideal* society ruled by convention, only the divine will operates, or perhaps the will of all individuals participating in a social decision. In principle, no conflict of will is involved in either case. But in *real* dictatorships (exemplified by the Nazi state and the USSR of Joseph Stalin), a great deal of bargaining, leverage, and coalition formation occurs, much of it involving coercion and fear of reprisal.

Hitler and Stalin provide vivid evidence of how a totalitarian dictator can manipulate cognitions, affects, decisions, and behavior through leveraging. Skilled at manipulating his advisers, Hitler was also "a master of mass emotions. To attend one of his meetings was to go through an emotional experience. . . . Nothing was left to chance. . . . every trick of the theater was used." He grasped what he could do with "a combination of propaganda and terrorism," along with the "compulsive power of the Gestapo, the SS, and the concentration camp" (Bullock, 1959:340–373). In addition to his capacity for instilling fear (relying on the SS and other instruments of leverage), however, Hitler was able to inspire support from many people through his personal magnetism and oratorical powers.

Stalin used Communist Party personnel files and secret police capabilities as specialized instruments for leverage. As indicated by Khrushchev, Stalin put the party "and the NKVD [People's Commissariat of Internal Affairs] up to the use of mass terror," at first against the "exploited masses" and then against the "honest Communist" and even the Leningrad NKVD. When a man went to Stalin "on his invitation as a friend," he did not know where he would be sent next, "home or to jail." Even an "old comrade" might confess to being an "enemy of the people . . . because of . . . physical methods of pressuring him, tortures . . . deprivation of his judgment, taking away his human dignity" (Khrushchev, 1956:1–89).

Decisions, Options, Plans,
and Implementations

In this chapter, we are concerned primarily with decisions affecting critical issues pertaining to economic, political, or strategic security. To one degree or another, all societies are subject to continuous interplays between demands and responses from domestic and external environments. Private individuals and firms make many demands and responses across national frontiers, but regimes and their agents are responsible for trying to synchronize and optimize events and outcomes in the two environments. Regimes try to ensure at least some measure of law, order, livelihood, "fair play," and possibilities for advancement in the one environment and trade and other accesses and security from attack in (or from) the other. Yet much that a regime may propose at home ("butter," protection for domestic production, or whatever) is likely to constrain to some degree what can be done abroad ("guns" on land, on the sea, or in the air; access to external resources and markets; and so forth), even as military costs constrain investment in capital-generating production, health, education, basic science, and general welfare.

At the same time, however, the more the commercial and other capabilities and activities are strengthened at home, the more widely they are likely to expand abroad, and, understandably, the greater is likely to be the domestic demand for the defense of these interests overseas. Governmental activities in the two environments thus demand complex planning, organization, implementation, capacity for making painful choices, and sufficient monitoring to keep track of what is, or is likely to be, available (extraction), how the more pressing demands and bargaining and leverage activities are distributed, and how much can be allocated to each undertaking.

Comparatively, the regime has vastly more influence and power than any private citizen does. Members of the rank and file continually generate demands, however, and because in principle such individuals can enhance their bargaining and leveraging potentials by forming coalitions, the ruling elite and their bureaucrats confront the necessity of making certain that at least some proportion of rank-and-file demands are met. In the external environment, moreover, there are other states to deal with, and whatever a leadership does—especially leaders of a powerful state—is likely to contribute to the shaping of the international system.

In modern industrial states, individuals through their votes and in combination through lobbies and interest groups make special demands for much more than domestic law and order and security from outside threats, attacks, and invasions. Farmers in many countries want subsidies. Workers have their demands, and corporations have theirs. Some industries want protection from outside competition, others need assured access to raw materials, and still others want to sell freely in foreign markets or to take advantage of cheap labor in developing countries. In Third World nations, peasant populations demand agricultural land of their own, whereas large landowners insist on government protection from peasant revolution and land seizures.

In responding to such demands, individuals in a decision group can be constrained or otherwise influenced by what other group members think or are perceived as thinking. Pressures for conformity (referred to as groupthink) are often associated with smaller groups, but "smallness per se is not necessarily disruptive of effective information processing" (Janis, 1972:36–49). Groupthink occurs as group members, feeling uncertain (or perceiving themselves as possessing less leverage potential), defer to those whom they perceive as more authoritative or possessing greater leverage. In formal policymaking, decisionmaking groups tend to be small—often from two or three to a half dozen or a few more. In times of crisis, the membership of such a group tends to be reduced (Snyder and Paige, 1958:36–49).

There is no certainty that those with superior knowledge and skills in the issue area under consideration can compete successfully with those who have an advantage in other aspects of bargaining, such as power and access to information or resources. More specifically, advantage in bargaining and leverage is likely to derive from budgetary controls, the power to hire and fire, and control of implementation measures. Bargainers and leveragers can also seek advantage by controlling the particular information that defines a problem at issue, by identifying options available to other bargainers (within or outside the bureaucracy), and by developing the ability to control (or confuse) the objectives of their opponents within other (but related) issue areas.

In general, the bargaining and leverage advantages of a national leader or other highly placed decisionmaker will depend not only upon available sanctions but also upon the presence or absence (as within many dictatorships) of legal, cultural, ideological, or other constraints upon their use (Allison and Halperin, 1972:50). Lesser bargainers and leveragers in the decision process may have narrower, more specialized perspectives on the issues and may be defensive about their own contributions. Having weighed their personal costs and benefits of participation, however, they can demonstrate, by their active presence, a sensitivity to the national need (as articulated by the executive as well as by their own hidden agendas). Similarly, by demonstrations of loyalty and specialized knowledge and skills, these bargainers can appear to validate the chief executive's wisdom when he or she turns to them for advice. At the same time, each lower level bargainer is likely to be aware of a certain competitiveness dominating the group (as well as hidden personal agendas) and to apply whatever appropriate and reasonably safe leverages are available in order to protect, and further wherever possible, his or her own status and objectives in the coalition.

Marshaling Support in Preparation for Decision

Despite her or his status, prerequisite of office, and bargaining and leverage potentials, the prime minister, president, or dictator must strive for effective decisions and policies while maintaining sufficient support within the government (in the United States, the legislative branch, for example) and among influential interest groups and the public at large to keep the regime operating. At the same time, she or he must be sensitive to constraints of time and available resources (George, 1980b:1–2, 122). With allowance for the differences in procedure and hierarchical arrangements that characterize various forms of government and styles of leadership, every chief executive must observe these requirements or risk damaging consequences. The closer to decision a leadership advances, the more critical the issue of domestic support becomes.

The pursuit of effective leadership is further complicated by trade-offs associated with these requirements. Just as trade-offs between the pursuit of quality policy decisions and the need for consensus and support are often unavoidable, so, too, a prime minister, president, or even a dictator is likely to confront difficult trade-offs between quality policy decisions and the time and resources available. Other likely trade-offs include those between a desire to enhance the acceptability of the policy he or she has decided upon and the expenditure of the valuable time and further limited resources that would be required in order to acquire greater support for that policy. In addition, current demand has to be balanced against requirements of the future—a precept that is honored largely in the breach.

Authoritarian states, dictatorships, and tyrannies of other sorts—even those using the ballot—rely more directly and ostentatiously on police power, highly disciplined party elites and structures, controlled channels of information, and leverages of allocation in order to secure compliance, attract support, and ensure the regime's mandate. For their part, Western democracies tend to be characterized by institutionalized safeguards for the rights of political opponents and freethinkers—provided they do not actively threaten the regime with violence or threats thereof. Yet in their own terms, even dictators must assess their domestic support both outside and within the regime. And democracies may sacrifice human rights in favor of "practical realities."

With respect to crucial domestic/external issues, national leaders are well advised to take the dispositions of their populace into serious account. This is obviously true when external issues of strategic security are at stake, but external considerations often constrain (or exacerbate) domestic economic and/or political issues involving imports and exports, foreign aid, guns versus butter, citizens taken hostage, and so on. In modern democratic states, the secret ballot provides an organizational technique for recording individual mandates (leverages), which when aggregated confer the decisionmaking mantle on one set of leaders, rather than on another. Thus, the secret ballot conveys (with varying degrees of clarity or ambiguity) some indication of issue preferences, which leaders and bureaucrats may then transform into policies and actions. Hitler (better than many dictators) achieved some of the same outcomes by instilling uncertainty and fear among the populace and displaying representations of his own power and omniscience.

The options considered and the decisions reached will depend not only upon memories and experiences of the past and institutionalized habit structure but also upon perceptions of the situation at issue (relevant views of what is as well as preference orderings) and who in the leadership group (in terms of influence) sustains which perceptions and supports which options. Often, decisionmakers reach agreement that "something must be done" far more easily than they agree on a course of action.

To Go or Not to Go

Subject as they are to such realities, top decisionmakers, when confronted by a serious gap between their perceptions of fact and their preferences (or those of their most powerful and influential constituents), must first select one of two possible options: to act or not to act. In effect, such a situation requires a *go/no-go* decision. If there is general agreement within the leadership about the nature of the gap and a consensus about the preferred course of action—or if the ruling figure has sufficient leverage to "force" a consensus—a decision may be made with a minimum of debate. Such a decision may be a response to the "pull" of a strong preference or the "push" of an existing condition that seems intolerable.

Alternatively, there may be a consensus that something must be done but no consensus in support of a specific option. Bargaining and leveraging may continue for a long time before a concrete course of action can be agreed upon (Cyert and March 1963:29–30). Aware that the United States possessed capabilities superior to their own, but feeling pressed for oil and other resources required for their conquest of China, Japanese leaders debated among themselves for the better part of a year. Should they strike northward against the USSR, or should they occupy Southeast Asia? If they pursued the latter course, the United States would surely intervene, but there was not much readily available oil on the way to Irkutsk. Did Japan have the capability to withstand a U.S. attack? No one dismissed the serious risks (a long war against the United States would mean defeat for Japan). But during the autumn of 1941 the Japanese leadership decided with great reluctance that a preemptive strike against the U.S. Pacific Fleet was "the only way out of their dilemma" (Ike, 1967:133–286).

Sometimes the decisionmaker, confronting two or more options, has difficulty deciding which is most likely to yield the preferred outcome. Even more vexing and potentially immobilizing are circumstances in which all options appear to be unpromising or risky. Although political maneuvering on national decisionmaking levels tends to be competitive, participants may try to restrict their incompatibilities in order to protect each other's most important interests. Also, contrary to their stereotype as "empire builders," advisers and bureaucrats are not always eager to expand their domains. When their interests require it, they may avoid responsibility for an issue or narrow their range of participation in policymaking. Additionally, they may be unwilling to get involved in policy disputes on behalf of causes they consider unpromising or potentially costly to themselves (George, 1980b:2, 122). The Iran/contra affair during Reagan's second administration was replete with such avoidances, which with private empire-building can become a debilitating combination. Constraining, and in effect disciplining, policy on all levels of government is the budgetary process—the limited availability of time, human energy, and financial and other material resources that depend upon the regime's ability to extract (impose and collect taxes).

As in the making of decisions in general, we may expect each policymaker, in principle at least, to assess the optional courses of action as he or she perceives them; to calculate (however subjectively) the probable risks, costs, and benefits; and to favor the option that appears to offer the best cost/ benefit ratio. If they are wise, planners will try to identify ways in which the selection of particular means and ends may produce unintended consequences damaging to the national purpose. Competing values or preferences in the selection of an option may be described by a set of indifference curves. On the assumption that a state's capabilities are adequate, a regime is wise to make explicit preference orderings as well as possible trade-offs (optimal combinations of possible outcomes on a set of indifference curves) if means and ends are to be formulated and implemented within an established policy. The power-uncertainty concept reminds us, however, that the "adequacy" of a nation's capabilities is always problematic.

Establishing a Coalition in Support of an Option

In practical terms, the selection of an option is often an effort by the responsible decisionmaker to form a coalition in support of a course of action, a specific policy, an objective, and/or a means of implementation that he or she prefers or is willing to settle for. Depending upon the nature of the undertaking, planners begin considering what broad means to pursue in order to achieve what outcome. Crucial to such selection and planning are the bargaining and leverage strategies. In the making of foreign policy, these strategies are conditioned by definitions of purpose and by the extent to which the country's efforts to enhance its economic, political, or strategic security are expected to be perceived by other nations as threatening or damaging to their security or general well-being.

In many decisionmaking situations, the assessment of options is also critically affected by the leaders' perceptions and evaluations of recent policies and actions of friendly nations, as well as adversaries, and by their own uncertainties about the attitudes of domestic constituencies. While advancing an initiative or responding to actions of another state, the chief executive and his or her advisers may find powerful internal pressures or constraints coming to bear upon the decision process. In such complex circumstances, decisionmakers may find themselves searching for difficult trade-offs between domestic and foreign policy considerations (George, 1980b:26).

Of critical concern to a national leadership are the economic and/or military capabilities of the country relative to those of its adversaries. In economic policymaking, the interests of an import industry may conflict with the interests of export industries, and in issues of war and peace, the people of a country are commonly divided into "hawks" and "doves." In the latter instance, national leaders may exaggerate threats from the outside (and also the inside enemy suspected of collaborating with the outside enemy) in order to obtain greater cohesion and support for the regime.

National leaders favor a policy to the extent that they expect the benefits to outweigh the risks and costs. In reaching a foreign policy decision, they must balance their assessments of probable benefit of the external activities to the nation as a whole against probable costs to the domestic environment (basic productivity, health, education, welfare, and so on). If the external activities involve war or the risk of war, the leadership is wise to assess the willingness of the population to pay the price, including casualties, especially if the hostilities are likely to be intense and prolonged.

Often national leaders "trap" themselves into decisions that turn out to be contrary to their own (and the country's) best interests. One common trap involves uncritical pursuit of an option without continuing concern for serious doubts entertained before an implementing decision was made (Wilson's resistance to criticisms of his policy once he had decided to enter World War I). Many leaders in an international crisis are disposed to perceive their own acts as reasonable and nearly identical actions by an adversary as intolerably threatening (the tsar's order to mobilize Russia's Baltic Fleet in the July 1914 crisis leading to World War I).

The theory of cognitive dissonance may remind us how national leaders, like the rest of us, can be caught in psychologically disturbing situations characterized by perceptions, beliefs, or other cognitions that are inconsistent, contradictory, or seemingly without acceptable solution and hence are dissonance generating. A common tendency, for example, is to discount intelligence reports that do not fit beliefs or expectations (Secretary of State Dulles's inclination to accept information about the USSR that fitted his negative views of the adversary and to reject whatever contradicted his preconceptions).

Depending upon the strength of the dissonance suffered relative to the "costs" of relief, a decisionmaker may feel compelled to reduce the dissonance. Although the means selected may appear arational, the outcome may be functional. As indicated in Chapter 2, available responses to dissonance include (1) changing the perception or belief about what is real (Nixon's visit to China); (2) obtaining new information that alters the situation (new estimates refuting Kennedy's assumption that the United States was on the wrong side of a missile gap between itself and the USSR); or (3) acting to change reality (Kennedy's decision to take forceful action against the presence of Soviet missiles in Cuba).

In recent years, hostage-taking and other terrorist acts have produced dissonances that often defy either rational or acceptable solution. If a government does nothing, the hostages may be kept indefinitely; if it strikes back, the hostages may be executed (or passengers in an airliner bombed out of the sky); if it meets terrorist demands, the perpetrators are likely to take more hostages. In the long run, if the problem is to be solved, some of the economic and political conditions motivating terrorism may have to be eliminated.

As pluralists, many of us may assume that democratic procedures are more likely to yield "rational" decisions than are authoritarian or dictatorial procedures. In most situations, such confidence might not be misplaced, but economist Kenneth Arrow (1963:2–8, 18, 28, 30, 560; 1974:13–14) has warned us of a disturbing paradox. With respect to critical (and often highly controversial) issues, especially to the extent that strategic security options are under consideration, the generalized voting mandate cannot always be relied upon.

In discussing a possible voting paradox (or decision dilemma), Bueno de Mesquita (1981b:13) used U.S. deliberations during the Cuban missile crisis of 1962 as a hypothetical example. President Kennedy's EXCOM (the ad hoc Executive Committee debating how to resolve the crisis), in weighing possible U.S. responses to the installation of Soviet missiles in Cuba, had identified three leading options: an air strike, a naval blockade, or an invasion of the island. Suppose now that each of these possible responses had been supported by a constituency—A, B, and C. On a first ballot, the A's and B's choose an air strike over invasion, whereas the C's recommend invasion (which is now rejected). On a second round comparing an air strike with a naval blockade, the B's and C's favor a blockade, whereas the A's still prefer an air strike. We might then suppose that the blockade must be the majority preference. But in fact, if all the preferences are aggregated, a majority favors invasion over a naval blockade (supported so far only by the C's).

Disconcerting? Now comes the big catch: If the air strike and blockade had been considered first, the invasion option would have won, or if the invasion and the blockade options had been considered first, the consensus would have supported the air strike! But suppose all three options had been considered simultaneously? In that case, the EXCOM would have been deadlocked. (In Chapter 10, we shall touch upon one of Arrow's own examples, which looks toward an even more disturbing contingency that future leaders might confront.)

Policy or Plan for Implementing Selected Options

Some writers use the concept of policy to mean a plan, whereas others define it to include actions undertaken in pursuit of a plan. In order to avoid this ambiguity and to indicate how individual plans (psychological preparations for action) contribute to public plans (organizational "blueprints" for implementing collective action), we distinguish Plan (a policy formulation preparatory for action) from plan (the sequential transformation of blueprinted imperatives into action, together with feedback and responsive adjustments). Plans are debated and drafted in offices before the activity is initiated, whereas Plan-mandated plans are implemented in the field, usually under the direction of higher authority (cf. Miller, Galanter, and Pribram, 1960:98–101).

To the extent that a Plan begins to take shape, a large and complex (projected) undertaking is broken down into sequences of smaller tasks—

a procedure normally delegated to advisers and bureaucrats on various levels. In the course of these distributions of planning activity, information tends to move from top to bottom:

molar→molecular→molar→molecular.

In contrast, information for decisionmaking tends to move upward and inward:

molecular→molar→molecular→molar.

This movement corresponds to the operational hierarchy of molar goal and contributing means. At every molecular level, however, specialists are likely to draw upon their own individual Plans as they infuse the organizational Plan with technical details and applied field experience.

In order to translate a Plan into action, ministries, departments, and other agencies are assigned responsibility for mobilizing, training, and assigning personnel and for acquiring necessary resources. Then, as the Plan unfolds, national leaders issue strategic orders, and lower bureaucracies or commands attend to tactical problems and procedures. Each goal involves a hierarchy of contributing means—a hierarchy of "instructions" and matching actors for the control of some activity—and each act involves a hierarchy of implementing actions. Operational values (as opposed to values that are merely professed but not acted upon) are virtually synonymous with the means/end action hierarchy—the hierarchy of "instructions" and capabilities for control of the organizational behavior that occurs. Identified, distributed, linked, and integrated into a "battle plan," various tasks combine to accomplish larger purposes. As critical divisions of labor and levels of authority, responsibility, decision, and control are put into motion, each participant—down to the most molecular level—transforms his or her responsibility into performance.

Successful translation of a Plan into a plan (sequential action) requires mobilization of sufficient resources and the overall national capabilities to accomplish the specified task sequence. Insofar as resources and/or applicable knowledge and skills are limited, such implementation will be constrained. In principle, the plan works to the extent that collective capabilities translate into collective action in response to the collective purpose. If the Plan is oriented toward the external environment, however, new sets of constraints are likely to operate as soon as plans are implemented, often with quite unintended consequences.

Notable among great Plans contributing to unintended or, in the long run, self-defeating outcomes was the Schlieffen Plan, an order of battle developed in detail some years prior to govern the immediate mobilization of German forces; the necessary railway, naval, and associated arrangements for moving and safeguarding military supplies and personnel into position along the Western front; the over-running of Belgium; and the invasion of

France (and its ally Russia). The Plan was preprogrammed in ways that obliged the Germans to respond to the mobilization of an adversary not only by mobilizing itself but also by initiating hostilities, which in 1914 the leadership would have preferred to avoid. Also notable was the Maginot Line. In the aftermath of World War I, the French planned, built, armed, and manned the Maginot Line (extending deep underground) as a much-touted bastion against penetration of their eastern flank. In this case, the relevant "information" was flawed from the start. In 1940, Hitler merely routed his blitz around the northern terminal of the line and pushed through the low countries (at top speed for an invading army).

Four years later, a "dry run" amphibious assault of Western troops on friendly beaches (possibly forestalling a major disaster during the May 1944 landings at Normandy but incurring more casualties than the real invasion somewhat later) demonstrated the extent to which implementation of a massive plan of action could go wrong through faulty organization and communication. (On a much smaller scale, the U.S. Bay of Pigs operation collapsed as a result of bad information, poor planning, and insufficient capabilities committed to the task. On a much larger scale, U.S. operations in Vietnam were constrained by similar problems.)

One of the more notorious Plans leading to unintended consequences was Japan's attack on Pearl Harbor. In late 1941, Japan's molar objective—sketchily planned at best—was to establish a Greater East Asia co-prosperity sphere providing "protected" access to the resources and markets of China and Southeast Asia as far west as India. In order to implement this Plan, the Japanese had to win the war in China (a conquest that required more oil and other resources than were currently available) and occupy resource-rich Southeast Asia. But because a "southern expedition" into Southeast Asia would leave Japanese expeditionary forces vulnerable to flank attacks by the United States (with Great Britain and the Netherlands), Japanese leaders decided in late November (after more than a year of top-level discussions) that a preemptive strike disabling the U.S. Pacific Fleet was the only viable option. Given that the Japanese had been on a war footing for several years, naval and air units were already mobilized for the Pearl Harbor attack when the decision was finally made. In the longer run, however, Japan lacked the military and naval capabilities required to implement its co-prosperity plan.

In line with realist theory, national leaders (like many, if not most of their constituents) tend to perceive states—including their own and those of their allies and adversaries (and the international system)—as in a condition of being (an equilibrium) rather than as a set of interactive functions in a continuous process of becoming. What tends to become evident once a Plan is translated into action, however, is that its implementation and the inter-activities stemming from it begin to depart from and in a sense challenge the original version. For example, Thomas Schelling (1978:21) has shown how leaders, as well as their advisers and whole populations, acting in pursuit of their own interests, may fail to perceive (or remain indifferent to) the ways in which such activities combine with the efforts of others to produce results that may not have been anticipated by any of the actors. Often the accumulation of countless individual decisions, bargaining activities, and leverage applications (within a decision group or between national regimes) creates tendencies that were not planned or foreseen and that can limit a state's foreign policy effectiveness. This tends to be especially true of decisions leading into and made during international crises, in which, in effect, each move attributed to country A and each response attributed to country B are together so reciprocally generated that each can be characterized as an A/B act (Chein, 1962:15).

National Actions as a Source of Third Image Structures

As indicated in earlier chapters, the international system is a function of state capabilities, actions, and interactions, and strictly speaking, individual national leaders are the ultimately authoritative deciders and actors on the third image level, just as individual states and their relative capabilities are the sole source of international structure. As discussed in this chapter, however, chief executives and other authorized state officials, acting as they do in both environments, perform an even more critical function—namely, the two-way linking of domestic and international events (the latter consisting of actions attributable to other states).

National leaders, bureaucrats, and other agents of state do not provide the sole linkages between the internal and external environments of a society. On the contrary, through trade and other exchanges, private firms and individual entrepreneurs (to take one set of actors) engage in financial, commercial, and other exchanges with markets and individual consumers in other states, thus maintaining and expanding vast and increasingly intense networks of transnational exchanges. But to one degree or another, national leaders and bureaucrats characteristically attempt to regulate or otherwise constrain and/or facilitate such transactions. In practice this means that in view of the uneven growth, development, and other changes occurring in both domestic and external environments, the chief executive and his or her regime (constrained by the nation's power$_1$ and power$_2$ levels) are continually in pursuit of a tolerable dynamic equilibrium between the second and third images, even though much of what takes place may be and often is disequilibrating and beyond their direct control. In view of the uncertainties and diverse movements involved, it is small wonder that Plans of the past and present often court chaos when implemented in the "future."

The focus of this chapter has been on decision- and policymaking processes and some of the ways they can be constrained or distorted. Chapter 5 will discuss how states interacting with each other constitute and continuously shape the third image, which in turn constrains the states and influences the outcomes of their interactions.

Notes

1. George Tsebellis (1989:77–91) criticized the mistaking of a "rational opponent" for "nature" through use of decision theory in social situations but accepted game theoretical assumptions of rationality.

2. Arrow (1963:2) characterized voting and the market mechanism as "methods of amalgamating the tastes of many individuals in the making of social choice." A major problem confronting a democratic regime is how to harmonize or mediate the competing demands of the populace at large, special (and often powerful) interest groups, and the overall national interest.

PART 3

Third Image:
The International
System

5

Economics and War as Integrating Functions

As indicated in Chapter 4, the concept of the international system derives directly from the nation-state and its historical development. To avoid confusion, however, let us distinguish this usage from others that are commonly employed. Sometimes the term refers to empires of the past that encompassed more than one nationality, and in this sense the USSR and other multinational states might be designated international systems today. Any two or more intensely interacting states—the United States and the Soviet Union since World War II, for example—are also labeled an international system. But here we use the term to refer to the system that resulted from agreements reached at the Congress of Westphalia (this usage is central to the theories of modern realists and neorealists).

The focus of this chapter is less on theoretically derived concepts of the international system than on the ways in which the growth and development of states through millennia of history appear to have influenced its emergence and functioning. As will become evident in Chapter 6, some contemporary theories of international politics assume that the international system in effect explains, or even governs, the behavior of states. We take an opposite view: The logic of historical process—unevenness in human population growth, advances in knowledge and skills, access to resources and derivative capabilities within and among states—not only explains the emergence and shaping of the international system but also underscores the interactivities and interdependencies that characterize outcomes on both image levels.

Like realists and neorealists, we define the international system in terms of its interacting units (states) and its structure (distributions of power-as-capability and power-as-influence). Unlike Waltz and some others, however, we see the system's dimensions, structure, capabilities, and changes thereof originating within states and their component elements and processes, including individuals interacting with each other. From this it follows, as indicated in Chapter 1, that the international system (lacking a full-blown sovereign regime or government) is not a sovereign collective actor in the sense that a state is. Rather, it exists as an outcome of interactivity among its state components; the interactions constitute a major element of its structure. From this it follows that, with allowance for the United Nations and "partial" international regimes, which are not "sovereign" either, actions commonly attributed to the international system are in fact traceable to national leaders and representatives acting as spokespersons for their respective states on the third image level.

In Chapter 3, we discussed the emergence of the state and its sociocultural evolution from pristine forms to agrocommercial nation-states. Throughout that discussion, we drew attention to the dependence of states on interplays between domestic and external activities, but the international system was mentioned only in passing because until the appearance of agrocommercial nation-states during the European Renaissance, the international system as we know it today did not exist. Ancient and medieval states maintained diplomatic and trade relations with each other, and wars between them were commonplace, but there was no formal concept of an international system or an adequate basis for such a concept.

The Emergence of the Third Image

To a remarkable extent, this newly developed system—like the emergence of the agrocommercial nation-state itself—was an outcome of an explosive combination of the accelerating technological advances and population increases discussed in Chapter 3. By the time representatives of the European nation-states were convening in Westphalia (1648), the number of people in the world at the birth of Christ—about a quarter billion—had doubled to a half billion. The exponential implications of this increase become clearer when we note that the next doubling occurred in two hundred years (a world population of 1 billion by 1850), the doubling after that by the 1930s, and still another about thirty years after that. Even without a factoring in of technological advances, population growth of this order represents an extraordinary increase in demands for land, water, food, and other basic resources.

The advancement of western technologies during these centuries was also exponential. Insofar as we accept economic and political development as responsive to population growth and implemented through technological advancement, it was no mere coincidence that the Treaty of Westphalia marked at once the appearance in western Europe of full-fledged nation-states, the rapid expansion of state (and private) activities and interests beyond home borders, and formal recognition of an international system of states—a system that survived and expanded for the better part of three centuries.

The economics of the time was mercantilist, and in line with mercantilist precepts, the state, not the nation at large, absorbed mercantilist attention. To be successful in the new era, a state required more than the creation at home of an expanding commercial core and the defense of its population and domestic territory. Power and influence were the first requirements of the state, and statesmen of the era saw mercantilist practice as a system for enlisting economic policy into the service of these objectives. Medieval economics had focused on the maximization of goods available for consumption and on distribution issues, whereas mercantilist policies emphasized production and exportation (de Vries, 1979:237). A central aim of mercantilism was to maintain a trade balance that would provide an influx of gold and silver and thus contribute to the country's wealth and power.

The encouragement of exports and the discouragement of imports were the two great engines by which the mercantilist system sought to enrich the home country through an advantageous balance of trade. Colonies were relied upon to supply commodities that could not be obtained at home and would otherwise have to be imported and probably paid for in bullion (Williams, 1966:9, 30), and colonies required armies, navies, and power outreach. It followed that aggressive economic activity—made necessary for the achievement of commercial, military, and navy leverage—must become subservient to the state and its interests (Dorn, 1940:1). The ideal goal was imperial self-sufficiency under state dominion (Gilpin, 1975:25).

As might be expected, warfare (both internal and between states), which contributed to new second image forms, also played a major role in shaping the international system and determining the unceasing interplays between second and third image activities. A state's military capabilities enabled its regime to establish and maintain exclusive domestic rights and powers, to protect and expand national access to external resources and other advantages, and to influence the policies and activities of other states. Military capabilities and domestic security were dependent, however, upon the regime's ability to collect taxes, conscript personnel (largely peasants) for military service, and disarm the populace. With larger populations and more advanced technologies, the expansion of such activities required larger state bureaucracies, greater specialization and centralization of function, and (especially in wartime) the circumscription of public activities. Directly or indirectly, moreover, armies (especially in wartime) tended to live off the land (domestic as well as foreign), commandeering food, shelter, draft animals, and, often enough, women—activities that frequently generated resentment. Paradoxically, then, in pursuit of cohesion and security, external warfare sometimes led to domestic resistance (if not rebellion), the suppression of which required further strengthening of the state and further external expansion.

In the course of centuries, the expanded functions and specializations of the state—combined with competitions and changing capabilities among domestic estates and classes—led to structural differentiations within state regimes. These differentiations included cabinet offices, enlarged judiciaries, and parliaments or other legislative bodies. Externally, meanwhile, new developments in trade and warfare contributed to refinements in diplomacy and other forms of peaceful intercourse. With external expansion, conquest, and colonization, western European states transformed themselves into multinational empires.

Westphalia and the International System

The Congress of Westphalia marked a turning point in these trends. Convened to formalize the end of the Thirty Years' War (1618–1648), the assembled statesmen responded to developments of recent centuries by recognizing and formalizing the international system. The peace settlements redistributed national territories (and thereby resources) among the states and established rules of diplomacy.

Prior to the mid-seventeenth century, international treaties had been negotiated bilaterally and were limited to a narrow span of issues. The Congress of Westphalia brought together for the first time representatives from all the major powers of Europe in what had become an international system. During the sessions, they produced—through negotiation rather than coercion—two multilateral treaties (Osnabrück and Münster) legalizing a new order in Europe and thus formalizing the start of a new era in international relations (Mangone, 1951:21–22).

Between Westphalia and the Congress of Vienna (1815), the European system embraced roughly matched units (Great Britain, Holland, France, Prussia, Russia, Sweden, Poland, Austria, Spain, and Portugal), which were often able to maintain a rough "balance," although, as a result of uneven growth and development, they tended to leapfrog each other in power and influence. Expanding domestic demands led to expanding national activities and interests (exploration, colonization, mining, plantation management, commerce, banking, missionary activities, slave trade, and so forth) throughout the world and to additional demands for their protection by naval and military force.

As a result, regimes were more effectively organized, routinized, and bureaucratized. Foreign affairs were placed increasingly in the hands of professional ministers and diplomats; armies often consisted of mercenaries. States, through their leaders, tended to accept a conscious commitment to preserve a balance of power as they understood it. In fact, however, such balances were usually partial at best and were subject to adjustments (often violent) resulting from uneven growth and development and intense competition and conflict.

Consisting (by definition) of coequal sovereign states, the international system, according to the Congress of Westphalia, was to be regulated by a body of rules of international law coded by Grotius and disciplined by power balances. (According to one of several definitions, dominance by any single state, including the Hapsburg dynasties, was to be avoided.) The negotiations at Osnabrück and Münster were subsequently recognized as the first of many great conferences called to reassert the law of the international community and the relationships of member states. Law enforcement, however, was left to the states; there was no superior authority. Together, the codification of international law and emergence of the Westphalian conference system became forerunners of the nineteenth-century Concert, the International Court, the League of Nations, and the United Nations.

At this point, we need to emphasize that Westphalia and the Euro-centered international system as recognized and constituted there was essentially a western conceptualization. Paul Kennedy (1987:4–9, 23) pointed out that as late as the sixteenth century, the Ming, Mogul, and Ottoman empires were among the world's great civilizations and centers of power (as were two "outsiders," Japan and Muscovite Russia). These parts of the globe did not figure in the international system of Westphalia because, according to Kennedy, Europe's "free markets" and the emergence of competing states blocked possibilities for a centralized continental empire. Critical, also, was the West's economic and political capacity for organizing, refining, and implementing technologies (many having originated in the East) in ways the Chinese, Mogul, and Ottoman empires could not achieve at the time.

Although Westphalia may have marked the emergence of a new international system, the peace it established did not last. Market—and eventually industrial—developments played a powerful organizing role in overseas expansion, as did European armies and navies. Demands that could not be met domestically—for raw materials (including treasure), goods, services, land, adventure, and even religious converts—"spilled over" and were addressed to foreign lands. Competition for resources and markets, exchanges of coercive leverage, and the expansion of other activities and interests by actors originating in the various states often escalated into warfare on both sea and land (McNeill, 1982:150).

In the wake of domestic revolts and civil wars, Portugal—taking advantage of its shipbuilding and navigational technologies—captured Ceuta on the African side of Gibraltar (1415), Morocco (1458–1478), and parts of India and the East Indies (1500–1545) and thus achieved a head start in the spice trade. Then Spain embarked on conquests in Algeria, Tunis, Tripoli, (and by capitalizing on its sponsorship of Columbus) Puerto Rico (1508–1511), Mexico (1519–1521), Peru (1531–1533), and Chile (1540–1561). During the late seventeenth and eighteenth centuries, the five littoral states of western Europe—Portugal, Spain, Great Britain, the Netherlands, and France—fought against each other (by dyad and in various combinations) on the high seas, in Europe, in Asia, and in the Americas.

The advantages of colonizing the New World (where resources were abundant and labor scarce) were enhanced by a decline in the value of labor in Europe, an increase in the value of European resources, and efficiencies in ocean transport (emerging from the new technologies) that reduced transportation costs charged against goods from the Americas (D. North and Thomas, 1973:149). Thus, the productive capacities of labor were enhanced. Production increased in all the countries of Europe, as did the real revenue and wealth of the inhabitants (Kuznets, 1966:5).

Commerce, war, and "security" fueled each other. Requiring more treasure than could be extracted at home, the monarch or other head of state and the regime as a whole could use strong military and/or naval forces to obtain colonial resources and at the same time raise additional revenues through duties on trade. The larger and better equipped the armed forces, however, the more treasure was needed to support them. Hence, the larger and better equipped the forces, the larger was the bureaucracy required to administer the transactions, and the greater became the need for taxable trade. These interactive (and somewhat circular) sequences helped to build and shape both the international system and the states that constituted it (Tilly, 1981:112–117).

Some scholars have analyzed the growth and development of the international system in terms of war cycles and struggles for hegemony among major powers. Modelski, for example, identified five periods of "global" war, each giving rise to a hegemon: 1494–1517 (Portugal); 1579–1609 (the Netherlands); 1688–1713 (Great Britain); 1792–1815 (Great Britain); and 1914–1945 (United States). Others have included Spain as a hegemon (or have substituted it for Portugal), but Modelski identified Spain as a failed aspirant to hegemonic status, along with France, Germany, and possibly the USSR. There has also been disagreement about the length of war cycles— "long waves," "short waves," and so forth—and at which phase of a cycle war is most likely.

Competition for Colonial Empires

Encouraged by the voyages of Columbus financed by Ferdinand and Isabella, Spanish monarchs supported a series of explorations giving them access to the gold and silver of the Americas and opportunities for overseas colonization. From an economic perspective, Spain's empire long remained the envy of other Europeans, but ready access to unprecedented treasure— along with the Inquisitors, who persecuted Jews and Muslims (including large numbers of skilled artisans as well as entrepreneurs)—contributed to the neglect of domestic industry and the failure of capitalism to develop fully. Such longer term disadvantages of Spanish policy were often unrecognized by elites in other countries, however, and "hopes of finding precious metals spurred other European nations—notably England during the reign of Queen Elizabeth (1533–1603)—into sending explorers and settlers to the New World" (Williams, 1966:9).

With the defeat of its Grand Armada in 1588, Spain lost the preeminence that its exploration in the New World had established. Thereafter, Great Britain tended to frame policies against a renewal of its struggle with Spain, although within a decade Dutch merchants were sending out expeditions to Java (1595–1596 and 1598–1600) and posing a new threat to English trade. Dating from the latter half of the seventeenth century, England used navigation acts to try extending its shipping at the expense of Dutch competitors by restricting the importation of most goods to English vessels (or those of the country from which the cargoes originated) and by requiring English ships to be built and manned domestically.

Throughout the late seventeenth and early eighteenth centuries, an expanding range of long- and short-term investment opportunities opened up. During the reign of Queen Elizabeth I (r. 1558–1603), Walter Raleigh, Francis Drake, and other mariners had explored distant reaches of the globe, and soon commission merchants and colonial traders were exploiting opportunities created by growing governmental demands (arising from centralization and bureaucratization), increasingly efficient commercial networks connecting Atlantic seaports, and the cost-reducing potentials of rural industry (de Vries, 1976:237).

With the most efficient market in Europe and the cheapest ocean transport, Holland was a dangerous rival to England. Whichever country achieved full possession of the East India trade could "give law to all the commercial world." The power of Holland was formidable, but if Great Britain was to extend itself and enlarge its foreign trade, the nation had to surpass its rival and acquire wealth and power sufficient to deal with any state whatsoever (Lyall, 1893:43). Relying on their navy and the navigation acts as sources for leverage, the English tried to exclude the Dutch from English colonial areas. By 1700, after fighting three wars over the issue, they succeeded, and much of the colonial market fell into English hands (D. North and Thomas, 1973:149).

While the English and Dutch were disputing sea supremacy, another power had arisen to challenge them both. After the close of the Dutch war in 1674, the English fleet fell into decay. Dishonesty and incompetence spread, and even newly built ships were sometimes found to be unserviceable. The Dutch fleet also deteriorated. In less than fifteen years, the naval strength of the two nations combined was inferior to that of France, which had been enhanced under the administration of Jean-Baptiste Colbert (Egerton, 1903:57).

By the end of the sixteenth century, France had been seriously weakened by internal conflict and by external threats, and between 1635 and 1714 the country was at war for all but about ten years—against Spain, the Austrian Hapsburgs, Turkey, Holland, Germany, and Great Britain. But during that century of discord, three able kings—Henry IV (r. 1589–1610), Louis XIII (r. 1610–1643), and Louis XIV (r. 1643–1715)—transformed France into a formidable power.

The Seven Years' War (1765–1773) between England and France was largely the outcome of the expansion and collision of the commercial, military, and associated activities and interests of the two countries in India, North America, and other parts of the world (McNeill, 1982:146). This extended conflict provided a prototype for future global conflicts in which major powers and client states were both involved. In India, battles were fought by the troops of rival rajahs and sultans allied with one or the other of the two European powers (or with forces of their respective East India companies), and along frontiers between the British colonies and French Canada, the Iroquois were induced to join the English and the Algonquin the French (Williams, 1966:17, 73).

The Industrial Revolution and
the New Expansionism

In the mid-eighteenth century, Europe's economy entered a new phase characterized by growing populations, rising prices, a spread of rural industry, the expansion of settlers into forest areas and infertile lands, the development of cities of "unprecedented size and economic impact," and advances in the organizational (as contrasted with the mechanical) aspects of production (de Vries, 1976:243–245). Soon afterward, James Watt's steam engine and a series of other innovations transformed cotton manufacturing and thereby introduced the factory system—a new mode of production opening a characteristically "scientific" epoch that dominated "much of the first century of modern economic growth" (Landes, 1981:41).

Steam power and the Industrial Revolution required new products and commercial practices. Also needed for the new technology were iron, copper, manganese, petroleum, and wheat rather than the gold, silver, tropical plants, and naval stores that earlier mercantilist states had demanded. The new epoch provided a context for new patterns of expansionism (these came to be known as the new imperialism). With population increases and advancing technology, people raised new demands—some for new products and some for the materials needed to establish and maintain the new tools, machines, and production processes. Responding to such demands at home, people contributed to the development of new domestic institutions, activities, and interests abroad. These were the beginnings of the industrial state and an international system in which the industrial states of western Europe—and later Japan—became increasingly dominant (Kuznets, 1966:9–11).

The Industrial Revolution began in Great Britain, which had the world's highest agricultural productivity at that time—an accomplishment that provided a base for a growing industrial sector. While lowering food costs, these agricultural efficiencies also released labor and provided raw materials for industry. Rather than develop an industrial sector where none had existed before, the Industrial Revolution in England introduced new ways of producing old manufactures and thus transformed an industrial base that was already beginning to function (Lewis, 1978:10; deVries, 1976:252). The emergence of the Industrial Revolution in Great Britain was also the result of low-cost access to wool, coal, and other raw materials; the ability to shift productive resources into industries with relatively expanding markets; and, most importantly, the linking of industrial centers "with each other and with a highly efficient commercial and foreign trade center" (Gilpin, 1975: 28–31).

The material advances deriving from the Industrial Revolution took place in three major spheres: mechanical devices substituting for human skills; inanimate energy—particularly steam—taking the place of animal and human strength; and the obtaining and transforming of raw materials, especially in what were to become the metallurgical and chemical industries of modern times. Improved transportation and communications and the growing economies of the industrializing countries facilitated their penetration into parts of the world previously isolated and the opening of regions in Asia and Africa during the middle of the nineteenth century that previously had been closed to Western commerce (Kuznets, 1966:242).

The Industrial Revolution soon spread to the European continent. In command of the sea and in the lead in the productive technologies of the industrial era, Great Britain throughout much of the nineteenth century sought a world economy centered on its industrial and financial core. The ensuing collision of activities and interests between a declining France and a rising Great Britain triggered a series of wars during the French Revolution and the Napoleonic era. In this setting, Napoleon's turn-of-the-century goal was to develop Europe's economy through the instrumentalities of the continental system, with France at its center. Soon, however, the continuing growth of the British economy and the relative decline of French power created an increasing disequilibrium between France's aspirations and its capacity for maintaining the nation's integrity. After Waterloo, the British Empire—its leverage enhanced by industrial progress—was no longer one of several more or less similar competitors. On the contrary, "its pre-eminence in the colonial and maritime fields seemed obvious, and soon came to be taken for granted" (Parry, 1971:331).

Colonial Expansion and the Concert of Europe

With the determination of the Napoleonic wars, a more complex inter-national system emerged with five, and later six, main actors dominating European affairs. Insofar as the French Revolution and its aftermath had been a dynamic force destroying a perceived balance of power, the view was widespread that any revolution would launch a comparable threat. Convened by the major powers of Europe after the disruptions of the Napoleonic Wars, the Congress of Vienna (September 1814–June 1815) set out to restore the "balance of power" on the Continent, reestablish the principles of international law, and revive the notion of a Grand Design ascribed to Henry IV two centuries earlier. Like the conferences at Osnabrück and Münster, the Congress of Vienna assumed a role patterned after that of a lawmaking body. The announced intent of the great powers had been to end the years of warfare among the people of Europe and build a stable peace founded on a more equitable division of naval and military forces among the major powers as a guarantee of peace on the Continent. Succeeding events—including revolutions, colonial wars, and wars of liberation and restoration—belied these intents.

The winners of the Napoleonic struggle established themselves as the Concert of Europe—presumably to preserve the European status quo in-definitely. In principle, diplomacy by conference was to replace warfare among the great powers; they would respond to threat thereafter with collective action by the "grand coalition," which would invoke protocols put forward by the Concert of Europe (Rosecrance, 1963: 51). Meeting regularly to settle many issues, heads of state or their representatives frequently imposed major changes on lesser countries—often by force. As an outcome of such international conferences, Greek independence was imposed on Turkey, Belgian independence was imposed on Holland, and the autonomy of Serbia, Bulgaria, and Egypt was settled internationally by the major powers. "But when there arose direct and vital clashes between the great powers themselves—as between Prussia and Austria in 1866, Prussia and France in 1870, Austria and France in Italy, or Austria and

Russia in the Balkans—the system could no longer function collectively" (Luard, 1968:10).

The expansionist activities of Great Britain and other industrial countries included rising levels of foreign investment in each other's economies, in overseas colonies, and in nominally independent but low-technology, low-capability countries of Asia, Latin America, and elsewhere. Foreign investment often yielded limited benefits for the populations of target countries. Normally, investment enterprises were organized to serve the needs of foreign traders, rather than those of the domestic population. "In India," wrote political economist Charles Kindleberger (1970:76–77), "the railroads were laid to connect the major centers of the domestic economy. The same was true, of course, for railroads in countries producing bananas and meat." Did trade follow the flag, or vice versa? Sometimes one, sometimes the other. In either case, the nineteenth century, often characterized as peaceful, encompassed dozens of colonial confrontations, crises, and wars.

In North America, the people of the United States, eager for furs, timber, farmland, minerals, foodstuffs, and a variety of particular commodities, extended their activities westward from the Atlantic seaboard across the continent. "The Atlantic frontier," wrote historian Frederick Jackson Turner (1920:12–14), "was compounded of fisherman, fur-trader, miner, cattle-raiser, and farmer. Excepting the fisherman, each type of industry was on the march toward the West, impelled by an irresistible attraction. Each passed in succession across the continent." (Throughout many of the same generations, and for some of the same reasons, the Russians extended their activities eastward.)

With the rise of Germany and the Bismarckian Concert later in the century, "a temporary interlude of stability between periods of conflict" marked a distinct system of international relations; "it was not a return to the Balance of Power, but rather to its opposite" (Riker and Ordeshook, 1973:39). European monarchs saw the Concert as "an inchoate international government, designed to act at the first alteration of domestic institutions. They would act while the structure of material power was unchanged." But the British sought "an amended balance system . . . with political consultation under the conference mechanism" (Rosecrance, 1963:62). In the latter nineteenth century, the rise of Germany enhanced competition and conflict, and the turmoil of World War I put an end to the system.

Impressed by the power and influence of industrial capitalism, Marx (1962:346–358) identified cheap goods produced by industrialized nations as the "heavy artillery" battering down all "Chinese walls" previously impeding world trade and western political, economic, and cultural influences. He saw Great Britain smashing "the entire framework of Indian society" (including the institutions of an ancient Oriental despotism) and "causing a social revolution in Hindustan"—but without putting anything in its place. Only when "a great social revolution had mastered the results of the bourgeois epoch, the market of the world and the modern powers of production and subjected them to the common control of the most advanced people," only then would human progress "cease to resemble that hideous pagan idol who could not drink the nectar but from the skulls of the slain."

Marx was correct in his assessment of the revolutionary role Great Britain (and other capitalist countries) would play in what is now referred to as the Third (and sometimes Fourth) world, but he was wrong in his prognosis of early revolution in the advanced capitalist nations. Along with industrialization in Great Britain, the United States, the Low Countries (modern Belgium, Luxembourg, and the Netherlands), Germany, and elsewhere, powerful trade movements emerged, the franchise was extended, and democracy thrived. When revolution came to the West, it broke out in tsarist Russia, where industrial capitalism was weak and democracy undeveloped.

After 1860, the innovative capacities of Germany and the United States became evident, and those of Great Britain began to recede. During much of the nineteenth century, Great Britain's major trade rival had been France. But in total trade, merchant-marine tonnage, and number of commercial ships, Great Britain surpassed both France and Germany. In the course of the Franco-Prussian War (1870–1871), however, Germany gained territorial and other advantages at the expense of France, and during the remainder of the century, German capabilities increased rapidly, as did German demands for resources and colonies. Relative to Germany (and the United States), in fact, France and Great Britain were both declining in technological advancement, production, and shares of world commerce, although both countries continued to expand their territories outside Europe.

During the late nineteenth and early twentieth centuries, Germany, increasingly playing the role of Great Britain's major rival, had a faster growing population, a more rapidly advancing technology, and a greater acceleration of trade than Great Britain did. German economic growth depended on importing enormous quantities of raw materials as well as foodstuffs and luxuries paid for through exportation of manufactured goods. As German industry and overseas commerce expanded, moreover, the attention of the government, special interest groups, and sectors of the populace was increasingly directed overseas (Langer, 1962:287).

End of Colonialism and the Rise of the United States

World War I altered the apparent course of events, however. The tsarist government was overthrown, Germany went down in defeat, Austria-Hungary and Ottoman Turkey collapsed, France reasserted itself as the second largest overseas empire, and Great Britain, ruling 26 percent of the earth's land surface, was now the most extensive empire ever to exist. Nevertheless, there was also a growing recognition that colonialism's benefits were limited when balanced against the difficulties of obtaining adequate and peaceful economic returns from the colonies (Kuznets, 1966:342).

Prior to the last decade of the nineteenth century, the United States was insular and isolationist (there was, after all, a considerable part of a continent to explore and fill). During these decades, the Monroe Doctrine was more a symbol than a guide to action. The resources of the still expanding country were devoted to internal development and the relatively inexpensive conquest of Indian lands. By the end of the nineteenth century, however, U.S. companies were well embarked on the search for foreign raw materials. Between 1896 and 1941, the United States pursued an expansionist policy, directing its activities toward economic and strategic goals, primarily in the Caribbean and the Pacific. It was not until after World War II, however, that U.S. capabilities and ecopolitical expansionism became preeminent, and by then the era of territorial expansionism and colonial domination was almost over.

Until the outbreak of World War I, the international system had been dominated by a few European empires (the British, French, German, Russian, and Austro-Hungarian); by a number of extensive but less powerful European empires (the Dutch, Belgian, Spanish, and Portuguese); by three non-European empires (the Ottoman, Chinese, and emerging Japanese); and by the United States. With allowances for a few lesser states, the greatest part of the earth's land surface was occupied by these powers and their colonies and client states. By the end of World War I, however, the German, Austro-Hungarian, Russian, Ottoman, and Chinese empires had collapsed. During the interwar period, Nazi Germany, Fascist Italy, and Imperial Japan expanded their territorial holdings through armed conquest, only to be pushed back and eventually defeated.

In the last days of World War II, the Soviets expanded their territory until it was but slightly short of the high-water mark of tsarist holdings, and with the Maoist revolution of the 1940s, China reestablished most of the territory that had been lost after the empire's collapse in 1912—although the USSR held (and still holds) large areas that were detached from China through treaties perceived by the Chinese as imposed upon them by tsarist imperialism. With a few other, relatively minor exceptions, however, major powers since 1945 have not expanded territorially; almost all the former colonies have achieved independence. Within a decade or so after the close of World War II, the colonial system had all but disappeared, the nuclear age had begun, and the international system was in the throes of a major transformation.

By 1980, the developing countries of Asia, Africa, and Latin America accounted for 75 percent of the world's population, and by the year 2000 these countries are expected to encompass 90 percent of the total. Territories occupied by the "developed" countries of the world amounted to approximately 40.8 percent of the earth's total; the area of "developing" countries totaled about 59.1 percent of the global total.

Clearly, the international system of the late twentieth century was a far cry from the system of states discussed and conceptualized at the Westphalian Congress of the mid-seventeenth century. Except for the People's Republic of China and a few other large and/or influential states, however, developing nations have seldom been formally integrated in theories (or theory testing) in studies of the third image. The best way to analyze and understand the international system is to begin with systematic attention to its parts (component states), to their relative capabilities, and to other state attributes relevant to the encompassing image.

Postcolonial Configurations

Until recently, the economic and political development of Third World nations was treated as a linear process, divided into stages that proceeded from economic growth and a higher standard of living to increasing consumption and a narrowing of gaps between themselves and the industrialized countries. Analysts assumed that all Third World states began at the same point and had to solve the same problems, although at different rates (Hagen, 1962:10–16, 514–522). These analysts emphasized economic process and some of the relationships between economic and political phenomena.

National Profiles and Dimensional Structure

Economists and political scientists identify "size" as a major factor in determining differences between states and their capabilities. Size is assessed in different ways. Sometimes it means territorial extent, sometimes population size, sometimes level of technology, sometimes economic capability, and sometimes a combination of some or all of these factors. There are also different categories of size: the absolute size of a country's territory, population, or other dimension; the size of any one of these national dimensions as a percentage of the global dimension; the relative size of two or more of a country's dimensions; the size of one dimension of a particular country (territory, for example) relative to the same dimension of another country; the comparison between two or more countries on two or more dimensions; and so forth.

Countries often gain a degree of power status on the basis of their territorial extent and the size of their populations. The state with the largest territory in history was the British Empire, which in 1920 had an area of about 32,000,000 square kilometers, or 24 percent of the earth's land surface. The next most extensive states were the Mongol Empire, with a land area of about 24,000,000 square kilometers in 1309, and the tsarist Russian Empire, with some 23,000,000 square kilometers in 1905 (as compared with Soviet territory of 22,402,000 today) (Taagepera, 1978a:126). China ("the sleeping dragon") was accorded great power status during the latter days of the empire, at the close of World War II (when the Nationalist government ruled from Chungking) and as apprehensions rose with the establishment of Mao's control over the mainland. Such status is often unsupported by actual capabilities, however, as succeeding pages will demonstrate.

A country's profile—the proportional combinations of certain key dimensional variables within it—together with the size of these variables relative to the size of the same variables in other states contribute in major ways to the capabilities of that state and to the structure of the international system. Note that a country's overall size and its profile are independent (large, medium, and small states can have similar profiles). So, too, a seemingly large state (early twentieth-century China, for example) can have a weak profile (the small size of its technology and economy relative to its population and available resources). A small state with an advanced technology and economy can be surprisingly strong (modern Israel).

State profiles depend upon estimates of resource availabilities (as well as population, technology, and other dimension sizes). Unfortunately, it is impossible to measure a country's natural resources with accuracy. Most efforts in that direction assume that resources are randomly distributed in nature and that the larger a society's geographical area, the less specialized are its resources. Kindleberger (1962:231) proposed, however, that the extent of an economy from north to south is more significant in terms of its resource diversity than its east-west extent, especially if the country includes territory in both temperate and tropical zones. On the average, such countries will tend to import less than those of comparable extent with an east-west axis or with territory confined within a single zone.

Any extensive area can have potential resource value even though people to date have not found a way of adequately supporting themselves on it. As a first approximation, then, the larger a society's territorial base, the greater is the probability of its achievement of a tolerable domestic economy in industries not based on capital investment and labor skills and without reliance on foreign trade. In such circumstances, size above a certain level of skill and income per capita is a function of population rather than of geography.

This approach to resource availabilities, overall size, and distributions helps to explain why major objectives among state leaders throughout history have included acquisition of territory, whether by conquest or other means, as a means of enhancing national security, gaining influence over the activities of other states, and, to the extent feasible, gaining influence over the international division of labor and the global economy.

The first key size element in a country's economic capabilities, bargaining and leverage potentials, influence, and power is measured by the level of its GNP, the volume of its trade, and other "vitally important" considerations. Economic power is defined in terms of an actor country's ability to influence outcomes—to get others to do something that they otherwise would not do (and at an acceptable cost to the actor). A country with a high GNP and a relatively closed economy that nevertheless accounts for a large part of all international economic transactions becomes a prototype for the dominant power, or hegemon. GNP per capita and consumption of energy per capita tend to correlate closely.

Countries with relatively open economies, low GNPs per capita, low levels of energy consumption per capita, and small volumes of trade, capital movements, and other transactions tend to occupy weak power positions. In general, the smaller the national economy, the more skewed it is likely to be and the more it will trade outside its borders (Kindleberger, 1962:32).

A large part of the struggle for capability and influence amounts to efforts by nations to increase their size relative to other states. Within limits, their success depends upon how national resources are allocated—how much to basic production, to research and development, to defense, to education, to health, and so forth. Optimal allocation combinations differ, however, from one profile to another.

In using per capita indicators (GNP per capita, energy consumption per capita, per capita income, and so forth), we are relying upon averages that "hide" distributions within a society and thus can be dangerously misleading. In terms of income differentials, the richest families in any number of societies, both developing and developed, can earn thousands of times as much per annum as a poor family does. In a country with an annual per capita income of a few hundred dollars, the discrepancies can be much wider; the population is divided between poverty-stricken millions and a few of vast wealth.

With allowance for such limitations, country profiles provide graphic indicators of constraints on a nation's activities and offer possibilities for comparing diverse countries in terms of their capabilities and actions. Country sizes and profiles help define the relative positions of various countries in the system—developing nations, the lesser industrialized powers, the super-powers—as well as the roles of multinational corporations and other non-governmental actors. In spite of their many cultural, economic, political, military, and other differences, countries in the international system seem to fall into several primary categories according to these profiles.

None of these profiles should be taken too seriously. Clearly, each of the major dimensions (population, technology, territorial size, and so forth) is a continuum, and profile boundaries imposed upon nations in given cases at given times obscure many dynamic qualities. Alterations in profile result from events occurring in both domestic and external environments. Uneven growth and development among the master variables and their derivatives (capital formation and productivity, for example) can alter a country's profile, as can foreign trade, competition, or conflict with other nations. A profile serves as nothing more than a kind of high-speed snapshot of a society in continual change. The primary usefulness of the profiles is thus heuristic, rather than scientific—to provide rough illustrations of the differences that distinguish states and their relative capabilities within the international system. Profile studies become rigorous only as changes in population, technology, resource, and other relevant indicators are analyzed through time.

Given that these data come from different sources (and in some instances from slightly different years), they should be accepted as approximations only. In 1986, the aggregate GNPs of all the developed countries amounted to 77.6 percent of the global GNP aggregate, whereas the GNPs of all the developing countries accounted for about 22.3 percent of the global total. Per capita GNP for the developing countries in 1980 amounted to 29.4 percent of the world GNP per capita as compared with 70.6 percent for the developed countries, which, at $6,937, was more than ten times the amount for the developing countries.

For convenience in comparing clusters of states (each cluster composed of states with similar profiles regardless of national size), we shall assign

TABLE 5.1
Illustrative Profiles, 1984

Country	Area (km²)	Population (mil)	Density per km²	GNP (mil $)	GNP per Capita	Imports (mil $)	Exports (mil $)	Health Expenditure (mil $)	Education Expenditure (mil $)	Military Expenditure (mil $)
ALPHA										
U.S.	9,363,123	236.7	25.0	3,765,000	15,920	341,177	217,880	159,500	182,520	237,100
USSR	22,402,200	275.0	12.0	2,067,000	7,569	80,680	91,652	62,700	91,800	260,000
BETA										
Israel	20,770	4.0	193.0	26,570	6,233	8,411	5,804	834	2,002	7,206
GAMMA										
Japan	372,313	120.0	322.0	1,292,000	10,470	136,522	170,107	56,874	63,550	12,700
W. Germany	248,577	61.2	246.0	697,200	10,070	151,246	169,784	54,482	30,953	22,780
E. Germany	108,178	16.7	154.0	168,600	10,070	22,940	24,836	3,910	6,030	10,680
U.K.	244,046	56.4	231.0	482,500	7,590	105,961	94,502	26,525	6,030	25,410

DELTA										
Sweden	449,964	8.3	18.0	95,250	11,160	26,416	29,378	9,290	8,308	2,928
Norway	324,219	4.1	13.0	57,380	13,010	13,889	18,892	3,783	4,020	1,679
Iceland	103,000	0.2	1.9	2,541	10,150	839	740	228	119	0
EPSILON										
PRC	9,596,961	1,029.2	107.0	321,100	309	27,750	24,871	4,440	8,720	24,040
India	3,287,590	751.6	227.0	200,500	238	13,953	8,793	1,700	6,280	7,141
Brazil	8,511,965	136.3	16.0	212,300	1,447	14,935	27,005	3,180	7,763	1,778
N. Korea	120,538	19.6	163.0	23,000	1,172			200	720	5,200
S. Korea	98,484	42.0	426.0	85,300	2,034	30,631	29,245	222	4,092	4,590
Philippines	300,000	55.5	185.0	32,860	556	6,051	5,322	218	570	396
Bangladesh	143,998	98.6	685.0	13,050	142	2,042	934	57	270	248
Burundi	27,834	4.5	162.0	1,088	211	186	98	9	38	38
Mexico	1,972,547	76.9	39.0	161,300	2,097	11,280	23,602	892	6,160	1,081
Ethiopia	1,221,900	42.1	34.0	4,828	112	942	417	66	141	428
Haiti	27,750	5.7	205.0	1,716	307	472	179	19	21	27
ZETA										
Bolivia	1,098,581	6.0	5.5	5,576	1,342	631	773	40	126	120
Chad	1,284,000	5.1	4.0	564	118	162	110	4	11	9
ETA										
Saudi Arabia	2,149,690	10.8	5.0	104,400	8,061	33,700	36,834	5,243	8,123	22,220
Kuwait	17,818	1.6	90.0	27,030	16,280	7,699	10,751	655	1,141	1,438

Sources: Columns 1–5 and 10: U.S. Arms Control and Disarmament Agency, *World Military Expenditures and Arms Transfers* (Washington, D.C.: GPO, 1986); columns 6 and 7: United Nations, *Yearbook of International Trade Statistics* (New York: United Nations, 1986); columns 8 and 9: Ruth L. Sivard, ed., *World Military and Social Indicators, 1987–1988* (Washington, D.C.: World Priorities, 1987).

Greek letters to each cluster—alpha, beta, gamma, delta, and so on (see Table 5.1). Through time—and consonant with processes of uneven growth and development—states do not necessarily remain in the same profile categories. Whereas Japan approximated an epsilon profile in the late nineteenth century, by the 1930s, for example, it had developed into a beta state, and at some point after the end of World War II it achieved gamma status.

Alpha Profile Countries

Countries with knowledge and skills that are advancing rapidly combined with a relatively stable population and a substantial resource base are likely to be the most powerful and influential in the global system (alpha countries). The United States—characterized by a population that is "moderate" (relative to resource availabilities), an advanced technology, and an extensive territorial base—is a prime example.

A society exhibiting an alpha profile is a strong candidate for superpower status. The population of an alpha country is large enough to provide a substantial labor pool, the generation of high and increasing demands (combined with advancing technology), and technical and professional specializations of a high order. In addition, the country's extensive territorial (and resource) base is sufficient to ensure a reasonable access for industrial growth and public consumption. These conditions and processes contribute to the growth and domestic (uneven) distribution of specialized capabilities (agricultural, commercial, professional, and so forth) among the populace and its sectors. These conditions also contribute to the overall economic, political, and strategic capabilities relative to other states in the system.

Despite (and/or because of) the size of its master variables and to the extent that its population tends to increase (however moderately) and its technology continues to advance, an alpha country—*because of accelerating wants, needs, and demands*—will probably expand its activities, interests, and power outreach farther afield and more intensively than do states of lesser size. This expansion can be partially attributed to greater dependence upon an increasing volume and wider range of resources and markets beyond its own borders. Many other factors influence this expansion as well, notably foreign investment, access to foreign labor (the contracting of manufacturing processes to low-wage societies, for example), transactions with allies and client states (including economic, technological, and military aid). Whatever the intentions of an alpha state, any substantially weaker state intersecting with it intensely runs a risk of social, economic, cultural, political, and/or military penetration by the activities and interests of the stronger state. As a consequence of the discrepancy in their relative capabilities, the weaker state, somewhat like a colony, may suffer a kind of structural violence at the hands of the stronger.

In this connection, a Marxist-Leninist theorist would point to U.S. relations with Cuba prior to 1959 (or to the Philippines today) as an example of structural violence, dependency, and exploitation. We, on the other hand, could point to post-1959 USSR-Cuban relations and Soviet activities in several African countries as rough analogs (even though differences in U.S. and Soviet systems would yield quite different manifestations of structural violence, dependency, and exploitation). By 1959, the People's Republic of China had become deeply penetrated by the USSR, but the Maoist leadership was able to exert sufficient leverage to expel the Soviets.

In general, the greater the power and influence of an alpha nation, the greater is the range of its own public and private activities and interests (and on occasion those of its allies and client states). Insofar as such activities and interests appear to be seriously threatened, the leaders, bureaucrats, and many of the citizenry of the alpha country (especially those with personal interests) may be expected to assume a defense obligation roughly proportional to the nation's overall power, influence, and outreach. In line with the security dilemma, moreover, the wideranging efforts of an alpha country to fulfill its "international responsibilities" may be interpreted by another state (or states) as a threat to its (their) security.

Historically, leading alpha countries have tended to compete for hegemonic status (and allies) within the international system—the second-strongest nation often organizing itself to challenge, and if possible surpass, the hegemon. During their respective colonial periods, Great Britain, France, and other European countries achieved alpha status by expanding their activities, interests, territorial status, and access to overseas resources. As their capabilities began to taper off (in large part because of the rising costs of maintaining law and order in their colonial territories), these seemingly well-established empires lost their overseas territories (and alpha dimensions) and were overtaken and surpassed in power and influence by the United States and the USSR.

In seeking similar status, Germany and Japan tried to emulate France and Great Britain during the late nineteenth and early twentieth centuries by seizing territories of their own. As latecomers, however, they suffered the generally rising costs of maintaining nonadjacent, unassimilated, often densely populated colonies (already benefiting, however minimally, from the new technologies the colonizers brought with them). Germany and Japan also suffered from a lack of capabilities sufficient to overcome the aggressive resistance of the established alpha powers and their coalitions.

In their early growth and expansionist phases, both the United States and tsarist-Soviet Russia had the advantage of vast, sparsely inhabited, resource-rich territories that required no-more-than-appropriate knowledge and skills combined with motivation (furs, farmland, timber, minerals, fibers, fuels, defense, and so forth) for rapid development and the achievement of alpha status. The United States emerged from World War II in a position that was virtually unchallenged worldwide. The economy of the country was larger and more prosperous than that of any other country. After World War II, the fundamental political-economic objective of the U.S. leadership was to minimize barriers to the movement of goods, services, capital, and technology and to the maintenance of a world environment in which market economies and free trade could function optimally. Even before the termination of World War II, the United States and the Soviet Union began a new competition for power, influence, and hegemonic status.

Some broad similarities to the United States notwithstanding—large population, a larger and potentially richer territory-resource base, a high level of technology, and an "eastward movement"—the Russian/Soviet growth profile differs in important ways. Like U.S. growth, the Russian take-off dates generally from the last quarter of the nineteenth century, and from then on industrial growth, although lagging well behind U.S. trends, was nevertheless considerable and remarkably sustained. Since World War II, Soviet leaders have sought to maintain and extend an environment within which command economies and a network of bilateral arrangements could thrive. But economic growth and political development have been severely constrained by the society's domestic structure.

Despite considerable technological development, Soviet progress has remained uneven—in part because of decisions made in a highly centralized economy but for other reasons as well. It seems increasingly evident, for example, that highly structured political and managerial bureaucracies in the USSR have discouraged individual initiative and committed gross errors in the allocation of critical skills and resources within technological and developmental programs. Soviet progress, for the most part, has been pronounced in the grosser technologies required for heavy industry and military capabilities but at the expense of finer craftsmanship and more delicate and sophisticated modern control systems.

Agricultural technologies have encountered special difficulties in the USSR. In the coming decades, however, the Soviets can draw on some of the largest reserves of minerals and other critical resources remaining in the earth (aside from the ocean floors). The outcomes of policies of *glasnost'* (openness) and *perestroika* (restructuring) proclaimed in the 1980s (and other more specific economic and political reforms) are yet to materialize. In Eastern Europe, Soviet leaderships of the past had tried to dominate the weaker economies and at the same time constrain the capabilities of previously more advanced countries of the region.

Beta Profile Countries

The population of a beta society is large (relative to its territory), and its technology is advancing commensurately, but access to resources is significantly impeded because (1) the domestic resource base is perceived as too "small" or inadequately endowed; (2) trade capacities do not seem to provide adequate resources from abroad; and (3) efforts to expand the resource base (by exploration, conquest, purchase, or other means) have been inadequate or have not been undertaken. Countries with limited domestic resources and with levels of technology that advance at rates commensurate with population growth can be at a severe disadvantage, unless a trade network has been established to import (and pay for) resources from the outside.

A beta country is "driven" by rising needs, wants, and demands that the populace perceives as inadequately met. Under these "pressures," beta leaders, bureaucrats, and many private citizens are likely to sense the intense interdependencies among economic, political, and military capabilities for further development in their nation's circumstances.

Great Britain, France, the Netherlands, and other overseas empires approximated the beta profile during early stages of their territorial expansion. Bismarckian Germany qualified as a beta country aiming for alpha status. During the late 1800s and early 1900s, Japan became almost an ideal model of a beta nation. Its leaders, instructed by historical "progress" among western nations, consciously sought to emulate the expansionist successes of Great Britain and France and drew upon the rapidly advancing Germans to help them succeed.

A society with this profile type is under continuous pressure to expand its trade or, if that recourse is blocked in one way or another, to expand its territory. The latter was the situation of Japan in the 1930s. We should not conclude, however, that economic imbalances are the sole cause of a beta country's aggressive policies, only that the demand for resources and markets can exert a powerful impetus in that direction. Between 1870 and World War II, Japan was characterized by spectacular technological and economic growth. This trend was possible, in part, because the Japanese had a near monopoly on the manufacture and sale of silk. Additionally, the Japanese developed a capacity for importing raw materials in large quantities, transforming them into consumer goods, and exporting the finished products to foreign markets—thus acquiring foreign exchange for more imports.

During the later 1920s, this process of importing raw materials, processing them, and exporting them to foreign markets was partially interrupted by the western invention and production of rayon (and later nylon). The silk market collapsed, and the Japanese began selling other types of goods abroad. With the worldwide Depression of the 1930s, however, tariffs and other impediments to Japanese trade were erected to protect domestic production and employment in the United States and Europe. As a consequence of such barriers to its exports, Japan—finding itself hard put to obtain foreign exchange for its imports—undertook colonial expansion and military adventures as a solution (one that proved ill-fated).

Gamma Profile Countries

A gamma country differs from a beta country in that although its access to directly controlled resources (domestic resources or resources from its own colonial territory) is seriously limited, an extensive, high-volume, effectively secured trade network is in place. As a consequence, we may expect nations in this category to be economically motivated, sensitive to economic and political interdependencies within and without, and concerned about their relations with the hegemon and its challenger. The United Kingdom, France, and West Germany are examples of gamma countries today.

Gamma countries may exert strong lateral pressures, although usually more in economic than aggressively political or military modes (because of their relatively strong trade and financial networks) than beta nations do. Because gamma nations cannot easily escape the security dilemma, even in its strategic terms, they are likely to rely heavily on their alliance relationships.

Since World War II, Japan has been able to pursue a near-gamma course by further developing its industrial technology, relying on imports, and expanding its markets worldwide. In this way, Japan has supplemented its domestic resource base, which has been limited to the home islands as a result of the country's defeat in 1945. By contrast, Great Britain has declined since the turn of the century from alpha status (the British Empire) to gamma status, as has France.

Delta Profile Countries

Benefiting from a relatively low population and an advanced technology, a delta country is able to meet domestic demands through a combination of domestic resources and external trade. A central consideration here is the low population (as compared with gamma countries), which facilitates high levels of per capita consumption at relatively low absolute levels of acquisition and production. With a density of eighteen people per square kilometer, Sweden provides an example. In addition to significant domestic resources including iron and copper, Sweden for generations has maintained quality production, a strong merchant marine, and a far-flung and diversified trading network. Other delta countries include Norway, Finland, and Iceland (with densities of thirteen, fourteen, and two persons per square kilometer, respectively).

In recent generations, citizens and leaders in delta countries appear to have been "quality" motivated. To the extent possible, they have avoided external conflicts and focused on production of quality goods, services, and living conditions. Countries with populations that achieve a level sufficient to provide an adequate work force (while remaining sparse relative to technology) can develop a comparative advantage in economic growth and quality of life, provided their access to resources markets can be maintained. With world energy and other resource shortages, however, even Swedish leaders have been compelled in recent years to review their technological, industrial, and commercial policies. Citizens of delta countries have also discovered that economic and institutional social welfare cannot necessarily ensure social and psychological well-being.

Epsilon Profile Countries

A country fits into the epsilon profile insofar as its population is large relative to its technology and its access to resources is limited—either because its territory is small or poorly endowed or because existing resources cannot be extracted (or possibly even located) with available knowledge and skills. Gross discrepancies in access to resources (including elementary food and water), housing, education, health, and general welfare exaggerate the discrepancies and contradictions among social and economic classes, which can differ enormously in their interests, goals, and motivations. Often the advantaged become enormously rich while the poor remain grievously disadvantaged. If a collective motivation can be identified, it might amount to "modernization," but the idea of it may differ considerably according to class, education, income, and the like.

Epsilon societies in the past have often been overrun and absorbed by more powerful countries. During the nineteenth and early twentieth centuries, the colonial empires of Great Britain, France, Germany, Spain, Portugal, the Netherlands, and Japan consisted in large part of epsilon-profile societies that had been conquered or otherwise absorbed. Colonial India and semi-colonial China had epsilon profiles. Having achieved independence since World War II, most epsilon societies are now classified as developing countries.

The economic, political, and military penetration of India and China and their decline from great empires to colonial, semicolonial, and developing-nation status can be explained in part by the upsurge in population that appears to have occurred there and elsewhere around the middle of the seventeenth century. This decline can also be explained by the failure of Indian and Chinese knowledge and skills (technical, engineering, economic, and organizational) to develop commensurately. In both societies (India by the mid-eighteenth century and China by the early twentieth), the imperial structures of the past had already fractured. They were replaced by localized, warlord regimes that fought each other and often established themselves as clients of rival and rapidly intruding European powers.

With improved health services and nutrition, death rates in epsilon-profile countries of the world have fallen sharply in recent years without corresponding reductions in birthrates. Several epsilon countries (notably China) have undertaken Spartan modernization programs to move them toward gamma (or possibly alpha) profiles, but in spite of efforts to lower birthrates, the wide gap between population/technology levels and rates of change has remained a major obstacle. Continuing population growth in many of these regions threatens to nullify the effects of economic expansion on the available income per capita. In several epsilon profile nations, high fertility rates combined with reduced mortality rates, weak economies, and impaired access to resources have exacerbated the already existing poverty.

In addition to modern India and China (both making progress on several dimensions), epsilon countries (of varying sizes) include Bangladesh, Indonesia, Pakistan, Burundi, the Philippines, Vietnam, Lebanon, El Salvador, and Haiti. Aside from small city-states, Bangladesh in the early 1980s had the highest population density of any nation on earth (611 persons per square kilometer) and a per capita GNP of $129. By the mid-1980s an economic "basket case," the country was characterized by malnutrition, low rates of savings, large balance-of-payments deficits, and widespread poverty. The top 20 percent of the population received nearly half the national income, and only 8 percent went to the lowest 20 percent.

Energy per capita is universally low in countries with dense populations and low levels of technology. Per capita consumption in the United States in the early 1980s (10,204 kilograms of coal equivalent in 1983) ranged from five hundred to more than three thousand times the per capita consumption in countries such as Burundi (18 kilograms equivalent) or Bhutan (3 kilograms).

Aside from contemporary China, India, and a few other notable exceptions, epsilon profile countries tend to possess weak governments, weak economic systems, minimal bargaining potentials, and a vulnerability to economic, political, and military penetration from the outside. Famine is often endemic in such countries, and there may be a tendency, especially if the national territory is extensive, for some enclaves to "fracture off" and seek local autonomy, as warlord regimes did in China after the collapse of the Chinese Empire in 1911–1912. The challenge confronted by an epsilon country includes how to (1) hold population as constant as possible (zero growth), (2) develop technologies that are appropriate for enhancement of agricultural production and establishing the prerequisite foundation for basic industry, (3) train an effective work force and a critical mass of advanced and appropriately educated specialists, and (4) keep private consumption low and savings for productive investment high.

Zeta Profile Countries

Characterized by the low density of their populations and the relatively low level of their technologies, zeta societies tend to lack both the propensities and appropriately specialized levels of technology—including labor reservoirs, critical masses of innovators, and the special skills required for development. Although their problems are somewhat different, zeta populations (like their epsilon counterparts) differ significantly in motivations, expectations, and goals depending upon occupation, education, and income. Like many other Third World countries, those with sparse populations and underdeveloped technologies tend to be characterized by political instability.

Contemporary nations with zeta profiles include Chad, Zaire, Mali, Namibia, Somalia, Sudan, Bolivia, Guatemala, and Paraguay. The potentials tend to vary according to the proportion of the national territory that is arable, the availability of resources that do not require an advanced technology for acquisition and processing, and other limiting conditions. As a reflection of their inability to make uses of resources at hand, technologically deficient regions with low ratios of populations to potential local resources may exhibit characteristics common to dense population countries.

For example, the northern part of Chad, an extension of the Sahara Desert, is inhabited in large part by nomadic people who have very little in common with more settled populations in the south. This has rendered the country vulnerable to economic, political, and military penetration by some of its neighbors. Chad faces other barriers to economic growth. As late as the mid-1980s, the country possessed no outlet to the sea, no rail lines, little river shipping, and few paved roads.

Eta Profile Countries

A country with an eta profile differs from a zeta (or epsilon) in two major respects: An advanced technology and the specialists required to operate it have been admitted from abroad under one arrangement or another, and with these additions oil or some other valuable resource has become available. As a consequence, the GNP has reached a high level. The per capita GNP for some countries in the mid-1980s was higher than that of an industrially advanced gamma country with a much denser population or an alpha country like the United States. In some eta countries where the national wealth is high, the population is relatively small, incomes range from better than adequate to extremely high, and the management of the resource base can become an almost obsessive (but not necessarily well-ordered) concern. In less well-endowed states, this obsession is sometimes combined with uneasiness about radical movements.

The United Arab Emirates, Qatar, and Saudi Arabia are prime examples of eta nations. Characteristically, they have imported large work forces from more populated nations such as Pakistan (as well as highly skilled labor and engineering and management specialists from industrialized countries). Such countries have been able to achieve levels of trade and trade per capita that are among the world's highest, often with a strong export bias.

The apparent affluence of eta profile countries can be illusory. Because of the low level of indigenous technology and the limited skilled and unskilled labor force, the pace of industrialization is usually slow, the level of imports may be incommensurate with national revenues and exports, and there is serious risk that elements of the resource base (usually oil) may be seriously depleted before substitute industries can be developed. Depending on allocation policies, sectors of the populace may live in severe poverty. In eta nations, the challenge is to apply sufficient amounts of available capital to the development of an indigenous and properly trained work force and to the education of a critical mass of people with advanced and appropriately specialized knowledge and skills.

Uneven Growth and Development: Horizontal and Vertical Implications

The structurally derived capability gaps between themselves and more advanced nations leave epsilon, zeta, and even wealthy eta nations vulnerable to economic, political, and sometimes military penetration by alpha, beta, and gamma nations and their armed satellites. Because of these gross asymmetries, the effects can often be felt even when interchanges are "normal" and "peaceful."

This does not mean that epsilon, zeta, and especially the richer eta countries lack leverages altogether. During the eighteenth and nineteenth centuries, more than one colony learned how to twist the British lion's tail, especially with help from a rival alpha country. In modern times, Cuba (with outside help) has frequently harassed the United States in ways calculated to be irritating or threatening. North Korea (with outside help) kept the United States and South Korea at bay. With various types of leverage, Maoist China persuaded the Soviet Union to withdraw. North Vietnam squeezed the United States out by attrition, and the Afghans hacked away at Soviet troops for years. Overall, however, the less advanced a country's technology relative to its population, the lower are likely to be its capabilities and the less effective its bargaining and leverage potentials.

Any externally directed action by a state will be constrained and otherwise shaped by that state's profile, its capability (power$_1$), and leverage potential (power$_2$) and by the profile, capability, and leverage potential of the state on which it impinges. These considerations—including the gross differentials in capabilities and leverage potentials between the developing and industrialized countries as well as nuclear weaponry and other complexities in the contemporary international system (not excluding the volatility of cognitions and affects in the making of decisions)—raise serious questions about the adequacy of conventional balance-of-power approaches in the field of international politics today.

Decision and Action on the Third Image Level

As indicated in this and previous chapters, the international system, lacking an overarching regime, is more an ecological than an actor system; it provides an environment in which nations implement their external activities. This means that all decisions and actions on the third image level are traceable to states or components of states (private firms, for example, or individuals who in one way or another exert an impact upon the international system). A large proportion of third image activities are thus *internal*—that is, they are directed toward and in some way affect other elements of the international system.

As discussed in subsequent chapters, however, many third image decisions and activities have external effects in that they exert impacts on environments external to the international system—the ocean floors, for example, the outer atmosphere, and space. These concerns will be touched upon in the final chapters of this book. Chapter 6 will address power configurations and their implications within the international system.

6

The International Configuration

Chapter 5 revealed some of the intricate ways in which the emergence of agrocommercial and industrial nation-states contributed to the development of the international system and how the growth and development of the international system have constrained and shaped the evolution of states. The purpose of this chapter is threefold: to review a number of assumptions about the international system emerging from the Congress of Westphalia and diplomatic practice of the era that followed—notably the balance of power; to consider a number of conventional and more recent conceptualizations of the international system; and to compare these approaches with the third image perspective of Chapter 5 and with some of its implications for theory and practice in the nuclear era.

The chapter will in effect propose that issues of war, peace, and survival in an age of massively destructive weaponry require a perspective that makes explicit the reciprocal interconnectedness of the first three images. This perspective must be combined with an understanding that responsibility for third image outcomes resides ultimately with individual human beings through the policies and actions they implement in a state-centric world (rather than in any particular configuration of power).

Chapter 5 called attention to the Westphalian negotiations, the codifications of international law, and the succession of great conferences that occurred thereafter. Not only did these events prove to be forerunners of the nineteenth-century Concert of Europe, the League of Nations, and the United Nations; the Westphalian system conditioned the way generations of people conceptualized the third image and the implications for war and peace inherent in those various configurations, notably the balance of power.

Assumptions About Distributions of Power

Traceable to Thucydides and to ancient Chinese and Indian writers, balance-of-power principles were elucidated by Niccolò Machiavelli and others. These principles were used to describe, analyze, and guide the

133

implementation of inter-state diplomacy during the fifteenth century by the Medici, the Sforza, and other princely families of northern Italy. With advances in science during the Renaissance and thereafter, many Europeans perceived natural balances everywhere—a balance of heavenly bodies in the universe as seen by Galileo Galilei and Johannes Kepler; John Selden's balance of trade; and the balance of power assumed by James Harrington and John Locke to operate within the state. In diplomacy and international politics, balance of power and related concepts have been current ever since.

The Classical Balance-of-Power Concept

In classical form, the balance-of-power concept holds that each government will try to forestall the continuous expansion of any other state by balancing its power through suitable counteralliances. The rules of the system will treat its preservation, if challenged, as more rewarding than any individual national interest or combination of individual national interests. The destruction of the system, if threatened, must be treated as more penalizing than the thwarting of any individual national interest or the interests of any combination of national actors.

Beyond this core statement, however, many issues remain unsettled. Does a balance of power operate continuously, for example, or only under particular circumstances? Is there always a "balancer" nation determining the outcome of a neverending struggle for power (Morgenthau, 1968:187–189)? Theoreticians are not in agreement. Some proponents of balance-of-power diplomacy have seen the mechanism as "a tendency that makes itself felt from time to time" (Hawtrey, 1930:11). Theoreticians seldom make explicit the circumstances under which the balance of power operates, the reasons for its breakdown, or the viable alternatives when it fails to operate. Writers have not always been clear, moreover, about the extent to which balance-of-power outcomes are more or less deterministic and the extent to which they can be "managed." Hans Morgenthau (1968:202) saw politics, like society in general, as "governed" by objective laws rooted in "human nature" and operating in ways "impervious to our preferences." Yet he assumed that balance-of-power strategies would serve primarily as tools for the diplomat.

The term *balance of power* has been used several different ways (in some instances by the same author without warning to the reader). Despite their ancient heritage and widespread use by statesmen and theorists alike, balance-of-power concepts remain ambiguous and subject to varying and often contradictory interpretations. Does the term refer to a situation? A policy? A system? Hegemony? Equilibrium? Does it portend stability and peace or conflict and war? Disagreements have persisted for generations.

Insofar as balance of power is defined in terms of the distribution of national capabilities and influence within the international system, issues of systemic structure are central to serious discussions of politics on the third image level. Conventional definitions of structure include (1) a distribution of capabilities among similar units; (2) a set of constraining conditions; and (3) the form of interrelationships of states composing the international system. In Chapter 3, we discussed the emergence of the international system as a bottom-to-top outcome of interplays among states that were growing, evolving, and competing for territory and other resources, markets, and power$_1$. Prominent among these states were Austria and Spain (under Hapsburg rule), France, Sweden, Denmark, and Great Britain. In refining the international system concept, however, modern neorealist writers have tended to proceed from top to bottom, in part as a means of limiting the number of variables used in pursuit of parsimony.

Systemic Explanations of International Phenomena

In recent years, neorealist theoreticians have put forward new formulations of systemic theory, or *structural realism* (not to be confused with general systems theory), in studies of balance of power and other power configurations. Typically, proponents of this approach assume actor characteristics, rather than treating them as variables, and explain changes in outcomes not by variations in these actor characteristics but by attribute changes of the system itself (Keohane, 1982:327). From this perspective, the international structure is not a set of "deep, internal relationships" emerging "prior to and constitutive of" national actors "and their self-understandings." Nor does this interpretation of structure identify "precisely the boundaries, ends, and self-understandings that theorists accord to them [national actors] on the basis of unexamined common sense" (Ashley, 1984:234–235, 255).

Structural realism aims to correct the flaws of classical realism ("a refusal to define concepts clearly and consistently, or to develop a systematic set of propositions that could be subjected to empirical tests"), and, while drawing on insights and concepts of the "older" realism, to create "a more rigorous theoretical framework for the study of world politics" (Keohane, 1983:328, 510). Waltz criticized a tendency by Stanley Hoffman, Richard Rosecrance, and other realists to search for explanations "at the level of states and statesmen." As a result, the system level had become "all product" and not at all productive (Waltz, 1979:50, 53, 62). In response, Waltz and several others proposed a systemic top-to-bottom approach (cf. p. 000).

From this perspective, traditionalists and modernists alike were charged with reifying their systems by drifting to the "sub-system dominant pole" and thus reducing systems to their interacting parts. As an alternative, Waltz (1979) presented a theoretical approach inspired by microeconomic theory and derived by analogy. In Waltz's formulation, power is to the international system what money (profit) is to the market. Critics of this approach pointed out that power is not fungible in the sense that money is.

As a closed system, the micromodel is characterized by a structure consisting of states of different capabilities (abstractly conceived). Each state is assumed to pursue power (also largely an abstraction) but not to maximize it. Waltz (1979:50–53, 62) insisted upon a definition of structure "free of the attributes and the interaction of units" (states) as a means of distinguishing between systemic and unit-level attributes. The only second image phenomenon to link into and affect the international system is capability (power). But the *distribution* of capabilities is a systemwide (third image) concept.

Why did the micromodel admit *capability* at the second image level while excluding psychological variables and a wide array of other state-level phenomena? Proponents justified the decision by drawing an analogy between market theory and international politics, and between the commercial firm and the state—essentially the pursuit of profit and the pursuit of power—rather than by any logic internal to the problem. In this way, the micromodel avoided reductionism as defined but at the cost of analytic control over a number of potentially critical variables employed as constant assumptions.

The micromodel uses the concept of structure as a set of constraining conditions. Because structures select by rewarding some behavior and punishing others, outcomes therefrom "cannot be inferred from incentives and behaviors." The third image structure affects behavior within the system "but does so indirectly." The effects are produced in two ways: "through socialization of the actors and through competitions among them" (Waltz, 1959:18, 74, 100).

As defined in the micromodel, there are two sharply distinguishable types of structure—anarchical and hierarchical. Any other type must fall somewhere along a structural continuum between the two poles. In this view, the international system is anarchic. The argument might be made, however, that the international system (in spite of its lack of an overarching regime or world government) is several steps beyond anarchy. For example, rules agreed upon through the Treaties of Westphalia, the Concert of Europe, the League of Nations, the United Nations, international law, and other international arrangements amount to partial regimes that to some degree override anarchy, just as no market within a state is anarchic (or even strictly free). In any case, if the international system is anarchic, how can it function as an *actor* system constraining individual states in more or less predictable ways? In terms of the market analogy, it is a widely touted virtue of the free enterprise system that each person, firm, or other actor unit possesses the "liberty" to act according to its own interests without overarching constraint. It seems closer to the presumed reality of a market (or the international system) to assert what the neorealists carefully exclude: Constraints on individual actors are attributable in large part to a *recursive* process—that is, *personal (molecular) acts converge and "interlock" on the higher (molar) level.*

The underlying and determinant problems of the micromodel are an extended application of the rationality assumption, a "freezing" of cognitive and affective variables into unvarying assumptions, and a foreshortening of process. States act as a result of rational calculations about their positions in the system, thus enabling the theorist "to attribute variations in state behavior to variation in characteristics of the international system" (Keohane, 1986b:167). This is a tail-wags-dog assumption that results from a failure to identify interlevel (interbehavior) linkages—the uncertainty inherent in a regime's efforts at assessing the nation's power$_1$ and power$_2$ relative to the capacity of an adversary.

The issue is whether or not all unit-level attributes (other than capability) are usefully excluded by invoking the microdefinition of reductionism. Not only are cognitive and affective variables excluded (the consequences of advertising in a market, for example). Also excluded are the ways in which actions generated by individuals on a first image level, once they interpenetrate or converge, provide the constituent elements of second and third image phenomena. It is precisely through such transforming processes that "creators" become "creatures" (sometimes victims) of the market. Here and there, in fact, the micromodel—through its "assumptions"—smuggles first image variables into the picture. A market, once formed, becomes a force in itself that the "constitutive units, acting singly or in small numbers, cannot control." As each unit seeks its own good, "the result of a number of units doing so transcends the motives and the aims of the separate units." Out of the mean ambitions of the individual members, "the greater good of the society is produced" (Waltz, 1979:91). So, too, in international politics, "states act to ensure their survival," their *worry* [!] about it "conditions their behavior," they are "socialized." They "seek power," "prefer" survival, and "act to achieve that end." (Because the model excludes human beings, inclusion of such "assumptions" reifies the system.)

What, then, is structure as selector? Is the (anarchical) system anything other than states of different capabilities acting through their leaders and bureaucrats, constraining each other's actions? If not, then causality flows up, sidewise, and down, not just down. As theory, the assumptions of the micromodel suffer from an absence of recursive process linkages.

In subsequent debates, the second image–reductionist issue was also addressed through a concession that any "theory of international politics requires also a theory of domestic politics, since states affect the system's structure even as it affects them." Thus Snyder and Diesing's study of information processing and decisionmaking was recognized as "fully in accord with, rather than a departure from, realist assumptions" (Waltz, 1986:331), but aside from capability, the micromodel still did not indicate how the two images might be linked. Although ingenious and remarkably parsimonious, the micromodel is essentially mechanistic, deterministic, and costly in terms of explanatory depth and versatility. Although perfectly legitimate as an intellectual exercise (or a tentative probe into the international system), the model—if relied upon for clarifying the real world—could be seriously misleading.

In today's complex environment, a theory could fall considerably short of "billiard-ball" parsimony and still raise questions about its usefulness. If the state and the international system are simplified unduly, there may not be enough complexity left to further our identification and understanding of phenomena critical to the most basic issues of war, peace, and human well-being. Lacking government or regime, the international system, qua system, does not formulate policies or act in the ways that a state can be said to do. All the activities that occur in the international system are undertaken by states (through their leaders), by alliances (NATO, Warsaw

Pact), by representatives of states (including representatives acting for states in public international agencies such as the International Monetary Fund [IMF]), or by private organizations and individuals.

Alternatives to the Micromodel

A number of efforts have been made by critics—several of them within the structural realist school—to adjust for some of the micromodel's vulnerabilities. What might be called a "creeping adductionist" tendency has allowed for the reintroduction of several lower level, or molecular, considerations. In seeking to avoid treating states as billiard balls "whose internal components are impervious to foreign pressures," some writers have taken a state-centric, or statist, approach, proceeding from an assumption that the state-as-actor is a prime shaping element in the international system. This perspective makes possible an examination of a nation's policymaking process vis-à-vis foreign policy other lower level phenomena and, by implication, the relationship of states to the international system (Krasner, 1978:5–13, 55). Whether a major power suffers a diminishing of returns, for example, may depend not only on "systemic" constraints but also on domestic factors such as the variable capacity of its people to innovate given the incentives offered by its institutions.

A major source of uncertainty and debate stems from differing concepts of structure. A comparison of the following definitions of structure is revealing: (1) a set of constraining conditions (Waltz, 1979:73), a view that is relatively mechanical and static; (2) a distribution of capabilities among similar units (Keohane and Nye, 1977:20), implying "movement" (distribution) but not much sense of impulsion; and (3) spontaneously emergent structures corresponding to the systemic function—the totality of processes and vice versa (Jantsch, 1980:41)—a perspective allowing for continuous change and potentials for development.

Adductionist critics of the micromodel have tended to move from "a set of constraining conditions" toward a "totality of processes." But initiating analyses at the system level, according to one view, provides a baseline for future work. By seeing how well a simple model accounts for behavior, we understand better the value of introducing more variables and greater complexity into the analysis, which could begin with structural realism; then relax some assumptions; and finally develop "better theories of domestic politics, decision-making and information processing so that the gap between the external and internal environments" can be bridged systematically. In order to do this, however, we need "a multi-dimensional approach to world politics that incorporates several analytical frameworks or research programs" (Keohane, 1983:327–328).

Several neorealist adductionists have allowed for much more change than the micromodel encompasses, but so far these allowances have been restricted largely to oscillations and restorations of equilibrium rather than for "progressive" (in the Lakatosian sense, i.e., with reference to dynamic models allowing for recurrent testing, "falsification," reformulation, and retesting and presumably reflecting a dynamic reality) adaptation and long-term possibilities for transformation—phenomena that seem peculiarly relevant today and that Robert Gilpin (1981:121ff) has treated in his analyses of the nation and its historical emergence.

History Combined with Organizational Evolution

In developing a theory of the third image and its structure, why not proceed nature's way by assuming from the start that the history and sociocultural evolution of second image processes go a long way toward accounting for the international system? Why not open our investigations to the means (including trial, error, and complex feedbacks) through which first, second, third, and, increasingly, multilevel fourth image activities condition each other?

Earlier chapters have rooted human organizational development in prestate interplays of human populations, knowledge, skills, and resource accesses. Tracing these processes to the second image level, we watched the adaptive emergence and further growth and development of states manifested by centralization of power$_1$ and power$_2$ combined with the gradual recombination of pluralistic constraints. With (uneven) population growth, technological advancement, and resource accesses within and between states, their expanding activities and interests increasingly intersected in perseverant patterns and produced the international system. What could be more parsimonious and less reductionist than the historical, generic (presumably necessary and sufficient) processes (insofar as we can locate them) that produced the outcomes for which an explanation is sought?

From this perspective, a definition of the international system might include two inadequately examined provisions: those characteristics of a society that we believe to be the basic determinants of performance—namely, people, their cognitions, affects, knowledge, skills, actions, and institutions; and the form of the interrelationships of the human components insofar as they contribute to third (and eventually fourth) image patterns and outcomes.

In these terms, if we carry the state profiles of Chapter 4 a step farther, we can envisage an international profile of unevenly growing and developing states (each with its own profile) continuously interacting and competing with differential success. Alphas, betas, and gammas (with allowances for "size") are "out in front" in terms of power$_1$, etas are jockeying with indifferent success, the more "developed" of the epsilons and zetas are pressuring themselves to catch up while the lesser among them lag well behind, and the deltas are somewhat apart trying to run their own unique courses. This marathon metaphor has severe limitations, however, because the various runners are interacting and competing in ways that a simple race model fails to accommodate.

With a substantial change of perspective, we can envisage the states interacting and competing in very complex ways—some on balance positively, some threateningly negative, some almost neutral. Now we see the states in vibrant, shifting networks of bargaining, leveraging, forming and dissolving coalitions, and other interactivities. But what we now discern in four dimensions are perseverant, patterned, more or less institutionalized individual and organizational combinations stable enough to be traced through time, but never "standing still." These organizational combinations are always changing and now and then transforming as population numbers, knowledge, skills, resource accesses, capabilities, demands, and bargaining and leverage potentials of component actor units change (unevenly). Within this framework we can locate the sources of power$_1$ and power$_2$, identify the social and mechanical processes through which they are transformed, distributed, and put to use. In addition, we can assess some of the probable consequences, including who does what to (or with) whom with what risks, costs (to whom), and outcomes.

Interactions as Linkages and Manifestations of Conflict

In sharp contrast with the treatment of structure in the micromodel as the relative (but unspecified) capabilities (power$_1$) in the system, Morgenthau (1968:135) referred to diplomacy as "the art of bringing the different elements of national power to bear with maximum effect" on points in the international situation concerning national interest "most directly." Thus, diplomacy, he thought, constituted "the most important factor making for" that power. By that observation, he appeared by definition to have identified the "formation and execution of foreign policy on all levels" as an element of structure. There is a risk of confusion in this perspective, however. The formation (planning) of foreign policy can be construed as an element of power$_1$ and of domestic structure, thus providing a base for specialized economic, political, and military capabilities. Derivatively, however, the execution of power extends into the external environment and impinges on other nations, thus qualifying as a core element in the implementation of bargaining, leverage, and overall influence (power$_2$) and therefore of international (and global) structure.

Whether such interchanges are treated analytically as "friendly" linkages between individuals and/or organizations and institutions or as potentials or manifestations of conflict will depend in large part upon their quality and intensity. In practice, many economic policies and interactivities between nations rely upon economic resources for effective implementation, and many economic policies and activities exert leveraging effects upon relations between any two or more countries. This is true of normal peacetime commerce between nations, but manipulation of trade can be an instrument of conflict and war as well. In short, there is no juncture in second and third image interactions at which, in principle, states (acting through their leaders, diplomats, and private citizens pursuing transnational interests) cannot affect the direction and quality of international events. This tends to be true whether the second image activities are economic, political, or military—activities in one of these categories often having effects in either or both of the other two.

Albert Hirschman (1969) described how Germany just prior to and during World War II used foreign trade as an instrument in its policy of power expansionism and international control. His analysis was presented in terms of the supply effect (trade undertaken for commercial, industrial, and consumer purposes in general) and the influence effect (the employment of trade as a carrot or as a stick), which amounts to leverage.

The *supply effect* refers to the obtaining of access to the strategic materials required for power (power$_1$). This effect can be achieved through (1) policies that secure gains from trade, particularly the importation of strategic goods; (2) trade directed to countries from which there is minimal danger of being cut off; and (3) the control of trade routes. These aspects of national trade policy lead to a direct increase in the country's preparedness for war and provide protection in the event of trade interruptions. Just as war or the threat of war can be construed as a means of obtaining a particular result, so the supply effect may serve as an indirect instrument of power, the direct instrument being war or the threat of war. In its final result, therefore, the supply effect of foreign trade implies at least the possibility of war. With respect to the supply effect of foreign trade, Nazi Germany concentrated on imports needed for the war machine, accumulated large stocks of strategic materials, redirected trade to politically friendly or subject nations, and sought control of oceanic trade routes.

The *influence effect* refers to the leverage potential (power$_2$) a particular nation can exert over its trading partners to make them dependent on their trade with that country without a reverse dependency also being the case. The manipulation of trade to interrupt commercial or financial relations for strategic purposes dates far back in history. Thucydides identified the Megara Decree, which closed Athenian ports to the Megarians, as a factor in the outbreak of the Peloponnesian War. The influence effect can be accomplished by (1) developing a monopoly of exports and directing trade to countries requiring these articles; (2) directing trade to smaller, poorer countries and those with low mobility of resources; (3) creating vested interests in a trading partner's power groups; and (4) exporting highly differentiated goods to create dependent consumption and production habits.

From this perspective, the international structure in war or peace can be viewed as an aggregate of asymmetrical relationships among nations of differing interests, capabilities, and bargaining and leverage potentials and activities. State structures in turn amount to asymmetrical relationships among individuals and coalitions of differing interests, capabilities, and bargaining and leverage potentials and activities. Conceptualized in this way, the existence and characteristics of an international structure—including any particular configuration (balance of power, bipolar, multipolar, or what-ever)—"must be demonstrated . . . not prespecified" (E. Haas, 1982:242).

The problem of how much "reduction" and how much "system" (holism) is now resolved: The two perspectives are complementary, and outcomes are emergent therefrom and variable. In practical terms, the foreign policies and external activities of each nation are constrained not only by the capabilities, leverage potentials, and activities of rival states but also by their location within the global matrix of all the interactivities of all the states.

Power Configurations and
War/Peace Tendencies

A serious difficulty with systemic (as opposed to general systems) approaches to the international system is the tendency to predetermine processes and outcomes in terms of specific configurations that have had a long history in western diplomatic thinking: (1) loose bipolar, (2) tight bipolar, (3) multipolar balance of power, (4) hierarchical, (5) unit veto, and (6) universal (Kaplan, 1957:21–53). Because they are used so frequently in the analysis of war-prone dynamics, we are concerned primarily with the loose bipolar, tight bipolar, and multipolar balance-of-power configurations, which are widely thought to approximate international realities and are often taken seriously by theorists and statesmen.

Characterization of Subconfigurations

The tendency among writers in formulating bipolar and multipolar theory has been to deal with a limited number of great powers (or superpowers) whose potential military capabilities are roughly equal, together with particular weaker states whose systemic roles (for example, neutrality) are also relevant. This approach may have been adequate for the international system of earlier times when a few European colonial empires dominated most of the world, but it seems inadequate for the late twentieth century, especially with the proliferation of nuclear capabilities, cross-national political movements, and hostage diplomacy. A major problem with these subsystem types is that theoreticians have often used them to explain outcomes—the outbreak of war, for example, or the sustained preservation of peace—with notably inconclusive results. Attempts at formulation and application of the balance-of-power phenomenon have been especially inconsistent.

Theorists generally assume that multipolarity tends to be more stable and that polarization, or bipolarity, tends to be more conflictual and war prone. As used by some theorists, balance of power and multipolarity are virtually synonymous terms that imply stability. In this connection, insofar as each increase in the number of actors increases the number of possible dyads, the total system possibilities for cooperation and stability increase commensurately. This holds because in systems characterized by conflict-generating scarcities, each increase in opportunities for cooperation (that is, to engage in a mutually advantageous trade-off) will diminish the probabilities that a conflict will escalate to the threshold of war (Deutsch and Singer, 1964:396). (It may be equally true, however, that each increase in the numbers of actors in an international system also increases the possibilities for competition, conflict, and violence.)

Theorists assume that a multipolar system becomes unstable when "events which previously were unable to shift it from its existing equilibrium will now be sufficient to transform it into a different system." These potentially disturbing events include "inventions, construction of new economic facilities, discovery of new skills, and changes in communications and transportation in one national actor, if out of proportion to changes in other national actors" (Waltz, 1971:240). Such critically important events, although occurring almost continuously, are virtually excluded, however, by the micromodel's ultraparsimonious, static approach.

While recognizing the conventional wisdom that a world of many (presumably unequal) powers is "more stable than a bi-polar world," Waltz (1971:240) recalled a conventional theorem asserting that real partnership is possible "only between equals." From this contradiction, he then developed for an age of nuclear weaponry the proposition that "the relative simplicity of relations within a bi-polar world, the great pressures that are generated, and the constant possibility of catastrophe produce a conservatism on the part of the two greatest powers." The USSR and the United States, in short, may feel more comfortable "dealing *a deux*" than in contemplating a world in which "they vie for advantage with other superpowers."

Other writers in the field conceded that no major great power war had occurred under the strong bipolar configuration following World War II. At the same time, however, several recalled the Korean and Vietnam conflicts and pointed to peace-prone multipolar arrangements of the past. Notable among these were the years of European peace between the Napoleonic Wars and World War I. These years were characterized by relatively loose alignments that provided more favorable interaction opportunities, dispersed loyalties (Wallace, 1979a:76–77, 83–84), and multiple power centers less threatening to the system than to superpowers face to face (Gilpin, 1981:85). By contrast, tight bipolar configurations seemed to produce cleavages along a single axis that approximated a zero-sum game (Coser, 1956:76–77). According to a third perspective, however, any odd number larger than three "overmultiplied" relationships and invited attempts "at world conquest" (Burns, 1961:356). But other theorists in the numbers game suggested five as optimal—or more (up to an as-yet-unidentified limit) (Kaplan, 1970:130).

According to a fourth perspective, the optimal level of polarization and conflict was "somewhere between tight bipolarity and a loose multipolar system" (Wallace, 1979a:84). According to Rosecrance (1966:324), what he referred to as bipolarity—each of the two opposing alliances presumably being less cohesive than in a truly tight bipolar system—"does not eradicate violence, but it holds the prospect of limiting violence to far smaller proportions than either bipolarity or multipolarity. If peace is the objective, a system combining bipolar and multipolar features may be a means of reasonable approximation thereto."

Singer, Bremer, and Stuckey (1972:24, 45–46) summed up the controversy thus. From a classical balance-of-power perspective, "there will be less war when there is: (a) approximate parity among major nations; (b) change toward parity rather than away from it; and (c) a relatively fluid power hierarchy." From a hegemonic power viewpoint, however, "there will be less war when there is (a) preponderance of power concentrated in the hands of a very few nations; (b) change, if any, toward greater concentration; and (c) relatively stable rank order among, and intervals between, the major powers."

The clear implication seemed to be that a stable peace would depend upon the establishment of a powerful hegemon supported by a strong and reliable hegemonic alliance. But a quantitative study of wars in the nineteenth and twentieth centuries by these authors indicated that a power concentration did affect the incidence of war but that outcomes were "radically different" in the twentieth century as contrasted with the nineteenth.

How can this last inconsistency be explained? The authors speculated that "uncertainty—an intervening variable difficult to measure—plays a different role in the two centuries." When diplomacy was practiced largely by "small elite groups," the uncertainty factor may have been "modest in both its magnitude and its effects." With the opening of the twentieth century, by contrast, "industrialization, urbanization, and the democratization of diplomacy may have begun to erode the rules of the game." According to Singer et al., uncertainty was the outcome of three main variables: "the extent to which capabilities are highly concentrated in a very few nations; whether the distribution is changing toward higher or lower concentration; and at the rate at which relative capabilities are moving."

It may be, however, that whether a particular configuration of power is war prone or peace prone may depend upon other, more powerful conditioning variables that balance-of-power theorists have tended to overlook, discount, or ignore. A cynic might conclude that concern about particular configurations does little more than divert attention away from the *human* sources of conflict and violence.

Balance of Power and Its Many Definitions

Morgenthau (1968:161, 202–203) referred to balance of power in four different ways: "(1) as a policy aimed at a certain state of affairs; (2) as an actual state of affairs; (3) as an approximately equal distribution of power; (4) as any distribution of power." Overall, he saw two contradictory functions encompassed by the balance-of-power concept: to provide stability in the power relations among nations and "to insure the freedom of one nation from domination by the other," given that these relations are subject to change. Because nations desire to achieve a maximum of power, however, Morgenthau saw them facing the risk that "their own miscalculations" combined with increases in the power of other states might "add up to an inferiority for themselves," which they must avoid at all costs. This avoidance can be achieved (1) by bringing the "full weight" of diplomacy to bear on other nations in order to compel concessions from them" and thus transform a "temporary advantage into a permanent superiority"; or (2) by waging a preventative war, which however "abhorred in diplomatic language" and "abhorrent to democratic public opinion" remains "a natural outgrowth of the balance of power."

Morgenthau admitted, however, that all states do not at all times act in balance-of-power (or other power-politics) terms. If this is so, then we are left to find out, if we can, when they do and when they do not. Before these questions can be answered, however, we need to determine the true meaning of the term *balance of power*. A consensus in the field on this issue has not been reached; yet analysts in the field and in the literature regularly invoke the balance-of-power concept as if some agreement had been reached.

Ernst Haas (1953:446–456) identified eight distinct meanings for balance of power: (1) a distribution or configuration of power implying no particular "balance" unless explicitly stated; (2) "an exact equilibrium of power between two or more contending parties"; (3) hegemony, or a reach therefor; (4) stability or peace; (5) a condition favoring stability or peace; (6) realpolitik, competition, and balance of power merged into the concept of a struggle for power and survival; (7) a tendency of states to form alliances in common self-defense; (8) and "the formulation of balance of power as a universal law of history" encompassing "unplanned behavior which would defy any analysis in terms of motivations." Further confusing the issue is a tendency among writers to agree on a definition but to disagree about the consequences.

Does a balance-of-power system favor war or peace? One definition makes such a balance almost synonymous with stability and peace (this is probably a minority view). Some writers do not insist upon a power balance as a prerequisite for peace but nevertheless accept it as one of a number of possible strategies for resolving or avoiding international conflict. Whether by self-restraint attributable to a country's anticipation of unfavorable outcome from policy of aggressive adventurism, or by the responses of other states to such a policy, power-balance politics is often credited with restricting a major power (seventeenth-century England, for example, or Bismarck's Germany) from aggressive activities it might otherwise have undertaken (S. Hoffmann, 1968:13). This view runs counter to definitions (3) and (6) put forward by Haas. In any case, many, if not a majority, of theorists have considered a balance of power as at least one of several possible strategies for the maintenance of peace.

But other writers construe balance of power as "synonymous" with "war, intervention, competition and instability" (E. Haas, 1953:259). Inis Claude (1962:54) proposed that in reality the gulf "between those who envisage balance of power as a system designed to prevent war and those who do not is hardly as wide as it may appear. Both groups consider it a device for the creation and preservation of *equilibrium*." The main difference between them is that one group proposes that "war may be a necessary means to this end," whereas the other "stresses the expectation that equilibrium will produce peace by deterring aggressive action."

In general, balance-of-power theorists attribute changes in the relative capabilities of states and consequent changes in the power configuration more to alterations in alliance patterns than to differential growth and development within and between states. Morton Kaplan (1957:22–36) envisaged a transformation of balance of power relationships into a less stable, more war-prone, bipolar system resulting from new technologies and other "disturbing events"—a view that placed him at odds with Waltz's (1971:240) expectation that continuing pressures and a possibility of catastrophe in the international system would produce in the superpowers a stability of peace-biased conservatism.

Claude (1962:28) concluded that as a situation, balance of power maintains only that states in the international system will always be in a power relationship with each other but that to assert this as an axiom was a bit like saying that there will always be weather. A similar criticism can be made of balance of power as policy. To say that a nation maintains a balance-of-power policy leaves unclear when, how, and with whom the nation will act. If a country will act when the balance is not in its favor, to say after the fact that a particular action was taken because the balance was not in the country's favor amounts to a tautology. Some independent source of explanation is required. Essentially the same criticism can be leveled at the concept of balance of power as a system, i.e., to say that some kind of balancing process is occurring *without reference to the particular characteristics or actions of the states participating in that balance* is a tautology.

According to one generalized proposition, states in a balance-of-power system will act to "curb each other's ambitions and opportunities, to preserve an approximate equilibrium of power between them, and to reduce the level of violence" (S. Hoffmann, 1968:13). Many theorists would agree with this view, but some would not. According to Kaplan (1957:22), each state will:

- act to increase capabilities but will negotiate rather than fight;
- fight rather than pass up an opportunity to increase capabilities;
- stop fighting rather than eliminate an essential actor in the great power system;
- oppose any coalition or single actor that assumes a position of predominance with respect to the rest of the system;
- act to constrain actors who subscribe to supraorganizational principles;
- permit defeated or constrained essential actors to reenter the system as acceptable role partners;
- or act to bring a previously inessential actor within the essential actor classification, treating all such actors as acceptable role partners.

Like the micromodel, however, theorists have criticized these imperatives as structuring the problem so that behavior within it is determined by the international system itself—by the number of national actors and the power configurations among them (S. Hoffmann, 1959:246–247). This view discounts or ignores human cognitions, demands, and judgments.

Vagueness, inconsistency, and dogmatism continue to limit the usefulness of "power" concepts. Within a lateral pressure/disequilibrium framework, particular power configurations—bipolar, multipolar, balance of power (if rigorous definitions are agreed upon)—can play contributing roles, but these are rarely, if ever, sufficient and are almost always in close interplay with other variables.

Power Changes in the Third Image

In recent years, realists and neorealists have given new twists to the concepts of hegemon and hegemonic competition and conflict. Developed by a number of different "schools," some more economically oriented than others, hegemonic theory (broadly construed) does not easily lend itself to generalization. Hegemonic stability theory (our primary emphasis here) draws from political economy but places strong emphasis upon linkages between the idea of hegemon and the concept of the international security *regime*, which has subschools of its own. Commonly, proponents of hegemonic stability theory are influenced by structural realist assumptions.

Characteristically, proponents of hegemonic stability theory use the concepts of hegemonic actor, international regime, and complex interdependence in considering the international system. These theorists assume that the dominant, or hegemonic, state, through international regimes, seeks stability in the system through arrangements of complex interdependence. International regimes—"[the] sets of governing arrangements that affect relationships of interdependence"—comprise "networks of rules, norms and procedures" that regularize behavior, control its effects (Keohane and Nye, 1977:18), and shape relationships in the international system.

According to a commonly asserted neorealist perspective, "hegemonic distributions of power lead to a stable, open economic regime because it is in the interest of a hegemonic state to pursue such a policy and because the hegemony has the resources to provide the collective goods needed to make such a system function effectively" (Krasner, 1982:499). Accompanying changes in the international system alter "opportunity costs to actors of various courses of action" and thus contribute to further changes in behavior patterns (Keohane, 1982:329). As power is redistributed, power relations become inconsistent with the rules governing the system, especially the hierarchy of prestige (status inconsistency), which is replaced by a new hierarchy (established by war). This new hierarchy determines which states will dominate the international system (Gilpin, 1981:33).

At one pole, regimes are defined so broadly as to constitute "either all international relations or all international interactions within a given issue-area." At the other pole, regimes are identified as international institutions that "equal the formal rules of behavior specified by the charters of such institutions, and the study of regimes becomes the study of international organizations." From a middle view, a regime exists "when the interaction between the parties is not unconstrained or is not based on independent decision making" (Krasner, 1982:499).

According to a widely recognized definition, an international security regime consists of sets of principles (beliefs about fact, causation, and rectitude), norms (standards of behavior in terms of right and wrong), rules (prescriptions and proscriptions for action), and decisionmaking procedures (practices for making and implementing collective choice). Essentially in its own interests, the hegemon establishes and maintains its security regime as a means of regulating relations between itself and its allies, containing the adversary and its coalition, and to the extent possible "keeping the peace." Whereas some authors have tended to place more emphasis upon national market systems, drawing distinctions between those of advanced industrial states and those of developing nations, others—notably Gilpin (1981:177–179)—pursued the ideas of uneven growth and development and a world market economy (discussed further in Chapter 8). Whereas in the short run, the "world economy" has the effect of concentrating wealth in the more advanced countries, in the long run it may facilitate the spread of economic growth throughout the international system.

Hegemonic stability theorists postulate intense and often hostile competition and conflict in the international system between the hegemon (and its allies) and a challenger (and its allies) that is seeking to overtake and surpass its adversary. As defined by Robert Keohane (1984:32), hegemony involves a preponderance of material resources, and a hegemonic power must have control over raw materials, markets, sources of capital, and "competitive advantages in the production of highly valued goods." Criteria for hegemonic status include superiority in production, commerce, finance, and military capability; these superiorities may have been achieved in a grand sweep but are more likely to have developed interactively (and unevenly) during the course of generations.

By definition, hegemonic powers possess the capabilities for maintaining the international regimes that they favor. "They may use coercion to enforce adherence to rules; or they may rely largely on positive sanctions—the provision of benefits to those who cooperate." Changes in international regimes are the result of "changes in power resources specific to particular issue areas" (Keohane, 1980:131). Because of its superior capabilities, a hegemonial power "can change the rules rather than adapt its policies to the existing rules." Such an explanation is limited, however, by "the existence of inter-issue linkages." Solution of this problem therefore requires a "strong and sophisticated theory" that indicates under what conditions linkages between issue areas would be important and what their impact on outcomes would be (Keohane and Nye, 1977:44).

Like an empire, a hegemon tries to expand and strengthen its control over the international system—as long as it is profitable to do so—by providing "protection in exchange for revenue." In line with the theory of public goods and "free-ridership," however, Gilpin (1981:169) proposed that a hegemon will tend to "overpay" (because a dominant power in its own interests can be relied upon to defend the status quo, lesser states do not have much incentive to pay their "fair" protection costs) (Keohane, 1983:517). *Over the long run, as a result of the expansion of its defense perimeter and power outreach, the hegemon's military costs may be expected to increase and its returns to diminish with time.*

Within this framework, the challenger state may try to alter the rules impressed into the international system by the incumbent hegemon, the division of spheres of influence within the status quo, and territorial distributions among members of the international system. The probabilities of success for the challenger will depend upon the extent to which the capabilities and influence of the hegemon decline relative to the power of other states in the system. In response to a particular challenge, the hegemon may fashion new policies calculated to restore "equilibrium" to the system— the crux of the problem being the hegemon's ability to balance commitments and resources. To the extent that other members of the hegemonic regime approach parity with the declining hegemon and accept increasing responsibility for security costs, the regime may continue to prevail (Keohane, 1984:103–106, 195ff).

As capabilities of states and the structure of the encompassing international system change, the rules constituting international regimes also change. Meanwhile, insofar as their economic capabilities increase, secondary states no longer feel obliged to accept one-sided relationships and interchanges that threaten their national autonomy and status in the system. Thereafter, as they begin implementing policies more favorable to themselves, "the rule-making and rule-enforcing powers" of the hegemonic state further erode (Keohane and Nye, 1977:43–45). Eventually, the old hegemonial system collapses—whether by economic failure, major power shifts, war, or a combination of all three. As with prominent balance-of-power assumptions, hegemonic stability theory predicts that parity between hegemon and challenger is war prone and that asymmetry (hierarchy) is peace conducive.

Power Transition and Its War/Peace Implications

Because of uneven rates of growth and the possibility of increasing their capabilities through alliance formation, states within the international system compete for power and status and often engage in games of "catch up," "overtake," and/or "leapfrog" with each other. This tendency, which A.F.K. Organski and Jacek Kugler (1980:19–27) called the *power transition*, goes a long way toward shaping the interstate behavior, including alliances and adversarial relationships, that appears central to hegemonic competition and stability. Largely discounting alliance formation and a determinative source of power (and changing distributions thereof), Organski and Kugler identified each nation's relative socioeconomic and political development (and changes thereof) as the major source of power transitions.

Power transition theory also contrasts with realpolitik, structural realism, and (to a lesser extent) hegemonic stability theory; according to these, power changes among states and the outbreak of war derive primarily from power balances and deviations therefrom. Power transition theory, however, "provides no general rule" for explaining and predicting outbreaks of war and "warns that changes in the power structure will not, in and of themselves, bring war about." In this view, neither maximization of power nor a "single-minded urge to guarantee security in a narrow sense" is a strong incentive for war among major powers. On the contrary, nations that perceive themselves as "powerful and satisfied do not start wars"; they feel threatened only if they perceive that "the changing system challenges their positions, or if they no longer like the way benefits are divided." Power transition theory predicts that the weaker nation will be the attacker (Organski and Kugler, 1980:22, 27).

Underlying the power transition concept is the assumption that the international system is hierarchical rather than anarchic and that its dynamics derive from three central propositions: (1) states in the international system (especially major powers) are in continual competition—assessing, testing, and challenging each other's position in efforts to influence distributions of resources within the system; (2) the challenging and overtaking tendencies of one state against another will increase the probability of conflict and war; and (3) probabilities will be affected by rates of growth (and development)—that is, the faster the challenger overtakes the dominant country, the greater is the likelihood of war (Organski and Kugler, 1980:52–57). Like some of the more influential balance-of-power interpretations today, power transition predicts that the most favorable condition for peace is provided by an asymmetrical distribution of power between the two sides.

After empirical tests of their major hypothesis, Organski and Kugler (1980:61–63) modified their theory somewhat. They contended that differences in *rates of growth* between the dominant nation and the leapfrogging challenger sent the system sliding toward war, and the *relative speed* of the two powers on their respective trajectories was also important. Coalitions, moreover, were significant in two ways: The dominant nation's alliance was stronger in the cases investigated than was the coalition of the challenger, and the conflict between the two great powers waged through alliance commitments brought other major powers into the ensuing warfare.

A Lateral Pressure/Disequilibrium Approach

Although a lateral pressure/disequilibrium perspective is largely consistent with power transition theory, two exceptions exist. First, whereas power transition theory usually focuses primarily on major power competition, the lateral pressure/disequilibrium approach presents each nation in the international (and global) system as growing and developing unevenly and as competing in varying degrees with other nations in the system. Thus, the system is eligible in principle for power transitions of lesser scale. Second, lateral pressure/disequilibrium concepts place even greater emphasis on *acceleration of overtake* as a determinant of war-proneness. These concepts propose that a gradual "catch-up" by one nation is less likely than a rapid acceleration other nations perceive as threatening *and* that an established parity (or near parity) among nations, other things being equal, may turn out to be the least war prone among various possible international configurations.

The first perspective defines the international system in terms of the continually fluctuating capabilities, interactivities, and relationships of all nations in the system. Developing countries modernize and enhance their capabilities and influence, and unevenly growing and developing periphery nations often compete for local dominance (regional hegemony) among their kind. At the apex of this structure is the dominant power (the hegemon), which establishes the rules and oversees the working of the international system. Insofar as other major powers are "satisfied" with these arrangements, they tend to ally themselves with the dominant power. A major power dissatisfied with its position in the international system may be expected, however, to challenge the system—especially the dominant power and the rules it seeks to enforce—in an effort to obtain the place to which its increasing capabilities "entitle" it. But such a challenge will be made only to the extent that the dissatisfied power expects the benefits of such a change to exceed the costs.

Periphery nations, depending upon their respective levels and rates of development, will tend to establish relations as allies (or clients) of the dominant or the challenger nation. Which developing states ally with which major powers will depend upon varying combinations of geographical location, historical relationships (positive and/or negative), the ideological dispositions and relative capabilities and influence of domestic reform and/ or revolutionary movements, and so forth. To one degree or another, virtually all modern states are caught up in the dynamics of power transition and hegemonic succession.

Meanwhile, a challenger state will cease its opposition only if and when it perceives the costs of further effort to be greater than the probable benefits, whereupon a new challenger may emerge. When states in the international system widely perceive the benefits of further change to be greater than the costs, they will also perceive the costs of maintaining the status quo to be greater than the ability of the incumbent hegemony to do so. Thereafter, unless the trend is reversed, a new hegemonic regime (a new moving equilibrium and distribution of power) will be established.

To the extent that the dominant power perceives such a challenger to be overtaking it in capability and influence (which may result in part from the declining capabilities of the dominant state), the international system will experience a degree of destabilization, and the probabilities of war are likely to increase. Conversely, stability in the international system will tend to increase to the extent that the dominant state and its allies are stronger than any combination of challengers. In a sense, however, this "equilibrium" has been "imposed" by the superior capabilities and efficiencies of the hegemon and its "regime" and as such is founded upon (or within) a larger disequilibrium of uneven growth and development that is likely to portend future disruptions.

From the second perspective, therefore, the hegemonic "stability" is no more than a temporary set of relationships that in being are already and continuously in a process of becoming something else. The whole "moving picture" helps us see and understand "realities" that less dynamic "realism" obscures or defines outside the picture frame.

National Profiles and Constraints

One advantage of the lateral pressure/disequilibrium approach is the possibility of systematically locating and comparing the structures of all states in the international system according to the same measures (population, technology, resource access, budgetary allocations, and so forth). A second advantage is that bargaining, leveraging, and coalition formation provide a behavioral core that allows the horizontal and vertical linkage of states and their activities throughout the international system. In general, interactions within any dyad are conditioned in important ways by the profiles of the nations involved.

These capabilities facilitate the mapping, where appropriate, of interconnected activities in different parts of the system. Thus, for example, when two epsilon (or zeta) nations—one a client of the dominant power and the other a challenger client—go to war, the interactions of all four states, including tendencies toward conflict escalation, can be systematically traced and analyzed within a common theoretical framework. Relevant cases during the post–World War II era include the Korean, Vietnam, and Soviet-Afghan wars. (The same "four-cornered" model could be used in each case to study subsequent de-escalations if such should occur.)

Insofar as all nations are engaged to one degree or another in the (economic/political/strategic) game, the international system takes shape as an intensely dynamic environment of demands, leverages, reciprocations, and continuous change (wants satisfied and unsatisfied, new wants generated, and so forth). As individual states expand their activities and interests, their efforts are likely to intersect with the expanding activities and interests of one or more other states. To a large extent, the outcome of such an intersection will depend upon the bargaining and leverage modes and strategies employed by the two sides in pursuing their further activities and interests. The bargaining modes and strategies selected by the two sides are likely to be conditioned by the profiles of the two countries. It makes a considerable (even a critical) difference, in short, whether the relationship is alpha-alpha, alpha-epsilon, or epsilon-epsilon. Many other considerations are, of course, highly relevant (the needs, wants, demands, and capabilities of the two societies, for example), but these specifics are affected by each nation's natural (resource) environment and profile. For example, an alpha may be looking for raw materials and markets for its finished goods, whereas an epsilon may be reaching out for fertilizer, tractors, and exchange value for its sugar.

An epsilon (or zeta) country interacting intensely with an alpha (or other industrially advanced country) tends to be economically, politically, and strategically vulnerable, although the relationship may pay off in some much needed "currency." Prior to Fidel Castro's achievement of power, for example, Cuba—essentially a one-crop nation—sold its sugar to the United States and in so doing was penetrated economically, politically, and to some extent militarily. After Castro's victory, Cuba sent its sugar to the USSR and was still penetrated economically, politically, and strategically.

When the expanding activities and interests of two alpha nations intersect, they have the choice (in principle) of interacting positively or negatively. The selection can depend upon numerous factors, including how the leaders (and other elites) in the two countries perceive each other. If the two alphas are the dominant and challenger states in the international system, the probabilities are higher that their responses to each other will tend to be negative. But if the activities and interests of the two countries appear reasonably compatible (one being the dominant alpha, for example, and the other feeling threatened by the hegemonic challenger), the two may seek an alliance or the enlargement of an existing bloc. In practice, the dominant nation and the challenger both tend to maintain coalitions against each other. Major power allies are thus likely to establish arrangements of this kind founded on the principle of coalitional security.

The concept of an economic, political, and strategic hegemonic regime has been well developed. Normally, however, the challenger and its allies constitute a comparable, competitive regime (a theoretical consideration that has attracted less systematic attention). Either regime may be expected to include states of different profiles; betas, gammas, and possibly a lesser alpha are likely to predominate, but depending upon how either regime is defined or bounded, delta, epsilon, zeta, or eta nations may also be members or clients (as NATO and the Warsaw Pact demonstrate). A beta nation with a population that is large and growing relative to its territorial size, a rapidly advancing technology, and severely limited domestic resources (Japan prior to Pearl Harbor, for example) may fight for regional hegemony in order to acquire controlled access to raw materials and markets. On a lower level of capability, two epsilon states in competition for regional influence may interact similarly—one assuming the dominant role, the other challenging. Alternatively, a boundary dispute, common among agriculturally based societies, may initiate a conflict that is transformed into a struggle for regional hegemony.

A Partial Framework for Continual Change

Because of its extreme state-of-being, top-to-bottom assumptions, the micromodel is limiting, if not misleading, from historical, developmental, and policymaking perspectives. This does not mean, however, that a top-to-bottom approach is always anathema. On the contrary, once the *up escalators, down escalators, and lateral moving sidewalks* have been identified—along with a historically grounded, developmental, adaptive set of relative growth and decline processes—a top-to-bottom/bottom-to-top procedure can be useful (as later chapters on the fourth image will demonstrate). In this connection, a synergistic convergence of structural realist, power transition, and hegemonic stability approaches can probably take us a long way on the road of theory development.

As part of this same perspective, power transition and hegemonic stability theories overlap the lateral pressure/disequilibrium framework in significant ways. Implicitly, and to some extent explicitly, all three assume uneven growth and development within and between states, but neither of the first two takes into comparable account the intense and persisting interplays among population growth, technological advancement, and resource availabilities (including distributions). Surely, in combination, these were among the most powerful shaping and constraining forces in history and will continue to be so.

Moreover, in focusing on the uneven growth and development of (and competition and conflict between) major powers, neither power transition theory nor hegemonic stability theory has gone far enough toward including and linking up developing countries within the overall international system. Insofar as uneven growth and development within and between states are ubiquitous, it seems to follow that power transitions are also ubiquitous. From this observation we may conclude that whereas power transitions often lead to hostilities, at the current level of the theory's development they are not always reliable predictors of war. Many transitions pass unnoticed, some because the nations involved are too far removed from each other, others because on balance their relations are friendly (or at least not seriously conflictual). Such transitions, however, can have powerful effects upon interstate relations as well as upon the international system. Much the same can be said of hegemonic stability theory with respect to nations, whatever their location in the system, that are competing for dominance, however localized (Iran and Iraq, for example).

Power transition and hegemonic stability theories also place too heavy an explanatory burden on the power variable, which is central to competitions and conflicts but rarely sufficient. Also needed in most analytic cases is a valuational/affective indicator—*hostility, negative leverage, level of threat/ violence, or merely the record of past interactions conceived in these terms.*

As currently presented, neither power transition theory nor hegemonic stability theory takes adequate account of the logistics of power and influence: the effect, for example, of each country's capacity for expanding its activities and interests beyond domestic borders and each country's power outreach (its ability to bring power and influence to bear over the face of the earth). In fact, all states but one that were the hegemons in their respective eras (Portugal, Spain, the Netherlands, France, and Great Britain) expanded from territorially restricted, resource-limited (beta) nation-states into large overseas (alpha) empires that could be translated into vastly extended resource bases. The exception was the United States, which also expanded but primarily into contiguous land areas—the main exceptions being Puerto Rico, Cuba, Hawaii, the Philippines, and Alaska (purchased from expanding tsarist Russia). If it were to achieve hegemonic status, the Soviet Union would be comparable to the United States in terms of this particular set of dynamics.

Finally, neither the power transition approach nor the hegemonic stability approach has made sufficiently explicit the role, threats, and other implications (economic, political, and strategic) of the challenger and its regime in terms of client or surrogate competitions, conflicts, crises, and wars within an international system dominated by the hegemon and its regime. As a consequence, neither power transition theory nor hegemonic stability theory has gone far enough in developing a framework for (1) comparing competition, conflict, and other interactions between major powers *with the same processes* operating between lesser powers or making similar comparisons of such processes involving major powers interacting with weaker powers; (2) identifying processes that fuel and link competitions, conflicts, and crises in one part of the international system with other parts of the system (from "remote" developing nations to major powers, for example, and vice versa); and (3) revealing overlaps and congruences of the two (and other) theories, possibly merging them, and exposing the differences for further study.

The disequilibrium/lateral pressure framework provides explicit space for these phenomena. Before we discuss them, however, we need to recall briefly the somewhat elusive difference we see between an assumption of stable equilibrium and a moving equilibrium or disequilibrium. The former connotes a more or less "finished" system in balance with its internal and external environments and postulates action undertaken in response to a situational disturbance in its normal stability. We propose that a moving equilibrium is established from and in response to a condition of disequilibrium (or partial equilibrium at best). We further assert that an actor system, especially a collective system such as a state, normally pursues an equilibrium and may approach or approximate one from time to time (especially when growth and development are minimal), but it seldom if ever succeeds in maintaining an equilibrium because both internal and external environments are always changing and the system itself is necessarily changing. If one aspect of policy is stabilized, others soon demand attention—as the current tightrope walk by the United States between inflation and recession vividly indicates. Or if the system as a whole is stabilized (not changing in a changing world), that emerges as an issue in itself, and the disequilibrium becomes all the more apparent.

By contrast, a state pursuing a moving, or dynamic, equilibrium, while continually adapting to a changing external environment (or operating to bring its domestic and external environments into an interplay supportive of its own interests), can be characterized as stable even though (and in part because) it is continually adjusting and changing. Within this overall set of processes, gaps outstanding between the outcome of an implemented policy and a true equilibrium can vary from wide to narrow or even tolerable, but they rarely, if ever, reach zero. If a fixed stability is approximated too long, we may expect a deterioration of the system (which, in line with the entropy assumption of Chapter 1, occurs eventually in any case).

Many factors can contribute to constraints on efforts to achieve an equilibrium. Among these are the differential growth, development, and interplays within and between the states and the resource allocations that individual states and their respective societies make to various economic sectors and institutions and agencies of government (agriculture, industry, research and development, production, health, education, military).

With allowance for differences in capabilities and efficiencies, all states tend to be constrained in their activities by lag times between (1) the emergence of a "serious" (uncontrolled, runaway) disequilibrium and its recognition by a country's leadership; (2) recognition and formulation and acceptance of an appropriate policy; and (3) policy formulation and a reasonably effective program of implementation. In general, the strength of such constraints on a particular state tend to increase as the state passes through its apogee and to the extent that its efficiencies decline thereafter.

Insofar as a state's establishment of hegemony imposes upon other states its own characteristic bargaining, leverage, and disciplinary structures, a challenger's threat will initiate a period of instability, intense competition, and potentially disruptive conflict within the system. With a few relatively minor exceptions, major powers since World War II have not extended territories under their direct jurisdictions, but to one degree or another, most have expanded their activities and interests into many areas of the globe (including Antarctica, the ocean depths, and space). In the process, the major powers have often achieved strong measures of influence and even control through penetration of weaker states and regions outside the formal international system.

This chapter has dealt with differing perspectives on the third image and the international configuration of power as developed by and available to theorists and practitioners in the formulation and implementation of their foreign policies and actions. Chapter 7 will be concerned with international conflicts, arms races, crises, and outbreaks of war.

7

Deterrence, Crisis, and War

In previous chapters, we discussed some of the ways in which warfare contributed to the development of ancient states, the emergence of nation-states, and the establishment in western Europe of the nation-state, or international, system. In so doing, we described interstate wars as outcomes of uneven growth and development. We also specified that insofar as either country in a two-country relationship perceives the activities and interests of the other as threatening or injurious, the level of negative leverage exchanges is likely to increase. If the activities and interests of states with grossly unequal capabilities intersect, the probability of penetration of the weaker by the stronger is likely to be high. If the activities and interests of roughly equally powerful states intersect—especially if the adversary's activities and interests are perceived by one or both states as expanding— the probabilities of conflict, escalations, and crises are likely to increase. The outcome, however, will largely depend upon the positive and/or negative leverages used. To the extent that the capabilities and leverage potentials of the less powerful adversary are perceived as overtaking those of the stronger, the greater is the probability that negative leverage exchanges will escalate toward large-scale violence.

In this chapter, we consider some of the other factors that are likely to come into play when countries confront each other in a conflict (or potential conflict). For example, the wider the alliance commitments of each adversary, the higher is the probability that a crisis or war between them will expand. The chapter focuses first on a more or less generic approach to phenomena that may contribute to the escalation of conflict, to the dynamics of crisis, and to factors that may influence the outcome toward war or war avoidance. The chapter then discusses hegemonic wars and how they affect the international system.

International Conflicts and Their Escalation

Conflicts between states (as between individuals) are inescapable. One reason for this is the *security paradox*: In order to enhance its economic, political, or strategic (military) security, a state is likely to undertake defensive policies and actions that another country perceives as threatening to its security. In response, the latter state takes comparable measures of its own, which validate the anxieties of the first state, and so it goes. As a consequence, the two states—each acting to protect itself—jointly create the kind of outcome each was trying to avoid. In an international system in which all states are presumed to rely upon self-help for their security, relationships of this kind are likely to be accepted as normal. Once such a situation has been created, the critical question is how the conflict is to be dealt with—through bargaining (or comparable means) and nonviolent leverages or through the escalation of threats and violence.

The Threat of Force as Conflict Leverage

In principle, when the activities of a powerful country penetrate a weaker nation or collide with the activities and interests of another powerful nation, the leaders involved can proceed "rationally"—that is, they can rely on cost/benefit considerations. Numerous studies of bargaining and leveraging in disputes between states have indicated that national leaders engaged in crises tend to act rationally in this sense (Gochman and Leng, 1983:97); these findings were consistent with tenets put forward by Morgenthau and others. Yet evidence of nonrational elements in conflict decisionmaking also exists. This discrepancy derives in part from the fact that decisionmakers on both sides calculate the risks and probable cost of their responses according to their essentially subjective estimates (or those of their advisers) as the crisis unfolds.

In conflict situations, perceptions seem to be subject to an analog of Simon's concept of satisficing: The perceiver is less likely to compare a range of available information to ascertain which best fits the unfolding situation than to accept early reports that fit preconceptions or that otherwise appear persuasive (Jervis, 1976:101). Attitudes, beliefs, and stereotypical assumptions about opponents and enemies are active elements in "the polarized role which all men create," as is the tendency of human beings to create enemies and scapegoats (Rokeach, 1961:33). Thus, emotional feelings toward various foreign countries may take effect before even the most rudimentary "factual" knowledge about them has been assimilated. In addition, strong feelings of uncertainty, anxiety, fear, anger, or hostility can affect perceptions, attitudes, and decisions in deeply personal and subjective ways.

Ethnic, religious, and ideological differences (crusaders/Saracens, Catholics/Protestants, Communists/anti-Communists, United States/USSR, Arabs/Israelis, Sunni/Shiites) often exacerbate conflicts arising from economic, strategic, or other issues. In such situations, these differences help define the conflict, identify adversaries, and provide and justify motives. Thus, in effect, enemies tend to be those who are so defined (Holsti, 1967:25). Once formed, attitudes toward another country, especially an adversary, are not easily changed. When a national leader or bureaucrat has developed an image of another country, he or she will often sustain that view in spite of "objective" but discrepant information to the contrary (Jervis, 1976:146).

Because neither party in a bargaining relationship can read the mind of the other, each must contend with ambiguities, which may be interpreted quite differently by the two sides. Differing perceptions of the intentions of another state commonly underlie debates about policy or about the next move in a bargaining and leverage sequence. In the exchange of threats, each side often has extreme difficulty in ascertaining the extent to which its adversary may be bluffing. Normally, the truth of the matter cannot be established until the threat has been challenged by noncompliance. In conflict situations, most of us tend to evaluate our own intentions favorably and to assume the worst of our adversary. In fact, no one can know what the intention of another person (much less an organization) *really* is. A national leader may conclude that he or she has thwarted an adversary's aggressive intent when the latter had some other purpose. But when an adversary's behavior is undesired, a decisionmaker is likely to identify it as the product of evil intent rather than (for example) as a response to his or her own actions.

Conflict Spirals, Escalations, or Action/Reaction

A threatening, penalizing, coercive, or other potentially injurious move by one party (or state) in an interactive situation often evokes a comparable but possibly more threatening or punishing response from the other party. Such a response may occur regardless of the first actor's intent, that is, regardless of whether his or her purpose was to threaten or inflict an injury. This process is referred to as a *conflict spiral, escalation,* or *action/reaction phenomenon.*

Underlying this concept is the idea that change in one party's level of output on a given dimension "often produces *reciprocation* (also called reciprocative change), i.e., a resulting change in the other party's level of output on the same or another dimension." Such reciprocation can be either negative or positive. In principle, the exchanges may amount to an escalation of hostile thrusts or to a benevolent, cooperative, give and take (Pruitt, 1969:292). Frequently, the other party matches the mode and intensity of the first party's movement.

Relationships in an action/reaction process may be asymmetrical, and complementary or roughly symmetrical. Asymmetrical, complementary relationships are those in which the actions of A and B are different but mutually fitted to each other—one actor promotes or sustains reciprocal activity by the other (A's dominance promotes B's submission, and vice versa). Such interactions may be observed in relationships between major powers and their colonies or grossly weaker clients.

Symmetrical relationships are those in which the actions of A and B are on the same order of magnitude; action/reaction interchanges are often adversarial, highly competitive, and mutually but destructively emulative. A's threatening action stimulates B to act comparably (or raise the ante), which then results in similar responses by A. In these terms, an arms race or international crisis is an *escalation of a negative tit-for-tat exchange.*

Contributing to the degree of escalation characterizing "interstate bargaining in militarized disputes" are the nature of the issues in dispute and the leverages (threats of force) initially used. Hostilities are likely to escalate to the extent that initial physical force is linked to a vital issue and are less likely to escalate when either hostility or force is absent. The greater the bargaining power of one party, the higher is likely to be the conflict level of the adversary up to which the first party will be willing to escalate— and the greater is likely to be the response of the first party.

Such a conflict spiral can be triggered by a substantial or rapid change in the relative capabilities of the parties, by a move of one party that is perceived by the other as threatening or injurious, or both. We can therefore infer that the amount of resources, the level of technology, and the specialized capabilities available to the parties can affect the steepness with which an action/reaction escalates. Beyond some threshold, however, the lower the relevant capabilities of one actor compared with the other (the greater the asymmetry), the harder it is for that party to act in a defensive and challenging manner to provocations by the other. Also, the more likely is an underreaction to provocation, and hence the lower are likely to be the probabilities of a steep escalation.

Critical elements in an action/reaction process include each actor's capabilities, demands, contingency assertions (explicit or implicit), and applications of leverage. Also of fundamental importance are each actor's perceptions of and feelings about the other's capabilities, intentions, and leverage activities. The actual, as distinct from the perceived, intentions of each actor are more problematic. Neither actor (nor observer) can determine the true intent of the other, nor is either necessarily clear about his or her own intentions, which may be obscure or mixed.

Such an escalation is likely to continue until at least one of the parties perceives that the risks and probable costs outweigh the benefits (or until one party is completely incapacitated). Often, after costs have escalated on both sides, one actor mismatches the other's most recent initiative by showing a willingness to compromise or give in. This may (or may not) reverse the spiral in the direction of better relations.

The Arms Race as a Conflict Spiral

We can view arms races as an action/reaction process in which an increase in A's military capabilities is perceived by the leadership of a rival state, B, as a threat to its security. When the military capabilities of B are increased in order to reduce or close the gap, A's leaders perceive the increase as a threat to their nation's security and act to increase their capabilities. So the competition spirals. An arms race is also a "failed" deterrence as well as a defense capability phenomenon—that is, an increase in armaments by either side can function as leverage undertaken to inhibit the armament and other defense policies of the opposing side.

Theorists variously define the arms race phenomenon. Samuel Huntington (1971:499) referred to it as "a form of reciprocal interaction between two states or coalitions" or, more specifically, as "a progressive, competitive peacetime increase in armaments by two states or coalitions of states resulting from conflicting purposes or mutual fears." In parallel fashion, Michael Wallace (1979b:242) identified arms races as involving "similar simultaneous abnormal rates of growth in the military outlays of two or more nations." As the tendencies of A and B to respond in this way become more "intense and reciprocated," the bilateral competitive processes tend to "interlock," thus yielding the action/reaction process (Ashley, 1980:35). In such a competition, suspicion and fear may multiply with the armaments.

In the past, arms races have often been analyzed in terms of two divergent perspectives—the action/reaction, mutual-stimulation, positive feedback approach and the domestic, self-stimulation (bureaucratic inertia, technical momentum, economic and political vested interest) approach. Theorists have recently called the apparent dichotomy between these two perspectives "largely artificial"; according to this view, mutual stimulation and self-stimulation are susceptible to integration "within a unified theory which includes pure self-stimulation and pure mutual stimulation as limiting cases" (Lambelet, Luterbacher, and Allen, 1979:49–50). The action/reaction label for arms races is commonly associated with the work of Lewis F. Richardson (1960:13–17), who postulated that nations increase their armaments primarily in response to increasing arms expenditures of rival nations.

So conceptualized, an arms race is a demand and leverage process in which the bids—the communication of contingent terms, alternatives, and outcomes ("If you do this, we'll do that," or "Unless you stop increasing your armaments, we'll increase ours")—tends to be implicit, rather than explicit. Often the only messages sent or received are contained in the acts of leverage themselves—something like two mimes threatening each other in pantomime. Under such circumstances, the nonexplicit character of communications between the participants obscures the reciprocal aspects of the action/reaction process and contributes to the conviction on the part of each side that the other side is preparing for aggression (each side sees the other as aggressive and itself as defensive). As viewed by a participant, or by a power theorist, an arms race is an effort to achieve a favorable distribution of power and is therefore an integral part of the international balance-of-power process.

The more intense the arms race, the greater is likely to be the tendency of each adversary to interpret its own increases in arms expenditure as defensive and each increment of arms expenditure by the adversary as a measure of aggressive intent (rather than as a defensive response). Within the logic of deterrence strategy, a resulting escalation amounts to a counterintuitive outcome.

Common weaknesses in arms race studies include the failure of many models to link domestic and external variables systematically. Underlying such problems of conceptualization and design are difficulties of indicator selection (arms expenditures? fire power?), indicator construction (how to identify and aggregate relevant expenditures for and different weapons types, sizes, and purposes across countries), and validation of the accuracy of relevant data.

The domestic, self-stimulation explanation for arms increases was put forward by John Hobson (1938:xiii), a British liberal critic of twentieth-century capitalism, who identified a tendency that was later associated with the military-industrial complex. Enterprises connected with armaments production perform two relevant functions, according to Hobson: "They batten upon the public expenditure needed to sustain a spirited foreign policy" and contribute to the security dilemma by evolving "a corresponding 'defensive' policy in other countries to which they contribute by profitable supplies of arms and ammunition—thus producing a growing competition in costs of 'defense.'"

As identified by post–World War II observers, the military-industrial complex may include all those who invent, develop, build, or distribute armaments (and their components and replacement parts), including technical personnel, labor, suppliers, entrepreneurs, and contractors as well as managers and stockholders. Presumably, such special interest activities can help fuel the action/reaction competition once it is set in motion. Arms race studies emphasizing internal factors—including the building and selling of weaponry—have tended to de-emphasize, but not dismiss, the effects of competition between states in favor of the desire to build and sell new weapons systems and the development of industrial/military interest groups (Hollist, 1977:504–505).

Clearly, domestic factor approaches and action/reaction process approaches to the arms race phenomenon are not necessarily antithetical. Either can stimulate the other, and outcomes are likely to result from varying combinations of the two. The action/reaction process may be the dominant explanation of a particular escalation at one stage, whereas domestic factors may dominate at some other stage. We would not be surprised to find such variability taking place within the same countries through time as well as across any considerable number of countries at the same time. In any case, competitions in armaments *do* tend to create domestic constituencies for high levels of defense expenditure, and rising armaments bankroll contracts and jobs on many levels (Gray, 1974:219).

Richardson (1960:13, 35–36, 175–176) also proposed a rivalry model and a submissiveness model. In the rivalry model, he suggested that a country is not threatened by the total amount of arms possessed by the opponent but by discrepancies between the rival's arms and its own. In the submissiveness model, he postulated that if from A's perspective the threat from B's rate of arms increase is insignificant, A will lower its own rate. Conversely, if the rate of B's increase is so overwhelming from A's perspective that it cannot be countered, A will "give in" by lowering its rate of increase.

Other considerations may also contribute to an arms race. A competition between rivals may be fueled by the efforts of one party to improve its bargaining and leverage position. Alternatively, a state may take part in an arms race in order to increase its diplomatic influence or to achieve a more favorable outcome in case a war should occur. Conceptual complications arise when a nation races against more than one adversary at a time. At one point, the USSR apparently was racing with the United States and the PRC simultaneously. In three-cornered races, proportionate allocations directed toward each race become relevant (T. Smith, 1980:257).

Arms races do not escalate forever. Some de-escalate. Some eventuate in war. Perceiving the arms race process as fueled by hostile relations between countries, Richardson saw such hostilities dampened by fatigue associated with continued arms production. For one side or the other, the cost of continuing becomes intolerable (the USSR in the 1980s?). Alternatively, the arms escalation may slow down as constraints of fear or other costs become too strong. At such a juncture, positive peace measures are more likely "to bite" than at other times. A potential paradox is inherent in the situation, however. As the international climate cools down, the "submissiveness effect" may switch off, whereupon the nation may start escalating again (Smoker, 1969:63, 580, 723). In cost/benefit terms, an arms race participant is likely to withdraw from competition whenever it perceives the risk of falling behind to be preferable to the perceived cost of further armament.

Theorists have suggested three main types of modifications for Richardson's rivalry model and submissiveness model, which are composed of three major ingredients—a threat term, a fatigue and expense term, and a grievance term. Some writers have suggested the addition (or deletion) of variables. Others have introduced asymmetry into the equations (whereas Richardson had both states operating according to the same type of decision calculus, some writers feel it more realistic to represent opponents by different equations). The amount of arms in Richardson's submissiveness model can have varying effects on the armaments process either by speeding it up or slowing it down. Some writers have suggested that threat, fatigue, and grievance factors should be allowed to vary similarly. Other modifications have pertained to the equations themselves (Zinnes, 1976:272–273).

Deterrence and the Escalation
of Negative Leverages

Threats and other forms of coercion are often used in diplomacy well below thresholds of crisis or war. The application of threats implies that the adversary must be made to believe that the estimated consequence of noncompliance is more damaging than even the threatener may assume. Such an outcome is dependent upon the adversary's subjective interpretation and assessment of the threatener's intent, resolve, and capability, as well as its own intent, resolve, assessment of risk, and measure of relative capabilities. In making estimates, participants in an action/reaction process must often combine considerations that are not commensurable. Or the quantity of information relevant to decisionmaking may be so great that the leaders or bureaucrats suffer from "overload" and cannot come to grips with the details or their meanings.

Perception, decisionmaking, capabilities, and behavior tend to be intensely interactive in action/reaction processes. Each side must make decisions on the basis of its perceptions of the adversary's capabilities, bargaining power, and will as well as its sense of the overall diplomatic context. But changes in conflict behavior by either party (increases in threatening or violent leverages, for example) can affect the diplomatic climate, the bargaining power relationship, and decisionmaking. Often there are side effects and other outcomes of bargaining and leverage sequences that were wholly unanticipated by one or both parties. A coercive move that exacerbates the conflict and produces an outcome that is the opposite of what was intended is a commonplace occurrence.

Leverage strategies in the international arena include coercive diplomacy and deterrence, both defined as functions of the capabilities and will of an actor to carry out threats (negative leverages) and of the practical possibilities of implementing them effectively. Depending as they do on the perceptions and evaluations of the target actor, both strategies possess strong psychological components. A particular act by country A may, or may not be, intended as a threat against country B, but in either case it will function as a threat to the extent that B so perceives it.

Alexander George et al. (1971:21–32) developed protocols for the effective use of coercive diplomacy, which, in contrast to pure coercion, includes possibilities for side bargains and compromises. Coercive diplomacy requires finding a bargain—for example, arranging for an adversary to gain by compliance or risk serious loss by noncompliance (when the penalty is taken into account). Coercive diplomacy also requires threats or applications of force sufficient and appropriate for demonstrating an actor's determination to protect well-defined interests and readiness to use more force if necessary. By relying on lower levels of threat and/or applications of force (in combination with psychological considerations), coercive diplomacy is less risky and less costly than traditional military strategies as a means of achieving objectives—provided the strategy's merits are not allowed to prejudge its feasibility in any particular situation.

The purpose of coercive diplomacy is to instill in an adversary the expectation of unacceptable costs of sufficient magnitude to erode its motivation to continue whatever it is doing. If low-level leverage fails to evoke the desired outcome, inducement can be increased. Against a determined opponent, however, or one who perceives itself as about to achieve an important success, even a stronger threat or coercive sanction may be ineffective. Every move in a bargaining and leveraging situation can be interpreted, or misinterpreted, as a signal conveying information about subsequent moves or outcomes. Thus, a leverage used to achieve a particular outcome may contribute to its opposite—an irreversible escalation.

The Strategy of Deterrence

Whenever the activities and interests of two or more states intersect or collide (or are so perceived), possibilities exist for either peaceful or conflictual relations. Insofar as either side perceives its own activities and/or interests as threatened or under attack by the other side, however, leverages in the form of deterrence may be used in pursuit of security. Like coercive diplomacy, deterrence can be subsumed under the dictum put forward by Karl von Clausewitz (1943:3) that if "our opponent is to do our will, we must put him in a position more disadvantageous to him than the sacrifice would be that we demand." But the implications of modern deterrence are more military than diplomatic.

Often implicit in recommendations made by proponents of deterrence theory is the assumption that although we are peaceful, we are threatened by hostile aggressors. We remain at peace if we stay strong, but we invite attack if we stay weak (Jervis, 1976:75). According to this perspective, the most reliable (and least costly) way to contain aggression is to build our defenses and intelligently apply threats, sanctions, and force. Deterrence is thus concerned with the calculated exploitation of potential force—that is, with persuading an adversary that avoidance of specific courses of action is in its own interest (G. Snyder, 1961:5).

In the application of deterrence, a "defending" country's armed forces mount a psychological offensive to dissuade the adversary from attacking by confronting it with possible costs in excess of probable gain. A theory of deterrence thus proposes something broader than a conventional application of military skills; in effect, it suggests the skillful *nonuse* of military forces (Schelling, 1960:9) as a mode of negative leverage. Credibility must be established, however, and maintained. A willingness to use force may have to be demonstrated. Essentially, then, deterrence is the effective persuasion of an adversary that the costs and/or risks of a course of action it might undertake will outweigh the advantages (George and Smoke, 1974:1)—in Karl Popper's terms, a strictly "plastic" (as opposed to mechanistic or deterministic) relationship. Thus, what an adversary *believes* is more critical than what is objectively the case. What is true of the adversary, moreover, is equally true of the would-be influencer, including its identification of the opponent as "aggressor." Each side thus tends to pin responsibility on the other.

If a regime is constrained only by the level of its own power relative to that of other countries, a state's leaders may be expected to rely upon threats, counterthreats, and other leverages (mobilizations, troop movements, armed attack) when other modes of interaction fail to achieve their purposes. In many conflict situations, the value (costs) of leverages exchanged in a sequence—together with the respective capabilities of the adversaries (examined in time series)—may be a better predictor of future trends than the proclaimed goals, intents, or policy statements of contending leaders.

In bargaining and leverage exchanges, whether with carrot, stick, or both, high determination may compensate for relatively low capabilities. The greater resolve shown by states in some disputes is usually the result of a wide range of factors—from the importance of issues as perceived by national leaders to their propensities for taking risks. This consideration often makes the outcomes of war difficult to predict—the conclusion of the Vietnam War provides a recent example.

A weaker state may try to demonstrate resolve by making a tit-for-tat response or by raising the ante. In conflicts between states of relatively equal capabilities, however, one state may be more cautious than its adversary and may thus create a degree of asymmetry in the action/reaction process. A strategy of deterrence may be complicated, especially in a democracy, by the fact that national leaders must often communicate with two audiences at once. In demonstrating to their own citizens (as well as the adversary) a determination to "stand firm," national leaders may incite their adversary to raise the ante in retaliation.

In regard to conflict situations in which carrots and sticks are combined in a unified strategy, a review of John Kennedy's modest successes in Laos (organizing indigenous people against North Vietnamese incursions, for example) or of his more spectacular persuasion of the Soviets to withdraw their missiles from Cuba would call attention not only to his threats but also to his willingness to give the opponent a substantial quid pro quo. Thus, behind selection of a deterrence strategy may be the desire to use force in flexible, psychologically oriented, subtly creative ways.

Linkage Between Deterrence and Possible Escalation to War

To be effective, a deterrent must be stable as well as credible. Stability requires invulnerability—that is, the would-be attacker must be persuaded that any increase in its force level would be futile. Credibility means that the potential aggressor must come to the conclusion that the deterring nation has both the capability and the will to carry out its threat if it should not be heeded. In any situation of potential armed conflict, a defender's decision about whether to pursue a firm policy that risks war will depend upon the defender's calculations of the value and probability of conceivable outcomes (Russett, 1969:366).

In general, the greater the potential attacker's will and relative strength, the greater is the leverage that will have to be applied to the attacker. Deterrence is considered more likely to be successful to the extent that two sets of criteria are met: (1) The "defender" must persuade the "attacker" to believe that the defender's motivation is high, that the defender possesses adequate capabilities, and that the defender is free from domestic constraints; and (2) deterrence measures will be more successful insofar as the defender supplements threats, evidence of superior force, and/or other measures calculated to deter the attacker with positive inducements designed to soften the attacker's determination to attack (George and Smoke, 1974:264). But the attacker will determine whether to press an attack according to its estimate of the calculations of the defender. If the attacker considers the chances that the defender will fight to be substantial, the attacker will be likely to attack only to the extent that it expects the prospective gains from doing so to be great (Russett, 1969:367).

Credibility may decline rapidly as the value of an objective diminishes or to the extent that the ability and resolve to make good on threats are not adequately demonstrated. A country with high values at stake is likely to be under strong pressure to act in ways that will reinforce its declining credibility.

While generally denying that threats set off "self-fulfilling spirals of fear," hostility, and violence, deterrence theorists do not claim that deterrence always works. They may explain a failure as the target country's unwillingness to believe the adversary's threat or the application of leverages by the initiating country in circumstances in which the target country has situational advantages and can "design around" them to reach its objective without having to resort to any of the proscribed actions (Jervis, 1976:79–80).

Raoul Naroll, Vern Bullough, and Frada Naroll (1974:331) drew upon historical records from China (five separate dynasties), the Caliphate, the Byzantine Empire, Rome, Russia, France, England, Spain, and Switzerland to determine how deterrence worked during a period of some twenty-five hundred years. In general, the findings were "not encouraging to those who suppose that military preparations are likely to lead to peace." Sometimes deterrence worked, but often it did not. Often the power$_1$ and power$_2$ of the deterring nation were less effective than its leaders expected. We may thus conclude that although the purpose of deterrence is to discourage the adversary from some course of action by "posing for him a prospect of cost and risk outweighing his prospective gain" (G. Snyder, 1961:3), when deterrence and spiral (or action/reaction) theories are compared, "they give opposite answers to the central question of the effect of negative sanctions." By applying a crude version of deterrence theory, national leaders may thus contribute to outcomes contrary to their intent that are nevertheless explained and predicted by spiral theory (Jervis, 1976:78–81).

If the parties to an action/reaction process are coalitions (or coalitions of coalitions), the course of the escalation may be constrained by relationships that are internal to one or both participants. When two countries are in confrontation, for example, and ethnic or other special interest groups in one country have severe grievances, these groups may seek, or anticipate seeking, support from the opposing country (or fellow ethnic or other interest groups within it). Hence, special interest groups may resist the escalation effort of the country in which they are located. Something similar can take place when domestic coalitions (rival political parties, for example) are in bitter dispute over foreign policy. During the late 1960s and early 1970s, national leaders in the United States found it more and more difficult to increase military efforts in Vietnam as larger and larger numbers of the populace opposed the intervention.

Proponents of deterrence theory implicitly assume that both the deterrers and those to be deterred maintain tight, centralized control over the decisions they make. In this view, both defender and attacker are unitary, purposeful actors, and an overall rationality allows their choices and payoffs to be deduced. While elaborating a logic of bargaining that, as viewed by Jervis, may run "counter to common sense," deterrence theory generally supports the assumption that power must be met by power (George and Smoke, 1974:504; Jervis, 1976:78). As the target (or potential target) of a deterrence strategy, a nation (through its leaders) has three main options: to do nothing, thereby risking domination by the deterrer; to rely upon diplomatic negotiations; or to reply in kind (tit for tat). Because the first two seem to border on appeasement, compliance, or surrender, the third appears the only prudent, honorable course.

Theories of deterrence seldom take adequate account of the irrationalities of which the human being is capable, as when pride, determination, anger, hostility, or fear overrides reasonable calculations. These theories also overlook the human ability to rise to seemingly insurmountable challenges through which a whole society is galvanized against the adversary, even at the risk of devastating costs. Nevertheless, we continue to rely on deterrence in the nuclear era for the lack of a demonstrably more dependable alternative—evidence, if you will, of the "damned-if-you-do-damned-if-you-don't" implication of the security dilemma. Carried into the nuclear age, the logic of deterrence transforms inexorably into the logic of preemptive strike.

Crisis as an Escalation of Negative Leverages

An international crisis is an intense escalation, action/reaction, or schismogenic process (a runaway positive feedback situation) in which the exchanges of leverage and counterleverage between states become increasingly threatening and coercive or potentially coercive. Crises precede almost all wars, but not all crises lead to war. We can study a crisis from the perspective of a single state or of two or more states participating in the same confrontation. That we can view a crisis as a dependent, independent, or mediating variable, depending on our perspective, invites confusion (Allan, 1983:18).

Richard Smoke (1977:23–25) identified five possible sources of the tendency toward an escalation of conflictual and potentially violent reciprocations in crises and war: (1) a desire to win; (2) a desire not to lose; (3) a tendency by both sides to see the stakes increasing; (4) a tendency to define victory as a prerequisite for other objectives; and (5) a disposition to transcend for tactical reasons whatever constraints on action are seen to exist—the MacArthur proposal to attack supply bases in Manchuria during the Korean War, for example, or the U.S. bombing of Cambodian sanctuaries during the Vietnam War.

In simple behavioral terms, an international crisis amounts to an escalation of negative leverages. In cognitive, cybernetic, and action/reaction terms, crisis escalations come about in part because the leaders of one country, A, perceiving a gap between the nation's existing situation and their preferred state of affairs, expect a rewarding outcome from their action, X_1, which leaders of a rival country, B, perceive as opening a gap on their side (a threat or penalty of some kind). B's leaders consequently take some retaliatory action, X_2, by which they expect to close the gap (gaining some reward in the form of relief from A's punishing act). But B's response is perceived by the leaders of A as threatening, coercive, or otherwise punishing, whereupon they undertake action X_3, from which they expect to close the gap (gain reward in the form of relief from A's punishing act).

Again A's leaders see B's response as threatening, coercive, or otherwise punishing, whereupon they undertake action X_4, which they hope will deter B and thus bring relief as a reward or incentive. Or they may expect early changes in the crisis situation to be punishing but necessary enabling steps toward a more rewarding situation in the future. For example, by punishing Serbia in July 1914, Austro-Hungarian leaders expected to neutralize Serbian and Panslavic threats. Often the expectations of reward thus involve the avoidance or elimination of a punishing situation rather than the achievement of an outcome that might be intrinsically rewarding. Under pressure of intense interchange, each response is likely to be automatic and mindless, each move so swift as to appear reflexive. Oran Young (1968a:258) called attention to "test-of-strength" aspects of crisis interactions that often make the participants especially disposed toward communicating images of power, confidence, and resolution—and thus extremely reluctant to appear weak by dealing in an open and conciliatory mode or by taking the initiative in a forthright attempt to reach a settlement.

In sum, a crisis is likely to occur when at least one side perceives its security, immediate safety, or other vital interests threatened by an adversary. A crisis is likely to continue as long as the conceivable gains from further escalation are assessed by at least one side as preferable to the risks and costs of backing off or otherwise de-escalating. Being caught up in the anxiety of crisis, such a participant is likely to cling to its negative view of the other side, act (raise the ante) in order to contain or reverse the escalation, and interpret any positive messages from the adversary as a deception or a sign of weakness.

The playing out of the crisis is then strongly characterized by such factors as warnings, threats, hostile demonstrations, accommodations, concessions, and various other modes of communication and initiatives associated with bargaining and leverage strategies. In this connection, the question arises whether the military and industrial capabilities of adversarial powers have a significant effect upon the bargaining strategies and outcomes characterizing a crisis. When Anglo-German naval warfare exploded during World War I, considerable attention was focused on the possibility that the degree of reciprocity in crisis bargaining might be correlated in some way with the relative military and industrial capabilities of the adversaries. It is tempting to postulate that bargaining between adversaries of relatively equal capabilities may be more reciprocal in nature than bargaining between unevenly matched opponents. In a 1983 study, however, Russell Leng and Robert

Gochman (1979:232) found the relationship between parity and reciprocity to be weak, although they remained "reluctant to dismiss it out of hand, given findings in other studies."

Because they generate uncertainty, anxiety, fear, and other psychological pressures upon contending parties, crises contribute to shifts within the action/reaction process and to political realignments in the international system. The Berlin blockade (1948–1949) generated an intensification of interdependence among crisis participants along with perceptions by decisionmakers of a decline in their ability to control the course of events.

In an intense international crisis—the Cuban missile crisis of 1962, for example—deep feelings of tension, anxiety, anger, apprehension, or fear may penetrate all levels of society, including the press and the rank and file of the citizenry. Under extreme circumstances, even many avowed pacifists may become more belligerent. Thus, if individual attitudes toward positive and negative leverages within a society are envisaged along a distribution curve—from "dovish" on the left to "hawkish" on the right—we would expect that the more intense the perceptions of threat and possible attack from the outside, the stronger is the likelihood that the bias of the curve will shift in the "hawkish" direction. In a situation in which perceptions of threat are less widely shared, however, as in the United States during the Vietnam War, a bifurcation of the curve may occur; some previously complacent citizens may join the "doves," and others may reinforce the "hawks."

Participants in an action/reaction spiral, in seeking to avoid an escalation into war, commonly (but not universally) resort to some form of deterrence in an effort to "manage" the crisis. If the adversary backs down, the side that has applied deterrence is often said to have succeeded. If the adversary refuses to back down, the failure (and tendency toward escalation) is commonly attributed to insufficient capability or to poor crisis management. In most situations, however, the failure may also be explained in part by the adversary's decision to raise the ante (whatever the cost) rather than back down.

The tendency toward crisis escalation will be constrained by the relative capabilities and resolve (including the willingness to take risks and incur costs) of the participants. If the costs of continued escalation begin to exceed the expected advantage, either (or both) of the participants may decide to de-escalate or to withdraw. Otherwise, the crisis will probably escalate.

Insofar as the crisis continues, the higher the level of negative leverages, the greater is the probability that each side will view the other side as unprincipled, untrustworthy, hostile, aggressive, violent, barbarous, and bestial. As a result, the range of expectations tends to shrink; fewer and fewer possibilities seem plausible. Policymakers begin to feel that the future is closing in on them. This sense of a closing future—"the sense that the worst possibilities are the only ones to expect—then becomes its own additional source of anxiety" (Smoke, 1977:294–295). To the extent that policymakers are consciously sensitive to their feelings that time is "running out," they are less likely to recognize these feelings as their own psychic response to escalating exchanges of negative leverages than to something intrinsic to the intent and actions of the enemy. Such cognitive/affective tendencies may bias the course of crisis events in ways that the participants on both sides might have preferred to avoid. Schelling (1960:207–208) identified reciprocal lack of trust as a critical feature: "He thinks we think he thinks we think. . . . He thinks we think he will attack; so he thinks we shall; so he will; so we must."

In viewing the establishment of Soviet missiles in Cuba as a serious threat to U.S. containment policies, George and Smoke (1974:447–448) characterized the successful deployment of these missiles as "a major failure" of deterrence. According to the same criterion, however, Khrushchev's decision not to challenge Kennedy's naval blockade could be accepted as a classical instance of deterrence successfully applied—or even as the outcome of Khrushchev's good judgment.

Constraints on Crisis Escalation

As we would expect in an essentially plastic and equi- and multifinal situation, not all crises lead to war. "The analyst who undertakes a close examination of international crisis phenomena, in general," wrote Charles McClelland (1972:84), "faces the fundamental problem of accounting for the difference which would explain why many crises are begun and then abated, while some may lead on into war." From a simpleminded, but not irrelevant, perspective, for every crisis that escalates into war, there are many others that "cool down" or de-escalate. To the extent that both adversaries (or at least the more aggressive) perceive war risks and probable costs as outweighing the benefits, the crisis is likely to de-escalate.

This is essentially what happened during the Bosnian crisis of 1908–1909, when Russia—after a negative assessment of probable outcome resulting from its own lack of capability—backed off from military action against Austria-Hungary that might have triggered the war that actually broke out six years later. Thereafter, partly as an outcome of this sequence of events, Austro-Hungarian leaders assessed the probabilities of Russian intervention as lower than they otherwise might have, whereas some of the tsar's advisers were determined to avoid further indignity and reestablish the credibility of their own leverage potential (two opposing dispositions that fueled the crisis of 1914). This outcome contrasts with the Cuban missile crisis (a somewhat similar situation), in which Khrushchev's willingness to back off opened the way to (temporarily) improved relations between the USSR and the United States.

We can often attribute crisis de-escalation to relatively rational decision-making resulting from a comparison of the bargaining power of the adversaries. In an action/reaction process, the greater the bargaining strength of an initiating actor, the higher is likely to be the conflict level of the adversary up to which the first actor will escalate, and the higher will be the initiator's response level. Such response will become weaker, however, as the adversary's conflict level approaches the high point established by the initiating actor. Thereafter, the crisis activities of the adversary may de-escalate. A tendency toward de-escalation may result also from fears generated in both parties by the intensity of conflict, rather than from either side's evaluation of the opponent's capabilities or intentions (Allan, 1983:47–49). Conversely, an actor may confront a security dilemma: If the actor issues an accommodative bid (switches to positive leverage as a peace incentive), the adversary may take advantage of the bid as a sign of weakness or act preemptively, perceiving it as a deception. Assured de-escalation requires that *both sides* see the risk and costs of a continuing crisis outweighing probable benefits.

The Prisoner's Dilemma

A two-player, one-move-each, mixed motive or non-zero-sum "game" (one player's gain need not require a loss by the other), Prisoner's Dilemma is often cited as a way of clarifying arms race dynamics and conflict escalation. As in a crisis situation, each player would like to escape from a difficult situation with the least possible "cost" (or the greatest possible advantage) (Tedeschi, Schlenker, and Bonoma, 1973:16–17).

When used by theorists in the field of international politics, the "lesson" that is often emphasized as an instructive game theoretical analogy for the study of crisis is the lack of mutual trust generated by players who, in a high-stress milieu, cannot communicate with each other. But the game also elucidates problems of rational choice (cf. Rapoport, 1960:173 and Rosenberg, 1988:103–105). As Anatole Rapoport anecdotally illustrated, a district attorney—lacking enough evidence for conviction—separately questions two suspects whom he knows to be guilty and who are both convictable for a lesser offense. He presents to each of them, A and B, options with the following outcomes: If both confess, both get severe sentences that are reducible because of confession. If one confesses and turns state's evidence, the informer goes free whereas the other "gets the book." If neither confesses, both will be convicted for their lesser offenses.

What will (should) A and B do? If A could be sure that B would "stand his ground," A would, too. But if B were not to confess, why should not A do so and "go scot free"? Beyond this, A reasons, "no matter what B does, I am better off confessing. If he does confess, I would be a chump not to and take the whole rap. . . . If he doesn't, I stand to gain by confessing. . . . Either way you look at it, I am better off if I sing." The problem is that B may reason the same way, in which case both end up with a "somewhat commuted severe sentence," whereas, if they were to trust each other's "underworld" concept of integrity, they would end up with mild sentences for a misdemeanor.

Although the Prisoner's Dilemma "game" is widely cited in arms race and crisis escalation literature, it tends to obscure personal responsibility in international crisis situations and is analogically misleading on three counts: (1) the district attorney, a third party (with physical control over the other two), dictates the options and outcomes, whereas in international arms races and crises, the parties interactively generate their own options and shape their own outcomes; (2) although the prisoners are held wholly incommunicado by the district attorney, the two countries, through their leaders, ultimately control their own communications or lack thereof; and (3) whereas the prisoners are limited to one move each without possibilities for drawing inferences from the other's behavior, participants in arms races and crisis escalations (even if not speaking) are exchanging actions sequentially. A mode of communication, a series of reciprocations very precisely create the process we are seeking to understand. These considerations are taken into account by Robert Axelrod (1984:92–95, 109–110) in developing tit for tat as a strategy for reducing conflict.

From these considerations we are forced to conclude that action/reaction processes involve psychological considerations different from and significantly more complex than the dilemma of the two prisoners, who each make one judgment in their "crisis" (within the purview of the game). National leaders, through sequential reciprocations, not only create (jointly) their own sequences of choice points but also, with each interchange, create the parameters of the next option set. In these terms, Smoke (1977:278) described each escalation as undertaken on the basis of expectations likely to be at least partly unknown by the party who undertook it. As a consequence, each side's field of expectation "shifts with the leverage of every escalation," and each side's Plan is partially hidden from the sight of the other but is also changeable in response to the other's last move. Misinterpreting their respective feedbacks, each side may minimize its own contributions to the escalation and maximize the contributions of the adversary. What we see are the security dilemma and its corollary activated in sequences of such potentially high intensity that in a worst-case analysis, neither trust nor rationality is likely to be recovered until one side or the other (or both) is exhausted or overcome.

War as Ultimate Leverage

According to Clausewitz (1943:596–599), wherever war breaks out, policy has created it. Yet in some cases, war seems to occur (or not to occur) in spite of policy or (in line with the paradoxes of deterrence and crisis) contrary to the original intentions of the participants. Although some adversaries appear to be swept into war by intense interchanges of an action/reaction process, such an outcome is not predetermined. Despite innumerable assertions in history books and political science texts, war is never inevitable. For every crisis that escalates to war, there are others that cool off or de-escalate (and also wars that occur without a clearly ascertainable crisis). In principle, there is always a choice, however unpleasant. But how can the difference be explained? How is the balance between war and no war tipped?

In reaching for "a general history of war and foreign conflict initiation and escalation," Bruce Bueno de Mesquita (1981b:ix, 28) used expected utility concepts to put decisions for war under a microscope, so to speak, and thus "to distinguish between systemic patterns and incidental occurrences related to war." He sought to explain why under certain circumstances each of the many contradictory statements about war initiation may be supported. Given the problem that Bueno de Mesquita was trying to solve, his approach was rigorous, parsimonious, and elegant. But as he fully conceded, there were trade-offs not easily avoided, including some fundamental aspects of decisionmaking that he purposely excluded.

The first explanatory element Bueno de Mesquita (1981b:47–48) used in his theory is the difference or gap between actor A's utility for his or her preferred view of the world and A's utility for the policy of the adversary, B. Other elements include A's perception of what might be gained by succeeding in a conflict with B in which A can then impose new policies on B; A's perception of what might be lost by failing in a bilateral contest in which B might impose new policies on A; B's perception of how much B would seek to alter A's policy in the future compared with B's current perceived policy differences with A; A's current perception of the probability of succeeding against B; and A's current perception of losing to B.

Bueno de Mesquita derived his theory from the following propositions.

1. War decisionmaking is dominated by a single strong leader.
2. Leaders are rational, expected-utility maximizers.
3. Differences in leaders' orientations toward risk-taking influence decisionmaking.
4. Uncertainty about the likely behavior of other states in the advent of war affects decisionmaking.
5. The power a state can use in war declines as the site of the war becomes geographically distant from the nation.

This is a bold start, but in developing his theory Bueno de Mesquita wisely qualified these five propositions. He recognized, for example, that the "strong" or "key" leader, acting as a "gatekeeper," may be advised by cabinet members, advisers, and specialized staff, but emphasized that he or she assumes the "ultimate responsibility" of approving or disapproving an option to go to war.

In identifying the "strong" leader as a "rational expected-utility maximizer," Bueno de Mesquita also "softened" the concept of rationality. Given a set of goals, for example, a rational actor will choose the option that maximizes his or her expected utility. Thus, according to Bueno de Mesquita's perspective, Adolf Hitler can be treated as a rational actor because his goals as well as the logic of the actions he took to reach those goals can be judged as rational or irrational. Also, contrary to commonplace concepts of rationality, Bueno de Mesquita asserts, two or more rational actors may sustain quite different preference orderings and therefore act differently under similar circumstances. Choices between war and peace, moreover, are made as if to maximize not only the welfare of the strong leader, but also the "welfare of those at whose pleasure the leader remains in a position of leadership" (1981b:28).

So far so good, but if Hitler, Churchill, and Roosevelt were all rational actors (because their goals and actions can be judged as rational or irrational), how useful is the concept of rationality for explaining differences between their policies and actions? Suppose a critic were to decide that one or another of these leaders was irrational. What difference would this make in the explanations or predictions?

Sources of Irrationality

Depending on one's definition of rationality, there are at least three possible sources of "irrationality" in any national decision: (1) The ultimate decisionmaker cannot escape filtering information through his or her cognitive and affective systems, assessing capabilities subjectively (especially when sources are in disagreement) and calculating risks subjectively, regardless of how many statisticians, specialists, and experts are advising the decisionmaker or how many computers are used; (2) advisers, bureaucrats, information gatherers and assessors, military men, and others are all subject to comparable influences (and are sometimes inclined, perhaps quite unconsciously, to report and advise what they think their superiors expect or want to be told, especially if the boss is a Hitler or a Stalin); and (3) all information filtered through organizational levels, from individuals through one coalition to another, whether "vertically" or "horizontally," is subject to selection and interpretation according to the "logic," "organizational rationality," interests, and purposes of each level (in addition to the "subjective rationality" of every individual selector, interpreter, and evaluator involved).

With regard to uncertainty and risk-taking, according to Bueno de Mesquita, not all rational actors respond to the same information in the same way, one reason being that "each individual has his own tastes and preferences" (1981b:33). A risk-averse leader, moreover, will be less likely to make a decision for war than a risk-prone leader—a useful reminder but almost a truism within Herbert Simon's concept of "subjective rationality."

There are other issues along similar lines. Utility, according to Bueno de Mesquita, is determined by the "congruence of policy ends" between states. In this connection the probability of either side's success in a contest with the other is a "direct, positive function of each relevant nation's power compared to that of each other relevant nation" (1981b:29–30). All thing being equal (and Bueno de Mesquita concedes that all things are not always equal), a state has a higher probability of winning over a weaker nation than it does over a stronger. But if individual, "rational" leaders often assess the same phenomena differently, as Bueno de Mesquita clearly recognizes, then their assessments of their own capabilities and those of their adversaries (especially if "softer" capabilities such as national will are admitted) will be highly subjective and susceptible to the influences of belief, hostility, anxiety, fear, and the need to attract and bolster support from cabinet members, staff, and even the general public.

These considerations are not meant to denigrate an innovative, imaginative, and challenging theory. But once Bueno de Mesquita had opened the door to Popper's "cloud-like" phenomena, these phenomena themselves became a theoretical challenge that cannot be wished away. In the long run, if this challenge is picked up, Bueno de Mesquita's theory as a whole is likely to be strengthened—with a consequent increase in its congruence with the "realities" of war and peace decisionmaking and a reduction of the distance between his "model" and what are often thought of as the "softer" concepts of Jervis (1970 and 1971) and other more "psychologically" (and/or less "quantitatively") oriented theoreticians in the field. In the long run, a general theory will require the integration of both "hard" and "soft" variables (for assessments of the problem see Bueno de Mesquita, 1985a and b, Krasner, 1985, and Jervis, 1985). The conclusion to be drawn from these considerations is that the intricacies of conflict processes leading to war are pervasive, elusive, and difficult to integrate into what Bueno de Mesquita referred to as a "general theory." In this regard, the main wars of this century provide ample evidence.

Documents of the 1914 crisis that led into World War I reveal Austro-Hungarian, German, British, and French decisionmakers in almost hourly sessions with their cabinet members and with their political and military advisers. Historians have characterized Tsar Nicholas II as weak and vacillating, Kaiser Wilhelm II as arrogant, stubborn, impulsive, and wavering. Both were often at odds with their ministers and military advisers, and decisionmaking in major European capitals was less the outcome of clear-cut national interests than of a confusion of leverages undertaken by anxious, arrogant, and often bumbling diplomats and heads of state in pursuit of shortsighted concerns and expectations. For these reasons, the Cyert and March approach to group decisionmaking as bargaining and leverage for the formation of a coalition in support of a particular option, however poorly defined, appears to have advantages over Bueno de Mesquita's strong leader assumption in the analysis of decisions for war.

Directions in the pushing and hauling within national leaderships during the summer of 1914 were influenced by events in the international environment. Following Gavrilo Princip's assassination of Austro-Hungarian Archduke Francis Ferdinand, the escalation accelerated. Austria-Hungary was bent on "punishing" Serbia through what it envisaged as a localized war. Great Britain urged mediation. Russia ordered, canceled, and reordered a general mobilization in support of Serbia. The British Admiralty dispatched a standard "warning telegraph" to the fleet. Germany proclaimed a "state of imminent danger of war." Great Britain decided that if Germany and France were to declare war, Great Britain would be drawn in, but it made no commitment to France. Belgium ordered a general mobilization. Austria-Hungary called up remaining Imperial Army corps and activated the militia. France ordered general mobilization. Germany ordered mobilization minutes later and ordered troops into position along eastern and western fronts. Churchill mobilized the British Fleet. Turkey mobilized. On learning from his ambassador in London that Great Britain was about to make him a proposal for resolving the crisis, the kaiser ordered champagne. King George sent a telegram, received at midnight in Berlin, asserting that the German ambassador had been misinformed, that the situation would be clarified in the morning.

We often attribute more coherence and cold-blooded calculation to decisions for war than history will support. Insofar as Kaiser Wilhelm II had a coherent policy, it surely had something to do with German hopes of succeeding to British hegemony. Around midnight (August 1–2, 1914), disconcerted by his cousin George's telegram (and after painful hours of irresolution), Wilhelm decided to mobilize German forces and, in accordance with the Schlieffen Plan, to march through Belgium and attack France (as well as Russia, France's ally to the east). Deeply agitated, standing "in vest and underpants, with a mantle thrown over his shoulders and withered arm," he faced his chief of staff Helmuth von Moltke. Already a victim of lesser events triggered by Princip, a little-known Serbian terrorist with objectives of his own, the kaiser, tired and disturbed by his cousin's failure to send a concrete proposal, told Moltke, "Now you can do what you like" (Bülow, 1931:165). In coming to this decision, the kaiser scribbled in the margin of a document the warning that if Germany were "to be bled to death," he would see to it that Great Britain would "at least lose India."

Immersed in rationalization and self-justification, adversaries often cling, or are blind to, the deeper roots of their own antagonisms and behavior. With the outbreak of war, Prince Bernhard von Bülow asked Chancellor Theobald von Bethmann Hollweg, "Well, tell me at last how it all happened." The chancellor "raised his long, thin arms to heaven and answered in a dull, exhausted voice, 'Oh—if I only knew'" (Bülow, 1931:165). The question today is as pertinent as it was then: "How could a second-rate Balkan plot set off a first-rate catastrophe?" (Remak, 1967:60).

Patterns of decision were different in World War II, but they were, if anything, more problematical. Hitler, who on paper exercised absolute power if anyone did, and Stalin, whose power was nearly absolute, used carrots (grants of privilege, immunity, power) and sticks to get mindless compliance and whatever advice, active support, and life-or-death loyalty they wanted or needed from their henchmen—although the counsel they received was often overridden and scorned. According to Paul Kennedy (1987:306) (and contrary to many assumptions at the time), National Socialist decisionmaking was "quite chaotic" in structure, a condition that Hitler appeared to encourage in order to maintain his own ultimate authority. Hitler was a chronic opportunist who did not hesitate to reverse his goals and policies when a new and seemingly favorable option presented itself. Neither Hitler nor Stalin was reluctant to use threats, imprisonment, exile, or death as leverage against high-ranking party and government officials.

In Japan, the military-civilian oligarchy responsible for the Pearl Harbor decision wavered for months—some proposing a northern expedition against the USSR, others advocating a southern thrust to seize oil and other vital raw materials in Southeast Asia. The constraint against moving north was a lack of raw materials, which could not be picked up during a drive against Irkutsk. The risk against a southern thrust was the near certainty that the United States would launch a strike against Japan's eastern flank. Ultimately, the attack on Pearl Harbor was undertaken—with deep misgivings—as a preemptive measure (Ike, 1967:199–207, 260–262). (We can only speculate what outcome a Japanese "march to Irkutsk" might have produced.)

Many, if not most of these idiosyncracies of leadership are difficult to analyze or predict. Nevertheless, such arationalities, irrationalities, and random disturbances need to be allowed for in second and third image theories and models—or at least when findings are interpreted.

Hegemonic War

In this book our overall approach to war has been generic—that is, we have considered differential capability, expansionist, negative leverage, and disequilibrium functions relevant for explaining the outbreak of any international war regardless of the size, intents, or other particular attributes of the participating states. In recent years, however, theorists have paid a great deal of attention to a particular type of war—the hegemonic war—which derives from hegemonic stability theory (as discussed in Chapter 6). Some theoreticians of hegemony have tried (with indifferent success) to connect hegemonic change and hegemonic war with economic waves, or long cycles. (We will touch upon that in Chapter 8. Our concern here is with hegemonic stability theory.)

As indicated in Chapter 6, hegemonic stability theorists propose that if neither the declining hegemon nor those states constituting its security regime can respond effectively to the "dissatisfied" and "overtaking" challenger nation, the resulting disequilibrium will be resolved by force through a hegemonic war. Depending upon two critical variables—dissatisfaction and relative power—this theory is both parsimonious and logically persuasive, but does it stand up empirically? Conditions pertaining to the outbreak of World Wars I and II provide a simple test.

Presumably, World War I occurred when Great Britain, the declining hegemon, proved unable to balance commitments and resources effectively enough to restore "equilibrium" to the system (see Chapter 9 for further discussion). War broke out, and the disequilibrium was resolved by force (in favor of the hegemon and its security regime) (Keohane, 1984:103–106, 175, 195ff.; Gilpin, 1981:188–189). There are problems with this analysis, however. Depending on which set of data we use, the United States (not Germany) should have been the challenger (or possibly even the hegemon). If we use GNP as a rough indicator of power, for example, the United States prior to the outbreak of World War I was already the second (if not the first) most powerful country in the system. Why, then, did not the United States (as challenger) fight Great Britain (as hegemon)? Keohane's conclusion that a member of the incumbent hegemon's "regime" can challenge and accede without resorting to force may be relevant here. But if so, then why was not the United States, rather than Great Britain, the target for Germany (as challenger) in 1914 and again in 1939?

From these observations, we conclude that although contributing to international conflict, a power transition is not necessarily sufficient to explain a hegemonic (or for that matter any other) war. Dissatisfaction (or hostility) and power may be the most parsimonious (and for some purposes sufficient) variables for explaining an outbreak of war, but these data by themselves do not predict (or account for) the identity of the adversaries involved. But power combined with activities and interests can go a long way toward prediction and explanation of war, whether or not hegemony is at issue. Perceived threat and violence, in short, tend to induce further threat and violence between actors on any organizational level from the first image through the fourth.

So far we have been concerned with the first three images—the individual, the state, and the international system—and the characteristic ways in which they are "nested" and interact with each other. Chapter 8 will show how these three images fit into, interact with, and depend upon the fourth image, the global system.

PART 4

Fourth Image:
The Global System

8

The Structure of the Global System

So far we have examined the nesting of three images—the individual, the nation, and the international system. In this chapter, reversing the perspective of earlier ones, we approach the global system and its components "from above"—as if we were riding an observation satellite with the whole planet and its people spread out beneath us—in order to consider how the first three images "fit into" and interact with the fourth, or global, image.

Our intent in this chapter is threefold: (1) to see how a growing world population characterized by expanding knowledge and skills and multiplying demands for resources (and services) and acting in pursuit and defense of their interests contribute to a *globalization* process that affects the planetary environment and the living beings dependent upon it; (2) to determine how processes of the natural environment and actions and interactions of the global population combine to constrain and facilitate human pursuits and interests; and (3) to examine how much we contribute to our most threatening problems by the ways we deal with the natural environment and with each other. In recent times, at an exponential rate, our spectacular interventions into and transformation of the natural environment have made our lives easier, healthier, longer, and in many respects much more rewarding. But with advances in scientific knowledge and skills we are also increasingly aware of our dependence upon the finely tuned, ever-fluctuating natural forces that allow us to live on the planet. Concurrently, moreover, our unprecedented successes reveal rising costs in damage to natural and social environments. We increasingly perceive that in pursuing new equilibria we create new and troublesome disequilibria. Some people advocate establishment of a world government to bring order to the planet.

High-tech lenses in our observation satellite magnify the global topography and reveal astonishing details, but there are no national boundaries to be seen. Fortunately, we have a late-twentieth-century computerized *Baedeker* to help us understand what goes on below. Our purpose is to piece together what we already know about the global system and what we can gain from observing it as a whole.

Is the Fourth Image Necessary?

The idea of global governance is not new. During the last six or seven centuries, more than one hundred international "peace plans" and proposals for world government have been formulated—some of them providing for a global kingdom, empire, federation, or world parliament. Of known designs for the uniting of nations, only two—the League of Nations and the United Nations—have been implemented with some degree of success, but neither qualifies as a world government. As indicated in earlier chapters, the global system today is a more encompassing environment than a world government would be.

George Modelski (1972:42–46) developed the concept of globalization as the process through which "a number of historical world societies were brought together in one global system." Fixing the "opening" of the process at "about 1000 A.D.," he identified the Muslim world following the Arab conquests of the seventh century as the nearest approximation of a worldwide political order in the ancient past. But Modelski saw Portuguese and Spanish navigators initiating the major drive during the Age of Discovery by extending communications around the world and preparing the way for others.

In developing a "structural theory of imperialism," Johan Galtung (1971) characterized the modern world—derived in large part from colonial relationships and the industrial revolution—in terms of global divisions of labor between what he identified as core states (producing secondary manufactured goods) and periphery nations (producing primary raw materials), each with its own domestic contradictions and conflicts. In addition, Galtung identified "go-between" nations exchanging "semi-processed goods with highly processed goods upwards and semi-processed goods with raw materials downwards" (Mexico, Argentina, and Brazil "going between" the U.S. and Central America, South Korea and Taiwan going between Japan and Southeast Asia) (1971:104). He saw such "semiperiphery" nations as "one cycle behind the Center as to technology but one cycle ahead of the Periphery as to degree of processing" (1971:104). While generalizing to three classes (center, go-between, and periphery), Galtung saw also the possibility of generalization to continuous chain (or network) linkages, "which would then serve for considerable distance between the extreme Center and the extreme Periphery" (1971:105).[1]

Another political economist working with global (rather than state) economic aggregates, Immanuel Wallerstein (1984:38, 85), developed the idea that capitalism had been a world-system from its start. Under capitalism, economic development had created each of the three zones—core, semi-periphery, and periphery—each with its own mode of production and form of labor (wage earners, serfs, and slaves). Wallerstein's essentially neo-Marxist approach differed from classical Marxism in that his focus was on international (rather than domestic) contradictions and struggles. He saw core states competing among themselves for economic advantage and expanding and contracting in long waves, or boom-and-bust, cycles (Bergesen, 1983:9–17).

World-system specialists do not have a monopoly on wave, or cycle, theory, however. Nicolai Kondratieff, whose book *The Long Wave Cycle* became something of a classic, was a pioneer in the field. According to Kondratieff (1984), whose concern was essentially economic, overinvestment in an economic upswing leads to a downswing and capital depreciation and thence to a reinvestment upswing. Subsequently, several European scholars applied cycle, or wave, concepts to warfare initiation. In their view, war-generated inflation and/or gold production, which shocks the economy, creates long waves resulting from or otherwise connected with major wars. More recently, numbers of theorists have looked for correlations among economic cycles (waves), the rise and fall of hegemons, and hegemonic and other major wars. The results have been ambiguous.

Since the two world wars, the global concept has been invoked with increasing frequency by the United Nations, national leaders and bureaucrats, the media, and academics. This invocation has taken the form of discussion about global population, world resources, world economy, world trade, the World Bank, the World Conference on AIDS, problems of world ecology, world culture, and world order. There has been talk of a global "village" emerging from and contributing to global consciousness.

We think that globalization began long before Arab expansionism. Earlier chapters have indicated how human beings in early prehistoric times saw themselves as a part of nature, but later, with enhanced technologies, they began to accept themselves as nature's master. Much the same is true of our adaptations to natural processes on earth. Our hunting and gathering ancestors depended upon the riches of the planet for survival, but their interventions in nature were necessarily limited by the level of their knowledge and skills. They had no choice but to adjust themselves to and seize what advantages they could from winds, rains, tides, climate, and other planetary functions and features. Today, however, because of vast increases in population and spectacular advances in technology, we have intervened in ways that affect natural features and processes and, in combination with them, accomplish feats that even our recent forebears could not have imagined. We increasingly make use of natural laws to achieve new ends, but they do not come free of cost. In our efforts at co-opting natural forces to enhance our capabilities, we find ourselves contributing to outcomes we do not intend. For centuries, we proceeded as if we were out to conquer nature. Today, with an increasingly global perspective, we begin to recognize ourselves again as creatures of nature.

Global Theory for the Twenty-First Century

Let us suppose that since starting this chapter we have ridden the observation satellite several thousand miles in a circumnavigation of the earth. Our itinerary takes us around and around in an ever-changing orbit much the way a string wraps around and around the core of a baseball. This way we view the whole earth from many different vantage points, but so far we have seen mostly water. Forty-five minutes ago we left the North

Pole, traveling "south" (is there any other direction from that pole?) over the Diomede Islands in the Bering Strait, where U.S. and Soviet territories are within sight of each other. Then we moved along a bearing that approximates the international date line but allows us to veer a trifle to the southwest. After bypassing the South Pole on our left, we plan to steer a trifle northwestward over the western bulge of Africa and on toward Greenland.

Baedeker informs us that of the earth's total surface of approximately 197,000,000 square miles, a whopping *70.8 percent* is ocean—its depths and floor are still largely unexplored but are known to be rich in resources. Aided by spectacular graphics beyond the imagination of *Baedeker* readers of the past, the computerized "handbook" demonstrates to us through maps and animations the extent to which we all depend for our existence and well-being upon the earth and the planetary system of which it is a component. In combination, the whole and even the minutest parts constitute the natural and social environments that constrain and help to shape us and that we act upon and alter. Viewing the earth from above (with *Baedeker's* visual aids), we can comprehend better how the four images interact.

If from the observation satellite our sweeping view of the earth infuses us with a momentary sense of power, awe, and omniscience, the vastness and laws of space remind us of nature's dominion. Newly acquired understandings of natural forces have enabled us to hitch this ride into orbit, but viewing the world from up here reminds us of how dependent we are upon nature (take away the planet and where are we?) and how complex the interactivities are between ourselves and the natural environment. Because of our knowledge of natural forces, we can circle the planet, but we still have to obey nature's basic laws.

Baedeker is programmed to brief us on some of the relevant issues: how our demands increase with our numbers, how we depend upon energy in its many natural forms, and how our advancing skills in transforming and applying energy have revolutionized our capacities, our dependence upon resources, our ways of living, and our self-images—but always at a price. One of nature's cost accountants is the second law of thermodynamics, which reminds us that although basic energy cannot be "consumed" or "destroyed," neither can resources be used nor "work" performed (actions taken) without some measure of energy degradation from more usable to less usable (and often toxic) forms. The consequences are twofold. First, the greater the use of natural resources in a given environment, the greater are likely to be the costs (in terms of local depletions and/or degradations) and the greater the disposition to find substitutions or explore other environments. Some resources are potentially renewable (forests, for example), provided we facilitate renewal. Second, the greater the amount and the wider the range of resources used, the greater is the production of wastes in general (garbage, trash, junk) and the higher is the risk of toxic consequences (direct, as when fumes or other ingested residues contribute to cancer or other diseases, or indirect, as when wastes alter the natural environment in ways that endanger human health). Yet we can adapt to the second law of thermodynamics through creative initiatives.

Feeling it too early in our voyage to confront such dismal considerations, we call up *ecosystem*, which has a more cheerful connotation. Here *Baedeker* is eloquent and brightly graphic. Together with their physical surroundings, we can see the plants, animals, and people in any part of the world as an ecosystem characterized by biocenosis (self-regulation). Different species, through their diversities, activities, and mutual correlations, induce circulation of energy and matter. Underlying *all* living activities on earth is an inter-dependent, delicately balanced economy requiring genetic diversity. Loss of this natural diversity could damage the ecosystem in ways threatening to human welfare throughout the globe.

As our first orbit carries us over the mid-Pacific, the satellite's observation equipment enables us to identify a sulphurous smog obscuring a wide expanse of ocean below us. We punch CO_2 into *Baedeker,* which identifies carbon dioxide emissions as the principal factor in changing the earth's atmosphere. Later, as the satellite approaches south polar regions, we enter *ozone*, which is immediately cross-referenced to *pollutants, nitrous oxides, methane,* and *chlorofluorocarbons.*

Even minor alterations in nature's dynamic but delicate biocenosis—a rise or decline of a relatively few degrees in the world's average temperature, for example—could strain or destroy the human order. From this perspective, all life seems disturbingly fragile. To pursue a dynamic equilibrium between global benefits and costs requires the knowledge, skills, sensitivities, and intuitive responses of a bird in flight among mountainous crags and down-drafts. The issue is, To what extent do human activities amplify the benign forces of nature and/or exacerbate those aspects of nature that threaten our well-being and possibly the survival of our own and other species? In this regard, we recall recent predictions of possible greenhouse effects and, at an opposite extreme, the warning that a global nuclear war might produce a devastating, worldwide nuclear winter. Question: What would be the effect of a worldwide nuclear war within a global greenhouse?

As we peer through a port of our observation satellite, the questions we want answered seem simple. How much of all that goes on down there is done by nature? How much by human beings? How much by people and nature conjunctively? More specifically, we want to distinguish among those global outcomes that for all practical purposes are beyond human control; those over which human control is partial; and (3) those for which humans are primarily, or wholly, responsible.

Fourth Image Structures

During our earthly orbits, as we speed our way over continents as well as oceans, we are struck by nature's global distributions—plains, mountain ranges, river systems, inland seas, to say nothing of flora and fauna. With its specialized equipment, the satellite maps not only the earth's topography but the location of metals, minerals, and other valuable resources beneath the surface. Unevenness in growth and development (resulting in part from natural resources distributions) contributes to an international system of states of radically different "sizes," profiles, and distributional capabilities. How we live depends to a considerable extent upon where we live.

We can identify the global structure in terms of two sets of distribution processes—natural and social. Natural distributions include geographical features, climate, weather, locations of natural resources such as flora and fauna. Social distributions (resulting from competition and bargaining and leverage within and between states, domestic allocations made by governments, reallocations imposed by victors after a war, and so forth) are determined by humans, even though we are offspring of natural forces.

In pursuit of resources and other "needs," wants, and demands, we humans "work" on all four image levels and move, distribute, redistribute, transform, and degrade resources. To a large extent, however, we do this through organizations—some "private" (stores, firms, industries, trading companies, and so forth) and some "public" (governments and government agencies, which regulate our activities, represent us abroad, and protect our national borders and our external, and generally expanding, activities and interests). Because nations are characterized by uneven growth and development, however, and by distinct size and capability profiles, their interactions on the third image level affect global distributions unevenly in terms of which products are produced where they are in demand.

Distribution patterns are constrained and otherwise influenced also by interactivities between social and natural activities (soil erosion caused in part by deforestation, overgrazing by domestic livestock, acid rain, damage to the air or ozone layer caused by humanly contrived operations *and* by air currents). Such distributions (lateral pressures) are directly traceable to the growth of human populations, the advancement of their technologies (including organizations), and their search for resources. The three great "engines" empowering these distributions (and related activities) are (1) the cumulative private activities (undertaken by individuals, commercial and industrial firms, and other organizations); (2) the activities of individual states; and (3) the impacts of the third image—resulting from interplays among all the world's states—on the global system. These distributions and impacts operate across national borders and register outside the international system and its formal jurisdictions—reaching into the ocean and its depths, penetrating the atmosphere, and expanding into outer space.

One way of dealing with distributions in terms of their social, economic, political, and military significance is to locate them, nation by nation (as in the profiles of Chapter 5) in percentages (or "shares") of global totals. How much of the world's territory, population, resources, production, and war casualties does each country "control"? Where are the concentrations? Where are the scarcities? What are the implications and outcomes of such distributions? In what ways are patterns changing? Why, how, and with what consequences?

Viewed from our observation satellite, we can envisage high-pressure "centers" within and among societies. These centers expand, penetrate, and often dominate low-pressure "peripheries" and intersect and sometimes collide with other high-pressure "centers"—all within circumscription of global boundaries. Or, from the perspective of terra firma, uneven growth and development within and between national concentrations (of population, technology, and resources) generate *transitions of power$_1$ and power$_2$* not only among core states in the hegemonic, King of the Mountain game, but among all states competing in the global system—each pursuing its own vision of social, economic, political, and strategic security. In these terms, alpha, beta, gamma, and delta nations constitute the developed world; the developing epsilon, zeta, and eta countries are strung along the "mountain" slopes, each struggling according to its own capacity, some overtaking and passing others, a few pushing ahead in spurts, others falling behind. At any given time, some are trying to dominate, block, dislodge, injure, or destroy others that they construe as adversaries. Some, such as Taiwan and South Korea, appear to be well along toward transforming themselves from epsilon to beta or gamma profiles. Since the late 1930s, social (as distinct from natural) distributions have been attributable to three interactive "event systems": World War II and its immediate outcomes, the cold war, and the uneven growth, development, and competitions among all of the world's states.

Human Agents of Distribution

Earlier chapters have shown how wars of the past have contributed to the emergence, rise, decline, and evolution of states, ancient agrarian empires, commercial city-states, agrocommercial nation-states (and derivative empires), and the international system—all manifestations of major redistributions of one kind or another. World War I challenged the centuries-old great power system of nation-states-transformed-into-empires and effected redistributions that appeared cataclysmic at the time but turned out to be only a preliminary shake-up as compared with World War II.

The 1945 end of hostilities marked a major historical transition and the opening of a new era, the shape of which is only now beginning to emerge. Within a few years, remaining overseas empires of the past were dismembered, and new nations emerged. The movement of these old colonies toward independence was facilitated by the United Nations and its member states, which established a monitored trusteeship system to assist the new nations in achieving self-government. But revolutions in countries of the periphery also played a major role, and global events and future expectations everywhere were conditioned by the inescapable reality of humanity's first nuclear war over Japan.

Life went on, but with some rapid and major alterations. Postwar distributions depended in large part upon where the victorious troops were when hostilities ended and what the strongest victors wanted. Almost overnight certain allies became enemies, and yesterday's enemies became today's new friends—an ancient story. A world of many new states, new national boundaries, new economies, new polities, new conflicts, new diplomacy, and new strategies was emerging—a world that appeared to be increasingly riven and off balance. Occupying vastly extended lines at war's end, Soviet and Western forces confronted each other from the Barents Sea to the Dardanelles, in China, and wherever their vessels passed at sea. In global terms, however, the activities, interests, and power outreach of the United States and its emerging international regime were the farthest extended.

Post–World War II international politics was largely shaped by the cold war, which was manifested by economic, political, psychological, military, and covert competition among the expanding activities and interests of the United States, the USSR, and their respective allies, clients, and international regimes. Preeminent among global actors during these years were the United States, now the acknowledged hegemon, and the USSR, the prime challenger. Playing a King of the Mountain game throughout the cold war years, these two superpowers (and their international regimes) competed, or struggled, for advantage while developing countries tried to accomplish in decades what the industrial nations had required centuries to achieve. Many of these weaker players were, and still are, severely constrained. The less developed their technologies, the narrower were the possibilities for product substitution, favorable trade, and the accumulation of surpluses required for modernization. Despite these and other constraints, the economic and social fabrics of many developing nations, already deeply penetrated by industrialized nations, changed with blurring rapidity as modernization accelerated. During these years, several traditional, formerly vulnerable agrarian societies achieved diversified economies with interactive agricultural, commercial, and industrial sectors (but often not without severe environmental costs). In view of such successes, the failures were all the more striking.

During the postwar years, the United States, through the Marshall Plan, the Point Four Program, and the establishment of NATO, rendered large-scale aid to Western European nations and to Third World regions of the globe. Among U.S. purposes were (1) to rebuild Western European nations into a market strong enough to absorb U.S. exports and thus stave off a postwar depression; (2) forestall the expansion of Soviet influence; (3) generate economic growth and development in the Third World; (4) prevent the Third World from moving into the Soviet orbit; and (5) rebuild Japan in order to ensure Japanese access to Asian resources and markets and block Soviet penetration of the Japanese islands. In those days, the United States possessed a near monopoly of nuclear weaponry, world monetary reserves, and petroleum.

The position of the USSR was difficult to assess. At the time of the Bolshevik Revolution, Russia, in spite of a growing industrial capacity in major cities west of the Ural Mountains, was still a developing country with relatively small bourgeois and proletarian classes (the principal contenders, theoretically, in a proletarian revolution). Because Marx had expected "proletarian" revolutions to erupt in advanced capitalist countries, Leninist leaders and their Stalinist successors were forced to combine ad hoc development programs with bureaucratic practices held over from the tsarist past. In succeeding decades, the results were mixed at best, especially with respect to agriculture.

Despite reasonably steady growth since World War II, the USSR, being especially weak in agricultural production, trade, and finance, has been unable to overtake the United States and has remained in part "an under-developed country." The rigidity of its five-year plans made it difficult for the Soviet Union to take advantage of trade opportunities, the quality of Soviet goods was often not competitive, the regime played almost no role in the international financial system, and the nonconvertibility of the ruble further separated the country from the global economy. The specialized sector of notable Soviet growth was the military.

Soviet trade and trade per capita were also constrained by the characteristics of the command economy. In regard to some resources, the USSR was self-sufficient; in others it was not. Much of its trade with other countries was arranged through barter agreements, the sale of gold, or reliance on dollars or other so-called hard currencies. The arms trade became a sphere of rapid expansion. In the meantime, Lenin's vision of world revolution and his understanding of revolutionary dynamics served as powerful but not decisive instruments in the hands of Stalin and his successors.

Concurrently, by printing dollars, the United States (and U.S. taxpayer) financed the overseas investments of U.S. corporations, the importation of goods, foreign aid programs, the maintenance of troops overseas, and the fighting of wars in Korea and Vietnam. Through specialized international regimes, global monetary and trade arrangements were regularized under virtually undisputed U.S. economic hegemony. Under the Bretton Woods Agreement of 1944, which prescribed how various nations dealt with each other financially, gold and U.S. dollars became major reserve assets, and exchange rates were fixed. Arrangements under the regime underwent a continual process of financial, political, and economic adaptation. Movement toward currency convertibility led to a regime transformation, which lasted until the 1971 U.S. suspension of convertibility of the dollar into gold. Similarly, the General Agreement on Tariffs and Trade (GATT) implemented policies favoring nondiscriminatory trade practices.

The Marshall Plan and Point Four Program distributed U.S. IOUs (credit and technology) throughout much of the global system. The success of both programs was evidenced by a decade and a half of growth and expansion in the economies of the United States, the nations of Western Europe, parts of the Third World, and Japan during and following the U.S. occupation. The same years saw an expansion of the cold war, the development of the H-bomb, and Soviet achievement of nuclear capability. Toward the end of this period, however, the presentation of Marshall Plan and Point Four Program IOUs in the form of U.S. dollars contributed to a run on the U.S. gold supply in the early 1960s (reaching peaks in 1965 and 1967) (United Nations, Department of Economic and Social Affairs, 1981:1027).

During the late 1950s and early 1960s, U.S. direct investment in overseas manufactures increased dramatically, and global exports grew at a remarkable rate (Keohane and Nye, 1977:21, 55, 81). The U.S. economic and military hegemony was such that financing the nation's dominance was less a problem than ensuring financial resource flows to other countries sufficient to keep the international economy in balance—a dollar shortage problem (Gilpin, 1981:173).

A major factor in the postwar generation and management of international trade was the multinational corporation, whose appearance in Third World countries was both welcomed and resented. Associated in people's minds with the United States and a handful of other industrialized countries, multinational corporations emerged from India, Brazil, Taiwan, Mexico, South Korea, and other developing nations as well. By the early 1980s, some five hundred multinationals and fifty thousand affiliates—through massive expansion of direct investments in many parts of the world—controlled more than 60 percent of foreign trade and accounted for a like proportion of the value added to all industrial production. To a large extent—up to 75 percent—their transactions replaced conventional exports (W. Goldstein, 1979:144).

Because they were basically incompatible with the controlled economies of Communist regimes, multinational corporations did not exist in those countries. Their closest counterparts were foreign trade corporations of the USSR, some of which dated back to the first decade or so following the Bolshevik Revolution (Quigly, 1974). As monopolies chartered by the government, these corporations were responsible for Soviet business abroad. Many corporations established subsidiaries in other countries, including in non-Communist states, but they also invested directly in foreign countries.

The United States dominated the postwar international monetary system, but Western Europe and Japan grew faster. By the 1980s, the revival of European and Japanese economies and the growth of Soviet military potentials were altering global capability distributions: U.S. trade balances had turned negative, current account balances were threatened (United Nations Conference on Trade and Development, 1983:336), and demands were made by spokespersons for the Reagan administration, some members of Congress, and various domestic interest groups for strengthening the U.S. arsenal.

Global Distributions in the 1980s

From whatever perspective we observed them, the world's people in the late 1980s numbered approximately 5 billion. Three out of four of these individuals—the largest share by far—lived in developing regions. These were spread unevenly over the continents but occupied roughly 60 percent of the earth's land surface. Their distributions were attributable in part to unevennesses in natural distributions of climate, weather, and materials indispensable to human life (water, basic foods) or prized for technological applications (timber, coal, oil, metals).

By the mid-1980s, the industrialized countries included only 24 percent of the global population, but they occupied 41 percent of the world's land area and generated 81 percent of its gross product. The developing countries, by contrast, with 76 percent of the world's population and 68 percent of its territory, accounted for only 19 percent of its total product. Global population density was estimated at thirty-five persons per square kilometer—less dense than the developing regions at forty-eight persons per square kilometer but denser than the developed countries at twenty.

Territories occupied by the developing countries were estimated as 11 percent arable (although more than 14 percent was reported as under cultivation), whereas the generally smaller territorial aggregates of the developed part of the world were assessed at about 12.6 percent arable. People around the globe were continually preparing more land for cultivation (draining marshes, clear-cutting vast forests), but at the same time expanses of once cultivated land were being lost annually to urbanization. According to estimates, only another 15 percent or so could be made arable. Many of these enterprises, along with the use of pesticides, oil drilling, industrial and military waste, were damaging, depleting, and/or polluting increasingly valuable land, water, and air resources—all were global problems (World Bank, 1983:29, 38).

During the same decades, a considerable percentage of rural populations moved into the cities, which were rapidly expanding in parts of Asia, Africa, and South America. Unable to find affordable housing, these rural immigrants (sometimes hundreds of thousands, including growing numbers of employed whose incomes were too low for going rents) were settling for space under stretches of thatch or canvas or in packing cases squeezed between urban buildings and the streets. (Because of high land and construction costs, homeless "underclasses"—including people holding jobs, however low paying—were also found in the United States and other industrialized countries.) Other Third World people were migrating to more developed countries, some for seasonable employment only, others for the purpose of settling. Higher wage and living standards accounted for some of these migrations, but large numbers of people left their native lands in order to escape revolution, civil war, or political oppression.

Since the post–World War II dismemberment of the British Empire, the USSR, occupying nearly 25 percent of the global land surface (22,402,000 km²), has been the largest country. In descending order, the next seven states—Canada (9,976,000 km²), the PRC (9,597,000 km²), the United States (9,363,000 km²), Brazil (8,512,000 km²), Australia (7,687,000 km²), India (3,255,000 km²), and Mongolia (1,565,000 km²)—are a mixed lot in terms of other dimensions. In population size, China and India rank first and second (the former with more than 1 billion people and the latter expecting 1 billion by the end of the 1990s and with population densities by the mid-1980s of 105 and 106 persons per square kilometer, respectively). Canada (rich resources) and Mongolia (with fewer, presumably) are sparsely populated—each with only 2 persons per square kilometer. Canada, the United States, and Australia are industrialized; China, India, and Brazil are industrializing, however painfully. Mongolia is developing, but data are in short supply.

TABLE 8.1
Global Totals, Representative Distribution, and Quality of Life, 1984

System/ Country	Area (%)	Population (%)	Density per km²	GNP (%)	GNP per Capita	Energy Consumption (%)	Energy Consumption per Capita	Imports (%)	Imports per Capita	Exports (%)
Global			36		2,862		1,859		410.00	
Developed	40.9999	23.5540	21	80.3310	9,823	74.7934	5,887	74.5810	1,300.00	73.1579
Developing	59.0000	76.4450	47	19.6680	741	25.2066	611	25.3190	136.00	26.8421
Finland	0.2537	0.1025	14	0.4011	10,240	0.2745	5,002	0.6340	2,546.00	0.7089
Japan	0.2801	2.5103	323	9.0133	10,470	5.1275	3,800	0.9525	1,135.00	8.9316
Sweden	0.3388	0.1736	18	0.7510	11,160	0.4399	4,703	1.3492	3,170.00	1.5463
Netherlands	0.0279	0.3012	390	0.9873	8,603	0.1425	5,853	2.1741	4,312.00	3.4658
Norway	0.2439	0.0858	13	0.4329	13,010	0.3072	6,570	0.7085	3,353.00	0.9942
Canada	7.5105	0.5251	2	2.4287	12,830	2.7923	9,773	3.9791	3,100.00	4.7479
France	0.4118	1.1485	100	4.0663	8,879	2.4130	3,923	5.3292	1,900.00	5.1355
Singapore	0.0005	0.0523	4,215	0.1365	7,387	0.1910	6,659	1.4635	11,336.00	1.2668
W. Germany	0.1867	1.2803	247	4.8992	10,070	3.8459	5,564	7.8101	2,501.00	9.0368
U.K.	0.1845	1.1820	231	3.5480	7,590	2.9895	4,760	5.3446	1,855.00	4.9411
E. Germany	0.0183	0.3494	154	0.9716	10,070	1.4296	7,600	1.1194	1,315.00	1.2921
U.S.	7.0565	4.9580	25	26.8140	15,920	25.4869	9,577	17.4170	1,442.00	11.4684
Israel	0.0158	0.0837	191	0.1727	6,233	0.1109	2,329	0.5003	2,446.00	0.3056
Cuba	0.0836	0.2092	90	0.1391	2,704	0.1651	1,467	0.4192	823.00	0.3249
Hungary	0.0700	0.2238	115	0.4600	7,492	0.4615	3,790	0.6605	1,213.00	0.6989
USSR	16.8660	5.7801	12	14.2880	7,569	18.6129	5,977	4.1046	291.00	4.8153
Philippines	0.2259	1.1861	189	0.2348	556	0.1884	312	0.3283	113.00	0.2776
China	7.2252	21.6390	108	2.3120	309	77.2390	664	1.3012	25.00	1.4547
El Salvador	0.0158	0.1025	234	0.0300	903	0.0105	174	0.0499	199.00	0.0382
Brazil	6.4083	2.8555	16	1.4399	1,447	0.9831	545	0.7764	112.00	1.4211
Iraq	0.3275	0.3180	35	0.2041	2,458	0.0916	535	0.5656	727.00	0.5421
Honduras	0.0843	0.0920	39	0.0218	683	0.0107	225	0.0487	219.00	0.0393
Zambia	0.5669	0.1360	9	0.0251	389	0.0431	339	0.0373	112.00	0.0344
Iran	1.2407	0.9498	28	0.5861	3,599	0.6567	1,328	0.7846	339.00	0.6595
Pakistan	0.6053	2.0125	120	0.2700	350	0.2404	215	0.2988	61.00	0.1348
Angola	0.9388	0.1548	6	0.0508	1,139	0.0115	120	0.0332	0.77	0.1057
Afghanistan	0.4879	0.2887	21	0.0354	270	0.0112	69	0.0710	101.00	0.0333

System/ Country	Exports per Capita	Health (%)	Health Expenditures per Capita	Education (%)	Education Expenditures per Capita	Military Expenditure	Military Expenditures per Capita	Quality of Life — Life Expectancy (yrs.)	Quality of Life — Infant Mortality (per 1,000)
Global	398		118		138.0		173	62	79
Developed	1,236	93.2080	469	84.7370	469.0	80.4920	589	73	16
Developing	140	6.7917	11	15.2620	11.0	19.5080	46	59	88
Finland	2,759	0.5156	598	0.4589	830.0	0.1103	158	74	6
Japan	1,414	10.0570	474	9.6383	529.0	1.6082	103	77	6
Sweden	3,524	1.6428	1,114	1.2600	997.0	0.4182	340	77	6
Netherlands	4,567	1.6078	631	1.4261	652.0	0.5703	276	76	6
Norway	4,563	0.6690	914	0.6097	971.0	0.2259	376	76	6
Canada	3,588	3.8017	855	3.7487	983.0	1.0119	286	76	9
France	1,776	6.5692	676	4.4752	537.0	3.0053	368	75	9
Singapore	9,518	0.0539	121	0.1506	393.0	0.1383	390	72	9
W. Germany	2,806	9.6343	891	4.6945	506.0	2.8558	329	74	10
U.K.	1,663	4.6905	478	3.8310	447.0	3.4500	400	74	10
E. Germany	1,473	0.6914	235	0.9145	362.0	0.8493	636	72	11
U.S.	921	28.2050	674	27.6810	771.0	30.8320	1,000	75	11
Israel	1,450	0.1475	208	0.3036	500.0	0.8359	1,609	74	14
Cuba	619	0.1167	66	0.1838	121.0	0.1769	159	74	16
Hungary	1,245	0.3095	164	0.4747	293.0	0.1808	303	70	19
USSR	331	11.0870	227	13.9220	332.0	29.3170	956	70	26
Philippines	93	0.0385	4	0.0864	10.0	0.0767	7	63	49
China	27	0.7951	4	1.3225	8.4	2.8875	23	67	51
El Salvador	148	0.0111	13	0.0188	25.0	0.0274	55	65	66
Brazil	198	0.5623	23	1.1774	57.0	0.2029	12	61	68
Iraq	676	0.0396	15	0.1444	62.0	1.8209	1,044	69	75
Honduras	171	0.0088	11	0.0182	28.0	0.0208	28	61	77
Zambia	100	0.0129	11	0.0282	28.0	0.0182	26	52	100
Iran	276	0.2274	20	0.9164	133.0	1.3917	257	53	112
Pakistan	27	0.0262	2	0.1034	7.0	0.2915	21	51	120
Angola	27	0.0149	11	0.0554	52.0	0.1285	NA	42	144
Afghanistan	46	0.0051	2	0.0129	6.0	0.0442	21	37	182

Sources: Columns 1–5, 12–15, 18, and 19: Ruth L. Sivard, ed., *World Military and Social Indicators, 1987–1988* (Washington, D.C.: World Priorities, 1987); columns 6 and 7: United Nations, *Yearbook of World Energy Statistics* (New York: United Nations, 1986); columns 8–11: United Nations, *Yearbook of International Trade Statistics* (New York: United Nations, 1986); columns 16 and 17: U.S. Arms Control and Disarmament Agency, *World Military Expenditures and Arms Transfers* (Washington, D.C.: GPO, 1986).

As a measure of pressure on agricultural resources, population densities can be misleading, especially in developing countries. In the PRC, the work force has had to support almost 25 percent of the world's people with about 7 to 8 percent of the earth's cultivated land. At first, Maoist leaders saw China's large population as a national asset. By the late 1950s, however, the PRC, learning from hard experience, had begun limiting population growth—with mixed success.

If we add technology (roughly indicated by GNP) to the preceding picture, distributions of capability and influence ($power_1$ and $power_2$) are more accurately represented. In the mid-1980s, when the gross global product was about $13,640 billion, developed nations accounted for about 80 percent of this total as contrasted with the 20 percent contributed by developing nations. The per capita distribution in the developed regions at that time was $9,782, as compared with a per capita distribution of $2,861 for all countries of the world and $751 in the developing world ($102 in epsilon Burundi, $122 in zeta Chad). A major concern for theorists, policymakers, and anyone else seriously concerned with war, peace, and survival at home and abroad is how these distributions (and consequent profiles) correlate, if at all, with economic, political, and military activities among nations on the global level—notably in terms of trade and warfare. We are concerned also with some of the consequences (intended and unintended) of fourth image activities for the well-being of individuals and communities worldwide (see Table 8.1).

Roots of Underdevelopment

The economic and associated disabilities of underdeveloped and developing nations have been explained in numerous ways. Marxism-Leninism has provided analyses based upon the production forces and class structures in imperialist and colonial or semicolonial nations and the investment in the latter of finance capital controlled by capitalist investors in the former. Drawing substantially from Marxist-Leninist theory, *dependencia* theorists have provided differing views as to whether the economic, political, and military ties of Third World nations to major capitalist powers are inextricable (short of revolution) or can be "outgrown" under progressive leadership. Those on the Left have tended to see the United States and other capitalist countries as exploiters that use market activities to displace territorial expansion and colonialism as a means of acquiring wealth and have seen the USSR (virtually by definition) as a "liberator." According to this view, trade relations established during the colonial era tied the economies of many developing nations to the "empires" of which they previously had been parts.

Westerners, while accusing the USSR and its allies (and clients) of practicing a Stalinist mode of imperialism, have attributed the spread of capitalist activities and interests to the greater efficiency of market institutions compared with other forms of organization. Even observers who saw most states benefiting (in absolute terms) from involvement in the capitalist world market economy might concede, however, that the more efficient and the more technologically advanced economies have tended to enjoy more favorable terms of trade, higher rates of profit, greater concentrations of wealth, and derivative benefits as compared to states with less developed technologies and economies (Gilpin, 1981:136, 176–177).

Characteristically, Marxist-Leninist regimes have maintained tight control—through bilateral treaties and similar instruments—over trade and monetary relations with other countries. After 1965, however, Soviet trade with non-Communist countries (both developing and developed) grew more rapidly than with Communist nations. The largest proportion of Soviet imports and exports consisted of machinery and equipment, with imports leading exports. Fuels and base metals ranked next among Soviet exports, with foodstuffs and other consumer goods taking second place among imports.

Modernization in the Third World

Because the international monetary capabilities of individual countries are functions of their overall economic and political capabilities (Bergsten, 1975:28), developing nations may find themselves trapped—unable to increase technological and economic capabilities without making costly commitments, incurring larger debts, and inhibiting development. Ultimately, whatever its ideology or form of government, a developing country may be forced to apply additional leverage internally in order to "squeeze" still more badly needed capital from domestic undertakings. Normally this cannot be accomplished, however, without severe alterations in domestic structure, such as the disciplined mobilization of labor, tight control over domestic consumption, rigorous methods of extraction, prudent investment in production and other basic functions of society including maintenance of domestic law and order, defense against attack from the outside, health, education, and so on. Rigorous birth control measures are likely to be a sine qua non in epsilon societies. In these terms, the People's Republic of China balanced high risks, benefits, costs, trade-offs, and often contradictory outcomes associated with extraction of capital in pursuit of rapid modernization (Loup, 1983:135)—often at high political cost.

Although relatively few Third World countries have been able to achieve successful land reform and industrialization programs, manufacturing industry has proved to be a remarkably dynamic sector of economic growth in those societies in which such changes have taken place. For a time, Chinese successes in land reform, establishment of rural industries, and steel production—despite serious setbacks—appeared to be "undoubtedly the most remarkable" in the Third World. By the early 1980s, however, the economic accomplishments of South Korea were taking many observers by surprise. Beginning from a relatively small base, the rate of growth in manufacturing production by developing states as a group has often been significantly higher than the corresponding growth rates of developed countries. Between 1950 and 1980, the world's developing countries more than doubled their per capita gross domestic products (GDPs). As these nations were still at much lower levels of industrialization, however, the absolute gain in manufacturing production per capita was no more than a small fraction of that obtained by nations with developed market economies (United Nations Conference on Trade and Development, 1982:71). Meanwhile, some forty nations, primarily in sub-Saharan Africa and south Asia, achieved only limited growth (about 1.3 percent annually) in per capita GDPs (Loup, 1983:19).

Among developing countries of Latin America, Africa, and Asia, a rise in domestic product per capita tended to accelerate as industrial shares in total output increased (and vice versa). In several of the more industrialized developing nations, the share of manufactures in total industrial output varied in the early 1980s from about two-thirds in large countries such as India, Mexico, and Chile to more than four-fifths in small territories such as Hong Kong. Overall, among seventy-six non-oil-exporting nations for which relevant data were available, approximately 75 percent of the populations lived in countries where the share of manufacturing represented 20 percent of domestic product and income per capita averaged $230 (1975 prices). The other 25 percent lived in developing countries where the manufacturing share was 20 percent or more and per capita income averaged $990.

A society's productivity depends upon factors that include investment distribution among economic sectors, rate of capacity utilization, and work force capacity for moving "rapidly down the learning curve" (Feinberg, 1983:225). Especially critical for long-term stability are the relative allocations to productive enterprise as contrasted with unnecessary consumption (by both public and private sectors), an ability to modernize in advance of population growth, and the will to pursue these ends without resort to dictatorship, either of the Right or the Left.

By the mid-1980s, the People's Republic of China, Taiwan, Sri Lanka, and South Korea were making remarkable advances in modernization. In China, despite periods of near chaos, the regime made notable progress in raising standards of living in terms of basic needs. At the same time, Chinese leaders were shifting toward an agricultural policy of increased production, specialization, and commodity production characterized by a new concern for "enriching" the peasantry as "fast as possible." This policy was followed by commercial and industrial policies promoting "entrepreneurship," which included the handing over of small, medium, and, to a lesser extent, large, state-owned enterprises to individuals and collectives—all within what was referred to as a socialist framework (Schram, 1984:454–457). The country seemed to have reached a plateau from which the next course of development was not yet evident. Meanwhile, as the 1990s approached, spontaneous student demonstrations, often cheered and even supported by the populace, raised new demands for "democracy" but were put down by military force.

In "private-enterprise" Sri Lanka during the 1970s, social welfare interventions contributed to improvements in several quality-of-life indicators (literacy, life expectancy, and infant mortality had improved substantially), but the annual growth rate, averaging 4.6 percent in the 1960s, dropped to 3.1 percent between 1970 and 1977, and the rate of gross fixed capital formation, which had increased until 1970, fell thereafter. Social conflict proved to be endemic during the 1980s. Pursuing its own variety of socialism, Tanzania made similar trade-offs—with benefit and cost outcomes roughly comparable to those of Sri Lanka.

Among a score or so of industrializing nations (having moved from epsilon toward gamma profiles since World War II), the Gang of Four— South Korea, Taiwan, Hong Kong, and Singapore—were remarkable for their success in combining high rates of growth with rapid expansion of employment and greater equality in income distribution. At the close of the Korean War, South Korea was "a half-economy in ruins," nearly two-thirds of cultivated land lay in waste, most of its limited industrial capabilities was destroyed, and more than one-quarter of its people were homeless refugees (Meier, 1984:57–58). The nation had a denser population and fewer natural resources than the Netherlands. Yet by 1978, the country had achieved in one generation a modern industrial economy with a per capita income of more than $1,000 and exports valued at more than $10 billion. Taiwan, another economically successful developing nation, achieved a growth rate exceeding that of any other country (except possibly Japan) and greater income equality than most developing economies. Like the People's Republic of China, South Korea and Taiwan were notably less successful with respect to democratization and civil rights.

Since independence in the late 1940s, India had doubled its population, which by the 1980s constituted 15 percent of the global population. For years, food production remained a bottleneck in India's development, and during the 1970s the country was importing more than 10 million tons of grain per annum. By the end of the decade, however, India had become virtually self-sufficient in wheat and rice. Such progress resulted from incentive prices for farmers, rural credit arrangements, and the introduction of high-yielding varieties of grain (Meier, 1984:60–67).

Global Exchange and Interdependence

Most nations rely on foreign trade to acquire resources, goods, labor, or specialized services that are not available domestically or that are obtained abroad at lower cost. Thus, global trade patterns are sensitive to natural distributions of resources and local resource depletions as well as to uneven distributions of knowledge and skills. In addition to returns from home production, societies gain income by exporting goods and services in exchange for imports.

In the mid-1980s, developing countries were responsible for 43 percent of global imports and 55 percent of exports as compared with the 55 percent of imports and 43 percent of exports accounted for by industrialized nations. World imports per capita amounted to $72, as compared with $109 for developed countries and $34 for developing nations. Global per capita exports stood at $46, as compared with $116 for developed countries and $21 for developing countries.

On a fundamental level, international trade derives from differences in relative production costs for various commodities within a country as compared with differences in relative production costs for the same commodities in other nations. These differences in costs also account for labor migrations from less efficient (lower-wage-paying) societies to more efficient (higher-wage-paying) societies and for the tendency of many industries to move their labor-intensive operations from more production-efficient home bases to less efficient (lower-wage-paying) countries.

Although the least developed countries export mainly labor-intensive products, more advanced countries such as Taiwan, South Korea, and Singapore export goods with higher coefficients of capital (material and human) (Kindleberger, 1962:183). As a developing nation increases its industrial capacity and enters further into the world economy, monetary exchanges expand, and consumption, formerly based upon subsistence, comes increasingly from abroad. At that point, the growth of manufacturing output often requires comparable expansion in foreign exchange availabilities for its support, which contributes to interdependence.

Unfortunately, in most developing countries estimated import requirements frequently exceed whatever expansion earnings have achieved (Sauvant, 1981:xxxvii). To meet these demands, such countries tend to export increasing amounts of food and other raw materials. Concurrently, the generation of export capacities and private investment flows is commonly cited by international economists and development specialists as an indispensable long-term corrective to such a country's economic development. In the short run, however, most developing nations have sought grants and loans from other nations and the World Bank in order to fill gaps in their foreign exchange resources. As goods are imported from industrialized countries, a developing nation may incur large foreign exchange deficits. Aid and loans can tie recipient to donor countries in various ways; the aggregate of such obligations creates global networks of political and economic significance. A shock in any part of such a network is likely to be felt throughout.

National Profiles and Uneven Exchange

A country's trade dependence tends to vary *directly* with population size and the level of technology and *inversely* with the size of its territorial base. Low levels of economic growth are a serious disadvantage. With respect to trade volume and bargaining and leverage potentials in the global market, there are differences between the more advanced and the least advanced of the developing countries. Import and export rates of growth depend upon a country's profile, its investment patterns (as between consumer and capital enterprises or between those enterprises in which the society is more and those in which it is less competitive), and its subsidy, tax rebate, and other incentive policies (World Bank, 1983:38).

In developed, resource-rich societies, the primary demand is for foreign markets where the country's goods can be sold. In order to secure such markets, however, resource-rich countries must maintain a sufficient level of imports so that foreign customers can obtain the exchange they require for purchases. Activities generating exports create jobs and incomes with multiplier effects, which are amplified to the extent that benefits are widely shared. Nations with above-average export growth often achieve above-average product growth (Loup, 1983:199).

Closely associated with international trade are international payments— both commercial trade dealings and noncommercial transfers. These payments are often, but not always, achieved through foreign exchange markets and, because of inadequacies in the system of data collection, are not satisfactorily recorded. In pursuit of technological and economic growth and development, Third World nations are often hard put to discover any feasible alternative to a continuing reliance on imports of capital and services as well as goods, which are commonly acquired through loans. This policy can exact high costs as well as benefits.

Developing countries tend to export natural resources or agricultural products and to import manufactured goods, technology, and weaponry from industrialized nations. Through such exchanges, developing nations may achieve product specialization, exploit economies of scale, and at the same time increase the foreign exchange earnings they need for payments on imports. Along with the benefits, developing countries—especially those with one-product economies—may also increase their dependence on a major trading partner or even on a particular import. With increases in the cost of oil dating from the early 1970s, the plight of many developing countries worsened.

Transitions in the Global System

For a decade or so after World War II, the global economic subsystem was "under repair," and the role of the United States as financial hegemon was not seriously questioned. During the late 1950s, however, a number of basic changes began to take place, and by the 1980s the U.S. ability to control the international monetary regime had decreased—although it was difficult to assess how rapidly the trend was moving and how far it would go from there. To some extent, this state of affairs followed logically from the successes of the various national rehabilitation programs.

Despite trade and aid programs, commerce in manufactured goods and raw materials remained concentrated among a few economically developing countries. In the mid-1960s, the U.N. Conference on Trade and Development offered criteria for establishing manufactures with export potentials in the Third World (Sauvant, 1981:42–46, 568–579). In subsequent years, comparable criteria were proposed by international agencies and individual specialists for orderly and accelerated diffusion of technology to developing countries, better access to patents held by enterprises in market-economy nations, improvement of conditions for trade and financial relations with Eastern

Europe and with command economies elsewhere, the cessation of nuclear testing in Third World areas, and so on (Meier, 1984:26).

In the course of their economic development, countries such as South Korea, Taiwan, and Singapore, in adapting to new comparative advantages, diversified their exports toward sophisticated, more capital-intensive products. Attracted by lower wages and other production costs, labor-intensive industries increasingly transferred from Japan (attracted there from the United States) to Hong Kong and thence to South Korea. Whereupon, the Koreans shifted to other developing nations some of the "low(er) tech" activities for which the latter now had a comparative advantage. The increasing strength, self-assurance, and self-awareness of many Third World states rendered them less controllable by the United States or any foreign power (Loup, 1983:199). As a consequence, "marching now to their own drummers," some developing nations moved further beyond effective U.S. influence. During the 1980s, a central foreign policy debate was how the United States should respond (World Bank, 1983:38).

By the late 1960s, most developing countries had gained political independence, which was largely consolidated during the next decade. Meanwhile, delegates from nations in the developing world known as the Group of 77 (later expanded to 122 members) became the principal organization through which developing countries pursued issues of collective economic interest. Members of the group urged replacement of an international system based on "colonialism" with a global system serving its members' interests while taking into account the special conditions and needs of developing nations (Codoni et al., 1971:13).

Third World spokespersons urged industrial nations to eliminate tariffs on raw materials from developing countries (Meier, 1984:36); urged the GATT to modify trade regulations in favor of Third World countries; urged the industrialized nations to buy more semimanufactured goods from developing countries; and urged the use of U.N. conferences to solve Third World trade and financial problems. A number of Third World leaders voiced dissatisfaction with the World Bank, with the International Monetary Fund, and with direct aid arrangements by the United States and other industrial nations. Through what was known as the Arusha initiative, a 1980 conference in Tanzania called for a U.N. conference to provide for a "universal democratic and legitimate forum" for negotiating a new monetary system for global development. Pursuing development, a "group of 24" nations urged arrangements for accelerating concessional aid, expanding lending programs, and providing "for external debt reorganization" (Tinbergen, 1976:15–23).

Although manufacturing output increased in developing countries as a whole at a rate of about 6.5 percent per annum between 1960 and 1980, much of this growth took place in a few countries whose rapidly expanding exports of manufactures accounted for nearly half the value added in industrial sectors of the world's developing countries. Trade between developing countries as a whole, as well as between countries of a geographical region, remained low (Bergsten, 1975:108). Accounting for two-thirds of the developing world's population, Asian countries increased their per capita incomes in the three years of the 1980–1982 world recession, whereas with a few exceptions Latin American and low-income African countries suffered declines in per capita incomes.

A central problem of economic growth in developing nations was still the slow increase of exports. While exports stagnated, imports grew rapidly because of the industrialization efforts that had already been made. The developing nations with the most favorable terms of trade and export growth were those with expanding manufactures, such as Argentina, Brazil, Mexico, South Korea, and Singapore. Rates of import and export growth tended to be lowest among countries near the "bottom" in terms of technological advancement. Some of the highest growth rates were found among oil-producing countries. Even when import products in demand were available, however, they could not compete in terms of price, quality, or credit facilities with similar goods supplied by the developed countries (Codoni et al., 1971:213).

The continued growth of developing countries depends upon steadily expanding trade and capital inflows, both of which are closely joined to the level and stability of global economic activity. Interest payments, freight charges, private transfers, receipts from tourists, and the like often compensate for a trade deficit, but a balance-of-payment deficit implies that the economy is receiving foreign exchange in return for money balances. The domestic money stock is thus decreasing unless the effects are neutralized through purchase of private bonds by the central bank in exchange for money. What has been true in the past still holds in large part: The implications of balances of trade and balances of payments for national growth and global stability are not yet fully understood (Stern, 1973:356).

In large-scale trade and financial exchanges, the country with the more advanced level of technology and the stronger economy is likely to possess the substantially greater bargaining and leverage potentials and the greater possibilities for overall favorable returns. This is not to suggest that the weaker state never obtains an advantage, however. The terms (as well as the volume) of international trade, for example, can exert great influence on flows of income between countries and can function as a leverage mode. But to generalize about the distribution of terms of trade among developed and developing countries can be difficult and risky. In recent years, countries with favorable terms of trade have included some of the poorest (Chad, Ethiopia, Afghanistan, Rwanda) and some rich industrialized nations (Canada, Switzerland, Norway, Sweden, Finland, and East Germany). Nations with extremely unfavorable terms of trade have included India, Japan, Spain, and Chile. With an index value of 82, the United States in 1976 (base year 1970) ranked in the "lower lower-middle" among countries of the world (United Nations Conference on Trade and Development, 1982:8). Wherever they originate, exchange imbalances can expand into global dysfunctions.

Progress in most developing countries was much slower, but by the late 1970s, economic aid, the diffusion of technology, systematic alterations in tariff patterns, and other measures had contributed to efforts in numerous Third World countries to increase their industrial exports to Western Europe, Japan, and the United States. An important change in North-South relations had occurred. No longer did the more advanced of the developing nations "simply produce raw materials and food" for the industrialized countries (Meier, 1984:57–58). In spite of severe constraints, these developing countries began building economies of their own.

Challenges to the Global System

Despite the constraining effects of generally dense populations and lagging technologies, Third World nations as a category averaged 5.4 percent growth during the 1970s. This relatively strong performance was obtained, however, at the cost of rapid increases in external debt and domestic imbalances such as inflation, overvalued currencies, fiscal deficits, and distorted incentives for agriculture and industry. Following the second oil price shock in late 1979, oil-importing and oil-exporting nations suffered serious disruptions aggravated by a deterioration in the global environment (falling commodity prices, a trade slowdown, sharp increases in interest rates, reduced access to external financing, and economic policy failures among industrialized countries).

Weak demand in the industrialized countries contributed, moreover, to declines in the export prices of developing countries and to widespread recession. Within this context, the series of economic crises suffered in the 1970s signaled the beginning of a growing disequilibrium in the world economy. Included in these disruptions were two energy crises (1973–1974, 1979), double-digit inflation, high interest rates, an abnormally high dollar, the deepest recession since the Great Depression, unprecedented capital flows with attendant recycling problems, and, beginning in 1981, a progressive deterioration of the U.S. structural budget position. By 1982, the overall prices of primary goods in developing countries relative to prices of manufactures had reached a record low for the post–World War II period. With the exclusion of China, India, and a few other countries, the 1980–1987 average growth rate dropped to 3.9 percent.

By raising world savings and depressing investments, the two oil crises created a savings surplus "almost overnight." Subsequently, whereas the United States, resorting to budgetary deficits, created a severe shortage of savings, other Organization for Economic Cooperation and Development (OECD) nations cut their structural deficits by amounts that in the aggregate offset a large part of the U.S. expansionary shift. This created a dilemma: If the United States had followed suit, there might well have been a global recession, whereas if the others had followed the United States, there might have been a global boom leading to a new outbreak of global inflation. What transpired instead was in the aggregate a "reasonably satisfactory" world recovery, which, "because of its uneven distribution," led to a "massive disequilibrium" between the hegemon and its allies (notably Japan) that was "fraught with danger" for the world economy (Marris, 1985:33–35).

Disequilibria in the Global Economy

In one way or another, the continuing economic disequilibrium had impacts throughout the world. As markets in some more rapidly developing countries were expanding, competition for export markets among developed states was accelerating, and these states tended to favor protectionist strategies. U.S. attempts to influence the policies of developing countries by restraining certain categories of exports (embargoing certain types of nuclear technology in the absence of "sufficient safeguards," for example) were undercut by the trade activities of other industrialized countries.

Caught between increases in imports and decreasing exports, developing oil-importing nations in the mid-1970s (and some countries with oil of their own) experienced "an exceptional deficit in current account balances." After temporary improvement followed by the second price shock (1979–1980), the current account of these nations "reached $68 billion (more than five times the 1977 figure) by 1981." Only two options seemed to be available— to reduce imports of consumption and capital goods (at the expense of national populations and their possibilities for growth) or to seek massive external financing. Adjusting to the growing pressure on balance of payments, developing nations took steps to reduce the rate of growth of their imports and to increase the share of their exports (United Nations Conference on Trade and Development, 1982:72–73). Inflows of private and public capital from abroad enabled some nations to avoid severe cuts in imports and substantially increase gross investments.

From a U.S. perspective, however, the high level of U.S. imports was contributing to the nation's trade deficits, whereas the overall benefits to Europe and the developing countries tended to be disadvantageous. From the viewpoint of many developing countries, high interest rates were draining capital from their economies and financing the U.S. deficit while hampering growth in other countries and raising debt levels in a number of periphery nations. Having served the hegemonic power well in better days, free-trade ideology and policies were viewed by many in the United States as increasingly unsatisfactory as protectionism spread in other parts of the world. Trade balances for Japan, which was rapidly challenging the United States economically, were all positive (Japan had positive trade balances for twelve successive years, but payments deficits were incurred in four of them). West Germany was the only developed country with positive trade and payments balances for the period.

Meanwhile, developing countries were facing their most serious economic crisis since the Depression of the 1930s. Many of these nations, which lacked trade surpluses and were unable to break into world markets, found themselves incurring debts and mounting interest payments that they could not accommodate. This fundamental plight was exacerbated, moreover, by a malaise attributable to rising oil prices, sluggish economic growth in the developed market economies, the rising value of the U.S. dollar, and increases in real interest rates in world financial markets. Consequent reductions in the growth rates among developing countries and corresponding pressures to reduce their imports contributed to the shrinking of potential markets for Western goods. In sub-Saharan Africa, these problems were exacerbated by severe droughts in some thirty states. Third World countries increasingly turned to private banks in the United States and Western Europe for loans (Sauvant, 1981:42–46, 568–578).

Within the post–World War II Bretton Woods system, currency reserves were convertible, directly or indirectly, into gold at the central bank level; international exchange rates were "pegged" within comparatively narrow limits around declared par values; and "the main sources of external financing for balance-of-payments deficits . . . was the International Monetary Fund" (Meier, 1984:36). By the early 1980s, changes had occurred. No longer pegged, the exchange rates of major currencies "floated" and were not convertible into gold. To a notable extent, private banks had supplemented the IMF as a main source of balance-of-payments financing, a tendency exacerbated by oil-price increases after the 1970s oil shocks (Meier, 1984:36).

Between 1970 and 1981, at least thirty developing countries had trade imbalances and payments deficits for all twelve years, and many more incurred negative balances for half or more of the twelve-year period. The deficit states included the relatively high-growth states of Brazil and Mexico (with debts exceeding $100 billion each in 1987), South Korea, and Singapore as well as "basket cases" such as Burundi, Bangladesh, Chad, and Haiti. Third World debts had repercussions in the banks and treasuries of developed countries. Debtors during the 1980s included several of the richest as well as many of the poorest countries. (Normally a productive, "rich" country can redress a trade or payments imbalance by exporting financial, technological, or other services, but when several such nations incur serious trade and transfer imbalances, dysfunctions tend to become global.)

Problems of the international monetary system and those of the international trading system (including commerce in oil) were loosely interconnected. Never before had the global economy been so sensitively interdependent—especially as computerized communications between investment exchanges in various parts of the world became virtually instantaneous. At the same time, with the recession of the early 1980s and declines in imports among periphery nations, the United States and other industrialized countries found themselves confronted by developing nations on the verge of defaulting on debts owed to private banks as well as to government agencies in the West. A large proportion of World Bank and International Development Agency financial resources had come directly or indirectly from the central banks, the capital markets, and the governments of a handful of rich member countries. Meanwhile, as a proportion of GNP, the debt level of oil-importing nations had increased during the 1970s (from 12.3 percent in 1970 to 17.8 percent in 1979).

With increases in their demands for financing, many periphery countries sought new sources of external credit at a time when greater liquidity in financial markets was causing private banks to reach out for new customers (Codoni et al., 1971:202). During successive months, the ratio of debt service obligations to exports—boosted by higher interest rates—rose sharply in developing nations. Several of the larger debtor nations, which had relied primarily on private sources of finance, sought to reschedule (World Bank, 1983:7).

Incongruously, with rising interest rates and accumulated indebtedness, some developing countries, because of the magnitude of their loans, found their leverage potentials increasing as they dealt with banks in the United States or in other industrialized nations that were not prepared to risk the costs to themselves of large-scale default. But each one-point rise in the U.S. prime rate meant increases of billions of dollars in the interest costs of many developing countries, and rising interest rates in turn created financial outflows from countries that were already in desperate need of capital. Such outflows then contributed to increased unemployment, lower living standards, and slowdowns of development in the debtor nations. It was not uncommon for debtor regimes to find themselves caught between financial obligations and the economic demands of their constituents. In Argentina, for example, a newly established democratic regime (emerging after years of military dictatorship) felt itself fiscally endangered.

In Brazil, Mexico, and several other countries with debt-servicing difficulties, the problem was largely that of liquidity. In others, including Argentina, Bolivia, Jamaica, Nicaragua, Senegal, and Zaire, debt-servicing problems had arisen primarily from low returns on investment (Codoni et al., 1971:213). Insofar as debt servicing exceeded inflows, debtor countries as politically distinct as Turkey, Poland, Nicaragua, and Zaire chose to honor their debts and reduce the momentary burden by rescheduling part of them. Debt problems often intruded upon well-established commercial patterns. Argentina, for example, hoped to sell products to the United States in order to pay off its debt, whereas the United States, although wanting to see the debt reduced, hesitated to buy Argentine products, which were often in competition with its own.

As interest rates soared and exports stagnated, Third World debtor nations found the cost of servicing long-term external debts as a percentage of exports rising from 27.1 to 38.8 percent within a matter of months. The consequent drain of resources induced many countries to undertake stiff adjustments. Within a year or so, the recession began to give way to recovery, but prices remained low relative to those in more favorable times; food prices continued to rise, while prices of exported goods from developing countries tended to decline.

Among the more serious aspects of the Third World debt problem were the nature and terms of loans to debtor countries by private banks. Although major debtor nations took strong adjustment measures, and international economic recovery helped to expand Third World trade, the external debt problem continued to present serious risks to lender banks and to the global economy. It became increasingly evident to debtor countries and lender banks (and nations) that a certain amount of debt forgiveness was inescapable and generally beneficial to both sides. The questions were how and how much. Many debtor nations were unable to maintain debt-service payments, and there was widespread anxiety lest they be unable to honor their debts in the long run.

By the mid-1980s, growing numbers of observers and analysts were agreed that prevailing economic problems and the debt problem in particular were global rather than strictly national or regional phenomena. In considerable part, this disequilibrium was an outcome of uneven growth and development in the periphery, but it was also attributable to major alterations in the global configuration and to accumulating evidence that the United States might be entering a stage of economic, political, and military decline.

In many ways, the threat to U.S. economic hegemony was most readily clarified by comparing its circumstances with those of its primary economic challenger—Japan. By late 1985, competition between these two nations had become a critical issue in the world economy. Their global imbalances had reached levels of deficit (the United States) and surplus (Japan) "beyond anything ever before recorded by industrial countries." Among many factors contributing to the competition were a relative decline in basic U.S. industrial capacities and a rise in comparable Japanese capabilities, including spectacular challenges in high technology. Protectionism, while advantageous to Japanese farmers and industrial interest groups, was damaging to U.S.-Japanese relations, to the economies of both countries, and to the global system (as were the protectionist policies of other nations). Associated with these tendencies were an extremely low rate of national savings in the United States and correspondingly high rates in Japan. Also critical were the budgetary deficits (no country had "ever run deficits" as large as those of the United States) and surpluses (no country, except Saudi Arabia briefly) had "ever run surpluses like those of contemporary Japan." Sharp increases in the U.S. budget deficit contributed in turn to the country's trade deficit. Japan, however, had reduced its surplus, and this opposition of effort also contributed to the trade imbalance (Bergsten and Cline, 1985:1–9).

The spectacular economic growth of Japan was only one aspect of instabilities that were worldwide—with many Third World nations threatened by spiraling debts that in a number of cases appeared to put capitalist economies and democratic regimes in deep jeopardy. Several of these countries had borrowed heavily not only from the World Bank but also from private banks in the industrialized nations, particularly the United States. Much of the borrowed credit had been allocated to public payrolls (or to the military) rather than to education, health, development, or productivity—a trend decried by critics as evidence of fiscal indiscipline. Meanwhile the United States, a major creditor, had been meeting its military and public welfare charges through deficit financing—mortgaging the future, in effect.

Asymmetries in the Quality of Life

How has the world fared since 1945? How much progress has been made? With a relatively low population growth rate of 1.6 percent and a rising capita domestic product, the PRC reached literacy, health, and life expectancy levels similar to those of many middle-income nations. India's GDP growth averaged 5.0 (1980–1987), but agriculture suffered from bad weather and population growth remained high; as a result, per capita income averaged only a 2.8 percent increase per annum. Despite spectacular technological advancement and economic growth in many Third World nations, the numbers of people lacking food, water, shelter, health care, education, and other benefactions steadily increased. By the mid-1980s, an estimated 500 million people (roughly 10 percent of the global population) were under- or unemployed.

Famine was widespread in many nations of the developing world, especially in the poorest, and in 1984, 5 million children were reported to have died in Africa from hunger-related causes. At the same time, the world's nations had spent $17 trillion (in 1982 prices) on military activities. With 11 percent of the world's people, the superpowers accounted for 50 percent of the global military budget.

What about quality-of-life indicators worldwide? Insofar as indicated by life expectancy and infant mortality, quality of life within nations of the world tended to improve with increases in per capita consumption of energy (or, alternatively, GNP per capita—although the high-oil-production nations were somewhat anomalous). At the same time, paradoxically, each level and mode of technology tended to produce their own characteristic resource depletions, toxic wastes, and other pollutions. Soil erosion, deforestation, and desertification are age-old phenomena, but modern technologies were producing new problems, such as smog, acid rain, damage to ozone layers, and evidence of imminent (and potentially severe) climatic changes.

Let us consider the good news first. For the global population, the infant mortality rate in the mid-1980s was 112 deaths per 1,000 births, and life expectancy was sixty-three years. These numbers compare with 113 infant deaths per 1,000 and a life expectancy of fifty-nine years in the developing countries and 16.9 infant deaths and a life expectancy of seventy-three years in developed countries. Japan and Finland, tying for first among nations of the world with respect to infant mortality, each suffered 6 deaths per 1,000, and life expectancy in Japan and Sweden was seventy-seven years. In the United States, the infant mortality was 11 per 1,000, (ranking seventeenth), and life expectancy was seventy-five years (ranking seventh). In the USSR, infant mortality and life expectancy were 31 deaths per 1,000 and seventy years, respectively.

Year in and year out, the quality-of-life indicators for nations of the world tended to follow a technology "learning curve" represented by per capita energy consumption. The favorable effects of advances in technology were constrained, however, by populations that grew in advance of their acquisition of knowledge and skills. Countries with the least advanced levels of technology usually ranked near the bottom with respect to quality-of-life indicators: Nepal (110 deaths, forty-six years), Bangladesh (182 deaths, thirty-seven years), Burundi (119 deaths, forty-five years), and Chad (144 deaths, forty-three years) were representative of such countries. In general, nations with advanced technologies and relatively low population densities—Norway, Sweden, Finland, Iceland—tended to possess the most favorable quality-of-life indicators, but Japan's record demonstrated that through careful planning and resource allocation, a nation with a dense population and an advanced technology could rank near the top with respect to such quality-of-life indicators as longevity and low infant mortality.

Now for the bad news. Evidence of a bitter irony has accumulated in recent years: Some of the same technologies that have contributed to improvements in the quality of our lives increasingly produce dangerous unintended consequences. The greater the proportion of a population that can afford cars, the more highways are needed. But the more we build, the more cars we buy (two or more per family), the wider the gridlock areas expand, and the more toxics are spread.

Fertilizers and insecticides used in the Green Revolution have contributed to Third World pollution. Everyone benefits from the astonishing advances that have occurred in medicine since World War II, but access to many of the new regimens and surgeries are limited by technical availabilities and high costs—a reality raising difficult issues of triage (who, worldwide, gets the transplant, and who pays for it?). Concurrently, degenerative diseases of old age have increased with life expectancy. Drugs (alcohol and nicotine not excluded) and the AIDS virus have constituted major forces of invasion around the world; they have challenged life-saving advances in medical knowledge and skills everywhere and subverted many of the most advanced and poorest countries from within. (In many countries, the drug trade offers a quick ticket from rags to riches for the downtrodden, provided they are not shot first by Uzis or AK 47s.)

Meanwhile, the more plastics and other nondegradable products and toxics used—including medical supplies (toxic "disposables" awash on recreational beaches)—the more garbage we produce, the more costly its removal becomes, and the more bitter is the resistance to disposal sites in anybody's neighborhood (especially materials with a half life of thousands of years). Lately the shipping of wastes from industrialized to Third World countries may rank among the more galling global insults. Once touted as a clean and cheap energy source, nuclear technology has its own waste disposal problems.

Insofar as tropical rain forests and other woodlands absorb carbon dioxide, continued massive clear-cutting can only exacerbate the trend toward greenhousing. We can envisage these and other toxics released by human beings as "conspiring" with natural forces (winds, tides, river and ocean currents, and the like), which transport and distribute them beyond human control. Developing as well as industrialized nations increasingly suffer the consequences.

To the extent that these predictions are well grounded, we confront the possibility that more babies surviving today—with statistical prospects of living longer—will have to deal with a seriously deteriorating environment. Perhaps most disconcerting of all, as people live longer, more and more of them may burden their younger relatives (and taxpayers) by lingering on in a weakened, if not comatose, condition, unable to die. Finally, there is nuclear weaponry, which might turn out to be the terminal planetary waster. In order that we may understand better the complex relationships and interactions that might lead to an ultimate global conflict, Chapter 9 will "nest" the international "conflict system" within the fourth image.

Notes

1. This distinction between "class" and "chain," or network, linkage is somewhat similar to the distinction we draw in Chapter 5 between profiles as "horizontal" categories of nations at a time slice in the continuum in the progress and development of nations from one level of growth and development to another.

9

Global Competition
and Violence

Insofar as the global system encompasses the first, second, and third images, we would expect various manifestations of violence to be endemic on all four image levels—whether murder, assassination, terrorist attack, guerrilla activity, revolution, civil war, international war, or global war—and locatable within the fourth image framework. In this chapter, however, we are concerned primarily with organized violence used as leverage by individuals or collectivities on national, international, and global levels.

In previous chapters we have seen how organized, disciplined, and evolving modes of organized violence have played a major role in the emergence and sociocultural evolution of states virtually from their inception. Not surprisingly, therefore, just as economics (notably) and politics (to a lesser extent) have expanded and developed on a global scale, so has warfare. What are the implications of this expansion for the world at large as the twentieth century comes to a close?

In this chapter we briefly review the course of military globalization and some of its implications for the growth and development of states of differing profiles; identify the relationship, if any, between economic growth and global war; assess nuclear deterrence as the prevailing global "peacekeeper" mechanism of our time; and compare the global economic, political, and military configurations and processes following World War II with the configurations and trends today.

The Globalization of War

We have noted how warfare of a kind (prestate, more or less ad hoc collective violence) contributed to some of the earliest continental and intercontinental migrations. Such conflicts must have remained localized and severely limited, however, until our forebears achieved more advanced weaponry, means of transportation (horses, the wheel, ocean-going ships, and so forth), and organizational knowledge and skills enabling them to establish kingdoms and expanding empires. But the great accelerations of military (and naval) globalization occurred with the emergence of nation-states and the extensive sixteenth-century Portuguese, Spanish, and Dutch conquests (of India, the East Indies, East Africa, Mexico, and Peru); later with British and French expansionism; again during the twentieth century with the massive human involvements and destructiveness of the two world wars; and, finally, with developments in nuclear weaponry and missile technology (the first potentially "global" weaponry heralded by the U.S. destruction of Hiroshima and Nagasaki in August 1945).

With the development of long-range missiles, the weapon-as-vehicle became a surrogate for the horse, motorized weapons carrier, warship, aircraft, and other forms of lethal transport. Informed by global intelligence satellites, an attacker could fire to the far side of the earth from its own backyard and strike any target anywhere in the world within thirty minutes.

From our perspective, the core dynamics of conflict, violence, and war are essentially the same for all nations in the global system, but depending on individual profiles and associated capabilities, leverage potentials, and constraints, activities, interests, and responses to threat may differ from nation to nation and situation to situation. In today's world, however, the rapid advancement and uneven distribution of technology (including the knowledge, skills, and tools of warfare), combined with the intensities of interstate interaction, tend to one degree or another to induce, co-opt, or coerce nations of all profiles (including the weakest) into competing for position in the global King of the Mountain game.

This situation is more complex, however, than it may appear at first glance. Indeed, it is complicated by the horizontal competitions and conflicts between major powers; between regional powers of roughly comparable capabilities; and between "lesser," regionally dominant powers and the countries they tend to penetrate with their (locally) superior capabilities and (locally) expanding activities and interests. With a beta profile, for example, Israel's relatively dense population shared with its Palestinian neighbors historical and religious claims to the same territory—a recipe for lateral pressures and violent collisions.

In penetrating a periphery country with their own activities and interests, major powers and superpowers often compete for influence, if not control, over the economic, political, and military relationships that connect the weaker country's center with the outside world. This tendency can further encourage client-state arrangements and polarize or otherwise shape the global configuration of power and various connecting networks of economic, political, and military exchange in complex ways. During cold war decades, more and more nations of the Third World became pawns in the struggle between hegemonic and challenger nations (and their international regimes). Nicaragua, Afghanistan, and Angola are only three of the many examples. Lebanon, a small, multiethnic, multisectarian country, found itself caught in overlapping conflicts—the cold war, Arab-Israeli conflicts, Muslim-Christian antagonisms, and intra-Muslim struggles—as domestic warlords and intruding neighbors tore apart what had been a flourishing state and razed a city once known as the Paris of the Middle East.

New Postwar Linkage Patterns

As former colonies achieved independence in the aftermath of World War II, linkage patterns changed accordingly—up to a point. Most industrialized nations, especially the World War II victors, continued to play significant economic, political, and military roles in regions of the periphery. As in the past, a preponderance of wars (revolutionary, civil, and international) were fought in developing parts of the world—often with the direct or indirect involvement of industrialized nations. After 1945, moreover, the United States and the Soviet Union (hegemon and challenger), separated by vast distances (except across the Bering Straits) and constrained by the possibility of mutually assured destruction (MAD), concentrated many of their most aggressive competitions and applications of leverage in Third World areas where revolution appeared endemic. In pursuit of its own advantage, each superpower extended and defended its own activities and interests as far as the expansionism and defenses of the other allowed.

Since World War II, the USSR, the United States, and other major powers have developed and applied specialized strategies and tactics (political, economic, paramilitary, military, and combinations thereof) for dealing with conflicts within such inter- and cross-profile networks—with varying degrees of success, confusion, and failure. In this chapter we begin with the generic conflicts, violent leverages, and wars that are characteristic of nations in the global periphery (the epsilons and zetas, primarily) and work our way toward the major powers and hegemonic contenders constituting the center.

Unless a developing country makes strong efforts to remain nonaligned, there is high risk that it will be penetrated by the expanding activities and interest of stronger countries and will become dependent upon one or another industrialized nation (particularly a major or superpower) for trade, aid, and overall security. To the extent that this occurs, a client relationship may develop. Even the leaders of a nonaligned country may find themselves becoming "less nonaligned" with one power than with others. As a client relationship develops, the weaker country is likely to find itself increasingly penetrated economically, politically, and often militarily by the stronger nation. The tighter the bond, the greater is the probability that the dominant power will intervene in domestic and external conflicts of the client and that the client will be drawn into the dominant power's external conflicts.

To a large extent post–World War II relationships between the United States and the Soviet Union—and between each of them and countries of the developing world—were manifestations of global competitions between the hegemonic power and its primary challenger. From the beginning of the cold war, Soviet leaders made use of strategies and tactics that were ready-made. Drawing on combined economic, political, and military codes devised by Lenin and modified by Stalin, the USSR began supporting indigenous revolutionary movements in the colonies, former colonies, and semicolonies in Asia and later in Africa and South America. In the role of postwar hegemon, the United States, lacking experience with or understanding of these measures, initially found itself hard put to respond effectively.

Against a cold war background of sponsorship by the USSR and the United States of client states and proxy wars in far-flung parts of the world (but at risk of oversimplification), we can define our concern in terms of linkages between a conflict involving two center states (hegemon and challenger, for example) and a second conflict between the center of a periphery nation and its periphery (Chinese Nationalists and Chinese Communists, for example, supported by the United States and the USSR, respectively) or between periphery client states (South Korea supported by the United States and North Korea supported by the USSR). If A perceives B's client (or ally) threatening its client (or ally), A may decide in effect that an attack by its client on B's client may be the most effective (or least costly) solution to A's security problem (Soviet and U.S. clients in China, the Koreas, Vietnam, Cuba, Nicaragua, El Salvador, Angola, Afghanistan). Variations on these dynamics (from technical assistance to terrorism) and all manner of covert operations by both sides (tit for tat) go a long way toward accounting for the patterns characterizing global conflict during most of the last half-century. Such interaction networks also risk a low-level periphery conflict (U.S. forces into Vietnam, Soviet troops into Afghanistan, the Cuban missile crisis) triggering an escalation to hegemonic (and global) levels.

Local Revolutions and Global Wars

To the extent that developing nations are characterized by relatively low levels of technology and weak economies, there is a high probability of conflict between classes (primarily landlords, peasants, a relatively few big merchants, bankers, and professionals, small numbers of industrial workers), between rival political elites, and between competing military factions. Within such a profile, full-blown revolutions are most likely to occur as technological development (usually imported from the affluent West) accelerates and public expectations rise commensurately. The United States— often for lack of substantial middle-of-the-road elements to ally with—has typically supported ultraconservative, reactionary, oppressive regimes (big landowners, compradors, military cliques, and the like) as a counterforce to contain Soviet lateral pressures. The USSR has commonly aligned itself with emergent, challenging elites from the periphery of periphery nations (alienated intellectuals, peasant revolutionaries, emergent proletarians, and other "dispossessed"). The realities have been much more complex, however, and the results for both the United States and the Soviet Union have been uneven overall.

In principle, Communist leaders since Lenin and Stalin have advocated support for "bourgeois nationalist" leaders (Sun Yat-sen, Chiang Kai-shek) in alliance with the petty bourgeoisie, the peasants, and the emergent proletariat against the "imperialists and their "agents," or "running dogs," during early stages of revolutionary struggle. During later, more acutely revolutionary stages, Marxism-Leninism required direct support for the peasants and the workers (as the national bourgeoisie used its newfound power to defend its own special interests). In practice, however, the Soviet Union, beginning as early as the early 1920s in China, pursued a multilevel policy. While making overtures and eventually sending an ambassador to the legal Chinese government in Beijing, the Soviet Union acted concurrently through the Third International, which was supplying Chiang and the Kuomintang and training the latter's armed forces in an effort to overthrow the Beijing government. Meanwhile, the Third International also supported the Chinese Communists, urging them to join the Kuomintang in order to establish contact with the masses and eventually capture the regime from within or oust it from leadership of the revolution. In fact, it worked the other way: Chiang Kai-shek—as soon as he had acquired enough military strength—broke with Moscow and used Soviet-supplied weapons in an attack that nearly obliterated the Communists.

In trying to contain the spread of communism in countries of the periphery and to encourage democracy, the United States has suffered setbacks of its own in situations not entirely different from those encountered by the USSR in China and elsewhere. The middle classes tend to be small and "underdeveloped" in Third World nations. The industrial labor forces are usually limited in size and are relatively untrained. Capital is in short supply. The prevailing technology and the economy are not sufficiently developed to accommodate large infusions of sophisticated technical assistance from the outside. The more influential elites have no understanding of, experience with, or desire for democratic process. Whatever capitalist class may have developed is likely to have more in common with its counterparts in the "center of the center" than with the masses of people in its own "periphery of the periphery" (Galtung, 1971:81–118).

Characteristically, Mao Zedong, Ho Chi-minh, Fidel Castro, and other revolutionary leaders adapted, incorporated into, and institutionalized within their respective states many of the revolutionary, class-oriented strategies and tactics that had contributed to their successes in guerrilla warfare—with varying consequences. For example, after almost a decade and a half of domestic "victories" or partial "victories," Mao and some of his more radical supporters carried these "state-building" techniques to the nether edge of collapse during the Great Proletarian Cultural Revolution. Twenty years later, Mao's successors used the People's Liberation Army to put down—with tanks and assault rifles—peaceful student demonstrators calling for more democracy.

Land reform, a prerequisite in many societies if agriculture is to become more productive and contribute capital for industrial development, has been undertaken in a number of Western-oriented as well as Marxist-Leninist states (proceeding from quite different models, of course) with varying degrees of success. A central problem confronted by Western-oriented societies was well illustrated after Corazon Aquino and her supporters replaced the repressive regime of Ferdinand Marcos in 1986 with free elections and a democratic constitution. Like their predecessors, the new ruling elite was drawn primarily from the class of large, often absentee landlord families, which, along with the presence of extensive U.S. military bases, made reform difficult to achieve in a society where the commercial middle class was still underdeveloped and a left-wing guerrilla movement was strong in the countryside.

All of these considerations have profound and often frightening implications for the world at large in the nuclear era. Gross asymmetries between industrialized nations and developing nations (as well as gross asymmetries and conflicts within them) can encourage terrorist acts, contribute to revolutionary or civil wars, and help transform relatively small conflicts into elements of superpower struggle in which weaker states become surrogates for stronger states.

With allowance for their near-disastrous errors in China during the 1920s and elsewhere, Stalin and other Marxist-Leninist leaders avoided for decades what they dismissed as the "adventurism" of the United States and other industrialized countries in revolutionary China, Cuba, Vietnam, and elsewhere. They kept their own people prudently off the battlefield (and well to the rear, as in Vietnam) until the invasion of Afghanistan, a debacle rivaling or surpassing the U.S. experience in Vietnam.

In the meantime, with spectacular advances in communication, organizational, and weapons technologies, specialists in terrorism have vastly increased their capacities for destruction. There is nothing new about this specialty. Thucydides recorded how terrorism contributed to wars in ancient Greece, and the triggering of World War I by Gavrilo Princip's terrorist act has already been discussed. Modern practitioners, however, have transformed their "craft" from "an esoteric aspect of aggression and violence to a predominant means" of psychological and physical leverage (Ward, 1984:309). There is no reason to doubt, moreover, that the strategies, tactics, and destructive power of terrorist activities will continue to escalate with social unrest and new advances in technologies of violence.

Third World Military Spending Militarization

Military spending by Third World countries has tended to increase with GNP. In the 1980s, developing nations were responsible for only 20 percent of global military expenditures as compared with the 80 percent spent by industrialized countries. Nevertheless, many developing nations spent more on their military establishments than they did for health or education, whereas the reverse was true for industrialized countries. In 1957, the Third World share (China excluded) accounted for about 4 percent of total military expenditures; by 1977 the share was 14 percent. This increase could not have been achieved without the tolerance and often the connivance—if not the pressure—of industrialized nations and the arms trade. In expanding arms sales, the governments of exporting countries have tended to be active entrepreneurial partners—bringing buyers and sellers together, issuing licenses, and providing training for Third World forces that could ensure the purchase of sophisticated equipment for a long time to come. With the proliferation of weapons-producing capabilities throughout the world, there has been a trend toward the export of arms not only by industrialized countries but by numbers of Third World nations as well—China being only one of several.

In countries pursuing development strategies as different as those of Maoist China, South Korea, and Taiwan (and Japan under U.S. occupation), war in one form or another has preceded and/or functioned as part of the revolutionary tactics of land reform and the establishment of a new regime. Some theoreticians and policy advisers in the West also pushed the idea that militarization could be a useful tool for economic and political development in Third World nations. Under such circumstances, it was not surprising that many governments emerged as military regimes. Some of the military equipment (and the advisers and technicians who often went with it) was used for strategic defense, but in many Third World regimes national leaders relied upon such imports to maintain themselves in office and strengthen their grip on the government and the society as a whole. This raises the question whether modernization can be effected without dictatorial coercion, revolutionary violence, or the discipline of military rule. The answer tends to vary from society to society. Most Third World countries under military control were among the poorest, but several were relatively affluent—notably Argentina (four coups), Brazil (one), Chile (one), with per capita GNPs of $4,361, $3,301 and $2,506, respectively—and some had serious debt problems.

These realities should not obscure the responsibilities of center nations, especially those of the United States, the USSR, and their respective international regimes. Of 114 countries categorized in the early 1980s as developing, 56 (in Latin America, Africa, the Middle East, and Asia) were under military control. With the possible exception of two or three for which data were not available, 11 relied upon industrialized countries (the United States, the USSR, West Germany, France, Great Britain, Italy) as major suppliers. Between 1960 and 1982, these 56 nations accounted for eighty coups compared with the fifteen experienced by the other 58 Third World nations. Afghanistan, Uganda, Syria, and the Central African Republic (three coups each); Bangladesh, Upper Volta, Peru, and Benin (four each); and Ghana (five) had per capita GNPs of $240, $468, $1,481, $333, $129, $221, $1,056, $322, and $359, respectively. Warfare defended domestic "security zones" in the relations of some states but kept many others in military straightjackets. Between 1960 and 1980, the aggregate of regular forces in Third World countries increased from 8.7 to 15.1 million soldiers, and military expenditure in these countries increased threefold.

The effects of post–World War II militarization in both developed and industrialized sectors of the world are difficult if not impossible to ascertain. This much is certain, however: The combination of modern weapons, rising military budgets, and expanding arms trade represented critical diversions of material and human resources at a time when life for millions of people in developing countries was marginal and flows of technical and economic aid from industrialized to Third World countries were in competition with military assistance to regimes that were often corrupt as well as dictatorial.

In countries of the periphery, as in those of the center, we would expect technological development in advance of (or at least commensurate with) population growth to encourage external expansion of the society's activities and interests insofar as appropriate capabilities allowed. Foreign trade would be a commonplace manifestation of Third World lateral pressure, but external military activities might also occur, especially to the extent that such a country's military capabilities were strong relative to those of its neighbors. Alternatively, the lateral pressures of two countries of relatively equal capabilities (Iran and Iraq, for example) might collide and erupt into warfare. In these terms, we would expect competitions, conflicts, and power transitions to occur with some frequency among developing countries caught up, to one extent or another, in the King of the Mountain game.

Major Power Wars

With the dropping of U.S. nuclear bombs on Hiroshima and Nagasaki and the opening of the nuclear age, scholars, statemen, and military strategists began reexamining both the processes and the institutions of warfare—notably global warfare—from several new perspectives. In view of the many competing approaches to the global (or world) system, it is not surprising that explanations of global war have also differed. In recent years, theorists and empirical investigators—some from neo-Marxist or "revolutionary" perspectives, others from "liberal" perspectives, and still others from "conservative" perspectives—have looked for correlations between economic cycles, or waves, and global-scale war (J. Goldstein, 1988).

Marx saw warfare as an outcome of fundamental contradictions in the capitalist system, and Lenin, strongly influenced by World War I, explained modern warfare among the "imperialist" powers as a struggle for redivision of the colonial world among them. More recently world-system theorists, influenced by Marx, have characterized warfare among core states in terms of contradictions and conflicts within or (as in the case of Immanuel Wallerstein and others) between states competing among themselves for economic advantage and expanding and contracting in long wave cycles (Bergesen, 1983:9–17). In general, writers of the world-system school have been more inclined than others to include the Third World in their studies of the global economy and war. Among contemporary approaches to connections or linkages between the global economy and global (or hegemonic) war, three are especially influential. Each approach has a leading theorist and numbers of scholars with similar perspectives: the world-system approach (Wallerstein); the long cycle approach (Modelski and others); and hegemonic stability theory approach (Gilpin, Keohane, Krasner).

World-System Approaches

In specifying the powerful ways in which economic factors can contribute to uneven growth, hegemonic competitions, and war, contemporary world-system theoreticians focus upon capitalist imperatives to the virtual exclusion of more generic and universal economic processes (Wallerstein, 1980:38). Capitalist contradictions, which these theorists identify as fundamentally antisystemic, produce structural strains and crises such that "the only possible outcome is the disappearance of the system as such, either by way of gradual disintegration (leading in unpredictable directions) or through a relatively controlled transformation (aimed in a predicted direction and implying its replacement by one of several other systems)" (Wallerstein, 1983:21).

From this perspective, international conflict is of lesser relevance to the global system than is the evolving structure of the world economy. In short, attempts by capitalist states to restructure the world market to their own advantage during expansionist phases of the world economy have led to increased competition and warfare between core states during contraction phases. Within this framework, a powerful state rises through conflict to hegemonic dominance, then declines, and is eventually replaced by a rising challenger. Processes and events other than "capital accumulation," however, are often relegated to "subordinate, less central concerns" (Thompson, 1983:369–370). This approach encourages the view that hegemonic dominion, long-term economic cycles, and hegemonic wars are primarily, even exclusively, attributable to the capitalist system.

Long Cycle Approaches

While accepting the realist view that the world economy lacks any "sovereign" authority, Modelski (1972:13–14, 50, 88) maintained that this situation does not mean that political regulation is wholly missing. On the contrary, a web, or network, of transactions connecting producers and consumers of goods and services worldwide constitutes a global political system. This system is regulatory but not territorially based, and fluctuations in global governance can be traced to long economic cycles. Each global war determines the termination of incumbent authority and the emergence of a new world power.

Long cycle theorists have been criticized for a tendency to treat economic and political considerations separately and for their inability to decide what the system's fundamental motors of change are (Thompson, 1983:369–370). These theorists have emphasized "the alternative periodicity of phases of world power and global war" but, according to critics, have paid insufficient attention to linkages between economic and political elements (J. Goldstein, 1985b:411–444). Long cycle theorists have inadequately addressed "how unequal advances and distributions of technology within and across states" originate and "relate to alternations between competition and hegemony" (R. Weber, 1983:50).

On the whole, the success of the search for correlations between economic waves and war has been indifferent. Analyzing great power system data from 1495 to 1975, Jack Levy (1983:137) found "no hints of any cyclical pattern in either the occurrence of war or any of the other dimensions." Using Levy's data, however, Joshua Goldstein (1985:416–417, 431–432; 1988:250–265) obtained findings that were inconclusive but promising (in terms of unraveling the relationships, if any, between economic cycles and occurrences of major wars). According to Goldstein, during these years there was a decline in incidence of great power war (more and more "peace years" separating them); great power wars became shorter; great power wars became increasingly severe (annual war fatalities rose more than one-hundredfold in five centuries); and there seemed to be a lengthening of war cycles in successive eras. Inflation was an important variable, but wars seemed to "cause" it rather than the other way around. Throughout recent centuries, the military competed with and impeded economic growth—"a monkey on the back of the world economy."

Causal relationships between long economic waves and hegemonic cycles were weak. Goldstein found "the two cycles playing out over time, each according to its own inner dynamic but each conditioned by and interacting with the other." Demands would rise during upswings of the global economy. "Countries would expand" (in terms of their activities and interests); this expansion would then "intersect" (with the expanding activities and interests of another major power), and "competition and war" would increase. Over time, faster growth would contribute to increasingly severe great power wars, which tended to drain the global economy and dampen long-term economic growth. Lower growth then led to wars of less severity, which allowed for faster economic growth and the start of a new buildup toward war—all in one fifty-year wave.

These and other recent efforts at establishing causal linkages among economic waves, state building (and development), and war suggest that "real" interconnections between economics and organized violence are far more complex and more deeply imbedded in domestic structures and generative processes of individual states than most cycle or wave theoreticians have postulated.

Hegemonic Stability Theory Approaches

Hegemonic stability theory has much in common with long cycle theory. According to this view, during periods of strong domestic growth and consolidation, the activities and interests of the hegemon and its main allies expand externally. As their capabilities and bargaining and leverage potentials are enhanced, a partial and precarious international "peace-through-domination" may be established (the European "peace" of the nineteenth century, for example). As the hegemon experiences further growth and development, an increasing bureaucratization of production occurs, along with an expansion of public and private services and governmental extraction (tax collection and associated functions). Allocation activities and attendant trends then combine with the costs of external expansion to constrain social and economic efficiency, which results in a proliferation of domestic crises. The hegemon may succeed in checking this tendency through a "renewal" program involving new investment priorities, the development of new technologies, a reordering of budget allocations, or even a "peaceful revolution" of some kind. The historical record suggests, however, that sooner or later the hegemon is likely to decline and its hegemonic system with it.

Organizational growth and development are self-sustaining and self-limiting in that achievement of a more advanced level may reduce incentives, create new pressures on diminishing resources, and encourage entrenched interests to resist growth in competing sectors. As such tendencies accumulate, a "continuing disequilibrium" and "the financial drain it entails if it is not resolved" can lead to the "eventual economic and political decline of the dominant power" (Gilpin, 1981:106).

The probabilities of hegemonic war are likely to escalate insofar as (1) the leaders and influential sectors of the hegemon's populace perceive their country's economic, political, and strategic dominance and security mortally threatened by the increasing capabilities and negative leverages of the challenger nation and (2) the leaders and influential sectors of the challenger's population, aware of the hegemon's vulnerabilities, perceive an unprecedented opportunity for achieving economic, political, and strategic security for their own country by destroying the dominance of the hegemon. The "objective" circumstances conducive to the convergence of these two sets of perceptions occur as the incumbent hegemon, having passed well beyond its apogee, suffers decline relative to the expanding capabilities, activities, and interests of its challenger (Doran and Parsons, 1980:952).

For the most part, hegemonic theory *at its best* has explained hegemonic war in terms of power transition, the assumption being that a state with increasing power (economic and/or political and/or military capabilities) challenges the incumbent hegemon and, if successful in the struggle for dominance, replaces it. Undoubtedly, these dynamics account for a considerable proportion of the variance, but they are not necessarily sufficient; at least two additional variables may be required—lateral pressure (more specifically the major direction of the expansion of a nation's activities and interests) and the quality of relations (positive or negative) that an expanding nation has with whatever countries lie in the path of such expansion. An example from recent history will highlight the problem.

In 1914, Great Britain (according to subsequent agreement by theorists) was the incumbent hegemon, and Germany was the challenger. By that year, however, the United States had already surpassed both Great Britain and Germany on three commonly used indicators of power (in terms of relative capability indicators): industrial production (United States, 43 percent in 1910; Germany, 20 percent; and Great Britain, 19 percent); leading sector position (United States, 50 percent; Germany, 18 percent; Great Britain, 15 percent); and GNP (United States, 41 percent; Great Britain, 14 percent; Germany, 12 percent). In terms of naval expenditures, the relative strengths were different (Great Britain, 33 percent; United States, 19 percent; Germany, 17 percent). Only in the case of battleships was the United States not first (presumed hegemon) or second (presumed challenger). If we accept the validity of these indicators, we must ask ourselves why the United States was not the target of World War I (as the incumbent hegemon) or the overtaking challenger. Could the number of battleships have been so strong a differentiating variable? Or must other variables combine with rising capabilities to define the challenger (or the newly recognized hegemon)?

The relative capabilities of the three powers in the late 1930s are even more revealing: industrial production (United States, 39 percent; Germany, 13 percent; Great Britain, 11 percent); leading sector position (United States, 57 percent; Germany, 13 percent; Great Britain, 8 percent); GNP (United States, 41 percent; Germany, 13 percent; Great Britain, 11 percent); naval expenditures (United States, 17 percent; Great Britain, 27 percent; Germany, 20 percent; and battleships (United States, 20 percent; Great Britain, 20 percent; Germany, 7 percent). In this war, from a hegemonic perspective, Germany should have challenged the United States. But as it did not, we must assume that in many instances relative power by itself is not a reliable predictor of hegemonic or other wars.

As suggested in Chapter 6, concerted westward expansion helps explain why the United States did not play either a challenger or a hegemonic role in World Wars I and II. Lateral pressures—along with relative capabilities and focused negative leveraging (power$_2$)—help explain and predict the direction and target of a country's offensive (and/or defensive) military undertakings.

Military Expansionism

Since World War II, lateral pressures exerted by various countries have included the maintenance of military bases beyond domestic borders and the stationing of troops on foreign territory. The total of the world's armed forces on foreign soil in 1983 was reported at 1.6 million.

In the early 1980s, the United States had 360 major military bases (some adjacent to Soviet borders) and 1,600 installations in thirty-six nations—the largest and most advanced system of military, naval, and air bases in history. Of the 461,130 U.S. forces abroad, 319,000 were in Europe. The USSR had fewer established sites beyond its borders, but including its 115,000 troops in Afghanistan, Soviet troops accounted for a larger percentage (40 percent) than did any other country of the 1,937,530 global total of troops on foreign territory. A total of 700,880 military personnel were stationed abroad; 584,000 were in Warsaw Pact nations (Poland, Czechoslovakia, East Germany, and Hungary), 95,000 or more were in Afghanistan, and about 21,800 were elsewhere (Sivard, 1987:8–9; 1985:13).

Aside from Eastern Europe, the USSR stationed troops in Cuba (4,600 Warsaw Pact troops), in Vietnam, and in a dozen or so Middle Eastern and African nations. In the Far East, Soviet lateral pressures during the 1950s were manifested in the name of friendship, alliance, common interest, and shared goals by large-scale aid to the PRC and by its penetration by thousands of Soviet technicians, advisers, and industrial complexes. As an outcome of the Sino-Soviet conflict, however, this support was withdrawn, and during the 1960s, armed clashes occurred with some frequency between Soviet and Chinese forces along the Ussuri and Amur rivers and on the border between Chinese Xinjiang and the Soviet Republic of Kazakhistan. By the 1970s, the USSR and the PRC confronted each other along a common border with some 300,000 or more troops on either side backed by air bases, missile sites, and warships.

During these years, at least twenty other nations (including several developing countries) had troops stationed abroad, whereas ninety-three countries and territories had foreign installations or bases on their soil. The deployment of armed forces figured prominently in relations between core countries and periphery countries. Notable examples included Soviet relations with North Korea, North Vietnam, Cuba, and Afghanistan and U.S. relations with South Korea, South Vietnam, Israel, the Dominican Republic, Chile, Guatemala, and El Salvador. In Angola, the USSR used the armed forces of one client, Cuba, as surrogate "peacekeepers" in another client state. At times, the United States, Israel, and Lebanon found themselves in similar relationships. Meanwhile, the United States employed armed forces against Soviet influence in the Western Hemisphere—indirectly in Nicaragua (2.5 million people, 130,000 square kilometers in area, $830 per capita GNP, 75,000 troops) and directly in the Dominican Republic (6 million people, 49,000 square kilometers, $1,175 per capita GNP, 16,000 troops) and in Grenada. Between them, in the 1980s, the United States and the USSR had approximately 50,000 nuclear weapons—more than enough to destroy each other several times over (and possibly civilization as well).

Since the end of World War II, a large proportion of superpower conflicts and crises have involved developing nations in one way or another. In 1962, Soviet attempts to install missile bases in Cuba led to the Cuban missile crisis, which brought the USSR and the United States to the brink of nuclear war—a reality both sides have fully acknowledged in recent years (with agreement among surviving U.S. and Soviet officials that they came closer to a nuclear exchange than they fully realized at the time).

A comparison of sources indicates that approximately 130 major wars (each of 1,000 fatal casualties or more) were fought during the four decades following the termination of World War II. With one possible exception (the Soviet intervention in Hungary), all major wars during these decades were fought in developing countries. The average number of wars per year in the 1950s was nine, in the 1960s the yearly average was eleven, and during the 1970s and 1980s the average was fourteen. There was not a single year in which fewer than four wars were being fought (Sivard, 1983:15–20; 1985:9–10). The total of casualties suffered has been estimated at 16 million deaths (many more civilians than troops). The largest number of deaths by far occurred in Asia (see Table 9.1).

The Fourth Image and Hegemonic Instability

At once spectacular and universally threatening, twentieth-century knowledge and skills ushered in the nuclear revolution, nuclear proliferation, and the post–World War II "balance of terror." As a consequence, national

TABLE 9.1
Illustrative Distribution of Wars and Casualties, 1816–1980

Country	Total Years in System	Wars	Total Battle Deaths (000s)	Total War Months	Battle Deaths (000s) per Year	Wars per Year	War Months per Year	Months per War	Battle Deaths (000s) per War	Battle Deaths (000s) per Month
France	163	22	1,965.12	604.1	12.056	0.135	3.71	27.46	89.32	3.253
U.K.	163	19	1,295.23	409.8	70.850	0.115	2.48	21.57	68.17	3.161
USSR	165	19	9,731.20	285.8	58.977	0.115	1.73	15.04	512.17	34.049
Italy	165	12	759.50	154.7	4.603	0.073	0.94	12.89	63.29	4.910
China	121	11	3,128.50	207.9	25.855	0.091	1.72	18.90	284.41	15.048
Spain	165	10	195.90	276.3	1.187	0.061	1.67	27.63	19.59	0.709
Japan	114	9	1,371.45	197.9	12.030	0.079	1.74	21.99	152.38	6.930
Austria/Hungary	103	8	1,287.20	77.7	12.497	0.078	0.75	9.71	160.90	16.566
U.S.	165	8	664.82	262.3	4.029	0.048	1.59	32.79	83.10	2.535
Germany	130	6	5,353.50	139.4	41.181	0.046	1.07	23.23	892.25	38.404
Romania	103	5	639.50	65.2	6.209	0.049	0.63	13.04	127.90	9.808
India	34	5	14.00	17.3	0.412	0.147	0.51	3.46	2.80	0.809
El Salvador	106	4	1.05	4.3	0.014	0.038	0.04	1.07	0.38	0.349
Mexico	150	3	19.00	84.8	0.127	0.020	0.57	28.27	6.33	0.224
Brazil	155	3	101.50	80.0	0.655	0.019	0.52	26.67	33.83	1.269
Peru	140	3	11.60	59.2	0.083	0.021	0.42	19.73	3.87	0.196
Honduras	82	3	1.80	3.8	0.022	0.037	0.05	1.27	0.60	0.474
Canada	61	2	39.61	102.3	0.649	0.033	1.68	51.15	19.80	0.387
Denmark	160	2	6.50	11.5	0.041	0.012	0.07	5.75	3.25	0.565
Nicaragua	81	1	0.40	2.0	0.005	0.012	0.02	2.00	0.40	0.200
Sweden	165	0	0.00	0.0	0.000	0.000	0.00	0.00	0.00	0.000
Ireland	59	0	0.00	0.0	0.000	0.000	0.00	0.00	0.00	0.000
Iceland	37	0	0.00	0.0	0.000	0.000	0.00	0.00	0.00	0.000

Note: During their total "years in the system," at least 80 nations have avoided participation in any international war as defined by Singer and Small. Of these countries, more than 60 are Third World nations, most of which have "entered the system" since World War II. By definition, many major power interventions in colonial regions are excluded from this listing.

Source: Compiled from J. David Singer and Melvin Small, *Resort to Arms: International and Civil Wars, 1816–1980* (Beverly Hills, Calif.: Sage, 1982), pp. 167–173. Reprinted by permission of the authors.

leaders and rank-and-file citizenry alike have tended to rely upon their own nuclear weapons, or those of a more powerful ally, as the ultimate mechanism for survival in a thermonuclear balance of terror.

With Soviet and U.S. expansionism (lateral pressures) since World War II, the U.S. policy of containment, and the Soviet acquisition of nuclear capabilities, the problem was how to use the new weaponry to further national security and related interests. The answer recommended by some specialists was a combination of "massive response" capabilities and "flexible targeting." In the late 1940s, when Soviet forces appeared to be "posing a threat to Western Europe and Japan" and the United States had "only" about fifty atomic bombs, U.S. war plans emphasized strikes against industrial areas on the assumption that destroying them would also destroy the supplies essential for Soviet ground and naval operations. Although there was no deliberate counterpopulation targeting at the time, population damage was viewed as an inescapable by-product to such an attack. During the cold war years and down to the present and while thermonuclear weapons were being perfected, three major stategic concepts were developed—massive retaliation, mutually assured destruction, and flexible response.

Deterrence as War Prevention

The outbreak of war in Korea lent urgency to U.S. security problems. In 1954, Secretary of State John Foster Dulles announced a doctrine of "massive retaliation," through which the United States could respond "with large-scale attacks at a time and place not necessarily commensurate with Soviet provocation" (Martin, 1979:4–6). But although President Truman indicated to the press at the time of the Chinese intervention in Korea that an atomic attack on the PRC was under consideration, the USSR and European security remained the primary U.S. external concern (Bracken, 1983:77–79).

With the expansion of nuclear stocks in the United States, the USSR, and elsewhere, the term *deterrence* acquired two meanings: (1) a threat to discourage a strike by the adversary and (2) a generalized quantum leap in military capability calculated to enhance vastly the credibility and leverage potential of the leaders or diplomats of any nuclear power in the negotiation of sensitive issues. Deterrence theorists commonly point to the fact that in spite of the cold war the two superpowers have avoided a "hot war" as evidence of the efficacy of nuclear weapons as peacekeepers. The usefulness of nuclear weapons as a "diplomatic stock" for application in day-to-day diplomacy is less widely touted.

These considerations, combined with advances in weaponry (the development of advanced missiles such as Polaris and Minuteman), led to the concept of mutually assured destruction. MAD "encouraged the idea that the strategic arms competition was emerging on a plateau where, in the absence of any effective defense, mutual deterrence might be permanently assured by quite small arsenals of strategic weapons needing no further perfection." Capacities for assured destruction seemed to create a situation in which each adversary would be constrained by fear of what the other could certainly inflict in retaliation. The complacency was punctured, however, by the invention of "practical methods of defense against ballistic missiles." This led to the concepts of flexible response, selective targeting (Martin, 1979:4–6), second-strike capability, first-strike capability, limited nuclear war, and preemptive strike. All these concepts indicated that developments in strategic thinking were strongly influenced by changes that had taken place in the characteristics of the weapons themselves (the early shift in emphasis, for example, from bombs dropped from aircraft to warheads delivered by missiles, and thence from single to multiple warheads, and so forth). Each of these developments had implications not only for defense procurement and military strategy but also for the role (and fate) of noncombatants in the event of a nuclear war.

Dissatisfied with prevailing U.S. nuclear doctrines, Robert McNamarra, secretary of defense during the Kennedy administration, proposed a new approach that was concerned largely with damage limitation and that placed greater emphasis on counterforce—the selective targeting of a wide range of military targets. This approach involved the selection of targets apart from Soviet urban centers that could be struck with large numbers of warheads—but with allowance for "exceptions from the basic plan which could be fired later in the battle if desired" (Pranger and Labrie, 1977:85). Selective targeting and counterforce seemed to imply that a user could "win."

The next substantial change came during the later stages of the Vietnam War when President Nixon (1977:17), noting that the USSR had embarked on a formidable expansion of its nuclear arsenal, asserted unequivocally that massive retaliation alone was "no longer credible in all circumstances and decisive nuclear superiority was probably unattainable." Nixon's statement implied new opportunities for diplomacy. Nevertheless, he contended, in the event of a nuclear war, a U.S. president "should not be left with the single option of ordering the mass destruction of enemy civilians, in the face of the certainty that it would be followed by the mass slaughter of Americans." A "sufficient" nuclear capability must now be coupled with a "sufficient" conventional capacity to allow for the application of resources across "the full spectrum" of possible capabilities and conflicts.

Behind advocacy of the doctrine of flexible response combined with selective targeting capability was the assumption that the United States could strike pinpointed targets (nuclear installations) while relying on its own nuclear superiority (and capacity for massive retaliation) to deter retaliation from the Soviet Union. A narrowing of the U.S.-Soviet nuclear capability gap, together with the Strategic Arms Limitation Talks (SALT I) agreement banning antiballistic missiles and the development of multiple independently targeted reentry vehicles (MIRVs), undercut this assumption because each missile could hit several separate targets.

Consideration of this issue led to a round of debates between those supporting a flexible response capability—which set aside as a deterrence policy the use of nuclear threats against the civilian adversary (Rowan,

1979:131)—and those who, while critical of MAD, insisted that the "mutual hostage" relationship between the U.S. and Soviet populations was not only an inescapable "fact" but also the most persuasive deterrent available ("DOD Report FY72," 1977:33). In reality, according to the latter group, measures appearing to spare civilian populations might increase the probabilities of their destruction. In any case, the doctrine of flexible response revolved around concepts of "low-casualty," "controlled" nuclear warfare, thus removing one of "the most essential fears at the heart of deterrence" (Iklé, 1977:57–74).

As put forward by Secretary of Defense James R. Schlesinger (1977:107), a "selective targeting doctrine" opened possibilities for "limited-strike options"—a change calculated to "shore up deterrence across the entire spectrum of risk" and thus reduce the likelihood of nuclear war. The object was to keep levels of conflict as low as possible but to widen options to include, if necessary, a limited nuclear strike. Schlesinger conceded that it was difficult to identify circumstances in which such a strike might be considered. "What I am saying," he told the Senate Foreign Relations Committee, "is that it is easier to think of circumstances in which limited use might occur than to think of a massive all-out strike."

Physicist Sidney Drell (1983:14, 85) conceded that criticisms of deterrence based on "threatening tens and hundreds of millions of helpless citizens with annihilation" was "pretty strong and on target." But he also concluded with the caveat that "unless—or until—the human species makes that next great evolutionary advance by learning to resolve our differences peacefully," there will be "no escape from the mutual hostage relationship" of nuclear readiness and "no choice but to make deterrence work."

In support of flexible response, Fred Iklé (1977:58, 72), head of the United States Arms Control and Disarmament Agency, proposed that the United States design nuclear forces "almost exclusively for 'retaliation' in response to a Soviet nuclear attack" (second-strike capability). Such forces "must be designed and operated in such a way that 'retaliation' can be swift, inflicted through a single, massive and—above all—prompt strike," and "the threatened retaliation must be the killing of a major fraction of the Soviet population." In addition, for deterrence to work, the Soviets must be guaranteed the same ability "to kill our population" in retaliation.

Others challenged the assumption that "we know what will deter the Soviets (and eventually the Chinese or any other Johnny-come-latelies in the nuclear arena) from achieving their avowed objectives through nuclear aggression" once other means had failed. Would the Soviets or others let millions of casualties deter them from pursuing the interests of the "Communist cause"? (T. Powers, 1982:110).

Critics of the critics, while calling for refinements in MAD and the second-strike concept, took exception to the claim that the old doctrine, dating from the days of Robert McNamara, required "prompt, even instant" launching or that deterrence based on threats to the survival of civilian society had become outdated (Garnett, 1979:216). Such a view was fundamentally unrealistic. The hotline and other safeguards were designed to allow for delay, consultation, and exchanges of information with the adversary, and "the destructiveness of today's offensive arsenal of nuclear weapons is so overwhelming that deaths would number in millions or tens of millions if only a fraction of available weapons were delivered against the opponent's homeland" (Iklé, 1977:74–77).

Other informed critics were less confident. With many years of experience with issues of deterrence, physicist Wolfgang Panofsky (1979:83) warned that whatever plans were made to fight a "controlled" nuclear conflict, there could be "no certain methods to protect the U.S. population" if the adversary decided to respond with an "anti-population attack." To project an image of a "'clean' nuclear war generating minimum civilian casualties," moreover, "could make the use of nuclear weapons in limited conflicts more acceptable." In fact, the technology for counterforce, was "virtually indistinguishable from that needed for a first-strike threat to the opponents' strategic forces."

The concepts of flexibility, selective targeting, and limited nuclear strike suggested new potentials for negative leveraging that were largely absent in massive retaliation and MAD. Having come to view nuclear weapons in Europe as a possible "trip wire" for massive retaliation against invasion from the East, NATO leaders had built tactical nuclear weapons into their strategy, and they increasingly recognized possibilities for "transmitting diplomatic signals, inspiring confidence in allies, discouraging foes, influencing crises and signifying degrees of commitment" (Martin, 1979:16).

Concurrently, however, there was a growing fear among many citizens in Western Europe that employment of medium-range U.S. and Soviet missiles in the region, which were meant to provide a "lower level" alternative to the firing of intercontinental missiles by the two superpowers, might enhance the probabilities of limited nuclear war at the expense of Europeans upon either side of the East-West demarcation line. In general, critics of flexible response, selective targeting, and limited nuclear strategies saw no technological distinction between "weapons endangering the deterrent forces of the opponent in a first preemptive strike . . . and weapons designed for strategic retaliation" (Martin 1979:16). With shorter missile delivery times, there could be a tendency to reconsider first-strike options as "defense" against an offense that might not have been launched (Panofsky, 1977:83). This was an unparalleled milieu for the ultimate Game of Chicken. Finally, confidence in flexible response, selective targeting, and the possibility of fighting a limited war could be meshing ominously with the 1973 assertion by Soviet Minister of Defense Marshal Grechko (1977:207) that in the event of a global nuclear war, victory "would go to us."

One of the more disturbing aspects of the deterrence strategy was—and is—that *perceptions* by world leaders of the desired stability of nuclear deterrent forces can be as "real" as the real strategic arsenals themselves. Developing a theory of deterrence moves thus has involved a "tenuous relationship" between the United States and the Soviet Union that depends "not only on obvious objective factors" but also on "the perceptions, or misperceptions, of those who have the ability to induce Armageddon" (Zagare, 1987:177–178).

All in all, long-term reliance on mutual deterrence runs the risk of becoming a neverending, exorbitantly expensive struggle for dominance (requiring reassessment, readjustment, and strategic rethinking with each advance in weaponry). Such uncertainties, moreover, could involve increasing numbers of countries and their clients.

Star Wars

Early in 1985, President Reagan, reversing a widely shared assumption of the 1960s and 1970s, interpreted a tendency toward new, mobile MIRVs as undermining nuclear stability and the principle of mutual deterrence. Drawing on research begun in the Carter administration, he gave high priority to a new strategic defense initiative (SDI), often referred to as Star Wars, which attracted immediate attention as a potential umbrella against nuclear attack. Given that research in this direction had scarcely begun, the proposal was difficult to evaluate, even by highly trained specialists, but serious doubts arose.

Inherent in the SDI concept was a danger of relying upon computerized command and control systems requiring millions of programmed elements that could not be effectively debugged prior to firing. The planting of "worms" and "viruses," moreover, could become a new covert specialization. There was also the likelihood that even an optimally effective system would remain 5–10 percent vulnerable (50 to 100 missiles out of every 1000 might reach their targets)—an estimate that took no account of nuclear weapons delivered by aircraft, cruise missiles, or clandestine means. Arms control specialist Sidney Drell thought that SDI could be effective only if levels of available nuclear weapons were greatly reduced. SDI, meanwhile, could be a first step toward a militarization of space and an invitation for an adversary to forge a global sword to pierce the global shield. Some skeptics warned that by inviting attack, Star Wars could provide new incentive for a preemptive strike.

Relevant, also, was the observation that weapons, doctrines, and strategies considered "defensive" by the possessing nation might be viewed as offensive by the adversary (Drell, 1983:74–82). With relatively minor adjustments, an SDI installation might be converted to offensive purposes. There was also concern that regional populations living under an SDI umbrella might become vulnerable through complacency. Foreign Secretary Sir Geoffrey Howe (1985:8) of Great Britain warned against the creation of a twenty-first-century Maginot Line that could be outflanked by "relatively simpler and demonstrably cheaper countermeasures." Presumably, SDI would not defend a society from domestic nuclear "hijack" or a revolution triggering a nuclear exchange. Finally, in line with power transition assumptions (and peculiarly characteristic of power dynamics in the nuclear era), there was the additional risk that an adversary perceiving itself substantially behind in a Star Wars race might be strongly motivated to launch a preemptive attack before the leading adversary could operationalize its SDI capabilities.

What has been called the nuclear revolution brought about fundamental changes in global realities and strategies thinking. The first (and possibly the only) "defensive" volley may have to be fired before the first "offensive" volley reaches its target, even before the "offensive" volley is triggered (preemptive strike). Noncombatant societies may be destroyed along with the combatants. Civilians may replace military forces as prime targets for both sides. Casualties may be suffered generations after hostilities have ceased.

During the 1980s, the nuclear threat was put in a new and even more disturbing perspective by warnings of nuclear winter—a possible global consequence of multiple nuclear explosions. A group of U.S. scientists warned that "long-term exposure to cold, dark and radioactivity—when combined with prompt destruction from nuclear blast, fall-out, and the later enhancement of solar radiation due to ozone depletion—could pose a serious threat to human survivors and to other species" in the Northern and Southern hemispheres. Independently, a group of Soviet scientists reached similar conclusions at about the same time (Turco et al., 1983:203–204, 225–229). Subsequent studies modified details of this perspective, but the implications remained the same.

The crux of nuclear era is this: Modern warfare and preparations for it are global in ways far beyond "global" wars of the post-Westphalian era or of World War I and pre-Hiroshima World War II. Historical concepts of strategic security are obsolete—as obsolete as time-honored notions of hegemonic stability. But where do we go from here? There are no ready answers.

Tomorrow's King of the Mountain

In the past, serious challengers to the dominance of the hegemon have usually combined economic and military strength, but in its cold war challenge to the United States, the USSR has been militarily competitive but relatively weak economically. In the late 1970s and 1980s, the economic challenge to the United States came from Japan and the European Community (EC), not from the Soviet Union.

During the cold war, which plagued the post–World War II global system for decades, both sides soon learned that for purposes of realpolitik and coercive diplomacy, the usefulness of nuclear weapons as instruments of diplomatic leverage was severely limited. How far could a state nudge its rival with a weapon that threatened mass destruction if actually launched? This constraint put a premium on conventional forces, proxy wars, and covert operations for purposes of diplomatic coercion.

The Soviet-U.S. Competition for Military Hegemony

In the late 1960s and early 1970s, the emergence of a shaky Soviet-U.S. détente appeared to offer a respite in the cold war. In order to "maintain its momentum as a process" and to succeed, however, the relationship's competitive aspects had to be constrained and its reciprocal and collaborative aspects greatly strengthened. When the SALT II Interim Agreement was first being negotiated in the early 1970s, the balance of forces appeared unequal— with the United States still ahead in important ways. But by the end of the decade, a change for the worse had occurred, especially with the failure of Senate ratification of the SALT II agreements signed by President Jimmy Carter and Secretary General Leonid Brezhnev in 1979 (Breslauer, 1983:336). Yet the norms that had been agreed upon were minimal. Each side pursued policies and activities that supported its own activities and interests as the search for unilateral advantages continued to escalate (Smoke, 1984:176–177).

Although a subsequent worsening of Soviet-U.S. relations did not lead directly to anything like a war-threatening confrontation, it did contribute to dangerous instability and uncertainty between the two superpowers. The narrowing gap between the U.S. and Soviet nuclear and overall military capabilities could be explained in various ways. Because weapons scientists in the United States had determined years previously that "there was no good reason for large-yield weapons," they had therefore designed smaller weapons, although the USSR could "deliver more mega-tonnage." Although the Soviets had more missiles, U.S. missiles could be launched more quickly and were more accurate. U.S. bombers, moreover, "could deliver far more weapons than the small force of Soviet bombers," and U.S. missile-carrying submarines were difficult to track (Frei, 1982:212–215).

Some critics of détente attributed the narrowing of the gap to an inexcusably "soft" U.S. foreign policy and charged that the country had been hoodwinked. The debate was complicated by difficulties in the assessment and comparison of Soviet and U.S. capabilities. Buildups in Soviet conventional arms, moreover, had greatly extended the country's external influence. Insufficiently supported by economic and associated domestic assets, however, Soviet military power did not translate well into political bargaining and leverage potentials overseas. Although it would have been a mistake to underestimate Soviet strength, overestimation could also have deleterious effects.

Whereas increases in U.S. military budgets could be attributed to varying combinations of domestic and external influences, budgetary constraints could be construed to mean that pressures for incremental spending were being played down and that a substantial increase in any one year could offset trends toward further increases down the road. In the USSR, by contrast, this phenomenon appeared to be absent. In the early 1980s, according to one study of Soviet trends, there was no dynamic feedback between weapons stockpiled (or budgeted) and the tension level (Breslauer, 1983:336).

There was another source of uncertainty. On the basis of the military expenditure data used for analysis, one study went so far as to dismiss the Soviet-U.S. arms race as "a chimaera"—which it very likely was but not in the sense that the study intended. Although the two superpowers certainly were "building nuclear arms," they were not in fact competing or racing with each other (as they themselves alleged) (Smoke, 1984:215–216). A critic with an equally skeptical but opposing viewpoint charged that congressional debates provided evidence so sufficient that no "econometric study" was needed to prove that U.S. defense expenditures were geared to Soviet expenditure (Ward, 1984:309). Along the same lines, a 1983 content analysis of correlations between statements of the Soviet minister of finance in his annual budget speeches and actual military expenditures suggested that with respect to Soviet military budget changes, Soviet leaders acted as if they were responding to U.S. behavior of some kind, although not necessarily to U.S. military budget changes (Kugler, Organiski, and Fox, 1980:238).

A subsequent study provided evidence in support of this latter perspective. Rather than react to each other through defense budgets alone, the United States and the USSR each tried to equal or surpass the other in stocks of conventional and strategic weapons (Holzman, 1980:103). The analysis did reveal, however, that the United States tended to decrease its expenditures "in relation to a friendlier diplomatic climate with the USSR," whereas Soviet disposition was toward "increased investment in the face of a more cooperative international political climate" (Zimmerman and Palmer, 1987:365–366).

According to one view, by the mid-1980s the USSR and the United States appeared to have reached positions of relative military parity. One writer proposed that the lead in "a number of measures of strategic capabilities" had passed to the Soviets, but whereas the USSR had made advances in "all strategic components," the United States continued to maintain an advantage "in some strategic capabilities." In any case, whether or not the USSR had achieved parity or superiority, the strategic balance had become less favorable from a U.S. perspective than it once had been (Shulman, 1982:77–100). This did not mean, however, that either of the two superpowers, despite some 50,000 nuclear weapons between them, "could achieve mean-ingful—in the sense of militarily useful—strategic superiority" or that it would be politically helpful "to articulate such a goal" (Blechman, 1982:252–253).

Other observers from a different perspective maintained that the U.S. arms effort had leveled off more than a decade previously, whereas the USSR had pursued its military buildup through parity to substantial advantage. But according to a third perspective, the United States during the 1970s and early 1980s had targeted the Soviet Union with more weapons than the USSR had targeted on it. Thus, whereas some observers thought that the U.S. military establishment was holding its own at the very least, others asserted that the USSR, with an economy scarcely half that of the United States, was allocating more resources to its military establishment than the United States had been spending and steadily gaining the advantage.

By the 1980s, growing numbers of observers and analysts were concerned that the United States might be declining on all three core dimensions (economic [relative to Japan], political, and strategic) vis-à-vis the USSR. Clearly, a great deal depended upon the U.S. ability and determination to reduce its deficits to safer levels, to save more, and to recapture its command of the basic research and capital-generating production that had characterized its past growth and development. In a sense, leaders of the two superpowers, and through them the two societies, had been competing with enemies they themselves had fabricated—monster enemies that kept both sides committed to risks and costs that were potentially threatening to the political, economic, and strategic security that both sides pursued.

Glasnost' *and* Perestroika—*an End to the Cold War?*

Meanwhile, a remarkable "switch" seemed to be occurring. During some forty years of cold war, economies throughout the world had grown and developed while leaders of the major powers had interpreted strategic inabilities as the primary global threat. Yet by the late 1980s, evidence of economic overstrain was accumulating within both superpowers and in the world at large. Dating from the ascendancy of Mikhail Gorbachev, the Soviet leadership began to focus inwardly on problems of economic security at a time when national and trade deficits were widening in the United States.

In terms of the security dilemma and its corollary, new uncertainties were raised. By the late 1980s, many Western observers were interpreting Gorbachev's efforts toward *glasnost'* (openness), *perestroika* (restructuring), and renewed arms control negotiations with the United States as evidence of a personal sensitivity to fundamental Soviet problems and/or evidence of President Reagan's success in rebuilding a credible nuclear deterrent. With respect to an appropriate U.S. response, some U.S. analysts reasoned that economic security in both countries would benefit from the opportunity to divert capital from the arms race into potentially more productive sectors. Others suspected the USSR of protecting its own strategic capabilities while fostering complacency in the United States. A few saw an opportunity for the United States to secure a military advantage while the USSR restructured its economic foundations. More widely shared were serious doubts as to whether Gorbachev could overcome the stolid resistance of party apparatchiks and millions of workers apprehensive about the introduction of competition in the workplace. Concern also extended to the possibility that non-Russian nationalities in the Baltic states, the Caucasus, and elsewhere might seize upon the new openness to articulate long-suppressed aspirations for autonomy (if not independence). Many close observers suspected that only a confederation of some kind could hold the many nationalities together in the long run. Meanwhile, if Gorbachev were to fail, governance of the multinational state might fall into the hands of a military dictator.

At the same time, the United States faced difficult social and economic issues of its own—drugs, homeless people, unresolved civil rights problems, crime, an eroded educational system, and long-term indebtedness. Fortuitously for U.S. hegemony, just as the USSR was constrained by a flawed economy, Japan (the prime challenger to U.S. economic predominance) was limited militarily. There was no challenger on the horizon to compete with the United States on both dimensions. Although U.S. dependence upon external events was steadily increasing, the country, as pointed out by Fred Bergsten (1988:65), ran no immediate risk of "being overtaken and pushed into second class status by a new global leader," as the United States itself had succeeded Great Britain early in the century. There was good reason to believe, however, that the global configuration of economic power was almost certain to change. In terms of economic capabilities, for example, if the European Community achieved new unity, a three-cornered global distribution of economic concentrations seemed probable: (1) the EC, (2) the United States and Canada, and (3) Japan and the western Pacific rim. But Bergsten expected that the United States would still be capable of "blocking any conceivable economic initiative undertaken by others." At the same time, however, the United States could no longer compel other countries to "accept its views on major issues, or induce them to do so without financial and other rewards."

For those who hoped for a more constructive turn of events, the uncertainties were global rather than national. In the course of uncounted millennia of sociocultural evolution, the state had emerged as an ingenious and increasingly complex organizational device that relied upon concentrated capabilities and bargaining and leverage potentials (centering upon organized violence) for the maintenance of a domestic environment safe from internal disorder and external attack. Much as it had become difficult to conceive of a state without the sanctions of police power, so, too, the notion of a state without centralized military capabilities and negative leverage potentials for the exercise of coercive diplomacy, deterrence, and active measures of "defense" became virtually inconceivable.

Just as global economic interactivity and interdependence were now intensified, there was growing recognition not only that military costs were becoming a "monkey on the back" of many national economies (including those of the two superpowers) but that in many respects military leverages were losing much of their historical effectiveness. As the 1990s approached, the superpower military future seemed to depend to a large extent upon the readiness of the USSR to transfer capital from military to civilian production and the willingness of the United States to reciprocate.

Increasingly, the whole structure of global peacekeeping—founded on doctrines of coercive (military) diplomacy and deterrence—appeared outmoded to many observers. Because of their potentials for rapid escalation and global-level destruction (and, more immediately, if less spectacularly, their debilitating costs), weapons of the late twentieth century appeared to be losing, rather than gaining, day-to-day effectiveness in managing crises. The list was depressing—from China in the 1940s to Southeast Asia in the 1950s and 1960s, to recurring warfare in the Middle East, to obscure guerrilla activities in Africa and Central America. Costly to apply, the stick—whether wielded by the United States in Korea and Vietnam or by the USSR in Afghanistan (and indirectly elsewhere)—was an instrument that was risky to use and of uncertain effectiveness.

During these years the possibility of using nuclear weapons was seriously discussed on a number of occasions, but rejected. Whether the United States or the world would be better off now if nuclear weapons had been used against North Korea, the People's Republic of China, Vietnam, or the Vietcong is seldom raised as a policy consideration, but there must be some lesson to be learned from a retrospective examination of these close calls of the past.

In those days the United States and its World War II allies proclaimed the furtherance and defense—through the Marshall Plan for rebuilding European economies, Point Four aid to developing countries, and the sacrifice of lives on distant battlefields—of human rights, democratic regimes, and open markets. By the late 1980s, however, when millions of people in eastern Europe and elsewhere were bent on struggling to break out of totalitarianism, build market economies, and establish democratic governments, much of the world was burdened by indebtedness. At the same time, drug lords in South and Central America and parts of Asia and terrorists in the Middle East and elsewhere had become the new enemies as they flouted great powers and threatened the survival of lesser nations. And the United States—the generative hegemon of the twentieth century—found its creative capacities and "power outreach" seriously constrained, by massive deficits incurred in part by the cost of weaponry and decades of preparing for war, from moving the world at this unprecedented moment.

Suppose hegemon and challenger had been willing to negotiate their conflicts from the start. Suppose over the decades they invested even a fraction of their military expenditures in research, development, and planning for the future. Would either be worse off than it is today? Would their economies be weaker or stronger? Would they be better prepared for the twenty-first century? What about the rest of the world?

Does anyone know a better way to run the planet?

10

Global Survival

So far we have been examining and interpreting the past, but before we look toward the future, let us review briefly where we have been. Taking account of a splintered field of study and the unprecedented threats of a nuclear world, we raised possibilities for a unified conceptual framework in which critical problems and different, even contradictory theories could be located and compared. After a brief discussion of several classical paradigms that contribute to current theory and practice (mercantilism, liberalism, Marxism-Leninism, realism, and idealism), we presented a series of dynamic (change-sensitive) axioms linking together four (nested) images, or levels (individual, state, international, and global).

Our initial approach to these images was developmental—that is, we presented individuals as the only thinking, feeling, acting components of the other three systems. A central problem was to explain theoretically and historically how individuals could have combined and recombined to produce the values, institutions, and actions (including patterns of war and peace) characteristic of the other three images. Our approach in the first seven chapters was from past to present, from bottom to top, from inside to outside.

This investigative sequence identified developmental connections within the sociocultural evolution of our institutions from hunting and gathering bands and chiefdoms to ancient empires and city-states, agrocommercial nation-states, and modern industrial states. Also revealed were some of the ways in which human behavior (including war and peace activities) have changed with population growth and advances in technology—the engines of development and social transformation.

In Chapter 8, we moved outside and above the international system in order to locate it within and link it to the encompassing global, or planetary, system. This fourth image approach introduced the concepts of globalization and the global system, which provided a unified perspective on human dependence upon and relationships with nature. The concepts emphasized the intensely interactive and recursive relationships between ever-changing wholes and parts (see Figure 10.1).

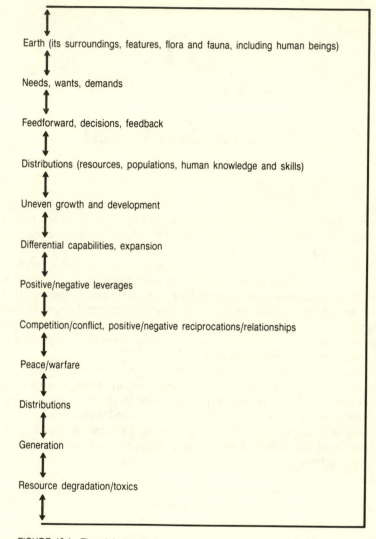

FIGURE 10.1 The global system

Contributory to this multidirectional, multicausal chain are human cognitive and affective phenomena. These include perceptions, beliefs, expectations, and the like as conditioned by anxiety, fear, hostility, ambition, suspicion, nationalism, ethnic and religious fanaticism, and so forth. These elusive considerations often exacerbate conflicts, which are also fueled by issues of economics and power. Such confusions complicate issues of war, peace, and survival and raise perplexing questions about decisionmaking and policy formation at a time when the whole world appears to be poised at a fateful turning point in human history.

In Chapter 9, we discussed deterrence as a time-honored defense of national security and the dominant strategic instrument relied upon by the United States and the USSR during post–World War II decades. Our discussion indicated that deterrence works much of the time but that it can also contribute to crisis and war. Nevertheless, in the course of arms reduction negotiations in the late 1980s, U.S. and other military planners warned against proceeding too far too fast. Yet in terms of the security dilemma, the more aggressively we pursue our own security without taking the security of others into account, the more likely we are to undertake measures that other(s) will perceive as life threatening to them.

The alternative—the pursuit of a program of peaceful diplomacy—seems an obvious solution to this dilemma. But it is not because in a potentially violent conflict, if either side makes a conciliatory move, the other is likely to perceive the effort either as deception or as evidence of a weakness to be exploited. Thus, *neither side can make peace with assurance unless the other side is willing to reciprocate.* This observation goes a long way toward explaining why after several centuries of peace-plan drafting, we still rely upon weaponry to protect ourselves from war.

The Security Dilemma:
Can We Evolve Our Way Out?

In previous chapters, we sketched the history of human collectivities and the pursuit of security set forth in terms of organized violence—that is, in terms of (1) force used as an ultimate sanction for maintenance of domestic law and order (institutionalized and/or structural violence); (2) force maintained by a society for its own defense and that of its (often expanding) activities and interests beyond its borders; and (3) the constraint or penetration sensed by a substantially weaker state as the result of the economic, political, and/or military activities and interests of a powerful state that appear threatening, coercive, exploitative, or otherwise damaging.

In terms of adaptation and sociocultural evolution, human progress has been marked by a number of institutional transformations. One of these, the emergence of the state, amounted to a step-level change in organization and interpersonal relationships that made "civilization" possible. This transformation did not occur, however, without human cost, notably the replacement of what had once been the (extended) "family life" of the hunting and gathering band by the class structures of the state. Characteristic of early state institutions was slave (or serf) labor amounting to institutionalized violence. Slavery (and serfdom) allowed for economic and political exploitation through the centralization of power in the hands of ruling elites. By providing cheap labor, slaves and serfs created economic surpluses that helped make early states viable. And the concentration of armed force in state regimes provided societies with economic and political "security" within and defense against attack from without.

Central to the sociocultural evolutionary story over the many millennia since the emergence of early states has been the painfully slow emancipation of human beings at large from the institution of slavery and various manifestations of serfdom. As recently as the middle of the nineteenth century large sectors of the United States economy still relied upon slave labor, and thousands of young Americans gave their lives in its defense. Some people who opposed slavery resigned themselves to the notion that years or generations might be required to eradicate the practice. But today, although slaves are still kept in some parts of the world (according to reports that are difficult to authenticate), the institution is no longer relied upon, supported, or defended by modern states, by their economies, or by public opinion in general. Through adaptation and sociocultural evolution we have found substitutions for slave labor and have left the institution behind us.

Is there any basis for believing that in some analogous way we might grow up and out of our dependence upon state-centered monopolies of violence for the maintenance of "security"? Some historians, sociologists, and others maintain that slavery was successfully renounced precisely as it ceased to be economically useful, i.e., as it ceased to be profitable for those who had once relied upon it for their "security." Is there an analogy between slavery and "legitimized" violence for the resolving of disputes, or between economic surpluses derived from slave labor and economic, political, and physical "security" derived from war and preparations for war? Here, parenthetically (but not incongruously), it needs to be noted that "legitimized" armed force also performs "legitimate" economic functions. People in many walks of life (not just the makers of aircraft, tanks, and missiles and their parts but also the suppliers of uniforms and vast arrays of other equipment and supplies) rely for their livelihood upon war (or preparation for war). This is not the only (or the foremost) "cause" of war by any means, but as with slavery, some people gain while others pay heavily—in one currency or another—when warfare is on the agenda.

The critical question is this: In an age of saturation bombing, nuclear weapons, and as yet unfathomed potentials for bacteriological instruments of death, has war become "uneconomical"? As with slavery, have the probable long-term costs outrun the probable benefits? In recent years, defense expenditures have contributed to trillions of dollars in debts and deficits—IOUs for the future citizens of the United States and many other countries. In this regard, Paul Kennedy (1987:532) warned in the late 1980s that if the United States continued to devote 7 percent or so of GNP to defense while Japan and West Germany concentrated on basic research and development, U.S. development rates would be slower than those of "countries dedicated to the market place and less eager to channel resources into defense." Consequently, the U.S. share of the world's manufacturing would "steadily decline."

These are only competitive hegemonic costs, however. In the late 1980s, the countries of the globe were spending about $900 billion a year on "defense" (war, deterrence, preparations for war). At the same time, several developing nations were reported to be planning (if not already building) plants for production of missiles, nuclear warheads, chemical weapons (the poor man's "nuclear" defense).

These economic and financial costs are only rough indicators of the knowledge and skills, natural resources, and human energy and extraordinary talents expended upon organized destruction at the expense of creative living. In the Middle East, parts of which are densely populated relative to the availability of productive land, societies with varying levels of technological and economic development compete and kill for territorial control, access to resources, security as they define it, or the right to pursue their own customs and beliefs unchallenged. People of different cultures and religious convictions put forward claims to the same territory dating back for millennia. The whole region could be viewed as a multidimensional Tragedy of the Planet in which all were at fault and none was to blame— a melancholy charge that could be leveled against many other parts of the world as well.

Since World War II, more than 1 million lives have been lost (largely in developing countries) in the service of deterrence, mutual containment of expansionist tendencies, persuasion, and defense, but insufficient time, money, or sustained effort has been invested in global health, education, the building of a world community, or the development of additional strategies for establishing and maintaining peace. In the past, war and preparations for war (or defense) appeared to soberminded people throughout the world to be advantageous, even necessary. But in the future, the waging of war (even war short of nuclear exchanges) is likely to be among the least profitable of all undertakings in human history, even less profitable than slavery became after the mid-nineteenth century.

Violence as a sanction is age-old. People of goodwill are often reluctant to condemn war altogether because of the role of "just wars" in opposing tyrannies and other manifestations of social injustice. We do not mean to overlook such realities. By the millions, people in the world suffer grinding poverty and profound injustice without prospect of relief. Tyranny still abounds. The rationales for just wars are beyond counting. Each of us, in short, could make a personal list of good reasons for fighting such wars. But as weaponry becomes incomparably more destructive and lethal and the risks (and potential costs) of armed protest escalating out of control more pronounced, people of goodwill and compassion might be pardoned for wondering whether effective and less costly ways could be found for righting social injustice short of "just" warfare.

By the 1980s, an awesome array of deep-seated threats to human security and effective adaptation were more and more widely recognized (population pressures, global debt, environmental depletions and toxicities, economic dysfunctions, drugs, AIDS, and other corrosions of a highly interactive, technologically advanced and mobile world society). None of these was resolvable by fiat or by the exercise of force within or between nations. Humanity was desperately in need of more creative solutions.

Three Action Strategies

In principle, there appear to be three interconnected, overlapping, and interactive courses of action—other than our age-old reliance on power and deterrence—to pursue a peaceful world: (1) to alter environmental conditions in ways conducive to peace; (2) to change our own day-to-day modes of dealing with family, friends, strangers, and adversaries in low-risk but peace-prone ways; and (3) to rely upon such strategies in order to develop and strengthen institutions conducive to peace. Clearly, these proposals are not trivial. Not only are we proposing to alter some of our own beliefs, habits, thinking, and favored activities, but we are also proposing to find ways of persuading others, including adversaries, to reciprocate in kind without resort to violence.

Given today's global complexities, is such change probable or possible? We have no guarantee. The answer lies with individual human beings throughout the world now and in generations to come. Many people are persuaded that gross inequities favor violence, that the world cannot continue indefinitely part rich, part desperately poor or on the nether edge of bitterly destructive competition. Many people assume, moreover, that terrorism, revolutions, international war, and other acts of desperation are outcomes, at least in part, of extreme social, political, economic, and other inequities. As long as the quality of people's lives varies tragically within and across nations, according to many observers and partisan activists, invoking peace on any image level is next to futile.

As we have seen, population, technology, and resources can be treated as master variables that influence people's actions and help explain second, third, and fourth image profiles. Within such simpleminded frameworks, we have explained many past human activities in terms of the pursuit of economic, political, and strategic security, as subjectively perceived and defined by individuals, groups, and whole nations. We have also indicated how as an outcome of (uneven) growth and development, a nation with one profile (epsilon, for example) may be transformed into another (beta, perhaps, or gamma), depending upon the growth and development rates of its master (and derivative) variables. As a starter, developing states might be given an added boost if the industrialized nations were to cooperate by investing some fixed percentage of their individual GNPs to launch a coordinated ten- or twenty-year development plan.

In the meantime, observers in the United States and elsewhere debate the hegemonic future. On the basis of recent rates of growth and development (average annual rates between 1970 and 1986), analysts project that the United States will maintain its economic preeminence for a decade or so but could be surpassed soon thereafter. As so projected, the third ranking country at the turn of the century will be Japan, which could achieve first place not long after. But such projections should not be taken too seriously. By altering its savings, investment, and production efforts, the United States— still several lengths in the lead—may well rejuvenate itself, just as either or both of its competitors (Japan or the EC) may lose ground or spurt ahead.

The argument could be made, however, that issues of economic, political, and strategic hegemony are overplayed. Historically, as we have seen, hegemony and hegemonic regimes played major roles in theory, diplomatic practice, and explanations of war and peace. Many theoreticians see hierarchy (and, inferentially, hegemony) as a prerequisite for global peace. But for the world of the 1990s and early twenty-first century, the security regime of some as yet unknown hegemon appears to be an uncertain, costly, and possibly disastrous "solution." Insofar as self-"liberating" Communist bloc nations turn to the West for assistance in "democratization" and economic growth, the "free world" may be put to an unprecedented test. How many of the vast resources poured into strategic defenses by both sides in the past can (and should) be mobilized now to assist in self-reconstitution (by us all)? Can we afford to fail? In such challenging circumstances a worldwide, synergistic (convergent, cooperative, win-win) effort may be worth a try.

In any case, at current rates of growth and development, the prospects for many developing nations appear extremely limited. Demographers are in wide agreement that the global population will probably double within a generation or so, and most of that growth will occur in the Third World. Without more successful diffusions of knowledge, skills, capital, and resources (notably fuels), productivity in many parts of the world is not likely to overtake the basic demands of increasing numbers of people. Under such conditions, poverty, hunger, and disease will undoubtedly remain endemic in these societies. Numbers of other developing countries may continue to modernize but while modernizing many may find their underclasses continuing to expand.

In addressing Third World problems, the World Bank (1980:69–71) referred to a "seamless web" of five critically interactive challenges: constrained *fertility*, adequate *nutrition*, equitable *income*, promotion of *health*, and effective *education* (and *environmental protection* through reduction of toxics). Each is a four image problem, and all are rooted in the activities of individuals, families, communities, and nations. The needs are clear: massive family planning; selective, continuously advancing knowledge and skills wisely and selectively implemented; and access to resources (fairly distributed, efficiently used, rigorously conserved, and, where feasible, regularly and systematically renewed).

In sociocultural evolutionary terms, we would expect a well-governed, productive, stable, and adaptive (self-learning) human species to emerge insofar as all short- and long-term benefits and costs were shared more or less equally by all the people of the world (as tended to be the case within hunting and gathering bands). This does not presage an end to competition so much as it signals a society in which the "rewards" of adaptive behavior are evident to and shared by all the citizenry and no one profits (makes millions or billions) from another's mortal disadvantage. In principle, a global plan for human survival seems to require initiatives falling into three primary clusters: (1) worldwide structural modifications leading to more favorable population/technology/resource access ratios and more nearly symmetrical distributions of quality-of-life benefactions; (2) the codification and implementation of more constructive modes of negotiation and persuasion; and (3) institutional adaptations favorable for peaceful adjustment and change.

For many regions of the world, population stabilization will be a priority and major challenge. Developing nations with technological advancement lagging behind population growth have found it difficult in the catch-up game to lower birthrates (poor people want sons for old-age insurance). As a consequence, many developing nations are trapped. Population growth hinders (or blocks) the technological advancement that could help stabilize their populations, but at the same time population increases consume production surpluses required to finance modernization. In practical terms, the constraining of population growth is an extremely difficult task. Confronting the 1990s and the beginning of the twenty-first century, Chinese leaders in Beijing reported that despite draconian measures during three decades, population growth in China was "out of control." Such observations provide somber implications for epsilon countries that have been unable to check population growth at all. In an effort to curb global "mismatches" between population and global "income-producing ability," the World Bank has urged a quadrupling of Third World family planning funds by the year 2000. Thereafter, technological advances, as in most industrialized countries, might be relied upon to exert "automatic" constraints on birthrates.

Along with population stabilization, developing societies require more equitable accesses to resources through acquisition of new technologies and the marketing of some surplus of home production in exchange for resources (and knowledge and skills) from the outside. Absolute equality is out of the question, but societies and humankind as a whole might be encouraged to adapt in the direction of multiimage-level equal accesses for individuals and whole societies to food, water, living space, health, education, useful work, democratic process, and possibilities for respect and self-esteem. Such aspirations must also be pursued in industrialized nations—including the United States, where some critics have charged that diminution of such accesses is contributing to the disintegration of families, the creation of an isolated underclass, and the erosion of national and global economic and political security and safety for the citizenry at large. Possibilities might include new approaches to enterprises (profit-sharing, worker ownership, and so on) through which costs and benefits are more evenly shared.

In most developing nations, technological modernization is a major goal that rivals population stabilization in importance. For some, the immediate need is for food or fuels. Successful adaptation in numbers of developing (epsilon) countries requires strong incentives for each of these criteria if poverty is to be eradicated and human development accelerated. Population constraints may be advisable for some industrialized countries as well, although for different reasons: to reduce demands for scarce resources, minimize toxicities, and stave off some of the effects of overcrowding (housing and potable water shortages, gridlock on land and in the air, and so forth).

Pressured by growing populations and rapidly advancing technologies, many countries are reaching farther and farther afield for basic resources—exploring the ocean bottom, for example, and investigating availabilities on the moon and elsewhere. Presumably the oceans and the floor beneath them encompass more basic resources than do all the world's land areas. Does this mean that nations and private interests are going to compete for, fight over, "plunder," and despoil these new frontiers as our ancestors fought over land frontiers? An ocean regime is in the making, but as of this writing the nations and private lobbies involved are still at odds over who should have what accesses and under what conditions.

We can imagine an arrangement transforming these regions into global reserves, monitored, regulated, and protected under the strict supervision of an empowered United Nations or an associated agency. A fundamental responsibility of the ocean regime could include the award, for a "catch-up period," of favored accesses through which developing nations could pay off debts with interest and finance and implement their own modernization. Such arrangements should facilitate more nearly equal accesses to nutrition, health, contraception, education, and productive work for people everywhere.

Here we need to remind ourselves that modernization and the meeting of human demands take tolls of their own in terms of local depletions and increases in toxic and other wastes. The use of scarce resources needs to be monitored and regulated worldwide and renewable resources replaced (a tree planted for each one cut). In addition, in order to protect the natural environment on which all life depends, the achievement of low-pollutant, energy-efficient technologies (fusion, solar, and other less damaging sources of energy) must become a high priority—along with controls on the production and disposal of toxic wastes and throwaway materials that are not biodegradable. So, too, technologies harmful to public health and the natural environment must be avoided and more benign technologies encouraged.

Access to Knowledge, Skills, and Information

Insofar as all four images and intervening organizational levels or environments are interactive and interdependent, a state's political capabilities are constrained by the strength of its economy. Conversely, its economic productivity is constrained by its political coherence and its ability to bring the knowledge and skills of its people to bear on its activities in innovative, efficient, and effective ways.

Something similar can be said about a nation's individual citizens. Production potential depends upon the interplay between the individual's access to information and decision processes and optimal access to resources (including access to health facilities, the best education appropriate for his or her talents and ambitions, socially valuable work, and income representing a reasonable share of the society's wealth). The more some people in a society lack optimal access to such resources, the more the society as a whole is likely to be constrained. Conversely, only the active and informed participation of its citizenry can legitimize the concentration of power in a democratic state. Everybody will benefit if everyone else is healthier, better educated, better off, and actively involved.

This means that the capabilities, productivities, adaptabilities, and quality of interactivities of molar actors will depend upon the capabilities, productivities, health, adaptabilities, and quality of interactivities of molecular actors, and vice versa. As in prestate times, individuals are dependent upon their societies, but societies are dependent (perhaps as never before) upon the quality and synergy of their human components. The world cannot afford underclasses of poorly educated, homeless, ill-nourished, all too often starving, and angered or hopeless people. If we are to make adaptive decisions on second, third, and fourth image levels, we need to take both individual and collective responsibility for the offspring we produce— ensuring the accesses they need for healthy minds in healthy bodies.

Knowledge, skills, information, and the right and opportunity to participate in momentous decisions affecting their lives can be viewed as vital resources and benefactions that are unevenly distributed worldwide, but more so in some societies (industrialized as well as developing) than in others. Through classification procedures, even democratic regimes severely restrict public access to information vital to effective checks and balances on the part of informed citizenries. Other problems result from neglect. In recent years, the U.S. literacy rate has been low for the world's richest and most powerful nation, many high school graduates are unable to read or write, and thousands of homeless (including many capable workers as well as others who are mentally ill) live in the streets, as do millions in cities elsewhere.

On the hopeful side, some authoritarian and totalitarian societies have made modest moves toward a *glasnost'* of some kind, if not democracy in the Western tradition, although most still have a long way to go. Although democracy imposed from outside seldom takes root, it does tend to work for people as they learn that their lives improve when they practice it. In the meantime, some avowedly democratic countries, partly in response to the cold war, domestic crime and violence, or both have become less zealous in their protection of civil rights at home. So, too, the overclassification of government documents has been so expanded (and tightened) and the planning and implementation of covert activities so detached from surveillance and public knowledge that accountability appears to have been irretrievably lost. In mid-1989, when Chinese student protesters erected a statue of styrofoam and plaster in Tiananmen Square, they reminded us that liberty carries a torch.

Then, before the year was out, millions of people in Poland, Hungary, East Germany, Czechoslovakia, and Romania, often at high personal risk, demonstrated how quickly dictatorial regimes, if sufficiently stressed by their own dysfunctions (and without supporting armed intervention from the outside), could be brought down—in all instances (except Romania, where army units joined civilians in putting down paramilitary "security" forces) without resort to arms. At the same time, however, the reliance of these people on—and their expectations of—market economies and democratic processes increased the responsibility of market-oriented democracies for persuasive evidence that they themselves were capable of pursuing and eventually maintaining social, economic, political and—increasingly—environmental security (including civil rights and open communications between citizens and their regimes).

A paradox of modern communication derives from the extent to which the new technologies, yielding massive and nearly instant "information," commonly constrain, tailor, distort, or trivialize conditions and events and misinform us, our leaders, and our adversaries. Such volume requires a capacity for scanning large amounts of information and an ability to distinguish professions and promises from actions. We need to learn that what we as citizens, business executives, politicians, bureaucrats, and national leaders *profess* is not as definitive as what we actually *do* and *how we do it*. Overall, we can expect the probabilities of peace to improve with open, unencumbered, "democratic" communications and our ability to discern the counterfeit.

In the long run, communications, along with diversity, social variability and trial and error learning, tend to be adaptation prone. By whatever means they are blocked, diluted, distorted, or manipulated, faulty communications limit opportunities for monitoring and participating in public decisionmaking and thus constrain adaptation and development on all image levels. In this connection, we can remind ourselves that individual citizens of the world's states, however democratic, have no legal standing or responsibility on the global level (except insofar as they speak or act in the name of states) and are thus limited in their ability to influence fourth image events.

To the extent that it could be achieved, activation of a multilevel equal access, positive bargaining, and positive leverage regime would amount to a highly developed manifestation of "open" democracy. Within such a structure, secrecy could be kept to a minimum. Attempts to use information classification for concealment of a regime's mistakes and of covert paramilitary activities would constitute a blocking of civil rights, as would reliance on covert agencies such as the KGB and CIA (whose activities commonly lead to corruptions of purpose, underworld alliances, and undemocratic, if not uncivilized, practices). Increasingly we have the technological means for monitoring each other's activities, but technological purpose can be circumvented or subverted by new applications. What we need in the interests of long-term adaptation is more open behavior more openly arrived at. In this connection, the modes through which individuals, groups, and nations deal with each other are of paramount importance, as are the ways in which our individualistic day-to-day activities (consuming resources and creating toxics, for example) aggregate by millions and billions worldwide.

Strategies of Negotiation and Nonviolent Persuasion

Earlier chapters identified means of negotiation and persuasion (positive and/or negative) as close to the crux between cooperation and conflict, peace and war, upon all image levels. In a world dominated by war/peace dilemmas and reliance upon weapons of mass destruction, the critical question is whether or not these deadly contradictions can be circumvented or resolved. The answer is both simple and complex. Often, we (and whole societies) fail to act until after we have allowed ourselves to collaborate in creating such contradictions. But there is more to the paradox. Because both sides of the conflict must be willing and determined to negotiate, each must assume that the other will respond to positive incentives with action that matches. The only reliable criterion either has is what the other does and consistently has done in the past.

To a large extent, our remote ancestors, face to face "for life" in small hunting and gathering bands, survived or perished depending upon their essentially peaceful negotiating skills. Insofar as they made these methods work, it may have been for lack of feasible alternative. Conceivably, we may have no other feasible option today. If that should be true, could particular patterns of bargaining, leverage, and coalition formation be adapted for human survival in the nuclear age?

From where we are today the possibilities still appear remote, although encouraging progress has been made, as evidenced by the Gorbachev-Reagan negotiations leading to the Intermediate-Range Nuclear Forces (INF) Treaty, the first Soviet elections since the Bolshevik Revolution of 1917, a discernable if precarious trend toward democracy in numbers of previously undemocratic countries, and new peacekeeping successes for the United Nations. As relevant organizations and institutions operate now, however, the United Nations and its agencies remain remote from and are not widely internalized by the people of the world. In any case, nationals of the world's various countries have no direct institutionalized communications or bargaining and leverage interchanges with the United Nations comparable to those institutionalized in democracies. This observation points to a major issue for the future. Can we expect the various nations to yield that much of their "sovereign" independence to a global government, or can more immediate steps be taken first? The theoretical protocols that follow are illustrative of strategies that if put into universal practice (a large order) would not require initial institutional change. If pursued long enough, however, these strategies might contribute substantially to the achievement of such change.

The Tit-for-Tat Strategy

We have been critical of Prisoner's Dilemma approaches to distrust and irrational choice in international conflict and crisis on the ground that as a one-move game, Prisoner's Dilemma tends to obscure the responsibilities of the participants for their own predicaments. In the 1980s, however, Robert Axelrod (1984:viii) proposed a sequential-move adaptation of Prisoner's Dilemma in order to find out how cooperation might emerge from among "self-seeking individuals when there is no central authority to police their actions." This situation is roughly analogous to that of a prehistoric hunting and gathering band. His basic idea involved small unilateral initiatives and agreements, each preceded by an announcement of intention and implemented "without promise of reciprocation" as moves to induce reciprocation and conflict resolution. Axelrod wanted a strategy in which either side could exploit or deny cooperation with the other but also have a possibility of achieving mutual gain from cooperation.

Axelrod's tit for tat was not the first strategy to be developed for the inducement of reciprocation, but it was certainly among the few to be tested rigorously. In order to assess alternate strategies, Axelrod invited experienced game-theory experts to submit programs for a(n iterated) computer Prisoner's Dilemma tournament—a sort of "computer chess tournament." Each program included a "history of the interaction so far," which the players could use in choosing "whether or not to cooperate on the current move." The most effective strategy was tit for tat—one player "starting with cooperation, and thereafter doing what the other player did on the previous move" (Axelrod, 1984:20, 30–31).

This finding led Axelrod to follow with an investigation designed to reveal how cooperation could "emerge among egotists without central authority." A second round tested different strategies. "The result was another victory for Tit for Tat," achieved in this instance by Anatol Rapoport, which persuaded Axelrod that tit for tat could lead to cooperation without "love," altruism, friendship, foresight, rationality, conscious choice, central authority, or even a great deal of trust. A few repetitive successes seemed to provide a stronger stimulus than trust did, although the presence of such phenomena could hasten the process. As demonstrated by the experiment, "cooperation can emerge even in a world of unconditional defection," but cooperation cannot occur if pursued only by scattered individuals who have no possibilities for interacting with each other (as in a single-move Prisoner's Dilemma game). To succeed, the moves must be widespread, persistent, and interactive. Substitution of "trust for distrust remains a never ending challenge," but repeated small successes can "work wonders" (Axelrod, 1984:89–91, 100).

Whether tit for tat is appropriate for application to intense arms races or intense crises, however, is a matter for further thought and experimentation. As compared with a computerized game played by academic specialists, the risk of applying a real-world tit-for-tat strategy during a crisis is that two adversarial heads of state, allowing themselves to be locked into an "unthinking" reciprocation, could trade sequential negatives into a classical action/reaction process—a runaway escalation triggering higher levels of violence. The 1914 events leading up to World War I could be viewed as a virtually unbroken tit-for-tat sequence. Retrospectively, we could argue that tit for tat worked in the Cuban missile crisis because Kennedy responded appropriately when Khrushchev backed down, but one extra tat in the prior sequence (a Khrushchev decision to smash through the blockade or a Kennedy refusal to wait another fifteen or twenty minutes) might have altered the course of human affairs in a major way.

A "Secret" of Human Interchange

If two people view cooperation as rewarding and mutual defection as punishing, an "opportunity for mutual gain from cooperation arises" when one person sees gains from the other's cooperation exceeding the costs of his or her own. Underlying several contemporary approaches to successful human interchange is a formulation proposed by sociologist George Homans (1961:62) that asserts in effect that *the open secret of human exchange is to give the other person behavior that is more valuable to him or her than it is costly to you and to get behavior in return that is more valuable to you than it is costly to the other.* This simple proposition seems eminently relevant to day-to-day negotiation and to bargaining and leverage processes (on all image levels) aimed at searching for common interests and the clearing of a path toward outcomes that both sides will consider acceptable. To succeed, however, the bargainers must share (or come to accept) some common and compelling interest. With respect to the Soviet Union and the United States, the Arabs and the Israelis, the Indians and the Pakistanis, and other adversaries in a nuclear world, we would expect even bitter enemies to pursue survival for their own kind, if not for themselves.

The Homans formulation places responsibility for war and the establishment of peace where it ultimately resides—within each individual (leader, bureaucrat, and rank-and-file constituent). At the same time, this formulation calls attention to behavior, which tends to be relatively overt and ascertainable, as distinct from motivations, intentions, values, and goals, which in adversarial situations are easily professed but difficult to ascertain and all too often distorted in action or honored in the breach. If the Homans formulation is to work, a major obstacle must be overcome or circumvented eventually— lack of trust between the adversaries. The more A wants B's trust, the more apprehensive A is likely to feel that B will distrust or take advantage of A. The more either side relies on coercion, threat, "dirty tricks," assassination, terrorism, or large-scale violence, the more the other is likely to respond in kind. By focusing on a search for common interests, the Homans formulation seeks to avoid this pitfall.

Conventional conflict, arms control, and crisis negotiations often begin with statements of position (threats included) by both sides. Conceived as a process, the Homans formulation starts at the other behavioral pole— with a proposition, offer, or bid that is based upon some tentative assessment of the adversary's needs, wants, and demands and is calculated to attract that country's interest. Thus, the objective of a country initiating positive leverage may be viewed as a first step, an exploratory probe, in an intense interactive search for a means of obtaining the outcomes that both of them prefer. (Conciliators, mediators, and other third-party negotiators normally try to help their clients achieve just such an outcome.)

A potentially powerful transformation can occur at the point where "my problem" and the problem of "my adversary" are recognized by both of us as *our problem* and our subsequent interactions become cooperative. These interactions then converge toward a joint solution and achieve an economy greater than that of our respective efforts implemented separately. In many real-world conflicts, however, the adversaries (as in the post–World War II arms race between the United States and the Soviet Union) are reluctant to make the first conciliatory move (a unilateral arms reduction, for example), lest the other side seize the opportunity to exploit the move. The Homans approach might also help to "level the playing field" when industrial states negotiate with weaker periphery nations.

Graduated Reciprocation in Tension Reduction

In the early 1960s, social psychologist Charles Osgood (1962) put forward an alternative to conventional approaches to the nuclear arms race that has much in common with the Homans formulation and that deserves more attention than it has received. Identified as Graduated Reciprocation in Tension Reduction (GRIT), Osgood's proposal was designed to reverse the action/reaction process characterizing conflict spirals, arms races, and international crises and thus offer possibilities for applying positive leverages without sacrificing security.

From Osgood's perspective, a basic, and defensible, objection to many arms reduction, disarmament, and peace plans is that unilateral initiatives appear to be involved. Who but a fool or a coward would throw aside his musket in front of the enemy's cannon? And who can be sure that the adversary will not take advantage of a conciliatory move? For decades, many people in the West have feared that once their guard is down, the Soviets will "overrun the world," whereas Soviets have perceived Westerners— especially Americans (in connivance with West Germans)—as poised to attack the USSR (the champion of global liberation and progress) at whatever opportunity presented itself.

GRIT was designed to deescalate conflicts, crises, or force levels by direct initiative and by eventual transfer of major forces, armaments, and final jurisdictions over international disputes to the United Nations or other conflict management and crisis prevention auspices. Tension reduction is pursued by inducing the adversary to take reciprocating steps; each step is graduated in risk according to the degree of reciprocation obtained from opponents. Neither side is *required* to give up anything (that is, incur vulnerability) until a mutually verifiable agreement has been reached. But success, according to Osgood, is facilitated insofar as reciprocations are diversified vis-à-vis "sphere of action" and "locus of operation"; prior to announcement, each reciprocation is unknown to the opponent in terms of sphere, locus, and time of execution. Meanwhile, any encroachment by the other side, any attempt to "take advantage," is resisted (cf. Mitchell:1986).

The purpose of GRIT can be described as a *reverse double ratchet effect.* By way of metaphor, we might describe GRIT as two window washers at opposite ends of a platform, each manning a block and tackle, lowering themselves down the face of a skyscraper while keeping the scaffold level (lest either or both fall off). Success may often require carefully monitoring, controlling, and verifying outcomes when asymmetrical relationships are being negotiated.

To induce reciprocation, country A—as initiator—persistently communicates a "sincere intent to reduce and control international tensions." Thus, in contrast to tit for tat, all of A's initiatives (in line with Homans) take advantage, wherever possible, of mutual "self-interests," mutual "self-restraints," and "opportunities for cooperative enterprise." All of these initiatives are "publicly announced at some interval prior to their execution and identified with the general policy" of tension reduction. Each announcement by A includes an explicit invitation for B to reciprocate, "but with form not necessarily specified." All initiatives announced by A are executed on schedule regardless of prior commitment by B to reciprocate, and unilateral actions—without incurring jeopardy (capacity for retaliation is kept intact)—must be continued for a period of time, "regardless of reciprocations given or even of tension-reducing events elsewhere" (Osgood, 1962:102–103).

Overall, Osgood's rules for calculated deescalation are much more "cerebral," interventionist, and "targeted" than tit for tat is. There are more behavioral options, but these are still relatively simple. (1) If B tries to alter the status quo by force, A will resist and restore the status quo. (2) If B tries to change the status quo by means that reduce tensions, A will take steps having similar intent. (3) If B seizes hostile advantage of initiatives taken in B's favor, A can shift to firm and punishing reciprocation. (4) If B responds to A's initiative with tension-reducing responses based on similar intent, A can reward B. Such controlled procedures are intended to facilitate conflict management, social learning, and openings for long-term adaptation.

Some theorists have objected that reliance on a backup nuclear capability during the arms reduction process can lead to a "bargaining chip" tactic for strengthening a nation's leverage—"the idea that weapons programs should be started in order to stimulate the other's interest in negotiations." This tactic can degenerate into an action/reaction process (Barton and Weiler, 1976:225). We should take serious account of this tendency, but GRIT, properly applied, should provide a reasonable possibility for discouraging the "chip" tactic or deflecting a tendency toward an action/reaction escalation.

Used in conjunction with a tit-for-tat strategy, GRIT's flexibility would provide possibilities for country A to respond to B's negative tat with a provisional positive (calculated to avoid an action/reaction crisis) without jeopardizing A's security or capacity for subsequent retaliation. (During the Cuban missile crisis, approximations of GRIT appear to have reversed the action/reaction spiral.) Combined with the Homans formulation, GRIT might refine some of the ways of presenting provisional positives.

The possibility of relying more heavily upon positive inducements should not be construed to mean that all negative leverages should be avoided. On all image levels, there are wide ranges of forfeitures and deprivations that can be imposed as disincentives and punishments. The objective is to reduce, minimize, and perhaps eventually eliminate violence as a means of persuasion.

During the years, GRIT has undergone a certain amount of "testing" through historical case studies, in which similar strategies appear to have been employed, and through laboratory experimentation. Much less "field testing" has been done, the Cuban missile crisis being one of the few (or perhaps the only) real-world crisis in which GRIT-like strategies were used. A major obstacle in the employment and testing of GRIT in such situations is the problem of distinguishing its moves from background "noise" or "interference." "Hard-liners" on either or both sides of a conflict can also present a serious problem (Mitchell, 1986:73–86).

Fortunately, early pursuit of positive leverage strategies—the development of more or less universally sanctioned institutions for constraining or heading off escalations, crises, and war—need not be at odds with either arms control (or disarmament) or with whatever level of security we now possess. Nor would GRIT-like moves require the total rejection of negative leverages. A large part of the problem involves the consensual establishment of limits beyond which threat and coercion will not be pressed. In this connection, judicious combinations of GRIT, tit for tat, the Homans formulation, and similar win-win exchange techniques can provide substitute strategies for locating common (and hidden) interests and for negotiating international and global conflicts without inviting escalation or requiring premature surrender of advantage. Suppose, for example, two former adversaries, having been on a positive tit-for-tat roll, slide off into a negative sequence—a potential action/reaction process. Under such circumstances, one or the other might change to a GRIT mode and shift back into a sequence of positive reciprocations.

In view of the size and complexity of the world, no combination of bargaining and leverage strategies can serve as a panacea. But one or another could be used to advantage in adaptive, sociocultural evolutionary modes to transform existing institutions into an appropriate global arrangement.

Such considerations suggest the desirability of controlled comparisons of and experimentation with tit for tat, Homans, GRIT, and other approaches in pursuit of a general theory of collective (family, neighborhood, community, workplace, nation, international, global) "negotiation." (If an understanding of cognitive dissonance provides a tool for identifying a "creative" or "adaptive" response to "predicaments" of choice, such a general theory could make available "creative" or "adaptive" responses for predicaments of action.) With sufficient built-in flexibility, a theoretical codification of these and other protocols might help to set new standards for human interchange and overall quality of life on all four image levels. In international and global environments, codification and integration of relevant protocols could proceed with, benefit from, and presumably contribute to real-world negotiations, statecraft in general, and institutional innovation. At the same time, this approach could move us in concert from where we are now to where we want to go. This could be done without abrupt, impulsive, or potentially disruptive structural changes. Once such an experimental regime had been embarked upon, institutional adjustments and refinements might take care of themselves as the protocols were put into practice.

In order to function effectively, however, nonviolent negotiations and incentives require an environment largely unknown today. What we need is a bootstrap operation through which the progressive employment of such negotiations and incentives from a limited base gradually opens up and enlarges congenial enclaves, which then further invigorate and expand tit for tat, Homans, GRIT, and similar protocols to continue widening the favorable institutional environment(s).

The Issue of Global Governance

Since World War II, there have been a host of grievous problems requiring attention, but during the latter 1980s numbers of observers throughout the world saw new and possibly epochal possibilities opening up. Despite serious domestic political constraints in both countries, the Reagan and Gorbachev leaderships during their INF negotiations seemed to support the view that arms reduction need not remain beyond the reach of superpower bargaining capacities.

Then Gorbachev went a step further. He proposed unilateral reductions of Soviet conventional forces that were not contingent on a U.S. reciprocation. U.S. leaders were left free to weigh the probabilities that Gorbachev would make good on his proposals (a major move toward breaking out of the "peace" paradox) and thus leave Western nations to decide for themselves whether to reciprocate. Some close observers thought that a door had been opened with possibilities for an unprecedented turn in human history. Others remained cautious, if not skeptical. Meanwhile, within the space of a few months, a prolonged war between Iran and Iraq wound down, progress was made toward peace in Angola, Soviet troops withdrew from Afghanistan after nearly a decade of futile intervention, and an uncertain peace seemed to be emerging after years of Vietnamese occupation of Cambodia.

In a world of endemic violence, however, all of this was only a small beginning. Israelis and Palestinians were still engaged in bitter violence on the West Bank and in Gaza, Sikhs and Hindus killed each other in India, and rival militias fought for influence in Lebanon. The Beijing regime put down demonstrations for independence in Tibet, major units of the People's Liberation Army turned their weapons against student demonstrators in China, the USSR used troops against ethnic unrest in Azerbaijan and Georgia, and 256 passengers, crew, and a score or more villagers were wiped out when a Pan American airliner was blown to pieces over Scotland by a terrorist's bomb. Two Libyan fighter planes crowding the U.S. counterparts over the Mediterranean were shot down by the U.S. pilots, and the United States threatened a "surgical strike" against a Libyan chemical plant thought to be dedicated to the production of poison gas (outlawed internationally since 1924 but finding favor again in several countries). The manufacture and testing of nuclear weapons continued, as did research and development in bacteriological warfare. News sources even indicated that unnamed weapons planners favored integrating elements of Star Wars with first-strike options—a seemingly lethal combination of sword and shield. In short, cold war premises and their inertia, rhetoric, and military leveraging were not easily set aside. Against this background, future probabilities were understandably assessed with great caution, and few leaders would have thought the times propitious for sweeping reductions in defense.

An End and a New Beginning

By the early 1990s the post–World War II era had receded into history, and the cold war order had collapsed. Could this unexpected turn of events be attributed to the Western policy of containment? Had the Communist dictatorships unraveled as an outcome of internal dysfunctions—an inability to adapt to domestic demands and those of a rapidly changing external environment? Or were both sides casualties of hegemonic struggle? Probably a combination of all three. For nearly half a century the two superpowers had exchanged deeply hurtful blows—economic, political, strategic and environmental—squandering their own potentials. There were ugly wounds on both sides, and many people throughout the world reached out for a different kind of future—an early global era in the planetary commons, perhaps, where long-term security (social, economic, political, strategic, and environmental) could be recognized as profoundly interdependent and indivisible.

If hegemonic theorists (and others) are right in asserting that "power inequality [hierarchy] leads to stability and power equality leads to conflict" (Kugler and Organski, 1989:126), only two "realistic" alternatives for global peace appear to exist: (1) the institutionalizing of a "fair-minded hegemon" (if not the incumbent, then a successful challenger) patterned after the legendary sheriff of the American West, who kept the peace on a lawless frontier; or (2) a world government (representative and thoroughly democratic, we would hope) entrusted with a global monopoly of "legitimized" force. But how feasible is world government as a solution? Many people are dubious. Clearly, the concept is diametrically opposed to the long-established principle of state sovereignty, and there is always the risk that a major power—a Hitlerian or Stalinist dictatorship—could achieve control and transform a peacefully inspired world government into a global tyranny. Can we afford to take such a risk?

As far back as the early 1960s, Edward Teller (1962:xii, 237, 290, 295), who as a physicist and the "father" of the H-bomb qualified as a charter "hawk," warned that although "we" would have to "stop" the Russians before we could "talk hopefully" with them, "military preparedness and the organization of the world for peace must go hand in hand." He thought at the time that an all-out nuclear war with the USSR could be avoided but not by "threat of massive retaliation or by mutual deterrence." He did not favor U.S. use of a first-strike strategy.

While convinced that the United States should be prepared to wage a war "limited in scope, limited in area, limited in objectives, but not limited in weapons" (arguing that nuclear weapons could be used with "moderation"), Teller urged the creation of a world community. The globe had become "too small, too crowded, too dangerous to accommodate many sovereign governments—each of them a law unto itself." Active and passive preparedness would buy us "nothing but time," which ought to be used "to establish a lawful and prosperous community of nations to ensure peace." The ultimate goal should be "nothing less than world government based upon principles of freedom and democracy." Meantime, the United States and other nations should make better use of the United Nations, despite its "many shortcomings."

Today, decades after the publication of Teller's imperative, the world has progressed in the design and manufacture of weapons, and global interdependencies appear to have intensified, but we have not proceeded very far toward a viable global community, let alone a world government. The formulation and testing of "security theory" have tended to focus more upon coercive diplomacy, refinements in deterrent strategies, the controlled employment of limited war, and Star Wars than upon the development of other, less violent options. The best that can be recorded is that to date a third world war (nuclear or conventional) has been avoided—an accomplishment that, in Teller's terms, has bought time that might be used more profitably than circumstances have allowed since World War II.

But clearly we need to give serious thought to safeguards and proceed with caution as well as ingenuity. In his presentation of the "voting paradox" (a minority preference can win when three coalitions vote up or down on three options in sequence—see Chapter 3), Arrow (1963:105–108) used the example of voter A preferring disarmament to cold war and cold war to hot war; B favoring cold war to hot war and hot war to disarmament; and C opting for hot war over disarmament and disarmament over cold war. This seemed to mean that a majority preferred hot war to disarmament (although if the order of voting were different, the outcome would be different). Arrow concluded that the only solution for this sort of dilemma was a constitution specifying those measures to be taken by a society "through its rules" and safeguards for making social decisions. Arrow's conclusion implies that a global arrangement of whatever shape would need to be founded upon a global-level "constitution" sufficiently universal in its assumptions and imperatives (and at the same time sufficiently parsimonious) to capture worldwide attention and approval. In view of our experience with the League and the United Nations, can we envisage a sovereign government of any kind winning the allegiance of a significant global constituency?

In spite of the practical problems constraining the United Nations, the concept of world government has a long history behind it. During the last several centuries, more than one hundred peace plans have been put forward, and a large proportion of them have included some proposal for a world empire, world confederation, world parliament, or some comparable arrangement (Wynner and Lloyd, 1944). Two of these—the League of Nations and the United Nations—have come to fruition, and the latter, as is widely recognized, operates today with considerable success. A part of its success is probable due to its shortcomings, however (Goodrich, Hambro, and Symonds, 1969).

Established in 1945, while the Pacific war was still in progress, the United Nations had as its proclaimed purpose the maintenance of international peace and security and the taking of "effective collective security measures for the prevention and removal of threats to the peace and for the suppression of acts of aggression or other breaches of the peace" (Article 1.1). In addition, the United Nations was dedicated to bringing about "by peaceful means, and in conformity with the principles of justice and international law, adjustment or settlement of international disputes or situations which might lead to a breach of the peace" (Article 1.1). Member states were enjoined to give the United Nations "every assistance in any action it takes" in accordance with the Charter (Article 1.5) but to "refrain in their international relations from threat or use of force" against other nations (Article 1.4).

Like the League of Nations before it, the United Nations was a major step in the direction of a more peaceful world, and it has played an important role in peacekeeping since World War II. Consonant with principles of international law dating from the Congress of Westphalia and before and in association with the International Court of Justice (and the Hague Convention for the Settlement of International Disputes), the United Nations provides a foundation and context for the ordering of a more peaceful world. Within the United Nations, all member states are under obligation to "refrain from the threat or use of force against the territorial integrity or political independence" of any other state and, in attempting to influence the behavior of other states, to act *only through diplomatic channels* (Article 1.4). In accordance with the Charter, member states agree also to accept and carry out decisions of the Security Council. Remarkably enough, these imperatives, if adhered to by all, or most, of the world would go a long way toward minimizing violence.

Consideration of U.N. strengths and limitations—and those of international law and the International Court—bring us back face to face with the security dilemma, issues of violence (the threat or use of force), the deterrence trap, and the issue of global order or governance. Conceptually and philosophically, the principles of the charter (and of international law and its institutions) have been encouraging developments, but they fall far short of world government. As a result, having neither resolved nor transcended the security dilemma, the United Nations (and within it, member nations) remains trapped in situations of violence or the threat thereof. The reasons for this predicament are simply stated: The states—notably the major powers (including the United States and other democracies)—have refused to relinquish their "sovereignty" and their preeminent right to take whatever unilateral measures they consider necessary in pursuit of their own national security. The assurance that principles of national sovereignty and voluntarism would be safeguarded in the charter (Articles 2.1, 2.7) has seriously weakened the United Nations as a keeper of global peace and at the same time has made membership acceptable to many nations (especially the United States and other major powers). Under Chapter VI, in effect, any government may ignore General Assembly or Security Council resolutions. In addition, the permanent members of the Security Council (essentially the "major powers") have created a convenient escape hatch for themselves—the veto—which renders invalid those council decisions that are not supported by "concurring" votes (Article 27.1).

For these and related reasons, the United Nations has been successful primarily in contributing to the resolution of conflicts involving small states. In a number of crises—Suez, Lebanon, the Congo, Cyprus, the Arab-Israeli crises of 1967 and 1973—the United Nations (and the U.N. Emergency Forces, using conflict-*containment* strategies) has played a major role in the constraint of violence, but its success in situations involving one or more major powers has been limited. (The U.N. "police action" in the Korean War during the early 1950s, for example, was to a large extent U.S. conceived and dominated.) With good judgment and good fortune on all sides, the major powers and the superpowers might achieve a consensus to limit their obstructionism to open, democratic means and submit themselves to U.N. and International Court decisions. With allowance for its limitations, the United Nations (together with associated agencies) provides an institutionalized precedent, reference point, body of principles, shared experience, and core framework through and around which reinforcing activities can be directed.

Sufficiently strengthened and supported by all the states, we could expect such institutions to relieve the major and superpowers of their largely self-imposed responsibilities for international "law enforcement" interventions (including "police actions" and "legal" sanctions).

The Decision of an Era: A Process of Discovery?

In the long run, achievement of a win-win world would almost certainly require some synchronizing and integrating of political and economic processes on the global level. The purpose of such activities would not be to reproduce national politics and economies on a global scale but to interweave and eventually institutionalize new political and economic networks worldwide. This process would borrow and adapt from many epochs and a wide range of cultures. When communications were open and trustworthy, and when interdependence existed between parties on a range of issues (and is so recognized), there would be a new and stronger incentive for transcending the security dilemma.

Acceptance of nonviolent diplomacy as an ultimate solution of international conflicts would seem to require a global-scale transformation in human values, beliefs, ideologies, policies, risk calculations, and habit structures. But given the ways of the world as we know them, the probabilities of ensuring security and optimal limitation of violence with minimal exercise of violence on all image levels are probably not high in the short run. The thrust of preceding chapters suggests that sustainable innovations in human relationships are more likely to emerge from trial-and-error adaptation (long-term sociopolitical evolution) than from inspiration or revelation. Conceivably the state as we know it today might turn out to be part of a violent but relatively fleeting stage in social evolution. But how could we get from here to there?

Pressures for Structural Change

Peaceful relations on a global level will undoubtedly require more than Soviet-U.S. détente or ad hoc applications of tit for tat, the Homans principle, or GRIT to superpower relationships. At the very least, global peace will require a global constitution as conceived by Arrow (possibly a strengthening of the U.N. Charter and a widening of its franchise) and a four-image-level reliance upon positive reciprocations. Over time, perhaps, the United Nations can be strengthened internally and by supporting institutions to provide safeguards when more proximate peacekeeping mechanisms fail.

Step-by-step evolutionary rejection of beliefs, habits, conditions, and institutions that encourage people everywhere to rely upon violence in its many forms (as a worthy, justifiable, effective, patriotic, even heroic way of influencing other people and whole nations) may well be the long-term sine qua non for a peaceful and survivable world. Such a program of learning would include not only the active participation of major states in strengthening international law and judicial institutions but also their readiness to observe international statutes, abide by judgments of global tribunals when their own activities and interests are subject to adjudication, and pursue "open" objectives "openly arrived at."

Adaptations on this scale will require active initiatives and support from peace-prone institutions outside of government (churches, schools, civic organizations) dedicated to the concepts and practice of nonviolent resolutions of conflict. Adaptations will also require a readiness to reward cooperation as well as individual initiatives in the workplace and elsewhere in day-to-day pursuits. Meanwhile, on third and fourth image levels, a generation or so of dedicated lines of access by developing nations to emerging technologies and access to the ocean floor and other sources of raw materials might help provide more level playing fields on which small states and major powers could negotiate to the advantage of both (for possibilities, see Borgese, 1968). Designed to reduce gross inequities among individuals, groups, and societies, such institutions might help to divert conflict into nonviolent channels; foster long-term social, economic, and political relationships inhibiting the rise of new Mussolinis, Stalins, and Hitlers; and replace war as the ultimate solution for crises within and between nations. Training and practical exercise in the use of positive incentives on all image levels might constitute the foundation for such efforts at adaptation.

Putting Old Institutions to New Uses

Institutions that are optimally "open" and democratic may be necessary for a more peaceful world, but in and of themselves, as Arrow's voting paradox (1963:105–108) suggests (where three coalitions are involved, sequential voting on three issues does not necessarily guard against a minority choice), they are not sufficient (at current levels of sociocultural evolution) to provide a "rational" device for aggregating billions of preferences, translating them into nonviolent bargaining and leverage moves, and at the same time, relying primarily on positive incentives for safeguarding the enabling and empowering constitution. Throughout the foreseeable future, sociocultural evolution toward a peaceful world may require the redundancy of institutional safeguards for augmenting and safeguarding democratic processes and the development of adaptive, more or less self-organizing coalitions supporting economic, political, and environmental survival worldwide. One way to institutionalize nonviolent mechanisms for mutual self-protection regulation on international and global levels is to establish specialized international regimes in conflicted issue areas (economic, political, cultural, and environmental) in order to complement and reinforce the United Nations and other international agencies.

Beginning in Chapter 2, we distinguished from time to time between organizational relationships characterized by coordination in the reaching of decisions (exemplified in nearly pure form by hunting and gathering bands and by Quaker meetings) and the centralized authority and reliance on negative sanctions used in varying degrees by all states and practiced to an extreme by absolute monarchs and dictators. We also indicated how, with the development of legislative assemblies and other "democratic" institutions, many states have combined coordinating and centralized processes (as exemplified, variously, by commons and prime minister/cabinet in parliamentary systems and legislature and president in federal systems).

In recent years, Keohane (1984:78–84, 89–92) and others have envisioned *nestings* and *networks* of specialized international regimes as providing an alternative to hegemonic discipline. These regimes would enable relatively small groups of nations to monitor each other's compliance with peacekeeping and other norms, rules, and practices that had been agreed upon as fundamental to national and global security and other interests. These theorists assume that such interests, perceived as shared rather than competitive, could provide the main incentive for establishing such regimes and that participating states would maintain their membership and support insofar as they found benefits from membership exceeding costs. Such arrangements would be a long way from a benign yet effective world parliament, but in the long run they might provide an interim stage in which a great deal of human trial, error, and adaptive retrial could be accommodated with reasonable safety.

To a large extent, international regimes as they currently exist reward for cooperation through economies of scale (and reduced transaction costs), relatively symmetrical accesses to high-quality information, and environments for orderly negotiation. Once a regime is established, the marginal cost of dealing with each additional issue tends to be lower than it would be if no such institution existed. As a consequence of such economies, specific agreements often become nested within regimes. Thus, in the economic sphere, an agreement among several nations to reduce a particular tariff will be affected by rules and principles of the trade regime (GATT), which will be nested in turn within some other set of arrangements, such as monetary relations, foreign investment, and so forth. EC developments throughout the 1990s may provide valuable precedents as well as pitfalls to be avoided.

Taken together, these arrangements could constitute an interlinked and complex pattern of relations (twenty-first-century sodalities, so to speak) through which center and periphery nations could deal with each other to the advantage of both. These arrangements would be additionally functional to the extent that issues of economic, political, and strategic security came to be linked formally. Appropriately designed global regimes could transcend narrow calculations of national interest and facilitate win-win agreements among states of vastly different capabilities. In time, moreover, increasing returns to scale might lead to extensive institutional backups upon crucial issues of national and global security on all image levels. The stronger the assessment of gain by participating nations of all "sizes" from such nestings and networks, the greater is likely to be the sense of shared "welfare dependency" among regime members and the stronger the constraining effect of the penultimate negative sanction—the threat of disruptive discord (a rough analog to ostracism among our hunting and gathering forbears).

International regimes are not surrogates for world government (although they may help us prepare for it), nor do they in themselves transform the state into some "higher" form. But we know from practical experience that they are feasible and effective for what they purport to do, and the process of regime nesting suggests the possibility, as yet largely unexplored, that it might substitute for power competition and deterrence in the furtherance of strategic and other manifestations of *shared security.* Nested regimes also seem to provide a rational instrument for exposing and managing the intense interconnections among economic security, political security, and environmental security (a prescription for the Middle East, perhaps, and other deeply conflicted regions of the globe). To the extent that nested regimes were to substitute for hegemonic stability, we would expect them to be highly dynamic, flexible, and sensitive to feedback and to function as powerful instruments for adaptation and social learning on and around the Peak of the Global Mountain and down and up its slopes. Perhaps in time the once disenfranchised people of the world could find themselves rendering functionally obsolescent the hegemon and its challenger(s) on that lofty promontory.

Suddenly, in the 1990s, there is pressing need for a new planetary view, new aspirations, and fresh visions for the future. For a moment, *tomorrow* is tactile in the hands of us all—wherever we are and whoever we are. If we allow these unprecedented opportunities to elude us, a denser, more pressured, technologically more "sophisticated" world of the early 2000s could easily produce new, more powerful adversaries, a more expensive and frightful cold war, and vastly more destructive weapons (some of them already on the drawing boards or in the minds of masterful designers). The 1990s appear to provide us with a historical instant that could be critical for the human species.

Over time, the security paradox generates a high probability of disaster, but if enough of us are ready to alter millennia of social habit and our own acceptance of violence, there are possibilities for change. We now have in hand—and our leaders have in theirs—some ideas, means, and opportunities for resolving (or transcending) the war/peace dilemma, avoiding the deterrence trap, safeguarding the environment, and expanding the hope that we may not have to face an escalation of environmental disasters or the next, possibly final, world war.

References and
Selected Bibliography

Acheson, Dean. 1944. "Statement Before the Sub-Committee on Foreign Trade and Shipping." Hearings Before the Special Committee on Post-War Economic Policy and Planning. U.S. House of Representatives, 78th Cong., 2nd sess. Washington, D.C.: GPO.

Adams, Richard N. 1975. *Energy and Structure: A Theory of Social Power.* Austin: University of Texas Press.

Adams, Ruth, and Susan Cullen, eds. 1981. *The Final Epidemic: Physicians and Scientists on Nuclear War.* Chicago: Educational Foundation for Nuclear Science.

Albertini, Luigi. 1957. *The Origins of the War of 1914*, vol. 1. London: Oxford University Press.

Aldrich, Howard E. 1979. *Organizations and Environments.* Englewood Cliffs, N.J.: Prentice-Hall.

Aldrich, Howard E., and Jeffrey Pfeffer. 1976. "Environments of Organization." In *Annual Review of Sociology*, ed. Alex Inkeles, James Coleman, and Neil Smelser, vol. 2. Palo Alto, Calif.: Annual Reviews.

Alker, Hayward, and Thomas J. Biersteker. 1984. "The Dialectics of World Order: Notes for a Future Archaeologist of International Savoir Faire." *International Studies Quarterly* 28, no. 2 (June).

Allan, Pierre. 1983. *Crisis Bargaining and the Arms Race: A Theoretical Model.* Cambridge: Ballinger.

Allison, Graham. 1969. "Conceptual Models of the Cuban Missile Crisis." *American Political Science Review* 63, no. 3 (September).

———. 1971. *Essence of Decision: Explaining the Cuban Missile Crisis.* Boston: Little, Brown.

Allison, Graham T., and Morton H. Halperin. 1972. "Bureaucratic Politics: A Paradigm and Some Policy Implications." In *Theory and Policy in International Relations*, ed. Raymond Tanter and Richard H. Ullman. Princeton, N.J.: Princeton University Press.

Allman, William F. 1984. "Nice Guys Finish First." *Science 84* 5, no. 8 (October).

Allport, Gordon W. 1958. "What Units Shall We Employ?" In *Assessment of Human Motives*, ed. Gardner Lindzey. New York: Rinehart.

Almond, Gabriel A., and H. Bingham Powell, Jr. 1966. *Comparative Politics: A Developmental Approach.* Boston: Little, Brown.

Ardant, Gabriel. 1974. "Financial Policy and Economic Infrastructure of Modern States and Nations." In *The Formation of National States in Western Europe*, ed. Charles Tilly. Princeton, N.J.: Princeton University Press.

Arrow, Kenneth J. 1963. *Social Choice and Individual Values*, 2nd ed. New Haven, Conn.: Yale University Press.

———. 1974. *The Limits of Organization*. New York: Norton.

Ashby, William R. 1960. *Design for a Brain: The Origin of Adaptive Behavior*, 2nd ed. New York: Wiley.

Ashley, Richard K. 1980. *The Political Economy of War and Peace*. London: Francis Pinter.

———. 1984. "The Poverty of Neo-Realism." *International Organization* 38, no. 2 (Spring).

Aspaturian, Vernon V. 1971. *Process and Power in Soviet Foreign Policy*. Boston: Little, Brown.

———. 1972. "The Soviet Military-Industrial Complex—Does It Exist?" *Journal of International Affairs* 26, no. 1 (Fall).

Atkinson, John W. 1964. *An Introduction to Motivation*. Princeton, N.J.: Van Nostrand.

Axelrod, Robert M. 1972. *Framework for a General Theory of Cognition and Choice*. Berkeley, Calif.: Institute of International Studies.

———. 1984. *The Evolution of Cooperation*. New York: Basic Books.

Axelrod, Robert, and Robert O. Keohane. 1986. "Achieving Cooperation Under Anarchy: Strategies and Institutions." *World Politics*, no. 4 (July).

Azar, Edward E. 1970. "Analysis of International Events." *Peace Research Review* 4, no. 1 (November).

Azar, Edward E., and Chung-in Moon. 1988. *National Security in the Third World*. College Park, Md.: Center for International Development.

Ball, George W. 1985. "The War for Star Wars." *New York Times Review of Books* 32, no. 66 (April).

Barry, Bryan. 1975. *Power and Political Theory—Some European Perspectives*. London: Wiley.

Barton, John H., and Lawrence D. Weiler, eds. 1976. *International Arms Control: Issues and Armaments*. Stanford, Calif.: Stanford University Press.

Bateson, Gregory. 1972. *Steps to an Ecology of Mind*. New York: Ballantine Books.

———. 1979. *Mind and Nature: A Necessary Unity*. New York: Dutton.

Beer, Francis A. 1981. *Against War: The Ecology of International Violence*. San Francisco: Freeman.

Befu, Harumi. 1977. "Social Exchange." *Annual Review of Anthropology*, vol. 6., ed. Alan R. Beals and Stephan A. Taylor. Palo Alto, Calif.: Annual Reviews, Inc.

Bennett, John W. 1976. *The Ecological Transition: Cultural Anthropology and Human Adaptation*. New York: Pergamon Press.

Benseler, Frank, Peter M. Heji, and Wolfram K. Kock. 1980. *Autopoiesis, Communication, and Society*. Frankfurt: Campus Verlag.

Beres, Louis R., and Harry R. Targ. 1977. *Constructing Alternative World Futures*. Cambridge, Mass.: Schenkman.

Bergesen, Albert, ed. 1983. *Crises in the World-System*. Beverly Hills, Calif: Sage.

Bergsten, C. Fred. 1975. *The Dilemmas of the Dollar: The Economics and Politics of United States International Monetary Policy*. New York: New York University Press.

———. 1985. *Global Economic Imbalances*. Washington, D.C.: Institute for International Economics.

———. 1988. *America in the World Economy: A Strategy for the 1990s*. Washington, D.C.: Institute for International Economics.

Bergsten, C. Fred, and William R. Cline. 1985. *The United States–Japan Economic Problem*. Washington, D.C.: Institute for International Economics.

Bergsten, C. Fred, William R. Cline, and John Williamson. 1985. *Bank Lending to Developing Countries: The Policy Alternatives*. Washington, D.C.: Institute for International Economics.

Bertalanffy, Ludwig von. 1933. *Modern Theories of Development*. Oxford: Oxford University Press.

_____ . 1950. "An Outline of General System Theory." *British Journal for the Philosophy of Science*, 1, no. 2 (August).

_____ . 1960. *Problems of Life*. New York: Harper.

_____ . 1968. *General System Theory*. New York: Braziller.

Bertram, Christoph, ed. 1981. *Strategic Deterrence in a Changing Environment*. Adelphi Library 6. Published for The International Institute for Strategic Studies. Westmead, England: Gower Publishing Company Limited.

Blake, Nigel, and Kay Poole, eds. 1983. *Dangers of Deterrence: Philosophers on Nuclear Strategy*. London: Routledge and Kegan Paul.

Blalock, Hubert M., Jr. 1964. *Causal Inference in Non-Experimental Research*. Chapel Hill: University of North Carolina Press.

Blau, Peter M. 1968. "Organizations." *International Encyclopedia of the Social Sciences*, vol. 11: 297.

Blechman, Harry M., ed. 1982. *Rethinking the U.S. Strategic Posture: A Report from the Aspen Consortium on Arms Control and Security Issues*. Cambridge, Mass.: Ballinger.

Block, Fred L. 1977. *The Origins of International Economic Disorders: A Study of the United States International Monetary Policy from World War II to the Present*. Berkeley: University of California Press.

Bohannan, Paul, ed. 1967. *Law and Warfare: Studies in the Anthropology of Conflict*. Garden City, N.Y.: Natural History Press.

Borgese, Elizabeth M. 1968. *The Ocean Regime*. Occasional Paper. Santa Barbara, Calif.: Center for the Study of Democratic Institutions.

Bosquet, N. "From Hegemony to Competition: Cycles in the Core." In *Processes of the World-System*, ed. T. K. Hopkins and Immanuel Wallerstein. Beverly Hills, Calif.: Sage.

Boulding, Kenneth E. 1956. *The Image*. Ann Arbor: University of Michigan Press.

_____ . 1978. *Stable Peace*. Austin: University of Texas Press.

Bracken, Paul. 1983. *The Command and Control of Nuclear Forces*. New Haven, Conn.: Yale University Press.

Braidwood, Robert. 1979. "The Agricultural Revolution." In *Hunters, Farmers and Civilizations*, ed. C. C. Lamberg-Karlovsky. San Francisco: Freeman.

Braudel, Fernand. 1979. *The Structure of Everyday Life: Civilization and Capitalism, 15th–18th Century: The Limits of the Possible*, vol. 1. New York: Harper & Row.

Breslauer, George W. 1983. "Why Détente Failed: An Interpretation." In *Managing U.S.-Soviet Rivalry: Problems of Crisis Prevention*, ed. Alexander George. Boulder, Colo.: Westview Press.

Brody, Richard A. 1966. "Cognition and Behavior: A Model of International Relations." In *Experience, Structure and Adaptability*, ed. O. J. Harvey. New York: Springer.

_____ . 1971. "Convergences and Challenges in International Relations." In *International Studies: Present Status and Future Prospects*. New York: Norton.

Bryen, Stephen D. 1971. *The Application of Cybernetic Analysis to the Study of International Politics*. The Hague: Martinus Nuhoff.

Bueno de Mesquita, Bruce. 1981a. "Power Distributions, and the Likelihood of War." *International Studies Quarterly* 25, no. 4 (December).

————. 1981b. *The War Trap.* New Haven, Conn.: Yale University Press.

————. 1985a. "Toward a Scientific Understanding of the Study of International Conflict." *International Studies Quarterly* 29, no. 2 (June).

————. 1985b. "Reply to Stephen Krasner and Robert Jervis." *International Studies Quarterly* 29, no. 2 (June).

Bueno de Mesquita, Bruce, and David Lalman. 1986. "Reason and War." *American Political Science Review* 80, no. 4 (December).

————. 1987. In "Modelling War and Peace," Seif Hussein, Bruce Bueno de Mesquita, and David Lalman, *American Political Science Review* 86, no. 1 (March).

Bull, Hedley. 1961. *The Control of the Arms Race.* London: Weidenfeld and Nicolson.

————. 1966. "International Theory: The Case for a Classical Approach." *World Politics* 18, no. 3 (April).

————. 1969. "International Theory: The Case for a Classical Approach." In *Contending Approaches to International Politics,* ed. Klaus Knorr and James N. Rosenau. Princeton, N.J.: Princeton University Press.

Bullock, Alan. 1959. *Hitler: A Study in Tyranny.* London: Odhams Press.

Bülow, Bernhard von. 1931. *Memoirs of Prince von Bulow,* vol. 2. Boston: Little, Brown.

Burke, W. T. 1969. *Towards a Better Use of the Oceans.* Stockholm: Almquist and Wiksell.

Burns, Arthur Lee. 1961. "From Balance to Deterrence: A Theoretical Analysis." In *International Politics and Foreign Policy,* ed. James N. Rosenau. Glencoe, Ill.: Free Press.

Burton, John W. 1972. *World Society.* Cambridge: Cambridge University Press.

————. 1983. "The Individual as the Unit of Explanation in International Relations." *International Studies Newsletter* 10, no. 2 (February).

————. 1984. *Global Conflict: The Domestic Sources of International Crisis.* College Park, Md.: Center for International Development.

Buzan, Barry. 1983. *People, States and Fear: The National Security Problem in International Relations.* Chapel Hill: University of North Carolina Press.

Campbell, Donald. 1969. "Variation and Selective Retention in Socio-Cultural Evolution." In *General Systems,* vol. 14, ed. Ludwig von Bertalanffy. Ann Arbor: Society for General Systems Research. Annual.

Carneiro, Robert L. 1970. "A Theory of the Origin of the State." *Science* 169, no. 3947 (August 21).

Central Intelligence Agency, Directorate of Research, Office of Political Research. 1974. *Potential Implications of Trends in World Population, Food Production and Climate.* Washington, D.C.: CIA.

Chein, Isidor. 1962. "Image of Man." *Journal of Social Issues* 18, no. 4.

————. 1972. *The Science of Behavior and the Image of Man.* New York: Basic Books.

Childe, Gordon. 1951. *Man Makes Himself.* New York: Mentor.

Choucri, Nazli. 1982. *Energy and Development in Latin America: Perspectives for Public Policy.* Lexington, Mass.: Lexington Books.

————. 1984. *Multi-Disciplinary Perspectives on Population and Conflict.* Syracuse, N.Y.: Syracuse University Press.

Choucri, Nazli, and Vincent Feraro. 1976. *International Politics of Energy Interdependence.* Lexington, Mass.: Lexington Books.

Choucri, Nazli, and Robert C. North. 1975. *Nations in Conflict.* San Francisco: Freeman.

Choucri, Nazli, and Thomas W. Robinson. 1978. *Forecasting in International Relations: Theory, Methods, Problems, Prospects.* San Francisco: Freeman.

Choucri, Nazli, with David S. Ross. 1981. *International Energy Futures: Petroleum Prices, Power and Payments.* Cambridge, Mass.: MIT Press.

Cipolla, Carlo M. 1965. *Guns, Sails and Empires,* New York: Pantheon Books.

———. 1988. *Before the Industrial Revolution: European Society and Economy, 1000–1700,* 2nd ed. New York: Norton.

Claude, Inis L., Jr. 1962. *Power and International Relations.* New York: Random House.

Clausewitz, Karl von. 1943. *On War.* New York: Modern Library.

Cline, William R. 1983. *International Debt and the Stability of the World Economy.* Washington, D.C.: Institute for International Economics.

Cobden, Richard. 1867. *Political Writings.* London: Ridgeway.

Codoni, Rene, Bruno Fritsch, Alex Meltzer, F. J. Oertly, Witgard Sieber, and Peter Weltser. 1971. *World Trade Flows: Integrational Structure and Conditional Forecasts.* Zurich: Schulthess Polygraphischer AG.

Cohen, Benjamin. 1983. "Balance of Payments Financing: Evolution of a Regime." In *International Regimes,* ed. Stephen D. Krasner. Ithaca, N.Y.: Cornell University Press.

Cohen, Ronald, and Elman R. Service, eds. 1978. *Origins of the State: The Anthropology of Political Evolution.* Philadelphia: Institute for the Study of Human Issues.

Cohen, Yousseff, Brian R. Brown, and A.F.K. Organski. 1981. "The Paradoxical Nature of State-Making: The Violent Creation of Order." Ann Arbor: University of Michigan, mimeo (April).

Communist International, Second Congress. 1920. *Proceedings of the Petrograd Session of July 17 and of the Moscow Sessions of July 19th–August 7th, 1920.* Moscow.

Corbett, Percy E. 1968. "International Law." *International Encyclopedia of the Social Sciences,* vol. 7.

Coser, Lewis R. 1956. *The Functions of Social Conflict.* Glencoe, Ill.: Free Press.

Cronbach, Lee J. 1975. "Beyond the Two Disciplines of Scientific Psychology." *American Psychologist* 30, no. 2 (February).

Cyert, Richard M., and James G. March. 1963. *A Behavioral Theory of the Firm.* Englewood Cliffs, N.J.: Prentice-Hall.

Deutsch, Karl W. 1963. *The Nerves of Government: Models of Political Communication and Control.* New York: Free Press.

———. 1965. "Preface to the Second Edition." In Quincy Wright, *A Study of War.* Chicago: University of Chicago Press.

Deutsch, Karl W., Sidney A. Burrell, Robert A. Kann, Maurice Lee, Jr., Martin Lichterman, Raymond E. Lindgren, Francis L. Loewenheim, Richard W. Van Wagenen. 1957. *Political Community in the North Atlantic Area.* Princeton, N.J.: Princeton University Press.

Deutsch, Karl W., and J. David Singer. 1964. "Multipolar Power Systems and International Stability." *World Politics* 16, no. 3 (April).

De Vries, Jan. 1976. *The Economy of Europe in an Age of Crisis, 1600–1750.* Cambridge: Cambridge University Press.

Divale, William T. 1973. *Warfare in Primitive Societies: A Bibliography.* Santa Barbara, Calif.: Clio Press.

"DOD Report FY72." 1977. In *Nuclear Strategy and National Security,* ed. Robert J. Pranger and Robert F. Labrie. Washington, D.C.: American Enterprise Institute.

Doran, Charles, and Wes Parsons. 1980. "War and the Cycle of Relative Power." *American Political Science Review* 17, no. 2 (June).

Dorn, Walter R. 1940. *Competition for Empire, 1740–1763.* New York: Harper & Brothers.

Drell, Sidney. 1983. *Facing the Threat of Nuclear Weapons.* Seattle: University of Washington Press.

Dunlop Illustrated Encyclopedia of Facts. 1969. Ed. Morris McWhirter and Ross McWhirter. Garden City, N.Y.: Doubleday.

Durkheim, Émile. 1960. *The Division of Labor.* Glencoe, Ill: Free Press.

Dyson, Freeman. 1984. *Weapons of Hope.* New York: Harper & Row.

East, Maurice, Stephen A. Salmore, and Charles F. Hermann. 1978. *Why Nations Act.* Beverly Hills, Calif.: Sage.

Easton, David. 1965. *A Systems Analysis of Political Life.* New York: Wiley.

Ebenstein, William. 1964. *Today's Isma,* 3rd ed. Englewood Cliffs, N.J.: Prentice-Hall.

Eccles, John C. 1977. *The Understanding of the Brain,* 2nd ed. New York: McGraw-Hill.

Eckstein, Alexander. 1966. *Communist China's Economic Growth.* New York: McGraw-Hill.

Egerton, Hugh E. 1903. *The Origin and Growth of the English Colonies and Their System of Government.* Oxford: Clarendon Press.

Ehrlich, Paul R., Anne H. Ehrlich, and John P. Holdren. 1977. *Ecoscience: Population, Resources, Environment.* San Francisco: Freeman.

Ehrlich, Paul R., Mark A. Harwell, Peter H. Raven, Carl Sagan, George M. Woodwell, Joseph Berry, Stephen J. Gould, Herbert D. Grover, Raphael Herrera, Edward J. Alenzo, Robert M. May, Ernst Mayr, Christopher P. MacKay, Harold A. Mooney, Norman Myers, David Pimental, and John M. Teel. 1983. "Long-Term Biological Consequences of Nuclear War." *Science* 222, no. 4630 (December 23).

Eisenstadt, S. N. 1963. *The Political Systems of Empires.* Glencoe, Ill.: Free Press.

Elliott, Kimberley Ann. 1988. *World Economic Problems.* Washington, D.C.: Institute for International Economics.

Engels, Frederick. 1959. *Anti-Dühring: Herr Eugen Dühring's Revolution in Science.* New York: International Publishers.

———. 1962. "The Origin of the Family, Private Property and the State." In Karl Marx and Frederick Engels. *Selected Works,* vol. 2. Moscow: Progress Publishing House.

Eudin, Xenia J., and Robert C. North. 1957. *Soviet Russia and the East, 1920–1927.* Stanford, Calif.: Stanford University Press.

Eulau, Heinz. 1963. *The Behavioral Persuasion in Politics.* New York: Random House.

Farb, Peter. 1968. *Man's Rise to Civilization as Shown by the Indians of North America from Primeval Times to the Coming of the Industrial State.* New York: Dutton.

Feinberg, Richard E. 1983. *The Intemperate Zone: The Third World Challenge to U.S. Foreign Policy.* New York: Norton.

Fenwick, Charles B. 1948. *International Law,* 3rd ed. New York: Appleton-Century-Crofts.

Festinger, Leon. 1957. *A Theory of Cognitive Dissonance.* Stanford, Calif.: Stanford University Press.

Finlay, David B., Ole R. Holsti, and Richard R. Fagan. 1967. *Enemies in Politics.* Chicago: Rand McNally.

Fisher, Roger. 1981. *Improving Compliance with International Law.* Charlottesville: University Press of Virginia.

———. 1985. "Beyond Yes." *Negotiation Journal* 1, no. 1 (January).

Fisher, Roger, and William Ury. 1981. *Getting to Yes.* Boston: Houghton Mifflin.

Frank, Phillip. 1961. *Modern Science and Its Philosophy.* New York: Collier Books.

Frankel, Joseph. 1973. *Contemporary International Theory and the Behavior of States.* New York: Oxford University Press.

Frei, Daniel. 1982. *Risks of Unintentional Nuclear War.* Geneva: United Nations Institute for Disarmament Research.

Fried, Morton F. 1967. *The Evolution of Political Society: An Essay in Political Anthropology.* New York: Random House.

_____.1975. *The Notion of Tribe.* Menlo Park, Calif.: Cummings.

Fried, Morton, Marvin Harris, and Robert Murphy, eds. 1968. *War: The Anthropology of Armed Conflict and Aggression.* Garden City, N.Y.: Natural History Press.

Friedman, David. 1977. "A Theory of the Size and Shape of Nations." *Journal of Political Economy* 23, no. 2 (January).

Friedrich, Carl J. 1938. *Foreign Policy in the Making.* New York: Norton.

Gaddis, J. L. 1974. "Harry S. Truman and the Origins of Containment." In *Makers of American Diplomacy: From Benjamin Franklin to Henry Kissinger,* ed. F. J. Merli and T. A. Wilson. New York: Scribner.

Galtung, Johan. 1971. "A Structural Theory of Imperialism." *Journal of Peace Research* 13, no. 2.

Gardner, Richard N. 1969. *Sterling-Dollar Diplomacy: The Origins and Prospects of Our International Economic Order.* New York: McGraw-Hill.

Garnett, John. 1979. "Disarmament and Arms Control Since 1945." In *Strategic Thought in the Nuclear Age,* ed. Laurence Martin. Baltimore, Md.: Johns Hopkins University Press.

Geertz, Clifford. 1960. "The Impact of the Concept of Culture on the Concept of Man." In *New Views of the Nature of Man,* ed. John Platt. Chicago: University of Chicago Press.

George, Alexander. 1969. "The 'Operational Code': A Neglected Approach to the Study of Political Leaders and Decisionmaking." *International Studies Quarterly* 13, no. 2 (June).

_____. 1980a. "Case Studies and Theory Development: The Method of Structured, Focused Comparison." In *Diplomatic History: New Approaches,* ed. Paul Lauren. Glencoe, Ill.: Free Press.

_____. 1980b. *Presidential Decisionmaking in Foreign Policy: The Effective Use of Information and Advice.* Boulder, Colo.: Westview Press.

_____. 1983. *Managing U.S.-Soviet Relations: Problems of Crisis Prevention.* Beverly Hills, Calif.: Sage.

George, Alexander, and Juliette L. George. 1964. *Woodrow Wilson and Colonel House.* New York: Dover.

George, Alexander, David K. Hall, and William E. Simons. 1971. *The Limits of Coercive Diplomacy: Laos, Cuba, Vietnam.* Boston: Little, Brown.

George, Alexander, and Richard Smoke. 1974. *Deterrence in American Foreign Policy: Theory and Practice.* New York: Columbia University Press.

Gerth, H. H., and C. Wright Mills, eds. 1956. *From Max Weber: Essays in Sociology.* New York: Oxford University Press.

Gilbert, Felix, ed. 1975. *The Historical Essays of Otto Hintze.* New York: Oxford University Press.

Gilpin, Robert. 1975. *U.S. Power and the Multinational Corporation: The Political Economy of Foreign Direct Investment.* New York: Basic Books.

_____. 1981. *War and Peace in World Politics.* Princeton, N.J.: Princeton University Press.

_____. 1987. *The Political Economy of International Relations.* Princeton, N.J.: Princeton University Press.

Gochman, Charles S., and Russell J. Leng. 1983. "Realpolitik and the Road to War: An Analysis of Attributes and Behavior." *International Studies Quarterly* 27, no. 1 (March).

Goldstein, Joshua S. 1985a. "Basic Human Needs: The Plateau Curve." *World Development Report* 13, no 5 (May).

———. 1985b. "Kondratieff Waves as War Cycles." *International Studies Quarterly* 29, no. 4 (December).

———. 1988. *Long Cycles: Prosperity and War in the Modern Age.* New Haven, Calif.: Yale University Press.

Goldstein, Walter, 1979. "Theory or Illusion? The New Nationalism as a Systems Concept." In *The New Nationalism: Implications for Trans-Atlantic Relations,* ed. Werner Link and Werner J. Feld. New York: Pergamon Press.

Goodrich, Leland, Edvard Hambro, and Anne P. Symonds. 1969. *Charter of the United Nations: Commentary and Documents,* 3rd ed. New York: Columbia University Press.

Gorney, Roderic. 1971. "Interpersonal Intensity, Competition and Synergy: Determinants of Achievement, Aggression, and Mental Illness." *American Journal of Psychiatry* 128, no. 4 (October).

Granit, Ragnit. 1977. *The Purposive Brain.* Cambridge, Mass.: MIT Press.

Gray, Colin S. 1974. "The Urge to Compete: Rationales for Arms Racing." *World Politics* 26, no. 2 (January).

———. 1979. "Nuclear Strategy: A Case for a Theory of Victory." *International Security* 4, no. 1 (Fall).

Grechko, Marshal. 1977. Report at the Fifth All-Army Conference of the Party Organization Secretaries. *Kraznaia svezda,* March 28, 1973. Cited by Colin Grey, "Soviet American Strategic Competition: Instruments, Doctrines, and Purposes." In *Nuclear Strategy and National Security,* ed. Robert J. Pranger and Robert P. Labrie. Washington, D.C.: American Enterprise Institute.

Grunebaum, G. E. von. 1970. *Classical Islam: A History, 600 A.D.–1258 A.D.* London: Allen and Unwin.

Guizot, M. 1869. *A Popular History of France from Earliest Times,* vol. 2. Boston: Dana Estes and Charles Lauriat.

Gulick, Edward V. 1955. *Europe's Classical Balance of Power: A Case History of the History and Practice of One of the Great Concepts of European Statecraft.* Ithaca, N.Y.: Cornell University Press.

Gyorgy, Andrew, and George D. Blackwood. 1967. *Ideologies in World Affairs.* Waltham, Mass.: Blaisdell.

Haas, Ernst R. 1953. "The Balance of Power: Prescription, Concept, or Propaganda?" *World Politics* 5, no. 4 (Summer).

———. 1982. "Words Can Hurt You; or Who Said What to Whom About Regimes." *International Organization* 36, no. 2 (Spring).

Haas, Jonathan. 1982. *The Evolution of the Prehistoric State.* New York: Columbia University Press.

Hagen, Everett E. 1962. *On the Theory of Social Change: How Economic Growth Begins.* Homewood, Ill.: Dorsey Press.

Halle, Louis. 1960. *American Foreign Policy.* London: Allen and Unwin.

Hammond, P. Y. 1966. "Prologue to Rearmament." In *Strategy, Politics and Defense Budgets,* ed. W. R. Schilling, P. Y. Hammond, and Glenn H. Snyder. New York: Columbia University Press.

Harris, Marvin. 1977. *Cannibals and Kings: The Origins of Cultures.* New York: Vintage Books.

Hart, Hornell. 1931. *The Technique of Social Progress.* New York: Holt.

———. 1945. "Logistic Social Trends." *American Journal of Sociology* 50, no. 5 (April).

Hartz, Louis. 1955. *The Liberal Tradition in America: An Interpretation of American Political Thought Since the Revolution*. New York: Harcourt, Brace.

Hawtrey, Ralph B. 1930. *Economic Aspects of Sovereignty*. London: Longman's Green.

Heckscher, Eli F. 1935. *Mercantilism*, vols. 1–2. London: Allen and Unwin.

Heider, Fritz. 1938. *The Psychology of Interpersonal Relations*. New York: Wiley, quoting F. H. Allport. 1955. *Theories of Perception and the Concept of Structure*. New York: Wiley.

Heider, Karl G. 1979. *Grand Valley Dani: Peaceful Warriors*. New York: Holt, Rinehart and Winston.

Heisenberg, Werner. 1959. *Physics and Philosophy: The Revolution in Modern Science*. New York: Harper & Row.

Herman, Charles F., Charles W. Kegley, Jr., and James N. Rosenau, eds. 1987. *New Directions in Foreign Policy*. Boston: Allen and Unwin.

Hirschman, Albert O. 1969. *National Power and the Structure of Foreign Trade*. Berkeley: University of California Press.

———. 1977. *The Passions and the Interests: Political Arguments for Capitalism Before Its Triumph*. Princeton, N.J.: Princeton University Press.

Hobbes, Thomas. 1950. *Leviathan*. New York: Dutton.

Hobson, John A. 1938. *Imperialism: A Study*, 3rd ed. London: Allen and Unwin.

Hoffmann, Erik P., and Frederick J. Fleron, Jr. 1971. *The Conduct of Soviet Foreign Policy*. New York: Aldine-Atherton.

Hoffmann, Stanley. 1959. "The Long Road to Theory." *World Politics* 11, no. 3 (April).

———. 1968. *Gulliver's Troubles, or the Setting of American Foreign Policy*. New York: McGraw-Hill.

Hollist, W. Ladd. 1977. "An Analysis of Arms Processes in the United States and the Soviet Union." *International Studies Quarterly* 21, no. 3 (September).

Holsti, Ole R. 1962. "The Belief System and National Images." *Journal of Conflict Resolution* 6, no. 3 (September).

———. 1972. *Crisis, Escalation, War*. Montreal: McGill-Queens University Press.

———. 1967. "Cognitive Dynamics and Images of the Enemy: Dulles and Russia." In *Enemies in Politics*, ed. David J. Finlay, Ole Holsti, and Richard R. Fagen. Chicago: Rand McNally.

———. 1976. "Foreign Policy Formation Viewed Cognitively." In *Structure of Decision*, ed. Robert Axelrod. Princeton, N.J.: Princeton University Press.

Holsti, Ole R., Randolph M. Siverson, and Alexander George. 1980. *Change in the International System*. Boulder, Colo.: Westview Press.

Holzman, F. D. 1980. "Are the Soviets Really Outspending the U.S. on Defense?" *International Security*, no. 4 (Spring).

Homans, George C. 1961. *Social Behavior: Its Elementary Forms*. New York: Harcourt, Brace and World.

Hopmann, P. T., D. A. Zinnes, and J. D. Singer, eds. 1981. *Cumulation in International Relations Research*. Monograph Series in World Affairs 18, Book 3. Denver, Colo.: School of International Affairs, University of Denver.

Howard, Michael. 1983. *The Causes of War and Other Essays*. London: Smith.

Howe, Geoffrey. 1985. Speech at the Royal United Service Institute, as reported in the *San Francisco Chronicle*, March 3.

Hume, David. 1889. *Essays: Moral, Political and Literary*. London: Longman's Green.

Huntington, Samuel P. 1968. *Political Order in Changing Societies*. New Haven, Conn.: Yale University Press.

———. 1971. "Arms Races: Prerequisites and Results." In *Power, Action and Interaction*, ed. George Quester. Boston: Little, Brown.

Hussein, Seif. 1987. "Modelling War and Peace." *American Political Science Review* 86, no. 1 (March).

Ifrah, George. 1985. *From One to Zero: A Universal History of Numbers.* New York: Penguin.

Ike, Nobutaka. 1967. *Japan's Decision for War: Records of the 1941 Policy Conferences.* Stanford, Calif.: Stanford University Press.

Iklé, Fred C. 1964. *How Nations Negotiate.* New York: Harper & Row.

———. 1977. "Can Deterrence Last Out the Century?" In *Nuclear Strategy and National Security,* ed. Robert J. Pranger and Roger P. Labrie. Washington, D.C.: American Enterprise Institute.

Inkeles, Alex. 1975. Emerging Social Structure of the World." *World Politics* 27, no. 4 (July).

Jahoda, Gustav, and Henry Taiful, as quoted by Ole R. Holsti. "Cognitive Dynamics and Images of the Enemy: Dulles and Russia." In *Enemies in Politics,* ed. David J. Finlay, Ole R. Holsti, and Richard R. Fagan. Chicago: Rand McNally.

Janis, Irving. 1972. *Victims of Groupthink.* Boston: Houghton Mifflin.

Jantsch, Erich. 1980. *The Self-Organizing Universe: Scientific and Human Implications of the Emerging Paradigm of Evolution.* New York: Pergamon Press.

Jervis, Robert. 1970. *Logic of Images in International Relations.* Princeton, N.J.: Princeton University Press.

———. 1971. "Hypotheses on Misperception." In *Power, Action and Interaction,* ed. George H. Quester. Boston: Little, Brown.

———. 1976. *Perception and Misperception in International Politics.* Princeton, N.J.: Princeton University Press.

———. 1983. "Security Regimes." In *International Regimes,* ed. Stephen D. Krasner. Ithaca, N.Y.: Cornell University Press.

———. 1985. "Pluralistic Rigor: A Comment on Bueno de Mesquita." *International Studies Quarterly* 29, no. 2 (June).

Johanson, Donald C., and Maitland A. Edey. 1981. *Lucy: The Beginning of Humankind.* New York: Simon and Schuster.

Jones, A.M.H. 1974. *The Roman Economy: Studies in Ancient Economic and Administrative History.* Totowa, N.J.: Rowman and Littlefield.

Kahn, Herman. 1960. *On Thermonuclear War.* Princeton, N.J.: Princeton University Press.

Kant, Immanuel. 1939. *Perpetual Peace.* New York: Columbia University Press.

Kaplan, Abraham. 1964. *The Conduct of Inquiry.* San Francisco: Chandler.

Kaplan, Morton A. 1957. *System and Process in International Policies.* New York: Wiley.

———. 1970. "International Law and the International System." In *Great Issues of International Politics,* ed. Morton A. Kaplan. Chicago: Aldine.

Keen, M. H. 1973. *England in the Later Middle Ages: A Political History.* London: Methuen.

Kelly, Rita M., and Frederick J. Fleron, Jr. 1971. "Personality, Behavior and Communist Ideology." In *Conduct of Soviet Foreign Policy,* ed. Stanley Hoffman and Frederick Fleron. Chicago: Aldine-Atherton.

Kennan, George F. 1954. *Realities of American Foreign Policy.* Princeton, N.J.: Princeton University Press.

Kennedy, Paul, ed. 1985. *The War Plans of the Great Powers, 1880–1914.* Boston: Allen and Unwin.

———. 1987. *The Rise and Fall of the Great Powers: Economic Change and Military Conflict from 1500 to 2000.* New York: Random House.

Kenny, Anthony. 1985. *The Logic of Deterrence: A Philosopher Looks at the Arguments for and Against Nuclear Disarmament.* Chicago: University of Chicago Press.

Keohane, Robert O. 1980. "The Theory of Hegemonic Stability and Changes in International Economic Regimes, 1967–1977." In *Changes in the International System,* ed. Ole R. Holsti, Randolph M. Siverson, and Alexander L. George. Boulder, Colo.: Westview Press.

———. 1982. "The Demand for International Regimes." *International Organization* 36, no. 2 (Spring).

———. 1983. "Theory of World Politics: Structural Realism and Beyond." In *Political Science: The State of the Discipline,* ed. Ada Finister. Washington, D.C.: American Political Science Association.

———. 1984. *After Hegemony.* Princeton, N.J.: Princeton University Press.

———. 1986a. "Reciprocity in International Relations." *International Organization* 40, no. 1 (Winter).

———, ed. 1986b. *Neorealism and Its Critics.* New York: Columbia University Press.

Keohane, Robert O., and Joseph S. Nye. 1977. *Power and Interdependence.* Boston: Little, Brown.

Kerbo, Harold R. 1978. "Foreign Involvement in the Preconditions for Political Violence." *Journal of Conflict Resolution* 22, no. 3 (September).

Keynes, John Maynard. 1964. *The General Theory of Employment, Interest and Money.* New York: Harcourt Brace Jovanovich.

Khrushchev, Nikita. 1956. "Secret Speech of Khrushchev Concerning the 'Cult of the Individual.'" In *The Anti-Stalin Campaign and International Communism: A Selection of Documents,* ed. the Russian Institute, Columbia University. New York: Columbia University Press.

Kindleberger, Charles. 1962. *Foreign Trade and the National Economy.* New Haven, Conn.: Yale University Press.

———. 1970. *Power and Money: The Economics of International Politics and the Politics of International Economics.* New York: Basic Books.

Kissinger, Henry. 1957. *Nuclear Weapons and Foreign Policy.* New York: Harper & Brothers.

Kistiakowsky, George B. 1981. "Preface." In *The Final Epidemic: Physicians and Scientists on Nuclear War,* ed. Ruth Adams and Susan Cullen. Chicago: Educational Foundation for Nuclear Science.

Klare, Michael T. 1984. *American Arms Supermarket.* Austin: University of Texas Press.

Knorr, Klaus, and James N. Rosenau. 1969. *Contending Approaches to International Politics.* Princeton, N.J.: Princeton University Press.

Kohn, George C. 1987. *Dictionary of Wars.* Garden City, N.Y.: Anchor Books.

Kondratieff, Nicolai D. 1984. *The Long Wave Cycle.* New York: Richardson and Snyder.

Krasner, Stephen D. 1978. *Defending the National Interest: Raw Materials Investments and U.S. Foreign Policy.* Princeton, N.J.: Princeton University Press.

———. 1982. "Regimes and the Limits of Realism: Regimes as Autonomous Variables." *International Organization* 36, no. 2 (Spring).

———. 1985. "Toward Understanding in International Relations." *International Studies Quarterly* 29, no. 2 (June).

Kugler, Jacek, and A.F.K. Organski. 1989. "The End of Hegemony?" *International Interactions* 15, no. 2.

Kugler, Jacek, A.F.K. Organski, and D. J. Fox. 1980. "Deterrence and the Arms Race: The Impotence of Power." *International Security,* no. 1 (Summer).

Kuhn, Thomas S. 1970. *The Structure of Scientific Revolutions.* Chicago: University of Chicago Press.

Kuznets, Simon. 1966. *Modern Economic Growth: Rate, Structure and Spread.* New Haven, Conn.: Yale University Press.

Lakatos, Imre, and Alan Musgrave, eds. 1970. *Criticism and the Growth of Knowledge.* Cambridge: Cambridge University Press.

Lambelet, Jean-Christian, Urs Luterbacher, and Pierre Allan. 1979. "Dynamics of Arms Races: Mutual Stimulation vs. Self-Stimulation." *Journal of Peace Science* 4, no. 1 (Fall).

Landes, David S. 1981. *The Unbound Prometheus: Technological Change and Development in Western Europe from 1750 to the Present.* Cambridge: Cambridge University Press.

Lane, Robert E. 1969. *Political Thinking and Consciousness.* Chicago: Markham.

Langer, William L. 1962. *European Alliances and Alignments, 1871–1890,* 2nd ed. New York: Knopf.

Lasswell, Harold D. 1958. *Politics: Who Gets What, When and How.* New York: McGraw-Hill.

———. 1965. *World Politics and Personal Insecurity.* New York: Free Press.

Leakey, Richard E. 1981. *The Making of Mankind.* New York: Dutton.

Leakey, Richard E., and Roger Lewin. 1978. *People of the Lake: Mankind and Its Beginnings.* Garden City, N.Y.: Anchor Press/Doubleday.

Leites, Nathan. 1951. *The Operational Code of the Politburo.* New York: McGraw-Hill.

Leng, Russell J., and Robert A. Gochman. 1979. "Behavioral Indicators of War Proneness in Bilateral Conflicts." In *Explaining War: Selected Papers from the Correlates of War Project,* ed. J. David Singer. Beverly Hills, Calif.: Sage.

Lenin, V. I. 1930. "Socialism and War." In V. I. Lenin. *Collected Works.* New York: International Publishers.

———. 1932. *State and Revolution.* New York: International Publishers.

———. 1939. *Imperialism: The Highest Stage of Capitalism.* New York: International Publishers.

Lenski, Gerhard. 1970. *Human Societies: A Macrolevel Introduction to Sociology.* New York: McGraw-Hill.

Leontief, Wassily. 1977. *Future of the World Economy.* New York: Oxford University Press.

Lessard, Donald R., and John Williamson. 1985. *Financial Intermediation Beyond the Debt Crisis.* Washington, D.C.: Institute for International Economics.

Lesser, Alexander. 1968. "War and the State." In *War: The Anthropology of Armed Conflict and Aggression,* ed. Morton Fried, Marvin Harris, and Robert Murphy. Garden City, N.Y.: Natural History Press.

Levy, Jack S. 1983. *War in the Modern Great Power System, 1495–1975.* Lexington: University Press of Kentucky.

Levy, Marion J., Jr. 1966. *Modernization and the Structure of Society: A Setting for International Affairs.* Princeton, N.J.: Princeton University Press.

Lewis, W. Arthur. 1978. *The Evolution of the International Economic Order.* Princeton, N.J.: Princeton University Press.

Link, Werner, and Werner J. Feld, eds. 1979. *The New Nationalism: Implications for Trans-Atlantic Relations.* New York: Pergamon Press.

Lilley, Samuel. 1973. "Technological Progress and the Industrial Revolution." In *The Fontana Economic History of Europe: The Industrial Revolution,* ed. Carlo M. Cipolla. London: Collins/Fontana.

Lotka, Alfred J. 1925. *Elements of Physical Biology.* Baltimore, Md.: Williams and Wilkins.

Loup, Jacques, 1983. *Can the Third World Survive?* Baltimore, Md.: Johns Hopkins University Press.

Lovins, Amory. 1976. "Energy Strategy: The Road Not Taken." *Foreign Affairs* 55, no. 1 (October).

Luard, Evan. 1986. *Conflict and Peace in the Modern International System.* Boston: Little, Brown.

Luce, R. Duncan, and Howard Raiffa. 1957. *Games and Decisions.* New York: Wiley.

Lyall, Alfred. 1893. *The Rise of the British Dominion in India.* New York: Scribner.

MacDonald, Norman. 1973. "The Biological Factor in the Aetiology of War: A Medical View." Anthropological and Ethnological Sciences. 1973. IX International Congress. Chicago. *Proceedings* (August-September).

MacKay, Alfred. 1988. *Arrow's Theorem.* New Haven, Conn.: Yale University Press.

Malinowski, Bronislaw. 1941. "An Anthropological Analysis of War." *American Journal of Sociology* 46, no. 4 (January).

Mangone, Gerald J. 1951. *The Idea and Practice of World Government.* New York: Columbia University Press.

March, James G. 1976. "The Technology of Foolishness." In *Ambiguity and Choice in Organizations,* ed. James G. March and Johan P. Olsen. Bergen, Norway: Universitetsforlaget.

March, James G., and Johan P. Olsen. 1976. "Organizational Choice Under Ambiguity." In *Ambiguity and Choice in Organizations,* ed. James G. March and Johan P. Olsen. Bergen, Norway: Universitetsforlaget.

Marris, Stephen. 1985. *Deficits and the Dollar: The World Economy at Risk.* Washington, D.C.: Institute for International Economics.

Martin, Laurence, ed. 1979. *Strategic Thought in the Nuclear Age.* Baltimore, Md.: Johns Hopkins University Press.

Marx, Karl. 1962. "The British Rule in India." In Karl Marx and Frederick Engels. *Selected Works.* Moscow: Foreign Languages Publishing House, vol. 1.

―――. 1965. "The Communist Manifesto." In *A Handbook of Marxism,* ed. Emile Burns. New York: International Publishers.

―――. 1967. *Capital.* Samuel Moore and Edward Aveling translation, vol. 1. London: Lawrence and Wishart.

Marx, Karl, and Friedrich Engels. 1947. *The German Ideology.* New York: International Publishers.

―――. 1962. *Selected Works,* vols. 1–2. Moscow: Foreign Language Publishing House.

Maslow, Abraham. 1978. *Motivation and Personality.* New York: Harper & Row.

Maturana, Humbertus H., and Francisco J. Varela. 1975. *Autopoietic Systems.* Urbana: Biological Computer Laboratory, University of Illinois.

―――. 1980. "The Organization of the Living." In *Autopoiesis and Cognition: The Realization of Living,* ed. Humberto Maturana. Dordrecht, the Netherlands: Reidel.

Mayr, Ernst. 1976. *Evolution and the Diversity of Life.* Cambridge: Belknap Press.

McClelland, Charles A. 1966. *Theory and the International System.* New York: Macmillan.

―――. 1972a. "The Beginning, Duration, and Abatement of International Crises: Comparisons in Two Conflict Arenas." In *International Crises: Insights from Behavioral Research,* ed. Charles F. Hermann. New York: Free Press.

―――. 1972b. "Some Effects on Theory from the International Event Analysis Movement." In *International Events Interaction Analysis: Some Research Considerations,* ed. Edward E. Azar, Richard A. Brody, and Charles A. McClelland. Beverly Hills, Calif.: Sage.

McClelland, David. 1969. *Motivating Economic Achievements.* New York: Free Press.

McGowan, Patrick G., and Howard B. Shapiro. 1973. *The Comparative Study of Foreign Policy: A Survey of Scientific Findings.* Beverly Hills, Calif.: Sage.

McNeill, William H. 1963. *The Rise of the West.* Chicago: University of Chicago Press.

————. 1982. *The Pursuit of Power: Technology, Armed Force, and Society Since A.D. 1000.* Chicago: University of Chicago Press.

Mead, Margaret. 1968. "Warfare Is Only an Invention—Not a Biological Necessity." In *War: Studies from Psychology, Sociology, Anthropology,* ed. Leon Bransom and George W. Geothals. New York: Basic Books.

Meadows, Donella, and Dennis Meadows. 1972. *The Dynamics of Growth.* New York: Signet Books.

Meier, Gerald M. 1984. *Emerging from Poverty: The Economics That Really Matters.* New York: Oxford University Press.

Midlarski, Manus. 1975. *On War: Political Violence in the International System.* New York: Free Press.

Mill, John Stuart. 1947. *Utilitarianism, Liberty and Representative Government.* London: Dent.

Miller, George A., Eugene Galanter, and Karl H. Pribram. 1960. *Plans and the Structure of Behavior.* New York: Holt.

Miller, James B. 1965. "Living Systems: Basic Concepts." *Behavioral Science* 10, no. 4 (October).

Mischell, Walter. 1971. *Introduction to Personality.* New York: Holt, Rinehart and Winston.

Miskimin, Harry A. 1969. *The Economy of Early Renaissance Europe, 1300–1460.* Englewood Cliffs, N.J.: Prentice-Hall.

Mitchell, C. R. 1986. "GRIT and Gradualism—25 Years On." *International Interactions* 13, no. 1.

Modelski, George. 1972. *Principles of World Politics.* New York: Free Press.

————. 1978. "The Long Cycle of Global Politics and the Nation State." *Comparative Studies in Society and History* 20, no. 2 (April).

Moll, Kendall D., and Gregory M. Luebbert. 1980. "Arms Race and Military Expenditure Models: A Review." *Journal of Conflict Resolution* 24, no. 1 (March).

Morgan, Lewis. 1963. *Ancient Society.* Gloucester, Mass.: Smith.

Morgenthau, Hans J. 1968. *Politics Among Nations: The Struggle for Power and Peace,* 4th ed. New York: Knopf.

Most, Benjamin A., and Randolph Siverson. Forthcoming. "Arms and Alliances: 1870–1913." In *New Directions in the Study of Foreign Policy,* ed. Charles Herman, Charles Kegley, and James Rosenau. New York: Allen and Unwin.

Naroll, Raoul, Vern Bullough, and Frada Naroll. 1974. *Military Deterrence in History: A Pilot Cross-Historical Survey.* Albany: State University of New York Press.

Neumann, John von, and Oskar Morgenstern. 1944. *The Theory of Games and Economic Behavior.* Princeton, N.J.: Princeton University Press.

Nicolson, Harold, 1946. *The Congress of Vienna: A Study in Allied Unity, 1812–22.* New York: Harcourt, Brace.

Nixon, Richard M. 1977. "U.S. Foreign Policy for the 1970s: Shaping a Durable Peace." In *Nuclear Strategy and National Security,* ed. Robert J. Pranger and Roger P. Labrie. Washington, D.C.: American Enterprise Institute.

North, Douglass C. 1981. *Structure and Change in Economic History.* New York: Norton.

North, Douglass C., and Robert P. Thomas. 1970. "An Economic Theory of the Growth of the Western World." *Economic History Review* no. 1.

————. 1973. *The Rise of the Western World: A New Economic History.* Cambridge: Cambridge University Press.

North, Robert C. 1963. *Moscow and Chinese Communists*, 2nd ed. Stanford, Calif.: Stanford University Press.

North, Robert C., Richard A. Brody, and Ole R. Holsti. 1964. "Some Empirical Data on the Conflict Spiral." *Peace Research Society: Papers, I.* Chicago Conference, 1963. Philadelphia: Peace Research Society.

Olson, Mancur. 1963. *The Logic of Collective Action: Public Goods and the Theory of the Theory of Groups.* Cambridge, Mass.: Harvard University Press.

———. 1982. *The Rise and Decline of Nations: Economic Growth, Stagflation and Social Rigidities.* New Haven, Conn.: Yale University Press.

Organski, J.F.K., and Jacek Kugler. 1980. *The War Ledger.* Chicago: University of Chicago Press.

Osgood, Charles E. 1962. *An Alternative to War or Surrender.* Urbana: University of Illinois Press.

Otterbein, Keith F. 1970. *The Evolution of War.* New Haven, Conn.: Human Relations Area Files.

Packenham, Robert A. 1983. "The Dependency Perspective and Analytic Dependency." In *North/South Relations: Studies of Dependency Reversal*, ed. Charles Doran, George Modelski, and Cal Clark. New York: Praeger.

Paige, Glenn D. 1968. *The Korean Decision.* New York: Free Press.

Panofsky, Wolfgang H. 1977. "The Mutual-Hostage Relationship Between America and Russia." In *Nuclear Strategy and National Security*, ed. Robert J. Pranger and Roger P. Labrie. Washington, D.C.: American Enterprise Institute.

Parry, J. H. 1971. *Trade and Dominion: The European Overseas Empires in the Eighteenth Century.* New York: Praeger.

Patchen, Martin. 1965. "Decision Theory in the Study of National Action: Problems and a Proposal." *Journal of Conflict Resolution* 9, no. 2 (June).

Petty, William. 1899. "Political Arithmatick" (1690). In *The Economic Writings of Sir William Petty*, vol. 1. Cambridge: Cambridge University Press.

Pfeffer, Jeffrey, and Gerald Salancik. 1968. *The External Control of Organizations.* Garden City, N.Y.: Doubleday.

Piaget, Jean. 1978. *Behavior and Evolution.* New York: Pantheon Books.

———. 1980. *Adaptation and Intelligence: Organic Selection and Phenocopy.* Chicago: University of Chicago Press.

Pierre, Andrew J. 1982. *The Global Politics of Arms Sales.* Princeton, N.J.: Princeton University Press.

Pinson, Kopel S. 1954. *Modern Germany: Its History and Civilization.* New York: Macmillan.

Plato. 1950. *The Republic of Plato.* A. J. Lindsay, trans. New York: E. P. Dutton.

Platt, John. 1971. "How Men Can Shape Their Futures." *Futures* 3, no. 1 (March).

Polackels, Solomon W. 1980. "Conflict and Trade." *Journal of Conflict Resolution* 24, no. 1 (March).

Polanyi, Karl, Conrad M. Arensberg, and Harry W. Pearson. 1957. *Trade and Market in the Early Empires: Economics in History and Theory.* New York: Free Press.

Popper, Karl R. 1972. *Objective Knowledge: An Evolutionary Approach.* Oxford: Clarendon Press.

Powers, Thomas. 1982. *Thinking About the Next One.* New York: Knopf.

Powers, William T. 1973. *Behavior: The Control of Perception.* Chicago: Aldine.

Pranger, Robert J., and Roger P. Labrie, eds. 1977. *Nuclear Strategy and National Security.* Washington, D.C.: American Enterprise Institute.

Prebisch, P. 1969. *Toward a Strategy of Development.* New York: United Nations.

Pribram, Karl H. 1976. "Self-Consciousness and Intentionality." In *Consciousness and Self-Regulation,* ed. Garry E. Schwartz and David Shapiro, vol. 1. New York: Plenum.

Pruitt, Dean G. 1969. "Stability and Sudden Change in Interpersonal and International Affairs." In *International Politics and Foreign Policy,* ed. James N. Rosenau, rev. ed. New York: Free Press.

Questor, George, ed. 1971. *Power, Action and Interaction.* Boston: Little, Brown.

Quigly, John. 1974. *Soviet Foreign Trade Monopoly.* Columbus: Ohio State University Press.

Rapoport, Anatole. 1960. *Fights, Games and Debates.* Ann Arbor: University of Michigan Press.

————. 1970. "Modern Systems Theory: An Outlook for Coping with Change." *General Systems* 15. Annual.

Rashevsky, Nicolas. 1959. *Mathematical Biology of Social Behavior,* rev. ed. Chicago: University of Chicago Press.

Rasler, Karen A., and William R. Thompson. 1983. "Global Wars, Public Debts, and the Long Cycle." *World Politics* 35, no. 4 (July).

Relf, William B. 1973. *Man and Future World Politics: A Study of Man and Its Implications for International Politics.* Singapore: Chapman Enterprises.

Remak, Joachim. 1967. *The Origins of World War I, 1871–1914.* New York: Holt, Rinehart and Winston.

Rich, Alexander, and John R. Platt. 1966. "How to Keep the Peace." *Bulletin of the Atomic Sciences* 22, no. 4 (April).

Richardson, Lewis F. 1960. *Arms and Insecurity.* Pittsburgh: Boxwood Press.

Richardson, Lewis F., and Carl C. Lienow. 1960. *Statistics of Deadly Quarrels.* Pittsburgh: Boxwood Press.

Riker, William H. 1962. *The Theory of Political Coalitions.* New Haven, Conn.: Yale University Press.

Riker, William H., and Peter Ordeshook. 1973. *An Introduction to Positive Political Theory.* Englewood Cliffs, N.J.: Prentice-Hall.

Robinson, James A., and Richard C. Snyder. 1965. "Decision-Making in International Politics." In *International Behavior: A Social-Psychological Analysis,* ed. Herbert C. Kelman. New York: Holt, Rinehart and Winston.

Robinson, Ronald E., and John Gallagher. 1965. *Africa and the Victorians: The Official Mind of Imperialism.* London: Macmillan.

Rokeach, Milton. 1961. *The Open and Closed Mind.* New York: Basic Books.

Rosecrance, Richard. 1963. *Action and Reaction in World Politics.* Boston: Little, Brown.

————. 1966. "Bi-polarity, Multi-polarity, and the Future." *Journal of Conflict Resolution* 10, no. 3 (September).

————. 1986. *The Rise of the Trading State.* New York: Basic Books.

Rosen, Steven J., and James R. Kurth, eds. 1974. *Testing Theories of Economic Imperialism.* Lexington, Mass.: Heath.

Rosenau, James N. 1961. *International Politics and Foreign Policy.* New York: Free Press.

————. 1969a. *International Politics and Foreign Policy,* ref. ed. New York: Free Press.

————. 1969b. *Linkage Politics.* New York: Free Press.

Rosenberg, Alexander. 1988. *Philosophy of Social Science.* Boulder, Colo.: Westview Press.

Rousseau, Jean-Jacques. 1916. *The Social Contract,* trans. Henry J. Toser, 7th ed. London: Allen and Unwin.

————. 1964. *Discourse on the Origin of Inequality Among Mankind.* New York: Washington Square Press.

Rowen, Henry S. 1979. "The Evolution of Strategic Nuclear Doctrine." In *Strategic Thought in the Nuclear Age,* ed. Laurence Martin. Baltimore, Md.: Johns Hopkins University Press.

Ruggie, John C. 1983. "International Regimes, Transactions and Change." In *International Regimes,* ed. Stephen D. Krasner. Ithaca, N.Y.: Cornell University Press.

Russell, Richard J. 1956. "Environmental Changes Through Forces Independent of Man." In *Man's Role in Changing the Face of the Earth,* ed. William L. Thomas, Jr., vol. 2. Chicago: University of Chicago Press.

Russett, Bruce M. 1969. "The Calculus of Deterrence." In *International Politics and Foreign Policy,* ed. James N. Rosenau. New York: Free Press.

————. 1983. *The Prisoners of Insecurity: Nuclear Deterrence, the Arms Race, and Arms Control.* San Francisco: Freeman.

————. 1985. "The Mysterious Case of the Vanishing Hegemony." *International Organization* 39, no. 2 (Spring).

Russett, Bruce M., and Harvey Starr. 1981. *World Politics: The Menu for Choice.* San Francisco: Freeman.

Sagan, Carl. 1982. "Foreword." In *World Military and Social Expenditures. 1982,* ed. Ruth L. Sivard. Leesburg, Va.: WMSE Publications.

Sahlins, Marshall. 1965. "On the Sociology of Primitive Exchange." In *The Relevance of Models for Social Anthropology.* New York: Praeger.

Sampson, R. V. 1964. In *A Dictionary of the Social Sciences,* ed. Julius Gould and William L. Kolb. Glencoe, Ill.: Free Press.

————. 1965. *Equality and Power.* London: Heineman.

Samuelson, Paul A. 1970. *Economics,* 8th ed. New York: McGraw-Hill.

Sauvant, Karl P. 1981. *The Group of 77.* New York: Oceana.

Schacter, Stanley. 1975. "Cognition and Peripheralist-Centrist Controversies in Motivation and Emotion." In *Handbook of Psychobiology,* ed. Michael S. Gozzaniga and Colin Blakemore. New York: Academic Press.

Schell, Jonathan. 1982. *The Fate of the Earth.* New York: Avon Books.

Schelling, Thomas C. 1960. *The Strategy of Conflict.* Cambridge, Mass.: Harvard University Press.

————. 1966. *Arms and Influence.* New Haven, Conn.: Yale University Press.

————. 1978. *Micromotives and Microbehavior.* New York: Norton.

Schevill, Ferdinand. 1961. *Medieval and Renaissance Florence,* vols. 1–2. Garden City, N.Y.: Doubleday.

Schlesinger, James R. 1977. "U.S.-USSR Strategic Policies." In *Nuclear Strategy and National Security,* ed. Robert J. Pranger and Roger P. Labrie. Washington, D.C.: American Enterprise Institute.

Schram, Stuart R. 1984. "Economics in Command? Ideology and Policy Since the Third Plenum, 1978–1984." *China Quarterly,* no. 99 (September).

Schrödinger, Erwin. 1956. *What Is Life? and Other Scientific Essays.* Garden City, N.Y.: Doubleday.

Schutz, Alfred. 1967. *The Phenomenology of the Social World,* trans. George Walsh and Frederick Lehnert. Evanston, Ill.: Northwestern University Press.

Seliger, Martin. 1976. *Ideology and Politics.* London: Allen and Unwin.

Service, Elman R. 1962. *Primitive Social Organization: An Evolutionary Perspective.* New York: Random House.

————. 1968. "War and Our Contemporary Ancestors." In *War: The Anthropology of Armed Conflict and Aggression,* ed. Morton Fried, Marvin Harris, and Robert Murphy. Garden City, N.Y.: Natural History Press.

_____ . 1978. "Classical and Modern Theories of the Origins of Government." In *Origins of the State*, ed. Ronald Cohen and Elman R. Service. Philadelphia: Institute for the Study of Human Issues.

Shamasastry, R. 1961. *Kautilya's Arthasastra.* Mysore, India: Mysore Printing.

Shils, Edward. 1968. "The Concept and Function of Ideology." *International Encyclopedia of the Social Sciences*, vol. 7: 66.

Shulman, Marshall. 1982. "U.S.-Soviet Relations and the Control of Nuclear Weapons." In *Rethinking the U.S. Strategic Posture: A Report from the Aspen Consortium on Arms Control and Security Issues*, ed. Harry M. Blechman. Cambridge, Mass.: Ballinger.

Simon, Herbert A. 1955. *Administrative Organization.* New York: Macmillan.

_____ . 1985. "Human Nature in Politics: The Dialogue of Psychology with Political Science." *American Political Science Review* 79, no. 2 (June).

Simpson, George G. 1949. *The Meaning of Evolution: A Study of the History of Life and of Its Significance for Man.* New Haven, Conn.: Yale University Press.

Singer, J. David, ed. 1979. *Explaining War: Selected Papers from the Correlates of War Project.* Beverly Hills, Calif.: Sage.

Singer, J. David, and Melvin Small. 1982. *Resort to Arms: International and Civil Wars, 1816–1980.* Beverly Hills, Calif.: Sage.

Singer, J. David, Stuart Bremer, and John Stuckey. 1972. "Capability Distribution, Uncertainty, and Major Power War, 1820–1965." In *Peace, War and Numbers*, ed. Bruce M. Russett. Beverly Hills, Calif.: Sage.

Sites, Paul. 1973. *Control: The Basis of Social Order.* New York: Dunellen.

_____ . 1986. "Theories of Hegemonic War and Soviet-American Relations." Paper presented at the Twenty-seventh Annual Meeting of the International Studies Association, Anaheim, California, March 25–29.

Sivard, Ruth L., ed. 1983. *World Military and Social Indicators, 1982.* Arlington, Va.: World Priorities.

_____ . 1985. *World Military and Social Indicators, 1984.* Washington, D.C.: World Priorities.

_____ . 1987. *World Military and Social Indicators, 1987–1988.* Washington, D.C.: World Priorities.

Smith, Adam. 1937. *An Inquiry into the Nature and Causes of the Wealth of Nations.* New York: Modern Library.

Smith, Theresa C. 1980. "Arms Race, Instability and War." *Journal of Conflict Resolution* 24, no. 2 (June).

Smoke, Richard C. 1977. *War: Controlling Escalation.* Cambridge, Mass.: Harvard University Press.

_____ . 1984. *National Security and the Nuclear Dilemma.* Reading, Mass.: Addison-Wesley.

Smoker, Paul. 1969. "Fear in the Arms Race: A Mathematical Study." In *International Politics and Foreign Policy*, ed. James N. Rosenau. New York: Free Press.

Snyder, Glenn H. 1961. *Deterrence and Defense: Toward a Theory of National Security.* Princeton, N.J.: Princeton University Press.

Snyder, Glenn H., and Paul Diesing. 1977. *Conflict Among Nations: Bargaining, Decision Making and System Structure in International Crises.* Princeton, N.J.: Princeton University Press.

Snyder, Richard C. 1962. *Foreign Policy Making.* New York: Free Press.

Snyder, Richard C., and Glenn Paige, 1958. "The U.S. Decision to Resist Aggression in Korea: The Application of an Analytic Scheme." *Administrative Science Quarterly* 3, no. 3 (December).

Soddy, Frederick. 1922. *Cartesian Economics: The Bearing of Physical Science upon State Stewardship.* London: Hendersons.

Sokolovskii, V. D. 1963. *Soviet Military Strategy.* Englewood Cliffs, N.J.: Prentice-Hall.

Sorokin, Pitirim A. 1957. *Social Change and Cultural Dynamics.* Boston: Porter Sargent.

Spencer, Herbert. 1891. *The Man Versus the State.* New York: Appleton.

Sprout, Harold, and Margaret Sprout. 1962. *Foundations of International Politics.* Princeton, N.J.: Van Nostrand.

———. 1965. *The Ecological Perspective on Human Affairs.* Princeton, N.J.: Princeton University Press.

Stebbins, G. Ledyard. 1971. *Processes of Organic Evolution,* 2nd ed. Englewood Cliffs, N.J.: Prentice-Hall.

Stegenga, James A. 1983. "Nuclear Deterrence: Bankrupt Ideology. *Policy Sciences* 16, no. 2 (November).

Stein, Arthur A. 1983. "Coordination and Collaboration: Regimes in an Anarchic World." In *International Regimes,* ed. Stephen D. Krasner. Ithaca, N.Y.: Cornell University Press.

Steinbruner, John D. 1974. *The Cybernetic Theory of Decision: New Dimensions of Political Analysis.* Princeton, N.J.: Princeton University Press.

Stern, Robert M. 1973. *The Balance of Payments.* Chicago: Aldine.

Steward, Julian H. 1977. *Evolution and Ecology: Essays on Social Transformation.* Urbana: University of Illinois Press.

Strayer, Joseph R. 1970. *On the Medieval Origins of the Modern State.* Princeton, N.J.: Princeton University Press.

Sullivan, John D. "Cooperation in International Politics: Quantitative Perspectives on Formal Alliances." Forthcoming. In *Behavioral International Relations,* ed. Michael Haas. San Francisco: Chandler.

Sullivan, Michael, and Randolph M. Siverson. 1981. In *Cumulation in International Relations Research,* ed. P. Terry Hopmann, Dina A. Zinnes, and J. David Singer. Monograph Series in World Affairs 18, Book 3. Denver, Colo.: School of International Affairs, University of Denver.

Taagepera, Rein. 1968. "Growth Curves of Empires." *General Systems,* 13. Annual.

———. 1978a. "Size and Duration of Empires: Systematics of Size." *Social Science Research* 7, no. 2 (June).

———. 1978b. "Size and Duration of Empires: Growth-Decline Curves, 3000 to 600 B.C." *Social Science Research* 7, no. 2 (June).

Taylor, A.J.P. 1975. *The Second World War.* New York: Putnam.

Taylor, Donald W. 1965. "Decision Making and Problem Solving." In *Handbook of Organization,* ed. James G. March. Chicago: Rand McNally.

Tedeschi, James T., Barry R. Schlenker, and Thomas V. Bonoma. 1973. *Conflict, Power and Games: The Experimental Study of Interpersonal Relations.* Chicago: Aldine Publishing Company.

Teller, Edward. 1962. *The Legacy of Hiroshima.* Garden City, N.Y.: Doubleday.

Thompson, William R. 1983. "World Wars, Global Wars and the Cool Hand Luke Syndrome." *International Studies Quarterly* 27, no. 3 (September).

———. 1988. *On Global War.* Columbia: University of South Carolina Press.

Thompson, William R., Robert D. Duval, and Ahmed Dia. 1979. "Wars, Alliances and Military Expenditures." *Journal of Conflict Resolution* 23, no. 4 (December).

Thompson, William R., and L. Gary Zuk. 1982. "War, Inflation, and the Kontrafieff Long Wave." *Journal of Conflict Resolution* 26, no. 4 (December).

Thurow, Lester C. 1980. *The Zero-Sum Society: Distribution and the Possibilities for Economic Change.* New York: Basic Books.

———. 1986. "The Economic Case Against Star Wars." *Technology Review* 83, no. 2 (February/March).

Tilly, Charles. 1981. *As Sociology Meets History.* New York: Academic Press.

Tinbergen, Jan, coordinator. 1976. *RIO: Reshaping the International Order.* New York: Dutton.

Tompkins, Sylvan. 1962. *Affect, Imagery and Consciousness.* New York: Springer.

Toynbee, Arnold. 1935. *Study of History,* vols. 1–6. London: Oxford University Press.

Truman, David B. 1971. *The Governmental Process: Political Interests and Public Opinion,* 2nd ed. New York: Knopf.

Truman, Harry S. 1945. "Letter to Heads of War Agencies, May 22." In *Public Papers of the Presidents of the United States: Harry S Truman.* Washington, D.C.: GPO.

———. 1949. "Radio and Television Report to the American People on the State of the National Economy, February 13"; "Address in Little Rock at the Dedication of the World War Memorial Park, June 11"; and "Address in Philadelphia at the American Legion Convention, August 29." *Public Papers of the Presidents of the United States: Harry S Truman.* Washington, D.C.: GPO.

Tsebelis, George. 1989. "The Abuse of Probability in Political Analysis: The Robinson Crusoe Fallacy." *American Political Science Review* 63, no. 1 (March).

Turco, R. P., O. B. Toon, T. P. Ackerman, J. P. Pollack, and Carl Sagan. 1983. "Nuclear Winter: Global Consequences of Multiple Nuclear Explosions." *Science* 222, no. 4630 (December 23).

Turner, Frederick J. 1920. *The Frontier in American History.* New York: Holt.

United Nations. 1981. *World Statistics in Brief.* Statistical Papers, Series 5, No. 6. New York: United Nations.

———. 1986. *Yearbook of International Trade Statistics.* New York: United Nations.

———. 1987. *United Nations Disarmament Yearbook.* New York: United Nations.

———. 1988. *Energy Statistics Yearbook, 1986.* New York: United Nations.

United Nations, Secretary General. 1989a. *Study on the Climate and Other Global Effects of Nuclear War.* Study Series 18. New York: United Nations.

———. 1989b. *Study on the Economic and Social Consequences of the Arms Race and Military Expenditures.* Study Series 19. New York: United Nations.

United Nations Conference on Trade and Development. 1982. *Trade and Development Report.* New York: United Nations Secretariat.

———. 1983. *Handbook of International Trade and Development Statistics.* New York: United Nations.

United States Arms Control and Disarmament Agency. 1986. *World Military Expenditures and Arms Transfers.* Washington, D.C.: GPO.

United States Department of Commerce. 1980. *World Population, 1979.* Washington, D.C.: GPO.

United States Department of Defense, 1971. *United States–Vietnam Relations.* Washington, D.C.: GPO.

United States Department of State. 1947. *Foreign Relations of the United States,* vol. 3. Washington, D.C.: GPO, pp. 202–219.

Valenta, Jiri. 1979. "The Bureaucratic Politics Paradigm and the Soviet Invasion of Czechoslovakia." *Political Science Quarterly* 94, no. 1 (Spring).

Väyrynen, Raimo. 1985. "Economic Cycles, Power Transitions, Political Management and Wars Between the Major Powers." *International Studies Quarterly* 26, no. 2 (April).

Viner, Jacob. 1937. *Studies in the Theory of International Trade.* New York: Harper.

———. 1952. *International Trade and Economic Development*. Glencoe, Ill.: Free Press.

———. 1958. *The Long View and the Short: Studies in Economic Theory and Policy*. Glencoe, Ill.: Free Press.

Voevodsky, John. 1969. "Quantitative Behavior of Warring Nations." *Journal of Psychology* 72, part 2.

———. 1972. "Crisis Waves: The Growth and Decline of War-Related Behavioral Events." *Journal of Psychology* 80.

Waddington, C. H. 1975. *The Evolution of an Evolutionist*. Ithaca, N.Y.: Cornell University Press.

Walbank, Frank W. 1953. *The Decline of the Roman Empire in the West*. New York: Schuman. Subsequently republished in 1969 as *The Awful Revolution: The Decline of the Roman Empire*. Toronto: University of Toronto Press.

Wallace, Michael D. 1979a. "Alliance Polarization, Cross Cutting and International War, 1815–1964: A Measurement Procedure and Some Preliminary Evidence." In *Explaining War: Selected Papers from the Correlates of War Project*, ed. J. David Singer. Beverly Hills, Calif.: Sage.

———. 1979b. "Arms Races and Escalation: Some New Evidence." In *Explaining War: Selected Papers from the Correlates of War Project*, ed. J. David Singer. Beverly Hills, Calif.: Sage.

Wallerstein, Immanuel. 1974. *The Modern World-System*. New York: Academic Press.

———. 1980. *The Modern World-System II: Mercantilism and the Coordination and the Consolidation of the European World Economy, 1600–1750*. New York: Free Press.

———. 1983. "Crises: The World-Economy, the Movements, and the Ideologies." In *Crises in the World-System*, ed. Albert Bergesen. Beverly Hills, Calif.: Sage.

Waltz, Kenneth N. 1959. *Man, the State and War*. New York: Columbia University Press.

———. 1971. "Stability of a Bipolar World." In *Power, Action and Interaction*, ed. George H. Quester. Boston: Little, Brown.

———. 1979. *Theory of International Politics*. Reading, Mass.: Addison-Wesley.

———. 1986. "Reflections on *Theory of International Politics*: A Response to My Critics." In *Neo-Realism and Its Critics*, ed. Robert O. Keohane. New York: Columbia University Press.

———. 1978. *Political Economy of Distribution: Equality Versus Inequality*. New York: Elsevier.

Ward, Michael D. 1984. "Differential Paths to Parity." *American Political Science Review* 78, no. 2 (June).

Weber, Max. 1968. *Economy and Society: An Outline of Interpretation Sociology*, vol. 2. New York: Bedminster Press.

Weber, Robert P. 1983. "Cyclical Theories of Crises in the World-System." In *Crises in the World-System*, ed. Albert Bergesen. Beverly Hills, Calif.: Sage.

White, Lynn, Jr. 1962. *Medieval Technology and Social Change*. Oxford: Clarendon Press.

Williams, Glendwr. 1966. *The Expansion of Europe in the Eighteenth Century: Overseas Rivalry, Discovery and Exploitation*. New York: Walker.

Williamson, James B. 1922. *A Short History of British Expansion*. London: Macmillan.

Winter, D. 1973. *The Power Motive*. New York: Free Press.

Wohlstetter, Roberta. 1962. *Pearl Harbor: Warning and Decision*. Stanford, Calif.: Stanford University Press.

Woodward, Ernest I. 1935. *Great Britain and the German Navy*. Oxford: Clarendon Press.

World Bank. 1980. *World Development Report*. New York: Oxford University Press.

————. 1983. *World Development Report.* New York: Oxford University Press.

————. 1984. *World Development Report.* New York: Oxford University Press.

Wright, Quincy. 1965. *A Study of War,* 2nd ed. Chicago: University of Chicago Press.

Wynner, Edith, and Georgia Lloyd. 1944. *Searchlight on Peace Plans.* New York: Dutton.

Young, Oran R. 1964a. "The Impact of General Systems Theory on Political Science." *General Systems* 9. Annual.

————. 1964b. "A Survey of General Systems Theory." *General Systems* 9. Annual.

————. 1968a. *The Politics of Force: Bargaining During International Crises.* Princeton, N.J.: Princeton University Press.

————. 1968b. *Systems of Political Science.* Princeton, N.J.: Princeton University Press.

————. 1983. "Regime Dynamics: The Rise and Fall of International Regimes." In *International Regimes,* ed. Stephen D. Krasner. Ithaca, N.Y.: Cornell University Press.

Zagare, Frank C. 1987. *The Dynamics of Deterrence.* Chicago: University of Chicago Press.

Zajonc, Robert B. 1968. "Cognitive Theories in Social Psychology." In *The Handbook of Social Psychology,* ed. Gardner Lindsey and Elliot Aronson, 2nd ed., vol. 1. Reading, Mass.: Addison-Wesley.

Zartman, William. 1976. *The 50% Solution.* Garden City, N.Y.: Doubleday.

Zimmerman, William, and Glen Palmer. 1987. "Words and Deeds in Soviet Foreign Policy." *American Political Science Review* 77, no. 2 (June).

Zinnes, Dina A. 1962. "Hostility in International Decisionmaking." *Journal of Conflict Resolution* 6, no. 3 (September).

————. 1967. "An Analytical Study of the Balance of Power Theories." *Journal of Peace Research,* no. 3.

————. 1976. *Contemporary Research in International Relations.* New York: Free Press.

Index